Rafael Núñez and the Politics of Colombian Regionalism

Rafael Núñez and the Politics of Colombian Regionalism, 1863–1886

James William Park

Louisiana State University Press
Baton Rouge and London

HOUSTON PUBLIC LIBRARY

Copyright © 1985 by Louisiana State University Press
All rights reserved
Manufactured in the United States of America
Designer: Rod Parker
Typeface: Melior
Typesetter: G & S Typesetters, Inc.
Printer: Thomson-Shore, Inc.
Binder: John Dekker & Sons, Inc.

Library of Congress Cataloging in Publication Data

Park, James William
    Rafael Núñez and the politics of Colombian regionalism, 1863–1886.

    Bibliography: p.
    Includes index.
    1. Colombia—Politics and government—1863–1885.
2. Núñez, Rafael, 1825–1894. 3. Regionalism—Colombia—
History—19th century. I. Title.
F2276.P25   1985   986.1'061   85-5256
ISBN 0-8071-1235-6

To my mother
In memory of my father

Contents

Illustrations

Acknowledgments

Research for this study was conducted during a one-and-one-half-year residence in Colombia in 1972 and 1973 and during the summer of 1978. The initial research period was funded by a Fulbright-Hays research grant and by the earnings of my wife, Cynthia, who with her customary élan taught a variety of classes at two universities in Bogotá; the Organization of American States provided funds for the 1978 research. My earlier two-year stay in Cartagena, 1967–1969, inspired a deep affection for Colombia's *costeños* and an interest in the nation's only costeño president, Rafael Núñez.

Among the many Colombians to whom I am deeply indebted I would like to express special gratitude to Horacio Rodríguez Plata for the use of his valuable library and manuscript collection, his helpful suggestions, and his warm hospitality. Although I became acquainted with Jorge Ancízar-Sordo only in my last months of research in Colombia, he was extremely generous with his manuscript collection. I also wish to express my deep appreciation for the excellent service provided by the staffs of the National Archive, National Library, Congressional Archive, Colombian Academy of History, Luis-Angel Arango Library, and Seminary Library of the Archdiocese of Bogotá, all located in Bogotá. The many courtesies extended by Alberto Lee López, O.F.M., Director of the National Archive, and Jaime Duarte French, Director of the Luis-Angel Arango Library, made my research efforts highly pleasurable and fruitful. Equally helpful were the staffs of the Cauca Central Archive in Popayán and the Biblioteca de la Universidad de Antioquia in Medellín as well as many friends in Cartagena. I especially enjoyed and benefited from an afternoon of discussion about Núñez with the late Gabriel Porras Troconis, an eminent Colombian historian who had studied Núñez extensively and who retained vivid recollections from his youth of his fellow *Cartagenero*.

Foremost among those in the United States to whom special thanks are due is Robert L. Gilmore, a scholar of uncommon courtesy and profound knowledge of Colombian history, for his advice in the interpretive aspects of this study. I also wish to express my sincere gratitude to Charles L. Stansifer and William J. Griffith for their support and their valuable counsel. Two eminent Colombianists, J. León Helguera and Frank Safford, helped move this study to its final stage by their timely encouragement; they also helped me avoid errors of fact and interpretation by generously agreeing to read and comment on the manuscript. For all of this I am grateful. Whatever errors may yet remain are exclusively my responsibility. And finally, but for the remarkable patience and quiet encouragement of my wife, Cynthia, this study would surely have remained unfinished.

Abbreviations

The following abbreviations have been used in the notes for libraries, archives, and document collections:

AC	Archivo del Congreso, Bogotá
ACdeH	Archivo de la Academia Colombiana de Historia, Bogotá
AN	Archivo Nacional, Bogotá
ASA	Archivo Sergio Arboleda (Sala Arboleda, Archivo Central del Cauca, Popayán)
ATCM	Archivo Tomás Cipriano de Mosquera (Sala Mosquera, Archivo Central del Cauca, Popayán)
BLAA	Biblioteca Luis-Angel Arango, Bogotá
BSM	Biblioteca del Seminario Mayor, La Arquidiócesis de Bogotá, Bogotá
CCM-ACdeH	Copiador de Cartas de Manuel D. Montúfar, Archivo de la Academia Colombiana de Historia, Bogotá
CdeHRP	Private collection of Horacio Rodríguez Plata, Bogotá
CdeJA	Private collection of Jorge Ancízar-Sordo, Bogotá
H-ACdeH	Pedro Alcántara Herrán collection, Archivo de la Academia Colombiana de Historia, Bogotá

Rafael Núñez and the Politics of Colombian Regionalism

UNITED STATES OF COLOMBIA, 1863–1885

PANAMA

• David
⁕ Panama

VENEZUELA

Sabanilla
Cartagena•
⁕Santa Marta
Barranquilla
•Riohacha

MAGDALENA
•Tolú
Valledupar•

Sincelejo•

BOLÍVAR

Magdalena River

Cauca River

Cúcuta•
•Bucaramanga

ANTIOQUIA
SANTANDER

Medellín⁕
•Rionegro
Socorro⁕
Vélez

Manizales•
Cartago•
CAUCA
Honda
⁕Tunja
Ambalema•

BOYACÁ

Buenaventura•
Buga•
Ibagué•
Girardot

Guamo⁕
⁕Bogotá

Cali•
TOLIMA

CUNDINAMARCA

Popayán⁕
•Neiva

•Barbacoas

•Pasto

ECUADOR

Preface

The central thesis of this study is that Rafael Núñez, dominant political leader of Colombia from 1880 until his death in 1894, laid the institutional basis essential for his nation's political stability and economic development and that he so acted largely in reaction against the debilitating forces of regionalism which he had earlier represented. This is not to exclude the interplay of other factors in shaping Núñez' behavior, but rather to give proper attention to the unexplored role of regionalism as a political force in Colombian history.

Colombia's period of extreme federalism, from 1863 to 1886, is a historical era which has generated a weak historiography, an abundance of controversy, serious misinterpretation, and polemical discussion. This period marked the heyday of nineteenth-century Colombian Liberalism which zealous reformers implemented under the inspiration of European ideological models of social equality, individual liberty, and laissez faire economics. Historians have only recently undertaken a serious evaluation of the consequences to national development of these years of Liberal domination. The bitter struggle for power between the traditional Liberal and Conservative parties has given rise to varied opinions about the underlying cause of these conflicts and about the basis of differentiation between the parties. Much of the disputation about the period stems from conflicting interpretation over the role of Núñez, the man most responsible for bringing the period to a close. An additional characteristic of these years, but one which has generated limited analysis despite its importance, was the trend toward regionalist exaggeration and national disintegration. The undermining of national institutions such as the church, the army, the national parties, and the central government together with incipient movements for independence by some regions all give evidence of the seriousness of the threat to national integrity. Although this study has as its focus an examination of the role of regionalism in Colombian history from 1863 to 1886 and of Núñez' action in reversing the trend toward national disintegration, the study touches upon all of the above questions still in dispute.

By mid-century the Liberal and Conservative parties had achieved clear definition. Colombian political history for the next half century was shaped by civil war and violence perpetrated by adherents of the two parties marching under distinctive banners of party ideology. Liberals gained power at mid-century following a controversial election and proceeded to enact in constitution and in law a program inspired by European reformers. This program was aimed at demolishing the restraints on individual freedom represented by state monopolies, tariffs, state patronage of the church, religious domination of education, press restrictions, and centralized government. Conservatives, on the other hand, harbored greater respect for their Hispanic heritage, sought to bolster the dignity and power of the church, saw the existing social hierarchy as essential for harmony, and fought to preserve a more centralized, authoritarian framework for governing society. Enactment of the Liberal program led to an unsuccessful rebellion by Conservatives in 1851 and a division in Liberal ranks which contributed to a short-lived military dictatorship in 1854 and to a Conservative election victory in 1857. Within three years Liberals took up arms against that government, and following a three-year civil war they gained firm control of the nation in 1863, when they issued a new constitution embodying their program.

Government remained in Liberal hands from 1863 to 1885, and the period was marked by extreme federalism, severe limitation on the church's roles in society, and provisions for wide-ranging individual freedom. Liberals were also the principal sponsors, during this period, of a free-trade program whose success required export expansion. But collapse of tobacco exports in the mid-1870s and the failure to fill the void with other reliable export commodities threatened their entire economic program. Also, Conservative opponents remained active and gained control of two of the nine states during these years, but they failed in their attempts to capture national power through a revolt in 1865, a civil war in 1876–1877, and through occasional alliances with one of the two Liberal factions. Liberal divisions, the result largely of ideological, regionalist, and personalist rivalries, posed as serious a threat to party domination as did the Conservative challenge. These divisions became critical to party fortunes beginning in 1875 when Rafael Núñez launched his unsuccessful first bid for the presidency as a Liberal.

Upon his election to the two-year term of president in 1880, Núñez began moving against key elements of the Liberal program and calling for constitutional reform. Following his election again in 1884, Núñez, faced with rebellion by the bulk of the Liberal party, summoned Conservatives to the aid of his administration, the Regeneration, and his faction of the Liberal party, the Independents. Núñez, the Independents, and the Conservatives were successful in the war of 1884–1885, and Núñez presided over implementation of the unitary Constitution of 1886, restoration of government protection of the church, and the undoing of the Liberal program. Liberals staged an insurrection in 1895 which was easily crushed. At the turn of the century, however, they plunged the nation into a major civil war, the War of the Thousand Days, which resulted in extensive property damage, heavy loss of life, and their own defeat. This conflict also contributed to the cession of Panama. The following three decades of Conservative rule brought political stability, economic recovery, and the beginning of industrial development. In those same decades the Liberal party sufficiently modified its ideology and program to exploit the social stresses inherent in the development process.

Núñez, twice elected president as a Liberal, thus occupies a central role in the decline of Liberalism. One of the most disputed questions about the life of Núñez concerns the reasons for his apparent betrayal of a life-long devotion to Liberalism. The reasons given in the historical literature for this change are nearly legion and include personal ambition, revenge, the influence of his second wife—a Conservative—the impact upon his ideology of his residence in the United States and Europe from 1863 to 1874, and the economic crisis in Colombia caused by foreign trade problems. Núñez also intrigues historians because of his impressive intellect, his voluminous writings, and, of course, his two marriages and his reputation as a philanderer. Regardless of how one assesses his motivation and character, Núñez left a major imprint on Colombian history by ending Liberal hegemony, inaugurating a period of Conservative rule which extended to 1930, and imposing upon the nation the still-surviving Constitution of 1886.

Many scholars who have studied Colombia have shown a clear awareness of the impact of regionalism at critical moments in the nation's history. Such moments include the early stages of the movement for independence and the crisis culminating in the separation of Panama. The extraordinary interest historians have directed toward Antioquia also indicates an appreciation of the very distinctive history of that particular region and of the contribution regional histories can make to an understanding of national development. But other regions have not been so carefully studied. Nor has there been a systematic examination of the relationship of the ebb and flow of regionalist sentiment and the development of nationhood. One of the observations repeatedly made by Colombians between 1863 and 1886 was the weakness of national feeling and the fragility of national ties. Many Colombians feared that the extraordinary degree of federalism granted by the 1863 constitution nourished regionalist sentiment to such a degree that it threatened national unity. Indeed, some Colombians openly advocated independence for their regions, and others looked forward to the day when their regions could maintain an existence separate from Colombia. This study attempts to specify the role of regionalism during this period, to assess its origins and strength, and to demonstrate that the reaction against exaggerated regionalism was spearheaded by Núñez following his election in 1880.

In recent years two major books related to the theme of this study have appeared. They are Charles Bergquist's *Coffee and Conflict in Colombia, 1886–1910* (Durham, 1978) and Helen Delpar's *Red Against Blue: The Liberal Party in Colombian Politics, 1863–1899* (University, Ala., 1981). Both books are essentially political and they necessarily examine the role of Núñez, though for neither is this the major focus. Delpar's book shares with this study an interest in intraparty disputes, but her analysis centers on the Liberal party, its decline, and its struggle as the party of opposition during the Regeneration. On the other hand, the present study gives greater emphasis to regionalist attitudes and conflicts, examines the considerable impact of regionalism on national political developments, and provides a more detailed history of the Conservative party during its nadir, 1863–1877, than here-tofore available.

More readily apparent are the differences in chronology, empha-sis, and interpretation between Bergquist's book and this study, al-though the two overlap thematically and chronologically. Bergquist argues that Liberal party success and failure in the last half of the nine-teenth century can be explained almost exclusively by economic fac-tors. He concludes that because of Liberal identification with the for-eign trade sector of the economy Liberal party fortunes prospered in the third quarter of the century when the export trade prospered and thereafter failed when the international market for Colombian exports failed. Somewhat more complex is the interpretation of the decline of Liberalism and the emergence of Núñez and the Conservatives in this study, for it incorporates economic factors as well as the dynamics of intraparty factionalism and regionalist rivalries. It also demonstrates that regionalist tensions, which had a variety of origins, were a deep-rooted, permanent feature of nineteenth-century Colombia and not a temporary result of the uneven effect of changes in the international market for Colombian exports.

Chapter I

Configuration of Colombian Regionalism to 1874

Regionalism has exerted a complex and profound influence on Colombian national development. In the early nineteenth century the urge for local and regional autonomy contributed to the movement for independence and then hindered its fulfillment by delaying united action. At critical moments in the nineteenth century some Colombians advocated independence for their regions, a goal achieved by Panamanians in 1903. A few years after that bitter loss, a Bogotá editor still found it necessary to call for the extirpation of "that stubborn regionalism which rests on the negation of the Fatherland."[1] The well-publicized demand during the 1970s by the department of Antioquia for greater departmental autonomy, a campaign popularized under the slogan "Antioquia federal," bears witness to the continuing vigor of regionalist aspirations.

Colombia is hardly unique in comprising sections distinguishable along geographic, economic, or cultural lines, but it differs from other countries of similar size in the deep imprint its regionalist sentiment has left on the pattern of national development. The delayed rise of a strong sense of nationalism must be attributed in part to the greater loyalty felt by most Colombians for the *patria chica*. Colombia's democratic tradition, superficial yet durable, owes much to the regionalist configuration. The nation's few dictators have been frustrated not only by the overwhelming physical barriers to firm national control but also

1. *El Republicano* (Bogotá), August 10, 1907.

by the regionalist reaction against perceived encroachment by central authority. Regionalism and the demand for effective local autonomy also nourished the centralist-federalist struggle which persisted for three-quarters of a century after the initiation of the wars for independence and which profoundly shaped national institutions during that period. Debate over the degree to which aspirations for greater local and regional autonomy should receive legal sanction provided an early basis for differentiation between the Liberal and Conservative parties. After these parties achieved national organization, they assumed the patriotic missions of counteracting regionalist dispositions and neutralizing the ever-present threat of fragmentation of the country. Rafael Uribe Uribe, when in a position to deal a crippling blow to the Liberal party by joining a third party movement, observed: "We who work for the preservation and organization of the great historical parties work for the maintenance of national unity; and on the other hand, those who fight for the dissolution and fragmentation of those parties unconsciously favor separatism and destroy a valuable tie which today unites Colombians."[2]

Geography has operated more forcefully than any other factor to encourage Colombian regionalism. Only in the last few decades has significant progress been registered in breaking down the physical barriers to national unity. Colombia lies in the tropics, but the three Andean mountain chains—the Western, Central, and Eastern Cordillera—that branch apart as they extend north-northeastward from the Pasto node provide a temperate zone of upland valleys and plateaus. It was in these temperate areas of difficult access where the bulk of the population chose to reside. There they were able to escape the discomfort and pestilence that plagued residents of the tropical lowland river valleys and the Pacific and Atlantic coasts. As a consequence of this pattern of settlement the majority of Colombians were isolated for centuries from frequent contact either with the outside world or with "neighboring" settlements.[3] Although many parts of Colombia underwent a highly autonomous development because of near in-

2.   Rafael Uribe Uribe, "La necesidad de los grandes partidos nacionales," *Revista Argentina de Ciencias Políticas*, IV (1912), 55–56.
3.   An interesting account of the difficulty in establishing governmental and ecclesiastical authority over Colombia's dispersed population is contained in the 1789

accessibility, substantial variations in the degree of isolation provided an important basis for regional differentiation. Bogotá is situated at the southeastern edge of the population cluster and is thus remote from most Colombians and incapable of imposing its cultural norms on the rest of the country. The llanos extending south and east of Bogotá are hot, humid grasslands falling within the Orinoco drainage basin. Although the llanos together with the forested Amazon drainage basin represent nearly two-thirds of the Colombian land mass, in the last half of the nineteenth century these two regions contained fewer than 2 percent of the population.[4]

Geographical factors not only sustained regionalism but also partly determined its configuration. The north-south orientation of the three Andean chains and their separation by the northward-flowing Cauca and Magdalena rivers guaranteed a communication system which generally followed the same orientation. Antioquia, astride the northern portion of the Central Cordillera, thus had closer ties with Tolima to the south than with Santander to the east, which together with Boyacá and Cundinamarca occupied the Eastern Cordillera and shared a common upland culture and geographical unity.[5] The gradual declension of the Central Cordillera northward into the coastal plains permitted overland contact between the two north coast states, Bolívar and Magdalena. Marshy lowlands in southeastern Panama made land travel impossible between that state and the rest of the country, and the snow-covered Sierra Nevada located near the coast in Magdalena hindered contact with the Guajira Peninsula in the country's northeastern extremity. The vast western state of Cauca contained the Western Cordillera, the upper Cauca River valley, the entire Pacific coast south of Panama, and the Amazon rain forests along the Putumayo River.

Colombia's racial pattern substantially contributed to regional dif-

report of Archbishop-Viceroy Antonio Caballero y Góngora to his successor. See José Manuel Pérez Ayala, *Antonio Caballero y Góngora, virrey y arzobispo de Santa Fe, 1723–1796* (Bogotá, 1951), Appendix 3, pp. 328–30.

4.   Fernando Gómez, "Los censos en Colombia antes de 1905," in Miguel Urrutia M. and Mario Arrubla (eds.), *Compendio de estadísticas históricas de Colombia* (Bogotá, 1970), Table 10, p. 27.

5.   In discussing regions, reference will be made to the nine states as they existed from 1861 to 1885: Antioquia, Bolívar, Boyacá, Cauca, Cundinamarca, Magdalena, Panama, Santander, and Tolima.

ferentiation. The centuries-long mixture of Spaniards with Indians from the advanced highland cultures had produced by the mid nineteenth century a white, Indian, and mestizo combination whose proportions varied considerably from region to region. The Indian element remained conspicuous in the eastern highlands, particularly in Boyacá, as well as in the mountains of southern Cauca. Introduction of Negro slaves to work in the mining areas of Cauca and Antioquia and the gradual migration of escaped and manumitted slaves to the sparsely settled lowlands gave rise to a white, Negro, and mulatto mixture along the coasts, within the river valleys, and in the mining zones of Cauca and the Central Cordillera. By the last half of the nineteenth century the Negro element predominated along the Pacific coast and in several north coast areas where fugitive slaves had established villages such as Palenque.

The administrative system inherited from Spain provided other elements conducive to regionalism. During most of the colonial period, Colombia, as well as the rest of Spanish South America, remained under the jurisdiction of the Viceroyalty of Peru but subject to the intermediate authority of presidents and *audiencias*, administrative-judicial bodies which shared and counterbalanced many of the presidents' powers. In some respects Colombia represented a departure from the desired rational pattern of jurisdiction supposedly in force in the Spanish Empire. Subordination to the Viceroyalty of Peru was minimal, and much of the territory that composed mid–nineteenth-century Colombia was governed by divided and often conflicting authority. Most of the area fell under the jurisdiction of the president of Santa Fe de Bogotá, but the Santa Marta and Guajira coastal areas were subject to Maracaibo in fiscal matters, Cauca directed its judicial appeals to Quito, and until the early eighteenth century Panama remained the seat of a separate presidency. Delay in the definite establishment of the Viceroyalty of New Granada until 1740 meant that distance, divided authority, and the usual bureaucratic devices of delay and requests for clarification permitted the growth over two centuries of a tradition of substantial local and regional administrative autonomy. The Comunero Rebellion of 1781 is properly classified not only as a tax resistance movement but also as an uprising in defense of local autonomy against growing royal authority which was about to be escalated by imposition of the intendancy system. This reformed system of governance was designed to achieve effective centralization of authority, economic development, and surplus revenues. Failure of the Bourbon reformers to implement in New Granada the intendancy system meant that the Hapsburg habits of laxity and casual compliance were never extirpated.

Colombia's hardly accessible mountain fastnesses and the flexibility of the colonial administrative system permitted the emergence of regions possessing distinctive subcultures shaped under the varied influences of climate, topography, and racial heterogeneity. Among the indicators of cultural differentiation along regional lines is the evolution of language. The educated *Bogotano*, proud of the purity of his Castilian, regarded the speech of a *costeño* as a gross defamation of the mother tongue. The nineteenth-century *cuadros de costumbre* and the use of regionalisms by writers such as Tomás Carrasquilla (1858–1940) reflect such a regional diversity in Spanish usage as to suggest the existence of true dialects. Religious attitudes also varied from one section to another despite a centuries-long Catholic presence. Laxity in religious observances on the north coast and their modification in Boyacá through the injection of Indian mysticism and practices offered striking contrasts to the strict observance of basic church regulations in nineteenth-century Bogotá, Medellín, and Popayán. Catholicism visibly reflected the impact of local tradition on compliance with regulation, quality of devotion, and content of belief. The rich variety of Colombian folk music suggests a spiritual diversity of enormous proportions ranging from the provocative, African rhythm of the north coast *cumbia* to the intensely morose and sentimental *pasillo* of the southern Cauca highlands. Varied patterns of life throughout Colombia provide a common theme found in nineteenth-century travel accounts. Regional differences in clothing, dwellings, and living styles are beautifully depicted in the watercolors of the mid–nineteenth-century traveler Edward W. Mark.[6] The Colombian love of carbohydrates also is manifest in different regional preferences, e.g., beans and corn-cake arepas in Antioquia, potatoes and wheat bread on the savanna of Bo-

6.   Eduardo Arias Robledo and Joaquín Piñeros Corpas (eds.), *Acuarelas de Mark, un testimonio pictórico de la Nueva Granada* (Bogotá, 1963).

gotá, and yucca and plantains in the tropical areas. It was such regionally diverse cultural traits as these—dialect, religious attitude, musi-
cal form, clothing, and diet—that marked an individual in the last half
of the nineteenth century not as a Colombian but rather as a costeño,
Antioqueño, or Santandereano.

The following caricature of a young Bogotano, proud of living in
the "Athens of South America" and of his affinity with European culture, suggests the difficulty with which a costeño or Caucano would
identify with a resident of the capital: "The stiff and conceited dandy
with a stride filled with affectation who walks along the principal
streets of the capital displaying in his clothing a total adherence to the
Parisian style and in his countenance a particular pedantic air of satisfaction, and in ecstasy with himself, that is the [Bogotano] returned
from Europe."[7]

A vigorous and sustained political expression of Colombian regionalist sentiment erupted during the opening phase, 1810–1815, of
the wars for independence. Central authority disappeared with the
elimination of royal government, leaving only municipal government
intact. The focus of political activity during that period resided in the
municipal governments of the provincial capitals such as Bogotá, Tunja,
and Cartagena where efforts were made to establish jurisdiction over
the surrounding province and to coordinate action with other provincial capitals. The repeated efforts by some patriots to reconstitute a
central authority roughly equivalent to that of the viceroy-audiencia-
real acuerdo, i.e., the coherent, well-articulated yet flexible system of
colonial governance, failed because of provincial rivalry and jealousy,
jurisdictional disputes, and a genuine distrust of centralism. Federalism was closely linked to republicanism in the ideology of the
early independence movement, and the provinces promulgated and revised constitutions containing these twin principles. The Spanish-
Americans engaged in a costly series of civil wars in attempting to
incorporate the Cundinamarcan portion of the viceroyalty into the
"United Provinces," but by the time the territorial association was con-
summated, the patriots lost access to the sea. Resort to a federal dictatorship failed to check the easy sweep of the Spanish reconquest
in 1816.

7.   Francisco de P. Carrasquilla, *Tipos de Bogotá* (Bogotá, 1886), 83.

As a direct result of the disastrous outcome of this outburst of local and provincial autonomy, federalism as a political force remained enervated for a generation. Successful achievement of the independence of Gran Colombia, composed of the modern republics of Venezuela, Colombia, Panama, and Ecuador, under the rigid authority of Simón Bolívar in 1819 as well as consolidation of independence in the 1820s under the unitarian Constitution of 1821 further assured the suppression of federalist aspirations. Two years after Venezuela and Ecuador separated from Gran Colombia, the Colombians promulgated the 1832 constitution, described at the time as mixed or centrofederal, which established a central government and divided the country into provinces administered by presidentially appointed governors and elected assemblies.[8] Victory in the 1836 elections by the so-called Moderate Liberals and other more conservative elements aroused fear among the more radical Liberals that a return to tyranny and monarchy loomed imminent. The assault on the authority of the national government, begun in 1837 and reaching its climax in the 1840–1842 civil war, was an expression of that fear. Proclamation of federalism by veteran Liberal officers supported by Liberal intellectuals played on two provincial attitudes—dislike of authority in Bogotá and the conviction that atheists controlled governmental exercise of the patronato. Despite the success of the national government in defeating the rebellion, the new Constitution of 1843 did not in practice affect local autonomy. During this formative period in the history of the two traditional Colombian parties, "Liberals" pinned the label of absolutism on the "Conservatives," and the latter replied by referring to the "Liberals" as anarchists.

Election of the Liberal candidate for president, José Hilario López, in 1849 initiated a period of rampant reformism, intellectual effervescence, and political and social turmoil. A group of young Liberal reformers inspired by prevailing European currents of thought formulated party ideology and directed it toward the liberation of Colombia from its ubiquitous Hispanic heritage. To accomplish that task of demolition they focused their attack on the pillars of traditional authority, the resources and roles assigned to central government and the church. The reformers intended to transfer most of these resources and

8. José de la Vega, La federación en Colombia, 1810–1912 (Bogotá, 1952), 135–37.

roles to provincial and municipal governments and to lay agencies. The assumed result was to be a broader base of participation in socio-political processes. Opportunity was to be further extended by abolition of monopolistic concessions in economic activities.[9]

Governmental decentralization became one device through which the Liberals attacked the power of central government. Legislation in 1850 abolished revenues from government monopolies and assigned other revenues and financial responsibilities to the provincial governments.[10] Between 1849 and 1853 the number of provinces into which the country was divided increased from twenty-two to thirty-six. The 1853 constitution eliminated the president's traditional power to appoint provincial governors and provided instead for their election. Anticlerical legislative and executive action of the early 1850s included extinction of the ecclesiastical *fuero*, expulsion of the Jesuits, and making civil marriage the only valid basis for inheritance and for determining civil status. The 1853 constitution also separated church and state, established freedom of religion, and ended the juridical personality of the church. To meet the demand for an end to economic privileges the reformers eliminated the tobacco monopoly and entailed property, removed subsidies on certain exports, and continued the nonprotectionist tariff policy begun in 1847.[11]

The sweeping nature of the reform program highlighted tensions in the Liberal party which deepened its division into Radical (*gólgota*)

9. For studies of the ideological nature of the reform movement see Robert L. Gilmore, "Nueva Granada's Socialist Mirage," *Hispanic American Historical Review*, XXXVI (May, 1956), 190–210; Jaime Jaramillo Uribe, *El pensamiento colombiano en el siglo XIX* (Bogotá, 1964), 173–80; Gerardo Molina, *Las ideas liberales en Colombia, 1849–1914* (Bogotá, 1917), 17–99.

10. Vega, *La federación*, 149.

11. Robert L. Gilmore, "Federalism in Colombia, 1810–1858" (Ph.D. dissertation, University of California, Berkeley, 1949), 237–38, 211, 214; Jesús María Henao and Gerardo Arrubla, *Historia de Colombia* (Bogotá, 1967), 664–66, 683. A recent, detailed study of ecclesiastical reform during the 1849–1853 period is found in Russ Tobias Davidson, "The Patronato in Colombia, 1800–1853: Reform and Anti-Reform in the Archdiocese of Santa Fe de Bogotá" (Ph.D. dissertation, Vanderbilt University, 1978), 271–307; Luis F. Sierra, *El tabaco en la economía colombiana del siglo XIX* (Bogotá, 1971), 87. The tobacco monopoly ended in 1850 in accord with a law passed in 1848, and the high taxes on planting and exports were also eliminated in 1850.

ment and blindly relying for support on the head of the army, General José María Melo, who "had insinuated himself into the counsels of government."[18]

The political crisis and social conflict marking the Obando presidency came to a climax on April 17, 1854, when General Melo overthrew the regime. Melo invited the president to remain at the head of the new government, but the enigmatic Obando declined. He offered no significant support or resistance to the *golpe*. As a political leader, Obando had proved ineffective and indecisive, unable to fulfill the obligations of office during times of stress. Núñez, who at the time was president of the House, later asserted with sarcasm that the coup "did not surprise . . . anyone, except General Obando."[19]

Melo's regime survived for only eight months because the Radical and Conservative upper classes actively cooperated politically and militarily in resisting it. José de Obaldía organized the resistance and, with the support of all living former presidents, assumed leadership of the legitimate government as vice-president. Melo received little support outside of the Bogotá savanna except from the populist governor of Cartagena, Juan José Nieto. While loyalist troops closed in on the Melo forces on the savanna, Obaldía entrusted Núñez with the task of checking disloyal elements in Cartagena. Obaldía removed Governor Nieto and named Núñez, the second designate, to replace him. Núñez elicited successful Liberal-Conservative cooperation against the *Melistas* and governed the province until the end of the year.[20]

A seriously tarnished and eclipsed Liberalism emerged from the debacle of 1854. Liberal party division, the extremism of many of the reform measures, and the disappointing performance of Obando all contributed to the decline in Liberal fortune and status. Conservative prestige, on the other hand, was enhanced considerably by the party's role in defeating Melo and restoring legitimate government. As an im-

18.   *La Luz* (Bogotá), March 21, 1882, reprinted in Rafael Núñez, *La reforma política en Colombia* (8 vols.; Bogotá, 1945–50), Vol. I, Pt. 1, pp. 147–48; *cf.* "Memoria testamental de don José de Obaldía, vicepresidente de la Nueva Granada," *Boletín de Historia y Antigüedades*, XXXI (March–April, 1944), 297–99.

19.   Lemos Guzmán, *Obando*, 394–99; *La Luz* (Bogotá), March 21, 1882, reprinted in Núñez, *La reforma*, Vol. I, Pt. 1, p. 148.

20.   Castillo, *El primer Núñez*, 194–95; Otero Muñoz, *Núñez*, 24–25; Gómez Picón, *El golpe*, 252.

and Moderate (*draconiano*) factions in the early 1850s. Led by Manuel Murillo Toro and Florentino González, the Radicals were a young intellectual elite who propagandized and crusaded for a society of scant structure above the municipal level. They favored such programs as civilian rule through minimal governmental power, abolition of the regular army and reliance on militia organizations, complete separation of church and state, and free trade. The Moderates, led by old-guard Liberals such as José María Obando and José de Obaldía and supported by existing artisan societies and the bureaucracy, sought retention of a moderately structured national society. They favored restoration of presidential appointment of provincial governors, retention of a small regular army backed by the militia, state supervision of the church, and protective tariffs.[12] Although the two factions cooperated in enacting many reforms, the areas of disagreement were profound and touched upon such controversial topics as centralism-federalism, trade policy, and church-state relations. These disagreements persisted.

Centralism versus federalism ranked as the principal item of debate throughout the 1850s. The course of this debate serves as one of the best indicators of the political convolutions of the period, because it delineated ideological boundaries between parties and factions and reflected the evolution of party doctrine. The struggle against centralism was fueled by the young reformers' zeal to eradicate authoritarian barriers to liberty as well as by the desire to fulfill longings for local and regional autonomy. Much of the experimentation of the period with governmental units of varying size and authority represented a groping for a level and pattern of decentralization sufficiently acceptable to the widening base of the politically active part of the population. This experimentation led from centralism to provincial fragmentation, then to federalism through the consolidation of provinces to form states, and finally in 1861 to the creation of sovereign states. The movement which began as an attack on centralism in the name of liberty and local autonomy ended as a quest for a stronger and more viable regionalist expression.

12.   Molina, *Las ideas liberales*, 63–64; Gustavo Otero Muñoz, *Un hombre y una época: la vida azarosa de Rafael Núñez* (Bogotá, 1951), 15; Aníbal Galindo, *Recuerdos históricos, 1840 a 1895* (Bogotá, 1900), 75.

Conflict in formulating the 1853 constitution focused on the extent to which the national government should be decentralized. The Radicals, in control of the Senate, called for the election of provincial governors, but a block of Moderate Liberals and Conservatives favoring presidential appointment of governors outnumbered the Radicals in the House of Representatives. Opposition to the decentralization measure was organized by the newly elected president, José María Obando, who objected to any measure tending to weaken his government, and by Rafael Núñez, a twenty-eight-year-old freshman congressman representing western Panama. These political allies had maintained a close association since 1849 when Núñez, a *Cartagenero*, accepted a position as Obando's secretary during the latter's term as governor of the province of Cartagena. Núñez subsequently supported Obando against the Radical candidate for president for the 1853–1857 period. Despite Núñez' youth and political inexperience at the national level, the House elected him its vice-president for the first month of the 1853 session and again in May.[13]

Núñez had never been to Bogotá prior to 1853. He nonetheless arrived in the capital with some well-formulated views on the question of decentralization which had been shaped by his experience as provincial assemblyman and secretary to four different provincial governors. In 1850 Núñez had endorsed the new national law decentralizing income and expenditures in the belief that "the effect of decentralization clearly will be to consolidate the provinces existing today, and even to reunite many of the sections which have recently been divided."[14] Shortly after Núñez arrived in Bogotá, however, he boldly challenged the well-publicized federalist position expressed by Florentino González. In two articles published in early 1853 Núñez concluded that "the logical consequence of federation would be, first disorder, then anarchy, and finally dictatorship." In subsequent articles he argued on behalf of "the triumph of the national cause," asserting that the election of provincial governors would seriously weaken the

---

13.   Nicolás del Castillo, *El primer Núñez* (Bogotá, 1971), 150–51, 158; Gustavo Arboleda, *Historia contemporánea de Colombia* (6 vols.; Popayán, 1919–35), III, 362, 384.

14.   Castillo, *El primer Núñez*, 78–83, 111, 117; *La Democracia* (Cartagena), May 23, 1850.

central government, lead to the predominance of individualism ov[e] community interests, and result in "democratic feudalism."[15] By thi he may have been warning against a continuance of caciquism, *i.e.*, p litical control by an entrenched local or regional boss.

The Radicals carried their point over the centralist opposition a established the choice of governors by election. A majority of t House members, including Núñez, issued a manifesto a few days fore the adjournment of Congress announcing their reluctant acqui cence in the Radical solution. The manifesto noted that by yielding this basic issue the new constitution could be sanctioned in the (rent year. In return for this concession, the centralist majority in House obtained the passage of article 53 of the constitution which mitted the president to remove elected governors from office f period to be determined by the Supreme Court.[16] Despite this cession, the Constitution of 1853 was, in political terms, both Conservative and anti-Moderate Liberal.

Implementation of the 1853 constitution and its many reform visions fulfilled most Radical ambitions. It contributed, howev the developing political crisis caused by the widening split in th eral party. President Obando was decidedly out of tune with th constitution, and his attitude tended to exaggerate party divisic enjoyed the support of the Moderate Liberals, the military, ar democratic societies—political clubs of artisans organized in th cipal cities to lobby against the free-trade program espoused Radicals. The army's support of Obando stemmed from fear th Radicals would suppress the standing army.

During the year-long Obando presidency, Bogotá was sha street riots, bitter clashes between Radicals and Moderates, an conflict pitting artisans against members of the upper class.[17] who was secretary of the interior for a few months in mid-1 later years criticized Obando for stubbornly resisting the reforr

---

15.   *La Discusión* (Bogotá), February 19, March 5, April 2, 9, 1853.

16.   *Neo-Granadino* (Bogotá), May 20, 1853; Manuel Antonio Pombo anc quín Guerra (eds.), *Constituciones de Colombia* (4 vols.; Bogotá, 1951), I'

17.   Alirio Gómez Picón, *El golpe militar del 17 de abril de 1854* (Bogc 135–41; A. J. Lemos Guzmán, *Obando, de Cruzverde a Cruzverde* (Popay 388–93.

mediate consequence of this shift in party status, Manuel María Mallarino, the Conservative candidate for vice-president, a position whose term overlapped the presidential term, defeated the Radical, Manuel Murillo Toro, in the late 1854 election. Mallarino thus occupied the vacant office of president from 1855 to 1857.

One of the apparent anomalies of Colombian political history in the 1850s was Conservative patronage of the movement toward federalism. Conservative governments supported creation of the state of Panama in 1855, the first formal step toward federalism, and promulgated the thoroughly federalist 1858 constitution. The principal reason for this Conservative apostasy was expressed by Mariano Ospina Rodríguez, Conservative president from 1857 to 1861, who wrote: "I ardently desire federation solely to see if it is possible to provide refuge in some provinces of the Republic for the victims of social reform in the rest."[21] In addition, many Conservatives liked the centro-federal constitutions of 1832–1853 with their provisions for local autonomy.

The tenacious desire to devise a pattern of government suitable to a fuller expression of regionalist sentiment contributed to the federalist movement of 1855. Writing years later, the chastened Radical publicist José María Samper described the regionalist basis for federalism in the following terms: "Very notable differences in race, very distinct customs and economies, climates so varied that they are opposite, formidable mountain ranges that separate the well-populated valleys and upper plateaus, enormous distances lacking good communications, a notable diversity in the conditions of wealth . . . all of this made it necessary to divide the nation into a reduced number of entities with their own independent administration[s]."[22] The persistence of weak, poverty-stricken provincial governments, however, thwarted regionalist aspirations as much as had centralism.

Federalism's strong appeal in 1855 is evidenced by the complete reversal of Rafael Núñez, who had launched his national political career two years earlier by combating the federalist ideas of the Radicals. In a pamphlet written in early 1855 Núñez presented two basic arguments on behalf of federalism: the need to consolidate provinces into

21. Mariano Ospina to General Pedro Alcántara Herrán, March 26, 1855, reprinted in Vega, *La federación*, 165.
22. José María Samper, *Historia de un alma* (Medellín, 1971), 396–97.

larger, more viable units and the desire to give legal expression to Colombia's regionalist configuration. He asserted that things could not be left in their present "insupportable state" of "discord and permanent struggle between the general government and the particular governments." Núñez concluded that because of political, economic, and cultural diversity, Colombia "is not a single nationality, but a group of nationalities, each one needing its own special, independent, and exclusive government."[23]

Provincial consolidation to form larger, more viable governmental units appealed to the anti-centralist Liberal reformers, to the Conservatives who wanted to preserve havens from Radical reformism, and to those who sought to give fuller rein to Colombia's regional diversity. The constitution posed no barriers to the reconstitution of larger territorial units, and consolidation offered a practical solution to the problems caused by provincial fragmentation without returning to centralism.

In early 1855 Congress took the first formal step toward federalism when it passed a constitutional amendment creating the state of Panama by consolidating four isthmian provinces. Panama was the first state formed because that remote region had special need of an effective, unified government capable of meeting the dangers and opportunities resulting from the enormous growth in transisthmian traffic in the years between the 1849 California gold rush and completion of the Panama Railroad in early 1855. The amendment that elevated Panama to status as a state also authorized the formation of other states by simple act of law. In 1856 Congress created the state of Antioquia, and in 1857 six new states were formed from the country's remaining provinces.[24] The Republic of Nueva Granada was thus reduced to a loosely associated group of eight states with a national government limited to largely symbolic powers and functions.

To ensure some basis for continued existence as a national society and to provide for interstate relations and comity, the new administration of Mariano Ospina Rodríguez moved rapidly and effectively to-

23.   Rafael Núñez, La federación (Bogotá, 1855), 7–8, 13.

24.   José María Samper, Derecho público interno de Colombia (2 vols.; Bogotá, 1951), I, 240; Pombo and Guerra (eds.), Constituciones, IV, 29–30, 127.

ward the promulgation of a new constitution. Although the Constitution of 1858, by associating the eight states as the *Confederación Granadina*, represented a step toward the recentralization of authority, it limited the national government to the exercise of specifically enumerated powers and reserved all other powers to the states. Besides embracing federalism, the constitution contained such Liberal doctrines as fully guaranteed individual liberties, unlimited freedom of the press, and separation of church and state, principles not unknown to the Conservatives.[25]

A process of testing the limits of function and authority assigned to the federal government in the new constitution began in 1859. A new law enacted by Conservatives called for the inspection of state militias by the national government. Another, the highly controversial election law, permitted the national government to exercise a decisive role in the verification of state election results.[26] The Liberals strongly protested the enactment of these laws, charging that they violated the federalist spirit if not the letter of the constitution.[27]

As the Conservative administration explored the possibilities for fullest exercise of federal authority, the Liberals, in control of several state governments, were determined to maintain state autonomy in the fullest degree.[28] Disturbances between the two parties broke out in several states in 1859, and Tomás Cipriano de Mosquera, governor of Cauca, announced his nonrecognition of the election law. Early the following year Mosquera overtly abandoned Conservatism and openly began courting the Liberals. By the time Congress met in early 1860 its greatest concern was how to contain the ambitious Mosquera who

25. Gilmore, "Federalism in Colombia," 378–84; Pombo and Guerra (eds.), *Constituciones*, IV, 55, 57–59, 73–74.

26. Antonio Pérez Aguirre, *25 años de historia colombiana, 1853 a 1878: del centralismo a la federación* (Bogotá, 1959), 94–95.

27. For example, see the formal protest from the president of the Panama Assembly, Rafael Núñez, dated October 13, 1859, in *El Tiempo* (Bogotá), #267, January, 1860 (date missing).

28. Ramón Espina to Tomás C. Mosquera, January 12, 1859, Mosquera to Espina, January 25, 1859, Espina to Mosquera, April 20, 1859, Espina to Mosquera, April 27, 1859, Mosquera to Espina, May 3, 1859, all in J. León Helguera and Robert H. Davis (eds.), *Archivo epistolar del General Mosquera: correspondencia con el General Ramón Espina, 1835–1866* (Bogotá, 1966), 283, 288–89, 297–300, 302.

had arrogated to himself leadership of the federalist forces. A congressional committee set to work drafting a compromise election law. It was enacted on May 10, but too late. Two days earlier Mosquera had declared the secession of Cauca from the Confederation and directed his army toward Bogotá.[29] Shortly thereafter a group of Liberals, including Manuel Murillo Toro, Aquileo Parra, and Rafael Núñez, attempted to forestall civil war by placating Mosquera with an endorsement of him as presidential "candidate of the federalists."[30] Despite this effort to appease Mosquera, he remained undeterred in his resolve to topple the Conservative government.

Mosquera's bellicosity placed the Radicals in a dilemma and caused division to resurface in the Liberal party. The Moderate Liberals, represented by Obando and López, dutifully followed Mosquera, but the Radicals initially resisted war and only reluctantly enlisted in Mosquera's ranks. Murillo, Salvador Camacho Roldán, and Núñez vigorously argued against war in mid-1860, but events made their position untenable. In a letter addressed to Murillo and published in *El Tiempo*, Núñez, although not a Radical, expressed the exasperation felt by many Radicals toward Mosquera: "General Mosquera surely must have desisted from all warlike thought since news of the electoral reform arrived; that is, since he lacked the only thing considered a *casus belli* in the present crisis. If he has not desisted, if he does not desist, the fault will not rest on those who accepted reform as a compromise for maintaining peace, but rather on his conduct in such a notably grave matter."[31]

The civil war of 1860–1862 was a violent statement by state political leaders determined to retain as much as possible of their near-sovereign independence of 1857–1858. Tradition and the language of the time make it difficult to avoid the simplistic label of a centralist-federalist struggle, but in reality the conflict still turned around the

29. Pérez Aguirre, *25 años de historia*, 95–115; Castillo, *El primer Núñez*, 244–47. For background information on Mosquera and insight into his character see J. León Helguera, "The First Mosquera Administration in New Granada, 1845–1849" (Ph.D. dissertation, University of North Carolina, 1958), 44–48.

30. *El Tiempo* (Bogotá), May 15, 1860.

31. *Ibid.*, June 26, 1860; Aquileo Parra, *Memorias de Aquileo Parra* (Bogotá, 1912), 211; *El Tiempo* (Bogotá), June 26, 1860.

problem of the allowable degree of local autonomy consonant with nationhood. In September 1860 the states of Cauca and Bolívar, the latter again led by Juan José Nieto, signed an offensive and defensive treaty directed against the national government. Shortly after his Liberal forces occupied Bogotá in mid-1861, Mosquera assumed control of the new government as provisional president, issued a series of virulently anticlerical war measures, and summoned state delegates to Bogotá to sign a pact of union. Seven of the nine states—the state of Tolima, formed from two Cundinamarcan provinces by a Mosquera decree during the war, brought the total number of states to nine—sent delegations. Participants were the "sovereign and independent states of Bolívar, Boyacá, Cauca, Cundinamarca, Magdalena, Santander, and Tolima."[32] This 1861 Pact of Union marks the formal implementation of the doctrine of state sovereignty, a doctrine later sanctioned when the Liberals gathered in convention at Rionegro and drew up the ultra-federal Constitution of 1863.

From 1863 to 1886 Colombian sovereignty was divided into nine unequal portions exercised by units called sovereign states. This period represented the culmination of a prolonged—perhaps particularistic—movement against centralization of authority. The movement had its genesis in the late eighteenth century resistance to the centralizing thrust of the Bourbon reforms. It then had found dramatic—if unsuccessful—expression in the Comunero Rebellion of 1781, and it would thwart any united action against Spain from 1811 to 1814. After 1831, the anti-centralist campaign was waged against the war-born absolutism of the first Republic of Colombia; it won acceptance in the rampant reformism of mid-century, and it found its ultimate expression in the Constitution of 1863. The national government and the church, institutions which in the past had provided a basis for national cohesion by articulating municipal and provincial interests in the capital, were debilitated during the 1863–1886 period. Political parties had yet to achieve a truly national organization. Absence of vigorous national institutions plus the lack of a national banking system and any extensive transportation network other than Magdalena steam-

32. Pérez Aguirre, 25 años de historia, 182–84; Pombo and Guerra (eds.), Constituciones, IV, 85, 89, 92–93. The 1861 Pact of Union was not signed by Antioquia and Panama and is therefore not considered a constitution.

boats and connecting mule trails made it certain that the states would become the foci of political and economic activity.

On the basis of propinquity and geographical unity, economic interest, and political identification the nine states periodically grouped into informal regions. During the latter part of the 1863–1874 period, the states aligned into these four regions: (1) Cauca; (2) the north coast, consisting of Panama, Bolívar, and Magdalena; (3) the Central Cordillera occupied by Antioquia and Tolima; and (4) the eastern mountain region of Santander, Boyacá, and Cundinamarca. The states composing these regions possessed distinctive economies and political traditions which determined the degree of internal cohesion and effectiveness of the regions in their struggle for influence and power at the national level.

Cauca had long enjoyed a position of prestige and national influence commensurate with its vast expanse. It was governed from Popayán, a tradition-minded city situated on the elevated southern extremity of the Cauca Valley. Cauca's widely varied climate and geographical features permitted the production of a great diversity of exportable commodities such as tobacco, cinchona, and rubber.[33] Gold mining had provided the key ingredient in Cauca's economic power during the first half of the nineteenth century, but the elimination of slave labor at mid-century had brought an end to large-scale mining operations. Cauca's exports registered no increase in value from 1862 to 1874. This stagnation led Aníbal Galindo, compiler of the 1875 *Anuario estadístico de Colombia*, correctly to conclude that Cauca "is in a lamentable state of backwardness and poverty." A major cause of the economic stagnation, aside from the sharp decline in gold mining, was the difficulty of access to neighboring states and to the exterior which seriously hampered large-scale production of bulky marketable agricultural and forest products. Completion of a reliable route between the port of Buenaventura and the Cauca Valley, an unrealized goal since the mid-sixteenth century, continued to offer hope for a brighter economic future.[34]

33. Aníbal Galindo (ed.), *Anuario estadístico de Colombia, 1875* (Bogotá, 1875), 142, 150–51, 180–82; Felipe Pérez, *Jeografía física i política de los Estados Unidos de Colombia* (2 vols.; Bogotá, 1862–63), I, 374.
34. Galindo (ed.), *Anuario*, 115, 136–37; Pérez, *Jeografía física*, I, 374; Vicente Restrepo, *Estudio sobre las minas de oro y plata de Colombia* (Bogotá, 1952), 76,

Table 1

State Populations in 1851 and 1870, Percentage Increase, and Populations of the State Capitals in 1870

	1851	1870	% Increase	Capital	1870 Population
Antioquia	243,388	365,974	50	Medellín	29,765
Bolívar	205,607	241,704	18	Cartagena	8,603
Boyacá	379,682	498,541	31	Tunja	5,471
Cauca	323,574	435,078	34	Popayán	8,485
Cundinamarca	317,351	413,658	30	Bogotá	40,883
Magdalena	67,764	88,928	31	Santa Marta	5,472
Panama	138,108	224,032	62	Panama City	18,378
Santander	360,148	433,178	20	Socorro	16,048
Tolima	208,108	230,891	11	Guamo	9,193
Colombia	2,243,730	2,931,984	31		

SOURCES: The state population figures are taken from Fernando Gómez, "Los censos en Colombia antes de 1905," in Miguel Urrutia M. and Mario Arrubla (eds.), *Compendio de estadísticas históricas de Colombia* (Bogotá, 1970), Table 13, p. 30. The population figures for the state capitals are from Aníbal Galindo (ed.), *Anuario estadístico de Colombia, 1875* (Bogotá, 1875), 28–46.

Although Cauca remained a *Mosquerista* bastion throughout the decade following 1863, the Conservatives made up a large minority concentrated along the border with Antioquia, in Popayán, and in the southern highlands around Pasto. The political threat posed by this Conservative minority helped maintain unity in the Liberal party but caused strained relations with Antioquia, a Conservative stronghold. José María Samper, the Liberal publicist, somewhat mistakenly considered Cauca "a model of stability" during this period, a view understandable in light of the state's patrician tradition.[35]

The three north coast states, in addition to their Atlantic coastline,

---

95–97. For a detailed history of the effort to open this route see James H. Neal, "The Pacific Age Comes to Colombia: The Construction of the Cali–Buenaventura Route, 1854–1882" (Ph.D. dissertation, Vanderbilt University, 1971).

35. Samper, *Derecho público,* I, 306.

shared a tropical climate, a low topographical profile along the populated littoral, and an orientation toward the exterior which was particularly pronounced in the case of Panama. Panama's extensive international contacts, remoteness from Bogotá, and loose ties with the other states led to a weak sense of national identity. An examination of the economic distance between Panama and Bogotá led one historian to conclude: "Panama was for all practical purposes an independent state between 1861 and 1885." Interstate economic ties consisted of little more than a light coasting trade with Cauca and Bolívar, for the land connection was impenetrable. Yet Panama was of considerable economic importance to the nation, because beginning in 1867 rental from the Panama Railroad Company provided a $250,000 annual income to the national treasury.[36] Panama's economy depended on the commercial activities of Panama City and employment provided by the railroad. The isthmian crossing was Panama's *raison d' être* and livelihood, but at the same time the cause of "a thousand conflicts and many other vexations." In view of the "decadence, not to mention the ruin" alleged to prevail throughout most sections of the state, it is hardly surprising that the projected isthmian canal would continue to be regarded during the following decade as an economic panacea.[37]

In contrast to Panama, whose exports were of slight importance, the economies of Bolívar and Magdalena depended primarily on production of goods for interstate trade and export. Both states produced cattle and large quantities of marine salt, which provided valuable commodities of trade with the interior states. Magdalena's exports consisted principally of dyewoods and hides which came from the interior between Riohacha and Valledupar. Bolívar possessed a more diversified economy than its eastern neighbor, and its 1863 exports were estimated at three times the value of Magdalena's.[38] The area around Carmen produced abundant tobacco of export quality; in 1874 only

36. William P. McGreevey, *An Economic History of Colombia, 1845–1930* (Cambridge, 1971), 162; law 46 of August 16, 1867, *Constitución y leyes de los Estados Unidos de Colombia espedidas en los años de 1863 a 1875* (Bogotá, 1875), 462, hereinafter cited as *Leyes de Colombia, 1863–75.* Note that "$" as used hereinafter refers to the Colombian peso.

37. Pérez, *Jeografía física,* II, 130; Galindo (ed.), *Anuario,* 115.

38. Galindo (ed.), *Anuario,* 123–24, 142, 158, 160; Pérez, *Jeografía física,* II, 128–29, 603–605, 637.

Cauca harvested a more valuable tobacco crop. Other commodities produced in exportable quantities included dyewoods, cotton, and rubber. Aníbal Galindo concluded in 1875 that Bolívar was one of only four states showing signs of a prosperous economic development.[39]

The Magdalena River, which formed the common border between Bolívar and Magdalena, was the main artery of trade linking the north coast and the Colombian interior. Both states' economies relied significantly on servicing the national import-export trade, and an intense commercial rivalry among Cartagena, Barranquilla, and Santa Marta focused on the struggle to capture the major portion of this trade. Cartagena had direct linkage to the river through the Dique Canal, and this had helped the city dominate Colombian external trade during the colonial period. Difficulty in keeping the canal open to navigation led to the emergence of Santa Marta as the most active port from the period of independence to the 1870s. Santa Marta maintained its dominant position until 1872, when Barranquilla, a Magdalena River port, captured the lead. Completion of a railroad connecting Barranquilla to the coast in 1871 catapulted it into a position of commercial dominance and gravely crippled economic activity along the seaboard of the state of Magdalena.[40]

All three north coast states were Liberal strongholds from 1863 to 1874. The political disturbances that they experienced were caused by party factionalism generally revolving around the question of loyalty to General Mosquera. Bolívar was the most politically tranquil of the three states. After Liberals ousted aging civil war caudillo General Juan José Nieto in 1864, no serious disturbances occurred. Magdalena suffered from many armed uprisings, all of them resulting from personalist struggles for power within the Liberal party. Mosquera had several clients in the state whose political fortunes tended to follow his own.[41] Insurrections and armed struggles for control of the state describe the political norm in Panama from 1863 to 1874. Ten factional

39. Galindo (ed.), *Anuario*, 116, 142.

40. Theodore E. Nichols, "The Rise of Barranquilla," *Hispanic American Historical Review*, XXXIV (May, 1954), 158–69; Alfredo Ortega, *Ferrocarriles colombianos* (2 vols.; Bogotá, 1920–23), II, 300; Galindo (ed.), *Anuario*, 115.

41. Gustavo Arboleda, *Revoluciones locales de Colombia* (Popayán, 1907), 9–12, 19–22; José C. Alarcón, *Compendio de historia del departamento del Magdalena de 1525 hasta 1895* (Santa Marta, 1898), 217–19, 227–28.

wars among Liberals racked the state, and three different constitutions were promulgated. José María Samper concluded that Panama excelled all other states in "its instability, the constant scandal of its barracks insurrections, and the immorality of its political circles and their governmental practices."[42]

Remoteness of the north coast from the Colombian interior heightened the region's conviction that it suffered from neglect by the national government. The great bulk of national revenue came from the Panama Railroad and the customs ports of Bolívar and Magdalena, and these states bitterly complained that they received little in return. Although the three states remained loyal to the Liberal party, the party gave scant recognition to the costeños in selecting its national leadership. Party factionalism contributed to the region's low political prestige and to the turmoil in Panama and Magdalena. In contrast to Panama and Magdalena, Bolívar exhibited political stability, and it possessed greater economic power. This relative strength enabled Bolívar to provide leadership for costeño regionalism in the decade following 1874.

Antioquia and Tolima, mountainous, landlocked states situated along the upper Magdalena River, shared a commercial orientation and an interest in mining activities. Antioquia ranked as one of the most economically dynamic of the nine states, causing many observers erroneously to attribute Antioqueño "race" and culture to Jewish origins.[43]

---

42. Arboleda, Revoluciones, 11–15, 18, 28–30, 34, 37–38; Samper, Derecho público, I, 308.

43. Controversy concerning the historical origins of the economic success of Antioqueños has nourished a debate up to the present. Antioqueño "uniqueness" in this regard has been attributed to a variety of factors including an ancestry containing a high proportion of Jewish and/or Basque blood, gold mining experience, absence of both a latifundista and serf class in the region, withdrawal of status respect by other Colombians, and a colonial tradition which favored investments in mining and commerce over agriculture. For a discussion of these and other factors see Everett E. Hagen, On the Theory of Social Change: How Economic Growth Begins (Homewood, Ill., 1962), 353–84; Luis H. Fajardo, The Protestant Ethic of the Antioqueños: Social Structure and Personality (Cali, n.d.); Frank Safford, "Significación de los antioqueños en el desarrollo económico colombiano: un examen crítico de la tesis de Everett Hagen," Anuario Colombiano de Historia Social y de la Cultura, II (1965), 18–27; Ann Twinam, "Enterprise and Elites in Eighteenth-Century Medellín," Hispanic American Historical Review, LIX (August, 1979), 444–75.

A relatively high rate of population growth contributed to a colonization movement into neighboring states which spread Antioqueño culture and influence. Gold provided the stimulus to Antioquia's economic activity. Mines in the northern part of the state furnished the bulk of national production, which in 1872 exceeded $2,000,000. Antioquia also conducted an active interstate trade, exchanging foreign merchandise obtained from the north coast ports and gold for provisions from neighboring states.[44] Small-scale agriculture contributed to the general economic well-being. Impressed by the Antioqueño countryside as he left the 1863 Rionegro convention, Salvador Camacho Roldán, a highly regarded Radical who remained prominent in Liberal circles throughout the last half of the nineteenth century, observed: "Land is well divided and the poor classes enjoy a comfort and independence which are equaled only in the State of Santander."[45] Antioquia maintained its closest commercial ties with Tolima. Except for Ibagué and Guamo, Tolima's important population centers were located along the Magdalena River, which provided a north-south means of transportation. The extensive borders shared with Cauca, Antioquia, and Cundinamarca as well as ready access to the Magdalena River permitted Tolima to concentrate on the cultivation of export crops and develop an overland trade in provisions. Tobacco from the northern area around Ambalema and cacao from the Neiva region in the south composed the first and second most valuable exports. Gold production became important in the northern mountain region during the early 1870s when Antioqueño settlers populated the area.[46]

No state surpassed Antioquia in its ardent support of the Conservative party and the Catholic Church. The Conservatives governed from 1856 when the state was formed until General Mosquera imposed a Liberal governor in 1862. During a brief conflict ending in January, 1864, the Conservatives replaced the Liberal government and wrote a new constitution which survived until the national government again imposed a Liberal regime in the aftermath of the 1876–

44. James J. Parsons, *Antioqueño Colonization in Western Colombia* (Berkeley, 1949), 87–89, 102–105; Restrepo, *Estudio sobre minas*, 199; Galindo (ed.), *Anuario*, 133, 135, 154–55; Pérez, *Jeografía física*, II, 539.

45. Salvador Camacho Roldán, *Mis memorias* (2 vols.; Bogotá, 1946), II, 230.

46. Pérez, *Jeografía física*, II, 54–55; Restrepo, *Estudio sobre minas*, 139.

1877 civil war. Pedro Justo Berrío, state governor from 1864 until 1873, cultivated friendly relations with the neighboring states and supported the federal system because it minimized interference from the Liberal-controlled national government. The religious disposition of the state leaders is revealed in the signing of an "adherence" to the pope by members of the legislature in 1873. In the same year the legislature vetoed the acceptance of national scholarships available for study at the National University in Bogotá because of the "materialist, utilitarian, and immoral teachings" at the university.[47]

In sharp contrast to its northern neighbor, Tolima lacked the unity and identity associated with recognition as a traditional political entity. The state consisted of two administrative units inherited from colonial days, the province of Neiva and the corregimiento of Mariquita; the latter had been absorbed by Cundinamarca during the wars for independence. Mariquita subsequently achieved separate provincial status, but both Neiva and Mariquita were incorporated into the state of Cundinamarca upon its formation in 1857. Creation of Tolima from these two Cundinamarcan provinces by Mosquera in 1861 caused serious administrative problems which were reflected in frequent shifts of the state capital among the cities of Ibagué, Neiva, Natagaima, and Guamo.[48] Despite such administrative difficulties, Tolima suffered few civil disturbances from 1863 to 1874. It remained a center of Mosquera loyalism until his ouster from the presidency in 1867 when the turmoil of national politics caused months of intermittent fighting in the state among Conservatives, Radicals, and Mosqueristas. The Conservatives emerged victorious, imposed a new constitution, and ruled Tolima for the following decade.[49]

Antioquia and Tolima shared similar topographical features and problems, maintained extensive commercial ties, and after 1867 oper-

47. Arboleda, *Revoluciones*, 8–9; Samper, *Derecho público*, I, 305; Estanislao Gómez Barrientos, *25 años a través del estado de Antioquia; primera parte, 1863 a 1875* (Medellín, 1918), 104, 180, 168(a)–69(a).
48. Felipe Pérez, *Geografía general, física y política de los Estados Unidos de Colombia y geografía particular de la ciudad de Bogotá* (Bogotá, 1883), 126.
49. *Memoria que el secretario de hacienda i fomento presenta al presidente de la república* (Bogotá, 1871), xxix, hereinafter cited as *Memoria de Hacienda* followed by year of publication; Arboleda, *Revoluciones*, 23–27; Carlos Holguín, *Cartas políticas publicadas en "El Correo Nacional"* (Bogotá, 1951), 77–79.

ated as close political allies. Both eagerly sought the improvement of overland travel and river navigation. Tolima's commercial and economic ties with Cundinamarca, however, were even more intimate because of its formation from portions of that state.[50] Tolima had long sold its products on the savanna of Bogotá and served as a main line of travel from the nation's capital to Popayán.

Colombia's Eastern Cordillera, which extended through Cundinamarca, Boyacá, and Santander, imparted a common upland culture to those states but minimized interchange among them. The three states shared leanings toward Liberalism, but the general nature of their economies was distinct. A network of internal trade radiating from Bogotá shaped the economy of Cundinamarca; a village-market economy prevailed throughout much of Boyacá, and Santander suffered a decline in its artisan industries while struggling to develop its exports.

The large variety of commodities produced in Cundinamarca contributed little to the export trade but provided the ingredients for a valuable internal commerce which distinguished Cundinamarca from other states. This commerce consisted of the exchange of hot-country products such as tobacco and sugar for goods produced in Bogotá and the savanna which included iron implements, salt, wheat, potatoes, and other foodstuffs. Shipment of foreign merchandise from Honda to Bogotá, from where much of it was distributed, added substantially to the value of this internal trade. State budget figures indicate the extreme importance of internal commerce in Cundinamarca. Road tolls provided the biggest single source of income in the 1874 budget—36 percent of the total.[51]

Boyacá's isolation, poverty, and bleak economic future offered a striking contrast to Cundinamarca. Major difficulties hindering development included the extremely mountainous terrain, the lack of anything resembling a transportation system, remoteness from the Magdalena River, and absence of exports. Production of simple textiles engaged about 30 percent of the labor force, but the bulk of these goods went to internal consumption. The few surplus commodities available for trade were exchanged for cattle from the llanos; salt, foreign mer-

50.   Samper, Derecho público, I, 309.
51.   Pérez, Jeografía física, II, 189–92; Galindo (ed.), Anuario, 220.

chandise, and iron tools from Cundinamarca; and provisions such as coffee, cacao, sugar, rice, and tobacco from Santander.[52]

Santander was considered one of the most prosperous states of the nation, and the Santandereanos enjoyed a reputation of being "hard-working and extraordinarily frugal."[53] The state produced a variety of commodities which sustained a limited but growing export trade based principally on cultivation of cacao and coffee in the region around Cúcuta. Production of common articles of clothing employed nearly a quarter of the labor force, and these goods together with to-bacco from the Girón-Piedecuesta area contributed to trade with neigh-boring states.[54] Because Santander possessed potentially valuable ex-ports, the lack of easy access to the exterior caused real concern. The Magdalena River on the western border and the Zulia River extending from near Cúcuta on the Venezuelan border to the Gulf of Maracaibo presented special problems. The Cúcuta-Maracaibo route required a combination of overland and water transportation and was subject to the whims of Venezuelan customs officials. A crude path connected the populated interior of the state with the Magdalena River, and its primitiveness caused growing demands for new, improved roads and for railroad construction. In the early 1870s Santander led Boyacá and Cundinamarca in calling for construction of an interstate railroad in Colombia's eastern mountain region which would link the region with the Magdalena River and with Bogotá.

Besides forming a geographical unity, the three eastern mountain states shared a Liberal political orientation and a relatively high de-gree of political stability. Cundinamarca was the least stable of the three states, partly due to "the concentration of all the agitations of na-tional politics in the [state] capital."[55] Mosquera had slight influence in Santander and Boyacá, but he enjoyed a strong following in Cun-dianamarca. Division in Cundinamarca's Liberal party contributed to instability and permitted the Conservatives briefly to gain control of

52. *Memoria de Hacienda*, 1873, 76; Pérez, *Jeografía física*, II, 337–38.

53. Galindo (ed.), *Anuario*, 115.

54. Pérez, *Jeografía física*, II, 442–44; David C. Johnson, "Economic and Social Change in Nineteenth Century Colombia: Santander, 1850–1885" (Ph.D. disserta-tion, University of California, Berkeley, 1975), 303–308.

55. *Memoria de Hacienda*, 1871, xxvi.

the state government in 1868 prior to Radical victory. Boyacá suffered only two significant disturbances during the period, and the Liberals had little difficulty in maintaining their domination there despite the presence of many large landowners and conventual establishments in the Tunja area which gave it a decidedly Conservative cast.[56] Santander was the most stable of the three states, experiencing no significant civil conflicts during the first decade under the 1863 constitution. It nourished the *comunero* tradition and ardently sustained Colombian liberalism throughout the nineteenth century. The Radicals were identified more closely with Santander than with any other state, and many Radicals of national prominence held public office in the state.[57]

Santander, with support from Cundinamarca and Boyacá, imposed its Radical Liberalism on the national government for a decade following 1867. Every Colombian president holding office during that decade had his political origins in one of these states. Forty-six percent of the Colombian population in 1870 resided in the region, and it elected twenty-seven of the sixty members of the House of Representatives.[58] Passage of legislation in the early 1870s supporting construction of the Northern Railroad, a route projected to link Bogotá with an unspecified port on the lower Magdalena River, represented the most conspicuous example of the region's exercise of its political power. That project expressed a principal aspiration of each of the three states—the provision of cheap, reliable transportation to the Magdalena River. It was designed to meet the commercial interests of Cundinamarca, ease the export problems of Santander, and offer a possible solution to the general economic distress of Boyacá.

Both the federal system of sovereign states and the informal grouping of states into regional blocs emerged in response to the unfulfilled aspiration for a medium capable of articulating regionalist ambitions. The opportunity to realize this aspiration arose when the mid-century surge of reformism debilitated central authority and national institu-

56. Holguín, *Cartas políticas*, 84–102; Arboleda, *Revoluciones*, 15, 23, 31–34.

57. Eduardo Rodríguez Piñeres, *El olimpo radical: ensayos conocidos e inéditos sobre su época, 1864–1884* (Bogotá, 1950), 164, 229–36; Eladio Mantilla, *Geografía especial del estado de Santander* (Socorro, 1880), 16. Examples include Manuel Murillo, Eustorgio Salgar, Francisco Javier Zaldúa, Nicolás Esguerra, and Aquileo Parra.

58. Pérez, *Geografía general*, 167.

tions. After the weakening of these barriers to regionalist expression, there occurred a decade of experimentation with governmental structure seeking to move the locus of power below the national level. Provinces consolidated into states in order to overcome their weakness and to exert pressure more effectively on the national government. The states repeated this process of combining into larger, more effective units in the late 1860s when they informally organized into regional blocs.

The four-region pattern did not achieve full definition until President Mosquera was overthrown in 1867. Prior to that date relations among the nine states were governed by competition between Mosquera, the Moderate Liberals, and Cauca on one hand and Manuel Murillo Toro, the Radicals, and Santander on the other. The considerable power which Cauca exercised through Mosquera's influence in Tolima, the north coast states, and Cundinamarca was dissipated the moment he left Colombia for forced residence abroad. Tolima joined Antioquia in its politically marginalized status as the only Conservative region amidst a sea of Liberalism. Mosquera's departure from the national scene rendered the north coast states more susceptible to Radical penetration but did not resolve the factionalism in the region's Liberal party structure. Panama's remoteness and the economic competition between Bolívar and Magdalena also complicated and delayed regional cooperation on the north coast. Cundinamarca and Boyacá followed Santander's leadership in the push for Radical dominance. This region's unity was enhanced by state economies which did not compete and by the ability to agree on mutually beneficial goals such as construction of the Northern Railroad. Such advantages permitted the Radicals who governed the eastern mountain region to gain control of the national government in 1867 and to retain it for the next ten years. The regionalist configuration which took form in Colombia during the first decade under the 1863 constitution decisively shaped the struggle for political power and the course of national development.

One of the keys to understanding the turbulence that Colombia experienced during the second half of the nineteenth century is the power of regionalist assertion. The results of that assertion became manifest in the aftermath of the mid-century reform movement which decentralized authority by shifting substantial governmental power from the national to the local and provincial levels. Reformers had hoped to eliminate civil war by reducing the opportunity for the abuse of power by the national government and by satisfying longings for greater local and regional control. Instead they merely decentralized civil conflict. In the context of weakened national authority General Mosquera found it opportune to initiate the war of 1860–1862 by ordering the secession of Cauca. And the secessionist threat was voiced more than once in subsequent years.

Chapter II

Colombian Liberalism, 1863–1874

Colombia's Constitution of 1863, its fifth after attaining separate independent status, allowed ample development of regionalist aspirations. It crippled national authority more severely than had any of the previous charters. Regionalism was an underlying cause of Liberal factionalism during the 1863 constitution's first decade of operation, but its more immediate causes were the uncompromising stance assumed by Tomás Cipriano de Mosquera and policy shifts by the Radicals. After Mosquera's removal from the national scene in 1867, the Radicals, with their base in the eastern mountain region, gained control of the national government. Firmly wedded to a policy of free trade, they discovered that its successful implementation required export expansion, which in turn could be achieved only if major federal expenditures were made for improved transportation. The resulting shift in Radical policy toward an enhanced federal economic and administrative power, a policy they had vigorously opposed in 1863, tended to blur the ideological differences between the two Liberal factions. At the same time regional rivalry as a cause of factionalism became more apparent. Challenges to Radical hegemony from 1869 to 1875 more and more suggested a struggle for power between the Colombian littoral and the interior.

On February 4, 1863, a constitutional convention composed entirely of Liberal delegates met at Rionegro, Antioquia, and began three and one-half months of deliberations on the document destined to govern Colombian political life until 1885.[1] Conservative exclusion from the convention was a direct consequence of Liberal victory in the civil war which had raged throughout the country since 1860. Aside from inaugurating more than two decades of Liberal rule, the 1863 constitution is significant for providing a governmental framework under which regionalist sentiment gained its fullest expression since Colombian independence. The Rionegro Constitution is less important for its doctrinal innovation, for it borrowed heavily from earlier constitutions and sanctioned elements of liberal ideology which had been in vogue for a generation. The ideological hallmarks of the 1863 constitution were its relatively extreme provisions protecting federalism and individual liberty and the high degree of state supervision it imposed on the church. Besides formulating a new constitution, the convention delegates also enacted laws and created a provisional ministerial executive to rule the country until the constitution was drawn up and a new president elected. During the closing sessions, the delegates elected Mosquera as president of Colombia for a term to end April 1, 1864.[2]

The very prominence of the delegates, who represented the nine sovereign states and the newly created Federal District of Bogotá, assured the convention of lasting historical significance. With few exceptions the men destined to assume conspicuous roles in Liberal party leadership from 1863 to 1885 were present at Rionegro. Among the delegates were seven men who during the next two decades would be elected to the presidency.[3] Prominent Radicals at Rionegro included Generals José Hilario López and Santos Gutiérrez as well as Salvador Camacho Roldán, Francisco Javier Zaldúa, and Justo Arosemena. The dominant position of the Radicals was reflected in the election of

1. Convention proceedings were published in *Anales de la Convención* (Rionegro), February 12, 1863, to June 5, 1863. Firsthand accounts by delegates are available in Parra, *Memorias*, 276–415, and Camacho Roldán, *Mis memorias*, II, 151–231. The best study of the convention is Ramón Correa, *La convención de Rionegro: Páginas históricas de Colombia* (Bogotá, 1937).

2. Parra, *Memorias*, 393, 402; Correa, *La convención*, 114–15.

3. Notable absentees included Manuel Murillo, Santiago Pérez, and Miguel Samper; the future presidents were Tomás Cipriano de Mosquera, Santos Gutiérrez, Eustorgio Salgar, Aquileo Parra, Julián Trujillo, Rafael Núñez, and Francisco Javier Zaldúa.

Zaldúa and Arosemena as convention presidents. The most conspicuous leaders of the Mosquerista faction, aside from Mosquera, were José María Rojas Garrido of Tolima, generally acknowledged the convention's best orator, and Ramón Gómez, also known as "El Sapo," political boss of Cundinamarca. Most commentators on the convention conclude that although the Mosqueristas were in a minority position the assertiveness of their leader partly compensated for numerical weakness.[4]

Colombia's outstanding mid–nineteenth-century political figure, Tomás Cipriano de Mosquera, was the most powerful delegate at Rionegro. Mosquera's power stemmed from his status as former president, his initiation of the civil war as governor of Cauca, his successful military leadership of the Liberal forces, and his position as provisional president of the revolutionary government formed in 1861. When the convention opened, Mosquera was a delegate from Cauca, provisional president of Colombia, supreme director of the war, and governor of the states of Cauca, Antioquia, and Tolima.[5] A division of loyal veteran troops accompanied Mosquera to Rionegro, a site he had selected for the convention because of the open enthusiasm of its citizenry for his wartime leadership.[6] His obvious power and his claim to be the savior of the Liberal party made Mosquera himself an issue upon which the delegates quickly formed into competing factions.

Although attitudes toward Mosquera appeared to be the basis for Liberal factionalism, at a more profound level the divisions derived from regional rivalry and ideological conflict. The regional basis of the disunity is suggested by the fact that the majority of the pro-Mosquera delegates came from one group of states and a majority of his opponents came from a different group of states. More than half of the Mos-

---

4. Pérez Aguirre, 25 años de historia, 189; Camacho Roldán, Mis memorias, II, 214, 217; Correa, La convención, 48; José María Cordovez Moure, Reminiscencias: Santa Fe y Bogotá (10 vols.; 6th ed.; Bogotá, 1942–46), VI, 8. Salvador Camacho Roldán judged that the convention was evenly divided between pro- and anti-Mosquera factions; see Camacho Roldán, Mis memorias, II, 160.
5. Camacho Roldán, Mis memorias, II, 154. Some states employed the title "president" for their chief executive, and others referred to him as "governor." The title "governor" will be used in order to distinguish the office from that of president of the republic.
6. Ibid., 157.

quera partisans came from his home state, Cauca, and the three north coast states of Panama, Bolívar, and Magdalena. The state origins of the anti-Mosquera faction show a greater degree of regional concentration. More than half of these delegates came from Santander, Boyacá, and Cundinamarca, with Santander providing the largest single block. Mosquera had few family ties and little economic base in the altiplano, and during the 1850s he had lost many of his clients in that area. Salvador Camacho Roldán observed that Mosquera wielded little influence in Santander and Boyacá because of the prestige of other Liberals in those states, whereas the strong military tradition of the north coast states rendered them susceptible to the caudillo's blandishments.[7] Division among delegates over loyalty to Mosquera thus followed a regional configuration. The coastal fringe tended to support him, whereas the eastern mountain region resisted his pretensions.

Debate on a proposal to transfer the capital from Bogotá to Panama City reflected the strength of regionalist sentiment and its disruptive effect on party unity. Four delegates from Santander—Aquileo Parra, Estanislao Silva, Felipe Zapata, and Alejandro Gómez Santos—and Camilo A. Echeverri from Antioquia presented the proposal to the assembly. The author of the accompanying report which argued in support of the proposal was Rafael Núñez, delegate from Panama.[8] Núñez asserted that the transfer to Panama City would increase foreign contacts and immigration, provide greater exposure to the beneficial influence of Europe and the United States, and reduce the isolation of the interior. He argued that the transfer would enhance national unity by strengthening the loose ties of the coastal states to the federation. Núñez' marked antipathy toward Bogotá is evident in the following passage from his report: "Bogotá, seat of the Viceroys and of the central governments, metropolis of ultramontane fanaticism . . . and general headquarters of all intrigues and political conspiracies, is, for these

7. *Ibid.*, 160–62.
8. *Anales de la Convención* (Rionegro), March 13, 1863; Parra, *Memorias*, 328; Camacho Roldán, *Mis memorias*, II, 220. Núñez did not sign the proposal, probably because he felt that sponsorship by a delegate from Panama would jeopardize its chance of passage. It is unclear why Echeverri and the Santandereanos sponsored this proposal, but it seems likely that they were concerned about separatist tendencies of the coastal region.

reasons, perhaps the last of the locations throughout the Union to which the capital of the new Republic can be entrusted."[9]

The proposal passed on first debate and then was sent to a commission headed by General Mosquera for further study prior to second debate. Mosquera introduced several modifications but left the basic proposal intact.[10] He earlier had revealed his feelings toward Cundinamarca and Bogotá when as provisional president in 1861 he decreed the formation of the state of Tolima from the Cundinamarcan provinces of Neiva and Mariquita and separated Bogotá from Cundinamarca by declaring it a federal district.[11] As though in competition with Núñez in expressions of hostility toward Bogotá, Mosquera described the Colombian capital as "a shored up convent, a refuge for the devout retired, an isolation hospital for friars and pious women with nothing to do."[12] Nevertheless, on the second debate the delegates defeated the proposed transfer of the capital because of fear of the unhealthful climate of Panama and concern over the great distance between the nation's interior and the Isthmus.

Aside from regional rivalry and attitudes toward Mosquera, Liberal factionalism derived from ideological issues which had divided the party a decade earlier into Radical (gólgota) and Moderate (draconiano) factions. The former, identified with the anti-Mosqueristas in 1863, focused on fully guaranteed individual liberty as the panacea for all social ills. To liberate the individual, the Radicals supported measures such as severely limited governmental power, civilian rule, antimonopoly laws, and minimum state supervision of the church once it was reduced in power and wealth. The Radicals' position on the church-state question at Rionegro, which exemplifies their general approach to social questions, was summarized as follows: "In the conflict between political opinions and religious beliefs there is no other solution than liberty."[13]

9. *Anales de la Convención* (Rionegro), March 13, 1863.

10. *Ibid.*, March 18, 1863.

11. Pombo and Guerra (eds.), *Constituciones*, IV, 88–89.

12. Pérez Aguirre, *25 años de historia*, 199. This is translated from "un apuntalado convento, un hospital de jubilados rezanderos, un lazareto de frailes y de beatas sin oficio."

13. *Ibid.*, 189–90, 206.

Both the Moderate Liberals of the early 1850s and the Mosqueristas at Rionegro inclined toward reliance on institutional authority in solving social problems. The Mosquerista remedy for the church-state problem in 1861 involved close state supervision of the church, forced exile of recalcitrant clerics, and confiscation of church land. Debate on the article on public order exemplified the Mosquerista attitude toward government. The proposed article authorized limited intervention by the national government in the affairs of the states, but the convention defeated the proposal because Mosquera, who favored it as a device which could be used to prevent the Conservatives from ever returning to power, could presumably use it to perpetuate his own power.[14]

The 1863 constitution, according to one Colombian historian, "was made, in large part, not for Colombia but against Mosquera."[15] The framers provided a high degree of continuity with the constitutions of 1853 and 1858, but at the same time their fear of the ambitious Mosquera in combination with distrust of the potential for growth inherent in any central authority induced a majority of the delegates to depart from principles established in the two previous constitutions. Even though Conservatives were excluded from the 1863 convention, the constitution that emerged was one of compromises. Doctrinal compromise sprang from the attempt to develop a fundamental law able to circumscribe the leader from Cauca.

By creating a weak executive branch and strengthening legislative authority, the delegates hoped to safeguard the country against the abuse of power. The constitution limited the president to a two-year term and declared him ineligible for immediate reelection, whereas congressmen, also restricted to two-year terms, were permitted immediate reelection. Senate approval was required for all appointments to the cabinet, diplomatic posts, and upper level military and civilian positions. Congress could override any presidential veto by a simple majority vote, and its authorization was required for federal intervention in the states.[16] The legislative branch retained the traditional powers of authorizing annual budget appropriations and electing the three

14. Camacho Roldán, Mis memorias, II, 186.

15. Rodríguez Piñeres, El olimpo radical, 74.

16. Articles 75, 79, 51, 57, and 19, Pombo and Guerra (eds.), Constituciones, IV, 154–55, 143, 145–46, 135.

presidential designates. Not so traditional was the judicial responsibility assigned to the Senate of making the final determination on the constitutionality of a state law on which the Supreme Court had ruled negatively. In addition to these powers, Congress played a significant role in the election of the president, who had to obtain the vote of an absolute majority of the states, each state having one vote. In case no candidate received such a majority, Congress elected the president from among the leading contenders.[17]

The delegates at Rionegro also provided constitutional sanction for a broad range of individual liberties in hopes of forestalling any tendency toward governmental authoritarianism. Liberties enumerated in the 1863 constitution resembled those of the two previous constitutions but were more absolute and extensive. Newly declared rights included the inviolability of human life and the consequent elimination of capital punishment, unlimited freedom of written and spoken expression, and the right to purchase, sell, and possess arms and munitions during peacetime.[18]

What most distinguished the system of government created at Rionegro was state sovereignty. The sovereign state was not just a constitutional expression. It was the limiting condition of national political life from 1863 to 1885. The nine states experienced in many respects during the war years from 1860 to 1862 an existence independent of the nation. They assumed a continuation of that state of affairs when they decided to "unite and confederate in perpetuity . . . and form a free, sovereign, and independent nation under the name of 'The United States of Colombia.'" All powers not specifically delegated to the national government remained the exclusive competence of the states. Delegated powers involved such matters as foreign relations and trade, national defense, coinage of money, regulation of weights and measures, and control over interoceanic routes. Any act by the Congress or president judged to be in violation of individual rights or state sovereignty could be nullified by vote of the majority of the state legislatures.[19] Each state had its own constitution, code of laws, legislature, and militia. As though to give the fullest expression to their sovereign

17. Articles 49, 53, 51, 72, and 75, *ibid.*, 142–45, 153–54.
18. Article 15, *ibid.*, 131–33.
19. Articles 1, 17, and 25, *ibid.*, 127, 134–35, 137.

status, some states reached the extreme lengths of signing treaties with other states and exchanging diplomatic agents as they had done in 1856 and 1857 when the states were created under the terms of the Act of Panama of 1855.

Failure to invoke the name of God in the preamble to the 1863 constitution signaled a major departure in dealing with the church-state question. Although the Rionegro charter, like the two previous constitutions, disestablished the church and declared freedom of religion, it departed from constitutional tradition by upholding Mosquera's anticlerical decrees of 1861. Thus incorporated into the constitution were his decrees placing the church under state supervision and disamortizing mortmain, i.e., normally non-marketable church, corporate, and community property.[20] By incorporating such anticlerical war measures into the constitution and wording the preamble in such a way as gratuitously to insult a significant segment of the population, the delegates at Rionegro perpetuated the acrimonious controversy surrounding the church-state issue.

One of the most serious defects of the 1863 constitution was the near impossibility of amending it. Article 92 provided for two distinct methods of reform. One required the summoning of a special convention by Congress at the request of all of the state legislatures. The other method required action in three stages: first, reform had to be requested by a majority of the state legislatures, then it had to be approved by a majority in both houses of Congress, and finally the Senate had to ratify it by unanimous vote, each state having one vote. Because each state had three senators, two senators from any single state could block reform. Consequently, the effort to amend the constitution succeeded only once.[21]

In creating an extremely federalist system of government, the delegates at Rionegro not only debilitated the administrative, judicial, and political authority of the national government but also economically crippled it. The constitution effectively weakened the fiscal power of the national government by permitting the states to exercise ample

20. Articles 6 and 23, *ibid.*, 128–29, 136–37.
21. *Ibid.*, 157, 176–77. The days on which each state voted for the president and published the results were made uniform throughout the country by an 1876 amendment.

taxing authority. The only constitutional restrictions on the ability of the states to raise revenue were prohibitions against taxing national property, exports, the use of naturally navigable waterways, goods in transit through a state, and goods subject to national taxation prior to being sold for consumption.[22] Such relatively few restrictions made it certain that the states, given their sovereign political character, would vigorously compete for tax revenue among themselves and with the national government.

Three of the most prominent members of the anti-Mosquera faction at Rionegro wrote extensive commentaries about the convention and the new Colombian constitution. All three expressed pride in the articles on individual liberties but strongly criticized other provisions. Aquileo Parra, the least critical commentator, deplored the difficulty of reforming the constitution and the weakness of the article on public order. Salvador Camacho Roldán concurred and added that the two-year presidency was another major weakness. Justo Arosemena, president of the convention during its last month, concluded a few years later that the constitution, "in defining sectional powers went too far toward authorizing perpetual sedition."[23]

The high degree of state autonomy alluded to by Arosemena gave the greatest license to regionalist forces endured by Colombia since the anarchic days of the United Provinces during the struggle for independence. At Rionegro these forces aligned in such fashion that Santander, followed by Boyacá and Cundinamarca, clashed with the coastal states led by Cauca. While Mosquera remained politically active the Cauca versus Santander pattern prevailed. Questions of ideology and personality overshadowed regional rivalry at Rionegro, but in the next two decades regionalism became an issue of greater moment.

A majority of convention delegates elected Mosquera as president for the truncated term ending April 1, 1864. The vote was far from unanimous because of widespread fear that as president he would not be bound by legal restraints. Justo Arosemena, as convention president, openly expressed this fear at the inauguration ceremony when

22. Article 8, *ibid.*, 129–30.
23. Parra, *Memorias*, 401; Camacho Roldán, *Mis memorias*, II, 188, 206–207; Justo Arosemena, *Constitución de los Estados Unidos de Colombia con antecedentes históricos i comentarios* (Le Havre, 1870), 75.

he warned Mosquera: "A single false step can ruin you forever in the esteem of your fellow citizens, the opinion of other nations, and the severe judgment of history."[24]

To the immense relief of the anxious Liberals, Mosquera as president comported himself in an exemplary manner. His good conduct may have been determined, at least in part, by the distraction of a brief war with Ecuador. From November until late February, 1864, he personally directed the military campaign which ended in a spectacular victory over the Ecuadorian army along the border in southern Cauca. While Mosquera and the army were thus gaining glory, Conservative insurrectionists toppled the Liberal government of Antioquia which Mosquera had imposed in 1862. The Conservatives failed to obtain recognition for their new government until Mosquera's successor assumed the presidency a few months later.[25]

Manuel Murillo Toro, president from 1864 to 1866, held political views decidedly antithetical to those of Mosquera. As former governor of Santander, editor of several newspapers, and Colombian president, Murillo was the intellectual spokesman and political leader of the Radicals. President Murillo's inclination toward compromise in resolving political issues affirmed his dedication to civilian rule and representative government which he had made manifest by his firm opposition to the 1860–1862 civil war. His pragmatism substantially contributed to the easing of church-state tensions during his first year as president. Murillo's willingness to reduce governmental supervision of the church represented a basic compromise; privately he expressed the conviction that the clergy was a retrogressive influence fully capable of "selling out the country as it has done in Mexico."[26] Another example of Murillo's pragmatism was his request of Congress

24. Parra, *Memorias*, 393; *Anales de la Convención* (Rionegro), June 5, May 22, 1863. The vote for president was thirty-seven for Mosquera, ten for other candidates, and fourteen blank ballots.

25. Cordovez Moure, *Reminiscencias*, VI, 62–101; Holguín, *Cartas políticas*, 75; Gómez Barrientos, *25 años de Antioquia*, 4–10, 23–27.

26. Manuel Murillo to Camilo A. Echeverri, August 28, 1863, in *Revista del Archivo Nacional*, II (January–February, 1942), 92–93; Gómez Barrientos, *25 años de Antioquia*, 70–71. For the change in governmental supervision of the church compare law 11 of April 23, 1863, with law 34 of May 17, 1864, in *Leyes de Colombia, 1863–75*, 37–38, 90–91.

that the national government be allowed to assume the burden of constructing a transportation network even though such action would be inconsistent with "the fundamental theory of our institutions." In spite of the animosity between the two Liberal factions and their leaders, Murillo succeeded Mosquera in the presidency in 1864 and two years later Mosquera again assumed the office.[27] Mutual restraint or a tacit understanding between the factions allowed peaceful alternations in power in the mid-1860s.

Murillo performed his most important act as president when, during his first month in office, he granted formal recognition to the Conservative government of Antioquia. In return for recognition, Antioquia agreed to reduce its army to 200 men and to withdraw fifteen leagues within its borders all *Caucanos* living on the Antioquia side of the border with Cauca. The latter provision expressed the traditional antipathy of Cauca toward Antioquia and a new fear of the contamination of Conservative doctrine spread by party activists. By legitimizing Conservative control of Antioquia, Murillo divided Conservative party leadership between Bogotá, site of its most "adventurous faction," and Medellín, where Pedro Justo Berrío presided over a stable government dedicated to peaceful progress and nonintervention in the affairs of neighboring states. Murillo held Governor Berrío in high esteem and privately described him as "a sincerely republican patriot and an enemy of reactions which could lead to civil war."[28]

The close understanding that developed between Murillo and Berrío helped stabilize the federal system from 1864 to 1874. Their cooperation contributed to the failure of a Conservative plot to topple the Liberal governments of Cauca, Cundinamarca, Boyacá, and Tolima in late 1865. The veteran leader of irregular forces, General Joaquín María Córdoba, operating in Cauca, served as one of the leaders in the plan,

27. *Diario Oficial* (Bogotá), May 2, 1864; Cordovez Moure, *Reminiscencias*, VI, 170. For an example of this animosity see Murillo to Mosquera, December 20, 1865, reprinted in Rodríguez Piñeres, *El olimpo radical*, 185.

28. Gómez Barrientos, *25 años de Antioquia*, 23-27; Eduardo Rodríguez Piñeres, "Páginas olvidadas en *El olimpo radical*: la liga de 1869," *Boletín de Historia y Antigüedades*, XXXVIII (April–June, 1951), 254; Murillo to Echeverri, August 19, 1867, in *Revista del Archivo Nacional*, II (January–February, 1942), 93–94.

but Conservatives in Cundinamarca provided the main support for the fighting in that state, Tolima, and Boyacá. Within a few weeks of the outbreak of the uprising, it was crushed in all of the states. Antioquia supported President Murillo in his efforts to end the revolt by refusing to supply the aid expected by the revolutionaries. The episode discredited the Conservative party but strengthened Antioquia's role in party leadership. Murillo correctly assessed that role in the following terms: "The Conservatives of the other states can do nothing without the support of Antioquia, but with Antioquia they can give themselves the illusion of winning and do much evil." [29]

During the fourth and last Mosquera presidency, 1866–1867, the Liberal party underwent an acute political crisis and the Conservative party bestirred itself to renewed activity. The brief period of accommodation between the Liberal factions ended, and a decade of political dominance by the Radicals began. After a several-months' stay in Europe as Colombian minister to England, Mosquera returned to Bogotá for his inauguration with a more exalted view of himself than ever, behaving in a way seemingly calculated to alienate his potential supporters. On one occasion Mosquera, attired in his masonic garb as Grand Master, led a procession from the presidential palace down the streets of Bogotá to commemorate the installation of the Masonic lodge. He further infuriated the Bogotanos as well as most Colombians from the interior when he decreed that the celebration of independence be held on November 11, the anniversary of Cartagena's declaration of independence, rather than on the traditional date of July 20, when the *cabildo* of Santafé moved toward autonomy under the Spanish monarchy.[30]

Deteriorating relations between Mosquera and Congress caused the political crisis of 1867. Control of Congress by the Mosqueristas in 1866 had temporarily averted a rupture in spite of many issues in dispute. For example, while in England Mosquera had contracted for a $7,500,000 loan to be used for public works, but Congress amended the contract to death.[31] In 1867 a coalition of Radicals and thirteen Conservatives gained control of Congress. Felipe Zapata in his mul-

29. Cordovez Moure, *Reminiscencias*, VI, 134–38; Arboleda, *Revoluciones*, 13–18; Murillo to Echeverri, August 19, 1867, in *Revista del Archivo Nacional*, II (January–February, 1942), 93–94.

30. Cordovez Moure, *Reminiscencias*, VI, 173–74.

31. Pérez Aguiree, *25 años de historia*, 261–62.

tiple roles as president of the House of Representatives, Radical spokesman, and editor of the stridently anti-Mosquera newspaper *El Mensajero*, was a principal organizer of the opposition to the president. Other prominent members of the opposition both in and outside of Congress included Santiago Pérez, Manuel Murillo, Pablo Arosemena, and Carlos Nicolás Rodríguez. Mosquera unsuccessfully tried to dissolve Congress by having the minority walk out leaving it without a quorum. He then attempted to regain control of the legislative branch by declaring that the House had too many members according to the last census, but a congressional committee firmly rejected this scheme.[32]

Aside from Mosquera's high-handed conduct, the dispute between the president and the Radicals centered on some fundamental issues. The Radicals objected to the violent manner in which Mosquera carried out the law on religious inspection and to his effort to justify his conduct on the basis of corruption among the clergy. Mosquera thus revived old church-state tensions which his predecessor had substantially reduced. Another dispute concerned a law on public order passed over Mosquera's strong objections which declared that the national government had to remain neutral in case of civil war within a state.[33] Conflict over Colombia's stance in the war between Spain and Peru precipitated the final crisis. In 1866 Colombia declared its neutrality, but shortly thereafter Mosquera signed a secret treaty with Peru. Then in the name of the Colombian government he purchased in the United States a war vessel which was to be transferred to Peruvian control. Shortly before adjournment, Congress learned of the transaction and launched an investigation. Mosquera retaliated swiftly. On April 29 he dissolved Congress, declared the nation in a state of war, and arrested several prominent Radical opponents including senators, congressmen, editors, and the governor of Cundinamarca.[34]

32. Cordovez Moure, *Reminiscencias*, VII, 31, VI, 182; Pablo E. Cárdenas Acosta, *La restauración constitucional de 1867* (Tunja, 1966), 20–21, 23; Parra, *Memorias*, 484–85, 490.

33. Cárdenas Acosta, *La restauración*, 26–27; Cordovez Moure, *Reminiscencias*, VI, 174, 178–80; law 20 of April 16, 1867, *Leyes de Colombia, 1863–75*, 434.

34. Cordovez Moure, *Reminiscencias*, VI, 180–81, VII, 38–40; Parra, *Memorias*, 489–91; Gustavo Humberto Rodríguez, *Santos Acosta, caudillo del radicalismo* (Bogotá, 1972), 127–30.

Colombia suffered the ignominy of dictatorship for less than one month. Radical leaders and key military figures quickly organized a plan to overthrow Mosquera, and they obtained assurances of Conservative cooperation. Antioquia and Santander assumed the leadership among the states in resisting the caudillo's pretensions. Governor Berrío of Antioquia within a few days raised a 7,000-man army, thus providing substance to the Radical-Conservative coalition. The dissidents overthrew Mosquera on May 23 with no significant resistance. Later in the year the Senate tried the ex-president, found him guilty of signing the secret alliance with Peru plus three minor charges, fined him twelve pesos, and sentenced him to three years in exile.[35] Upon his return to Colombia in early 1871, this remarkable man, at the age of seventy-two, resumed an active political career which continued until his death at eighty in 1878.

The Radical government of General Santos Acosta, installed to complete Mosquera's term, did not obtain immediate recognition from all nine states. Cauca briefly withheld approval. Bolívar and Magdalena offered stronger resistance, because in May Mosquera had sent military commanders to those critical states to assure their loyalty. Mosquera's adherents in Magdalena were defeated in battle, whereas in Bolívar peaceful negotiations elicited recognition of the national government. Minor fighting occurred in other states as a result of Mosquera's ouster, but only in Tolima did it produce significant change. The withdrawal of Mosquerista support from the Liberal government of Tolima precipitated several months of civil conflict which terminated in Conservative victory.[36]

The fighting in Tolima strained the Radical-Conservative cooperation which had developed during the contest with Mosquera, and events in Cundinamarca during 1868 brought it to an end. Ignacio Gutiérrez Vergara, a prominent Conservative leader who had publicly

35. Cordovez Moure, Reminiscencias, VII, 48, 97–111; Parra, Memorias, 491–92; Gómez Barrientos, 25 años de Antioquia, 82; Cárdenas Acosta, La restauración, 41–59, 61–69, 119–30.

36. Cordovez Moure, Reminiscencias, VII, 48–49, 114–15; Rodríguez Piñeres, El olimpo radical, 77; Rodríguez, Santos Acosta, 157–59; Arboleda, Revoluciones, 23–27. For details of the fighting in Boyacá see Rodríguez, Santos Acosta, 161–63; for the fighting in Cundinamarca see Arboleda, Revoluciones, 27–28.

supported the overthrow of Mosquera, was elected governor of Cundi-namarca in early 1868. His government enjoyed the support of some Cundinamarcan Liberals as well as friendly relations with President Santos Acosta and his successor, President Santos Gutiérrez. At mid-year the Radicals gained control of the state legislature, and the atmo-sphere of cooperation between the two parties changed to one of sharp conflict. As tension between the state executive and legislature inten-sified, the Radicals increased pressure on President Santos Gutiérrez to intervene. After the governor overturned some laws recently enacted by the legislature and summoned a constituent assembly, President Gutiérrez yielded to Radical pressure and on October 10 ordered the arrest of the chief executive of Cundinamarca. Besides assuring Radi-cal domination in Cundinamarca and strengthening that faction's con-trol of the national government, the intervention ended the brief period of Radical-Conservative cooperation.[37]

For a decade following the overthrow of Mosquera the Radicals controlled the national government. The presidents from 1867 to 1876, their terms, and the states with which each was politically identified are listed below:

Santos Acosta	1867–1868	Boyacá
Santos Gutiérrez	1868–1870	Boyacá
Eustorgio Salgar	1870–1872	Santander/Cundinamarca
Manuel Murillo	1872–1874	Santander/Cundinamarca
Santiago Pérez	1874–1876	Cundinamarca

Cundinamarca, Boyacá, and Santander continued to compose the core of Radical strength during the decade. By capturing the vote of only two other states the Radicals could retain control of the presidency. During the same period the Conservatives governed Antioquia and Tolima, and until the mid-1870s the Mosqueristas wielded political power in Cauca. Consequently, the three north coast states were of critical importance to Radical strategy for maintaining political domination.

During the decade beginning in 1867 the Radicals moved toward a

---

37. For details of the coup of October 10 see Parra, Memorias, 510–41; Cordovez Moure, Reminiscencias, VII, 115–26; Holguín, Cartas políticas, 81–102.

recentralization of authority on a de facto basis. In 1863 the Radicals had endorsed extreme federalism and a weak central government, and it was this position which best distinguished them from the Mosqueristas. But after the Radical-Conservative coalition vanquished the Mosquera threat in 1867, the distinction between the two Liberal factions on the issue of central authority tended to blur. This shift in the position of the Radicals was discernible on three issues: the law on public order, educational reform, and federal aid to public works.

Maintenance of public order was a euphemistic reference to the right of the national government to intervene in the states. Article 19 of the constitution, which expressed the Radical position opposing such intervention, required congressional approval for the use of national forces in case of civil conflict in the states. The Radical-Conservative coalition of 1867 further circumscribed the national government by passing a law on public order which remained in effect for more than a decade. This law began as follows: "When any proportion whatsoever of the citizens of a state revolt for the purpose of overthrowing the existing government and organizing another, the national government must observe the strictest neutrality between the belligerents."[38] Removal of the Mosquera threat moderated the Radical position to the extent of enabling the Senate in 1871 to pass a bill on public order which restored to the national government limited rights of intervention. The bill, however, failed in the House because of the opposition of Conservative representatives from Antioquia and Tolima who much distrusted a national government under Liberal control. Despite the lack of authorization to the national government to intervene in internal affairs of the states, the Radical administrations, nevertheless, did so intervene on numerous occasions, ostensibly to maintain public order.[39]

Achievements in the field of educational reform offer even clearer evidence of change in the Radical attitude toward government. Liberals at mid-century had implemented a series of reforms, applied to education as well as to other areas, designed to abolish privilege, reduce control by central institutions, and increase opportunity and competi-

38. Law 20 of April 16, 1867, *Leyes de Colombia, 1863–75*, 434.
39. Parra, *Memorias*, 580–84.

tion. Most of these educational reforms were directed toward higher education, where evidence of privilege was most conspicuous, and they included eliminating the need to obtain an academic degree to practice law or medicine, allowing *colegios* to avoid meeting standards on faculty and curriculum prescribed by Bogotá, reducing the status of the three national universities to *colegios nacionales*, and ending their subsidies. The results during the 1850s and 1860s of these "reforms" on higher education were a drastic decline in enrollments, destruction of the academic degree structure, severe weakening of the curriculum, and a decline in discipline.[40]

An early sign of change in Radical thinking came with the establishment of the technically oriented National University in 1868, but the thrust of educational recentralization was in the area of primary education. Legislation passed in 1870 focused on the areas of public primary instruction and teacher training. Public education was centralized under the direction and supervision of a national governmental agency, the General Directorate of Public Instruction, and federal funds were provided to support schools in the states that ratified the reform decree. The General Directorate of Public Instruction performed a number of services including the gathering of educational statistics, commissioning of textbooks, distribution of books and maps, and publication of a weekly educational journal. The organization of teacher training began in 1872 when nine German professors hired by the Colombian government arrived and inaugurated normal schools in each of the states. By 1875 twenty normal schools were functioning throughout the country.[41] The Radicals thus had substantially shifted their position toward the notion that the central government must assume major responsibility in the field of education.

The change in Radical policy toward recentralization of authority was most apparent in the area of federal aid to public works. Enactment of several laws in the early 1870s offering federal encouragement and money to railroad and other transportation projects provides abun-

40. Frank Safford, *The Ideal of the Practical: Colombia's Struggle to Form a Technical Elite* (Austin, 1976), 133–39.

41. Jane Meyer Loy, "Primary Education during the Colombian Federation: The School Reform of 1870," *Hispanic American Historical Review*, LI (May, 1971), 279–80, 286–87.

dant evidence of Radical support for an expanded role for the national government. That legislation was a logical response to both the persistent problem of budget deficits and an economic policy of free trade.

A prime goal of Radical policy makers was to enable the national government to escape the severe fiscal restrictions which the Radicals themselves had helped write into the Constitution of 1863. The pattern of federal expenditures from 1865 to 1874 testifies to the economic weakness of the national government.[42] Expenditures exceeded revenue for every fiscal year except 1867, when the government received $1,000,000 from the Panama Railroad Company for signing a new contract.[43] Payment of the national debt imposed the heaviest drain on the budget, especially from 1868 to 1873. The proportion of annual expenditures allocated for this item ranged from 27 to 56 percent, and the annual payment averaged about 39 percent.[44] After the allocation of funds for the debt and the normal administrative costs of government little or nothing remained for providing the kinds of services which would have enhanced the prestige of the national government.

A legacy of liberal economic measures enacted from the time of the first Mosquera administration in the late 1840s onward substantially reduced the resources available to the national government. In passing these measures, reformers had sought to extirpate the inherited Spanish revenue system, long odious to republican modernizers. The reforms included elimination of the tithe and the tobacco monopoly as well as national taxes on liquor, stamped paper, refining of gold, and use of national roads. In 1870 the secretary of hacienda correctly calculated that had the colonial tax system not been dismantled the revenue available to the national government for the fiscal year would have been nearly doubled.[45]

---

42. It should be noted that the fiscal weakness of the federal government in the 1860s and 1870s was also characteristic of the 1850s, when similar problems of budget deficits and large outlays for the national debt plagued the government. See José María Rivas Groot, *Asuntos constitucionales, económicos y fiscales* (Bogotá, 1909), 400, 414–15.

43. Law 46 of August 16, 1867, *Leyes de Colombia, 1863–75*, 462. A single-year reference to the fiscal year refers to the year in which the fiscal period ended. In Colombia the fiscal year extended from September 1 to August 31, so reference to the fiscal year 1867 means the period from September 1, 1866, to August 31, 1867.

44. Calculated from Table 2.

45. *Memoria de Hacienda, 1871*, vi–vii.

Table 2

Federal Expenditures by Fiscal Year, 1865–1874
Based on Annual Budgets and Supplemental Appropriations

Fiscal Year	National Debt	Treasury and Hacienda	War and Navy	Public Works and Development	Other	Total
1865	$ 760,200	$ 513,866	$774,968	$ 9,000	$ 532,375	$2,592,409
1866	882,000	871,227	398,385	33,000	530,516	2,715,128
1867	883,499	879,518	670,837	156,500	479,359	3,069,713
1868	3,235,098	1,496,989	248,023	253,000	525,097	5,758,207
1869	1,474,058	1,242,271	812,925	209,400	467,374	4,206,028
1870	1,800,156	799,079	377,358	274,100	694,138	3,944,831
1871	1,889,098	670,320	374,326	533,204	741,134	4,208,082
1872	2,298,563	697,355	463,456	580,660	739,643	4,779,677
1873	2,237,228	994,473	895,384	602,000	1,042,641	5,771,726
1874	1,290,891	824,740	538,319	737,770	1,076,472	4,468,192

SOURCES: These figures were calculated from the annual budgets and the supplemental appropriations laws for each fiscal year found in *Leyes de Colombia, 1863–75*. Note that the category "Other" includes expenditures for disamortized property, welfare, public instruction, postal service, justice, and foreign affairs.

Table 3

Federal Income by Fiscal Year, 1865–1874
Based on the Memorias de Hacienda

Fiscal Year	Customs	Salt Monopoly	Panama Railroad	Other	Total
1865	$1,337,946	$ 621,007	$ 34,000	$113,938	$2,106,891
1866	1,372,331	657,391	34,000	74,929	2,138,651
1867	1,148,668	1,066,615	1,000,000	166,138	3,381,421
1868	1,544,587	728,183	497,904	194,936	2,965,610
1869	2,089,065	686,935	250,000	263,079	3,289,079
1870	1,575,904	758,329	250,000	299,525	2,883,758
1871	1,561,082	790,009	187,500	278,202	2,816,793
1872	2,039,450	788,191	253,150	138,942	3,219,733
1873	2,775,450	799,213	250,000	168,831	3,993,494
1874	2,811,000	656,000	250,000	204,000	3,921,000

SOURCES: Memoria de Hacienda, 1870, iii; Memoria de Hacienda, 1871, 1; Memoria de Hacienda, 1873, 1–2, 32, 43, 46, 53–54; Memoria de Hacienda, 1874, 1; Memoria de Hacienda, 1875, 2. The Memorias de Hacienda of 1871 and 1874 include income from disamortized property which is not presented here because it was almost entirely in the form of greatly discounted bonds and treasury bills. Note that the category "Other" includes income from the mint, postal and telegraph service, and sale and rental of government land.

Despite limitations on revenue sources, federal income increased 86 percent from 1865 to 1874. Income from import duties provided the great bulk of the revenue and accounted for its increase. At the beginning of the period import duties furnished about 64 percent of all national revenue, and by 1874 that proportion had increased to 71 percent.[46] The trend toward greater dependence for revenue on import duties had begun at mid-century; during the first half of the 1850s customs revenue provided an annual average of 56 percent of total federal income. More than 90 percent of the total customs revenue collected from 1865 to 1874 came from four customs ports (listed in order of descending productivity): Santa Marta, Barranquilla-Sabanilla, Car-

46. Calculated from Table 3.

Table 4

Income from Customs Ports, 1865–1874

Fiscal Year	Santa Marta	Sabanilla-Barranquilla	Cartagena	Buena-ventura	Others
1865	$ 934,793	$ 50,115	$138,432	$ 68,008	$146,598
1866	948,535	83,253	107,390	58,375	174,778
1867	701,382	79,145	153,912	93,819	120,410
1868	1,083,231	139,550	121,966	108,330	91,510
1869	1,509,713	142,162	175,290	131,457	130,443
1870	1,100,008	93,119	144,893	115,643	122,241
1871	1,077,683	130,732	109,405	107,321	135,941
1872	911,851	665,009	115,870	177,896	168,824
1873	547,168	1,560,876	207,366	228,948	231,092
1874	294,436	1,877,100	182,711	242,972	213,781

SOURCES: Memoria de Hacienda, 1870, xxxiv; Memoria de Hacienda, 1871, 60; Memoria de Hacienda, 1873, 2; Memoria de Hacienda, 1874, 30; Memoria de Hacienda, 1875, 12.

tagena, and Buenaventura.[47] The economic viability of the national government thus depended on these four ports situated in the states of Magdalena, Bolívar, and Cauca, and this dependence increased during the decade.

The salt monopoly, a productive colonial survival, provided the second largest amount of national revenue for the decade.[48] In absolute terms the amount of income derived from it remained fairly stable during the period. Consequently, as total federal revenue increased the proportion obtained from salt declined from 29 to 17 percent. The origins of income from the salt monopoly displayed even greater regional concentration than did customs revenue. From 1864 to 1874 about 82

47. Luis Ospina Vásquez, Industria y protección en Colombia, 1810–1930 (Medellín, 1955), 199n; see Table 4.
48. More than 95 percent of the total income from the salt monopoly came from the sale of salt. The remainder came from the rental of small salt wells and mines and the tax on transporting salt. For a typical year see Memoria de Hacienda, 1870, lvii.

percent of the revenue from the salt monopoly came from salt works in Cundinamarca and another 17 percent came from Boyacá.[49]

Other producers of national income registered no significant growth during the decade. By 1874 they contributed no more than 12 percent of total federal income. Thus, in addition to being administratively circumscribed by the constitution, the national government was also economically restricted by the revenue pattern. The federal revenue system was marked by overdependence on customs and the salt monopoly and by too close a linkage between import expansion and revenue growth.

Although the Liberals deplored the lingering fiscal dependence on the salt monopoly, they regarded the growing importance of revenue from import duties as a major benefit resulting from implementation of their economic program. That program of laissez faire and low tariffs aimed at tying Colombia into a pattern of world trade expansion in which raw materials were to be exported in exchange for foreign manufactures. The Liberals enacted a purely revenue, non-protective tariff in 1861, and the principle of non-protectionism prevailed until the 1880s.[50] It should be noted, however, that, although the 1861 measure was authored and enacted by Liberals and Liberals are credited with the non-protectionism of the 1860s and 1870s, the impetus toward free trade began in the late 1840s, and it was bipartisan. The following average import duties calculated by William McGreevey in his history of the Colombian economy suggest the extent of Liberal eagerness to encourage imports through the 1861 measure:

1850–1859	13.7%
1862–1872	5.9%
1873–1884	11.4%

Upward tariff revision in 1873 and a 25 percent surcharge in 1874

49. These figures were calculated from the annual sale of salt reported in the *Memoria de Hacienda* for the following years: 1866, Table I, appendix; 1868, Table O, appendix; 1869, Table VIII, appendix; 1870, p. lx; 1873, p. 32; 1874, p. 46; 1875, p. 20.

50. *Memoria de Hacienda, 1871*, vi–vii; David Bushnell, "Two Stages in Colombian Tariff Policy: The Radical Era and the Return to Protection (1861–1885)," *Inter-American Economic Affairs*, IX (Spring, 1956), 4–5.

were enacted to increase revenue; consequently these measures did not violate the non-protective principle.[51]

In spite of the unreliability of Colombian trade statistics, particularly in relation to imports, some general trends stand out.[52] From 1864 to 1874 imports surged upwards causing trade deficits for at least half of the decade. Textiles composed approximately 70 percent of total import value. The free trade program of the 1860s and 1870s thus had its greatest adverse impact on the Colombian textile-producing region situated in Boyacá and Santander.[53] The impact is difficult to measure, but under the combined pressure of low tariffs and the gradual decline in the prices of European manufactures during the last three decades of the century, Colombian textile production, at minimum, was losing its share of the domestic market and shifting to the production of coarser goods.[54]

The proper functioning of the enacted foreign trade program required not only a non-protective tariff but also export expansion. For

51. McGreevey, An Economic History, 169–70; Law 104 of June 13, 1873, Leyes de Colombia, 1863–75, 1005–1009; Bushnell, "Two Stages in Colombian Tariff Policy," 7–8. For a discussion of the complex method of tariff collection employed during the 1860s and 1870s, the system of peso bruto, see Bushnell, "Two Stages in Colombian Tariff Policy," 6–7.

52. The principal source of Colombian trade statistics is Banco de la República, Informe anual del gerente, 1 julio 1960 – 31 diciembre 1962 (Bogotá, n.d.), Part Two, Table 127, p. 201, and Table 134, p. 216. All informed nineteenth-century Colombian economists agreed that trade statistics were highly inaccurate and that figures on imports, upon which tariffs were levied, were much less reliable than export data. McGreevey has confirmed those observations, and using foreign trade figures obtained from Colombia's major trading partners he has substantially revised the traditional trade statistics. For his revisions and a discussion of Colombian trade from 1845 to 1885 see McGreevey, An Economic History, 97–116. His work, however, has come under sharp attack. For a devastating critique of it see Frank Safford, "Reflexiones sobre Historia económica de Colombia, 1845–1930 de William Paul McGreevey," in Frank Safford, Aspectos del siglo XIX en Colombia (Medellín, 1977), 201–84.

53. McGreevey, An Economic History, 168. In 1870 more than one-fifth of Santander's labor force was engaged in artisan activities; see Galindo (ed.), Anuario, 22–26.

54. Bushnell, "Two Stages in Colombian Tariff Policy," 11; Ospina Vásquez, Industria y protección, 258–59. David C. Johnson concluded that Santander's artisan industry was in decline as early as 1859; see his "Economic and Social Change," 212.

this reason much attention was directed toward the encouragement of production for export, the search for new export commodities, and improvement of the externally oriented transportation system. Pamphlet literature of the 1860s through the 1870s is replete with propaganda and didactic material favorable to the cultivation of such products as coffee, cacao, rubber, and cinchona. Substantial growth of tobacco exports during the 1850s and 1860s following the abolition of the government tobacco monopoly at mid-century further encouraged the search for other export commodities.[55]

Table 5 demonstrates that the value of exports more than doubled from 1865 to 1874 and that tobacco continued to dominate the export picture as it had in the 1850s. The decline in tobacco exports which was only perceptible in the late 1860s became precipitous in the mid-1870s. By 1877/1878 tobacco composed only 5.1 percent of all exports as a result of declining leaf quality and competition from European colonies in the Far East. Three distinct regions dominated tobacco production in turn. During the boom years in the 1850s more than 90 percent of the tobacco exports came from the plains around Ambalema situated on the Magdalena River in northern Tolima. By the mid-1860s Carmen, Bolívar, had become the principal tobacco region, and a decade later it was replaced by the Palmira area in Cauca. Although the latter two regions became major producing centers, they never achieved the peak Ambalema production of the 1850s.[56]

Other important exports of the period included gold, cinchona, cotton, indigo, coffee, and hides. Gold in the form of coinage, dust, bars, and jewelry was the second largest export by value during the decade. Antioquia remained the undisputed center of Colombian gold

55. Nicolás Osorio, *Estudio sobre las quinas de los Estados Unidos de Colombia* (2nd ed.; Bogotá, 1874); C. Martínez Ribón, *Nuevo método para el cultivo de cacao* . . . (Bogotá, 1879); Evaristo Delgado, *Memoria sobre el cultivo del café en el municipio de Popayán* (Popayán, 1867); F. J. Madriz, *Cultivo del café o sea manual teórico y práctico sobre el beneficio de este fruto* . . . (Le Havre, 1871); Ospina Vásquez, *Industria y protección*, 243–44.

56. Luis Eduardo Nieto Arteta, *Economía y cultura en la historia de Colombia* (Bogotá, 1942), 284; Jorge E. Rodríguez R. and William P. McGreevey, "Colombia: comercio exterior, 1835–1962," in Urrutia and Arrubla (eds.), *Compendio de estadísticas*, Table IX, 208; John P. Harrison, "The Evolution of the Colombian Tobacco Trade, to 1875," *Hispanic American Historical Review*, XXXII (May, 1952), 165, 174; Sierra, *El tabaco*, 97–98.

Table 5

Principal Export Commodities as a Percentage of Total Export Value, 1865–1881

Fiscal Year	Export Total in Thousands of Pesos	Gold as Dust, Bars, Jewelry	Tobacco	Cinchona	Cotton	Indigo	Coffee	Hides
1865	5,043	23.5	48.7	8.7	6.3	0.1	2.0	1.5
1866	6,772	20.2	44.3	4.3	7.5	0.1	11.8	0.8
1867	5,494	*	51.2	3.7	10.3	*	11.1	0.7
1868	7,377	3.3	36.6	3.1	4.8	0.4	9.4	1.2
1869	8,137	27.8	37.0	5.4	3.7	0.5	7.5	1.1
1870	8,077	22.7	29.2	5.3	6.3	1.8	14.4	3.0
1871	8,248	20.1	18.0	10.9	3.5	*	11.8	3.2
1872	8,254	15.5	18.4	15.7	3.1	6.0	15.3	4.8
1873	10,478	24.1	19.4	19.4	2.5	3.7	18.4	4.7
1874	10,487	26.4	22.5	17.1	2.4	1.8	9.1	4.6
1875	9,984	20.5	27.3	15.1	1.4	0.6	7.3	4.7
1876	14,478	9.0	14.7	14.1	1.4	0.4	8.1	4.3
1877	10,049	6.5	13.7	8.4	1.2	1.2	7.5	3.0
1878	11,111	29.9	5.1	22.2	1.3	0.3	13.5	7.3
1879	13,712	26.6	6.6	19.4	0.7	0.1	*	*
1880	13,805	*	9.3	24.3	0.6	0.1	*	6.5
1881	15,837	*	6.9	32.4	0.2	0.1	*	6.0

SOURCES: For statistics through 1879 see Jorge E. Rodríguez R. and William P. McGreevey, "Colombia: comercio exterior, 1835–1962," in Urrutia and Arrubla (eds.), Compendio de estadísticas, Table IX, 208. For statistics for 1880–1881 see Luis Eduardo Nieto Arteta, Ecomomía y cultura en la historia de Colombia (Bogotá, 1942), 283, 301, 306, 309, 352, 383. Export figures on individual commodities do not exist for the remainder of the nineteenth century.

production, providing about 70 percent of the total. Cinchona bark, the source of quinine, was gathered from uncultivated trees usually located in sparsely settled areas of difficult access. Most of the cinchona exported in the 1850s and early 1860s came from Tolima and Cundinamarca, but during the 1870s Santander experienced a genuine cinchona boom. The increasing value of cinchona exports gave rise to the hope that it would become the principal export, filling the gap left by the drop in tobacco exports. Laws passed in 1870 and 1871 encouraged the search for stands of cinchona by declaring the national timberlands completely open and free for exploitation.[57]

In the mid-1860s Colombia took advantage of the shortage of cotton on the world market caused by the Civil War in the United States. Cotton exports remained significant until 1870, when they declined to their traditional minor status. Most of the cotton produced for export came from the region around Barranquilla. The export history of Colombian indigo is confined to the decade under survey. Production units could be found in all nine states by the late 1860s, but within five years exports had peaked and then declined to insignificance. Sustained production was not maintained because of the need for high capital investments for equipment purchase and maintenance, replacement of overworked land, and a large labor supply. Coffee occupied a minor position in Colombian export figures from the late eighteenth century (when first cultivated in Colombia) until the early 1890s, when it rose to a position of export dominance. In 1874 about 88 percent of the national production came from Santander, especially around the region of Cúcuta.[58] Hides represented a small but stable element in the export picture.

The quest during the 1860s for exports to supplement tobacco became an intensified search in the 1870s for new commodities to fill the void left by the collapse of tobacco exports. The problem was urgent

57.   Ospina Vásquez, *Industria y protección*, 243; Nieto Arteta, *Economía y culture*, 303; Pérez, *Jeografía física*, II, 54; 189; law 11 of April 6, 1870, law 51 of May 20, 1871, *Leyes de Colombia, 1863–75*, 624, 767.

58.   Ospina Vásquez, *Industria y protección*, 243; Nieto Arteta, *Economía y cultura*, 304–306; Diego Monsalve, *Colombia cafetera* (Barcelona, 1927), 630; William P. McGreevey, "Exportaciones y precios de tabaco y café," in Urrutia and Arrubla (eds.), *Compendio de estadísticas*, Table 2, pp. 210–11.

because only by sustaining a valuable export trade could the country support the high import level. From the latter, also, came the great bulk of federal revenue. Failure to maintain the momentum of export growth would undermine the entire economic program, which in turn could threaten the political position of the Liberals, principal champions of free trade in the 1860s and 1870s.

Export expansion required cheap, reliable transportation to the exterior. Without this essential ingredient no amount of pamphleteering could sustain export growth. The logical source of aid for transportation projects was the national government, but it was limited by article 17 of the constitution to "the maintenance of interoceanic routes which exist or which are opened in national territory, and the navigation of rivers which touch upon the territory of more than one state, or which pass into the territory of a bordering nation." [59] Government leaders during the 1860s generally respected the constitutional limitation on federal aid to the states because the federal treasury lacked funds and because in the one notable instance when they did not respect it—construction of a road from the Pacific port of Buenaventura to the Cauca River—the attained result was disappointing.

From the time of the conquest almost every generation had attempted to open this route in order to stimulate the export trade. [60] In the 1860s proponents also regarded the project as a means of helping Cauca recover from the heavy economic losses suffered during the 1860–1862 civil war. The project was approved by the Rionegro convention and funded by a special $1,000,000 loan contracted in London in 1863 on the initiative of Mosquera, who served as a founder, stockholder, and superintendent of the company formed to carry out the project. When the national government issued its last payment for the project in the early 1870s, the total amount granted equaled about $700,000. [61] Despite this large expenditure, the project was an igno-

59. Pombo and Guerra (eds.), Constituciones, IV, 134.

60. Gustavo Arboleda, Historia de Cali (2 vols.; Cali, 1956), I, 103–104, 139, 149, 181–82, 195–200, 274–75, 384, 406. The best summary of the history of efforts to open the Cali–Buenaventura route from the early colonial period to the mid-nineteenth century is found in Neal, "The Pacific Age," 1–31.

61. Law 33 of May 14, 1864, Leyes de Colombia, 1863–75, 89. The balance of the loan was used to pay the extremely high interest and servicing costs. Reports differ

minious failure. Salvador Camacho Roldán concluded in the 1870 *Memoria de Hacienda*: "This road is the most hapless indication that can be given of the system of giving money from the public treasury for the execution of enterprises not supported by private interests. From all the work and commotion caused by this project . . . only eight leagues of mountain road have resulted." [62]

The official role the national government might play in support of transportation projects from 1864 to 1871 was established by law 40 of 1864, which specified two methods for granting federal aid. One permitted the government to promote the formation of private construction companies and to buy shares in such companies. This method required a considerable outlay of capital, but the law authorized the government to obtain it through loans of up to $8,000,000. Because of the dismal results of the Cauca road project, this method of support soon fell into disrepute. [63] The government on occasion continued to support projects by buying shares, but it did so on a small scale and with funds available from normal revenue. [64] Under the second method the government could guarantee a 7 percent annual return on private capital invested in transportation projects. This became the preferred option because it minimized governmental intervention and expenditure. The Bolívar Railroad connecting Barranquilla and Sabanilla benefited from this type of aid. The company which undertook this enterprise received a guaranty from the government of a 7 percent annual return on its investment up to $600,000. [65] The striking success of the railroad offered another argument against contracting loans to support projects.

---

as to the exact amount received by the company. The *Memoria del secretario del tesoro i crédito nacional al congreso de 1873* (Bogotá, 1873), 27, states that "the account relative to this matter has been difficult to clarify [because of] the loss of some documents."

62. *Memoria de Hacienda, 1870*, p. ci. It should be noted that Camacho Roldán probably lacked proper objectivity in his assessment, for he had opposed this pet project of Mosquera since the 1850s; see Neal, "The Pacific Age," 105, 130.

63. Law 40 of May 28, 1864, *Leyes de Colombia, 1863–75*, 104–106; *Memoria de Hacienda, 1866*, lx. Law 7 of March 20, 1867, revoked the authorization to contract the $8,000,000 loan; see *Leyes de Colombia, 1863–75*, 427.

64. See the following examples: law 28 of April 30, 1869, law 59 of May 26, 1869, *Leyes de Colombia, 1863–75*, 580, 602.

65. Law 24 of May 23, 1868, *ibid.*, 519.

Law 40 also provided a guide for federal support of public works by enumerating fifteen projects deemed most worthy of federal aid. Eight of these projects involved the construction of roads to navigable rivers or seaports, four emphasized river and harbor improvement or establishment of river navigation, two projects were for building strictly interior roads, and one favored telegraph construction.[66] The government's understanding of "material improvements" clearly emphasized road and river transportation directed toward the exterior.

Because neither of the methods of aid specified in law 40 brought any of these projects to completion, the government resorted to other methods. In some cases it paid the salaries of engineers and technicians assigned to a project, allowed duty-free importation of necessary construction material and equipment, or granted land to the entity undertaking the project. An 1868 law granted Boyacá 5 percent of the federal income from the sale of salt in the state to be spent only on the construction of roads to the exterior.[67] By 1870 the most frequent form of federal aid had become the outright money grant for a specific project.[68]

State pressure for more federal aid increased notably in the early 1870s. In the 1870 *Memoria de Hacienda* Salvador Camacho Roldán strongly resisted the pressure, arguing that the constitution prohibited such aid and that the competition for it would endanger the federal system of government by causing a "struggle between federal and sectional powers." Among the factors leading the states to intensify their lobbying for federal funds was the apparent contrast between state poverty and federal prosperity. From 1865 to 1874 national revenue increased by 83 percent, whereas total revenue of all the states grew only about 50 percent.[69] A decree by President Manuel Murillo in 1872 further aroused state interest by declaring that henceforth the size of the

66. Other projects were added to this list by law 20 of April 26, 1866, law 3 of March 8, 1867, and law 27 of April 29, 1867, ibid., 272, 425, 439.

67. Law 3 of March 8, 1867, law 32 of May 11, 1869, law 24 of May 23, 1868, law 5 of March 13, 1868, ibid., 425, 583, 519, 503.

68. In addition to providing aid for specific projects, the national government granted general subsidies to Magdalena and Panama. See law 3 of February 26, 1868, law 3 of February 22, 1873, law 22 of May 8, 1863, law 68 of September 26, 1867, law 46 of August 16, 1867, ibid., 502, 906, 43, 482, 462.

69. *Memoria de Hacienda*, 1870, lxxxv; see Table 6.

national debt would be determined by the market value rather than the face value of government bonds, an act which constituted in effect a partial unilateral cancellation of the debt. As a result the outlay required to service the debt dropped sharply in the 1873/1874 fiscal period. Reports by the secretary of hacienda in 1873 and 1874 of budget surpluses for the preceding fiscal years seemed to presage the end of federal niggardliness.[70] The reports proved incorrect, however, when supplemental appropriations later were added to the original budget.

Growing interest in major public works projects, such as railroads, which could not possibly be funded by the states alone also contributed to the movement for more federal aid. Congress responded to initial pressures of this trend by enacting a law in 1871 analogous to that of 1864 which served as a guide for federal aid to public works projects.

Law 69 of 1871, like its 1864 predecessor, specified projects meriting federal aid.[71] Compared to the fifteen projects of 1864, the new law enumerated twenty-eight projects, some of which were duplications of the earlier ones, and it also emphasized road and river transportation to the exterior. The 1871 projects differed from the previous list by offering the option in some cases of building either a road or railroad. Thus began a protracted debate between the proponents of road versus railroad construction. Law 69 withdrew the government's option of buying shares in a construction enterprise but offered a guaranteed 7 percent annual return on private investment as the principal form of aid. It specified the maximum amount of capital for which the government could guarantee the 7 percent return, and the breakdown by region is as follows:

Antioquia, Tolima	$1,400,000
Cauca	1,000,000
Bolívar, Magdalena, Panama	1,500,000
Boyacá, Cundinamarca, Santander	9,400,000

The obvious regional discrimination in this distribution resulted from the anticipated construction of a road or railroad from Bogotá to the

---

70. Parra, *Memorias*, 599–602; *cf.* Table 2; *Memoria de Hacienda, 1873*, 1; *Memoria de Hacienda, 1874*, 1.

71. Law 69 of June 5, 1871, *Leyes de Colombia, 1863–75*, 783–89.

Table 6

Comparison of State and National Incomes in the Periods 1865–1866 and 1873–1874

	1865–1866	1873–1874	% Increase
Antioquia	$ 205,961	$ 396,564	93
Bolívar	159,169	201,800	27
Boyacá	120,280	122,100	1
Cauca	122,718	158,400	29
Cundinamarca	159,000	440,626	177
Magdalena	70,939*	78,801	*
Panama	249,926	318,000	27
Santander	173,801	235,957	36
Tolima	140,755	151,000	7
Total	$1,402,549	$2,103,248	50
National Government	$2,138,651	$3,921,000	83

*The earliest available budget data for Magdalena are for 1869 and appear in Memoria de Hacienda, 1870, xxi–xxii.

Sources: Income for the 1873/74 period is based on state budgets and is summarized in Galindo (ed.), Anuario, 220. Income for Boyacá, Cundinamarca, and Panama is for 1874; income for the other six states is for 1873. Data for 1865/66 are from the following sets of state laws: Leyes i decretos expedidos por la lejislatura del estado soberano de Antioquia en sus sesiones de 1865 (Medellín, 1865), 42–45; Leyes i decretos de Bolívar . . . 1865 (Cartagena, 1866), 61–69; Leyes i decretos de Boyacá . . . 1865 a 1867 (Tunja, 1868), 28–35; Leyes i decretos de Cauca . . . 1863 i 1865 (Bogotá, 1866), 246; Leyes i decretos de Panama . . . 1865 (Panama, 1867), 57–65; Leyes i decretos de Santander . . . 1864 (Pamplona, 1865), 79–97; Recopilación de actos de Tolima . . . 1862 a 1877 (Bogotá, 1879), 176–77; Recopilación de leyes y decretos de Cundinamarca . . . 1857 a 1868 (Bogotá, 1868), 402–408.

Magdalena River passing through Boyacá, Cundinamarca, and Santander. This project, which later became known as the Northern Railroad, called for an investment of $9,000,000.

Subsequent laws modified the landmark 1871 law by adding projects to the original list and by strengthening the commitment to railroads. A modification in 1872 declared that the Bogotá to Magdalena River route could be part railroad and part road, but by 1873 it was projected as a purely railroad route. The 1872 law also attempted to overcome any constitutional barriers to federal aid to the Northern Railroad by defining it as part of an interoceanic route which when completed would extend from Buenaventura to Bogotá and then northward to the Magdalena River. Enactment of the modifying law in 1873 exaggerated the regional discrimination inherent in the 1871 law by raising from $9,000,000 to $20,000,000 the amount of capital investment in the Northern Railroad which was eligible for the guaranteed interest. If that method of financing failed, the law authorized either a $20 million bond issue or contraction of a $20 million loan.[72]

The Northern Railroad project raised immediate controversy. Its regional focus, its anticipated high cost, and its dominance over other public works projects of the period gave it status in the 1870s analogous to that of the Cauca road project of the 1860s. The ensuing controversy amply justified Salvador Camacho Roldán's prediction of 1871: "The distribution among the nine states of projects supported by the general government eventually will become an apple of discord among them and between them and the general government, and this will produce bitter fruits of resentment and disunity." The 1871 law produced anguished cries of discrimination from Antioquia and Cauca, and even the governor of Santander complained that the Northern Railroad would bypass the most densely populated portion of his state. Commitment by the national government to the Northern Railroad nevertheless gained strength in 1872 when Aquileo Parra became secretary of hacienda, succeeding Salvador Camacho Roldán, a formidable opponent of the railroad. Parra, who held the post until 1875, was an export merchant from Vélez, Santander, and consequently an ardent supporter of the railroad which was projected to pass near his home town.[73]

The 1871 law on the one hand provided the initial sanction for the Northern Railroad but on the other it temporarily slowed the trend of aiding transportation projects through outright federal grants. Until 1874 new authorizations for such expenditures totaled only about $30,000, part of which was spent over a four-year period.[74] Congress

72. Law 52 of May 14, 1872, law 89 of May 30, 1873, *ibid.*, 858–60, 991–95.
73. *Memoria de Hacienda, 1871,* 138; Parra, *Memorias,* 592–95.
74. Law 58 of June 8, 1872, law 16 of March 22, 1873, law 88 of May 28, 1873, *Leyes de Colombia, 1863–75,* 877, 919, 990.

allocated only 11 percent of the federal budget for transportation projects for the 1872 fiscal year, but that proportion climbed to 18 percent three years later.[75]

Most of the increase in expenditures for transportation projects voted by the 1874 Congress came in response to the railroad fever gripping the nation. The Northern Railroad continued to dominate attention. In addition to renewing the authorization to issue bonds or contract a loan of up to $20 million, an 1874 law approved the expenditure of $125,000 for exploration, preparatory work, and the construction of feeder roads. Congress in 1874 also authorized the government to contract for the construction of a railroad connecting the cities of Piedecuesta and Bucaramanga in Santander with either Lake Paturia or the Magdalena River. Among the concessions granted to the contractor were subsidies of $100,000 for 1875, $125,000 for 1876, and $150,000 a year for the following eighteen and one-half years. Congress also approved construction of a railroad in Antioquia to connect Medellín with the Magdalena River and authorized an annual expenditure of $100,000 for a ten-year period.[76] Conversion of the Cauca road into a railroad represented the fourth railroad approved by Congress in 1874. No significant outlay of funds to the contractor was required until the railroad showed satisfactory progress, but in case of failure the law authorized the government itself to build the railroad.[77] All other public works projects approved in 1874 were for road construction and improved river navigation, but they were of minor importance in comparison with the four railroad projects.[78]

The nature of the national government's response to mounting state pressures for federal aid removed any doubts as to which region

75. For 1872 see law 86 of June 13, 1871, *Leyes de Colombia, 1863–75*, 812; for 1875 see law 64 of July 2, 1874, and law 62 of June 8, 1875, *ibid.*, 1103, 1194–95.

76. Law 31 of June 6, 1874, law 51 of June 19, 1874, law 18 of May 4, 1874, *Leyes de Colombia, 1863–75*, 1057–58, 1076–80, 1047–48.

77. Law 32 of June 6, 1874, *ibid.*, 1059–60. A contract for the construction of this line had first been approved in 1872, but the company's record was as dismal as that of the Buenaventura Road Company which the railroad company had absorbed. See law 66 of June 17, 1872, and law 64 of May 9, 1873, *ibid.*, 884–91, 955.

78. These projects included the following: $50,000 for a road from Cúcuta to the Magdalena River; $2,000 for navigation on the San Juan River in Cauca; $5,000 a year for four years plus an initial $3,000 exploration grant for roads in Cauca; $50,000 to remove obstacles from the upper Magdalena River. See law 21 of May 14, 1874, law 22 of May 14, 1874, law 62 of June 25, 1874, *ibid.*, 1050, 1101.

wielded the most power. Whereas Cauca had obtained the lion's share of aid in the 1860s, the most favored states in the early 1870s were Boyacá, Santander, and Cundinamarca. The coastal states, dominated by the Liberals, fared less well than Antioquia, a Conservative stronghold. In administering federal funds the Radicals showed themselves willing to place regional interest above party unity.

The Radicals continued to attach the utmost importance to a free-trade policy, but their commitment to a weak state and a laissez faire philosophy had weakened perceptibly by 1874. Such doctrines were found to be inconsistent with the exigencies of export expansion, which demanded a greatly improved transportation system. Private enterprise was unable to generate the capital to meet this demand, and state governments were unwilling to generate it through taxation. Consequently, the national government was relied upon as the only entity capable of responding to the need, in spite of the constitutional barriers to federal action. The increase in federal revenue from the 1860s to the 1870s, the decline in the states' share of the total revenue, and the changing emphasis from road to railroad construction were among the factors leading the states to rely increasingly on federal aid and to compete for it more vigorously.

Policies to which the Radicals committed the national government were largely shaped by economic pressures, but they also reflected the outcome of political conflict within the Liberal party. Until 1867 the Mosqueristas maintained a strong political position at the national level, although the two Liberal factions approached parity in terms of their influence in shaping federal policy. When the Radicals gained control of the national government their policies were free to evolve with few competitive restraints, but instead of moving forthrightly toward implementation of their model of a state limited in power and authority, the Radicals gravitated toward the ideological stance of the Mosqueristas. The recentralization of authority executed by the Radicals was more in harmony with the doctrines of their rivals than with their own stated positions. And yet the rivalry and animosity between the two factions did not lessen during the decade after 1867. This suggests that the basis for differentiation between the two Liberal factions was less ideological than regionalist or personalist.

Initiatives by the Radicals in the areas of educational reform and federal aid to public works released forces which threatened their continued political dominance. The federal aid program became an apple of discord, as foreseen by Salvador Camacho Roldán, because it too obviously favored the three eastern mountain states. The Radicals were vulnerable to the charge of blatant regional discrimination, particularly from the four coastal states whose port cities were the collection points for a large portion of federal revenue. The educational reform program also aroused political opposition. It intensified the hostility which Conservatives had harbored against the Radicals since the *golpe* of October, 1868. Although the Conservative party and the church hierarchy were each divided on the issue, the bishop of Medellín and the Antioquia wing of the Conservative party vigorously opposed the program.[79] Failure to strengthen the law on public order in 1871 deprived the Radicals of a legal device for coping with these new regionalist and religious forces of opposition. The temptation to resort to nonlegal methods would become compelling.

During the decade of Radical domination the opposition launched three serious campaigns to recover political power. In 1869 a group of Mosqueristas led by José María Rojas Garrido formally allied with dissident Conservatives including Carlos Holguín, former secretary of government in the overthrown Conservative regime of Cundinamarca, Recaredo de Villa of Medellín, and Leonardo Canal. Many prominent Conservatives of Cundinamarca, such as Antonio B. Cuervo and Manuel Briceño, supported the "league of 1869," but the vast majority of the Antioquia wing of the party refused to endorse it. A shared hatred of the Radicals provided the underlying basis of the league. Both partners had suffered from Radical golpes—the Mosqueristas in May 1867, and the Cundinamarcan Conservatives in October 1868. The league nominated the exiled General Mosquera for president and a mixed slate of candidates for lesser offices in several states. In the balloting for president the Radical candidate, Eustorgio Salgar, won with the votes of the three core Radical states plus Panama and Magdalena. Cauca, Bolívar, and Tolima voted for Mosquera, and Antioquia voted for its own Conservative candidate.[80]

An additional, noteworthy aspect of the 1869 election was the concrete evidence it produced that prominent Colombians were con-

79. Loy, "Primary Education," 281–85.

80. Pérez Aguirre, *25 años de historia,* 294–97; *Boletín Eleccionario* (Medellín),

templating national dismemberment. This threat was first voiced by Mosquera, who was reported to have written: "The Conservatives need a genius to lead them because it is necessary to begin by dissolving the republic, separating the states of Antioquia, Cauca, Bolívar, Magdalena, and Panama and moving the capital to the latter." At the same time a Conservative privately wrote: "The idea, or better stated, the proposal for the separation of some states from the union is gaining strength, and if I am not mistaken, it will probably not be long in coming." A few days later a Bogotá paper editorialized: "The movement which would certainly have a very serious and transcendental character for the future of the country is that which silently and tenaciously has been continuing for some years until the present for the purpose of organizing an independent nation from the states of Antioquia and Cauca; this project . . . has existed since 1859 in the mind of General Mosquera."[81] An early March edition of *La Prensa*, a Conservative Bogotá paper, circulated with an attached broadside entitled "Separation," which argued in favor of the separation of Antioquia and Cauca and invited Bolívar and Panama to join in organizing a new nation. The principal argument offered in support of such a drastic step was disgust with the existing Liberal government and its tendencies toward centralism. *La Prensa* editorialized: "Speeches, publications, and even proposals presented in one legislature are showing with a clarity which frightens us that we are rapidly marching toward the situation of Central America." Shortly thereafter the respected Medellín paper *El Heraldo* warned that if the national government did not permit free elections and respect state sovereignty the sister states of Cauca and Antioquia would be compelled to separate and form an independent nation. The paper argued that these two states had a sufficient territory, population, and resource base to sustain a prosperous independent existence.[82]

November 4, 1869; Cordovez Moure, *Reminiscencias*, VII, 128; Rodríguez Piñeres, "Liga de 1869," 255–72; Holguín, *Cartas políticas*, 116–20.

81.   Miguel Samper to José María Torres Caycedo, February 17, 1869, Manuel José Amaya to José María Torres Caycedo, February 17, 1869, in Ignacio Gutiérrez Vergara collection, Archivo de la Academia Colombiana de Historia, Bogotá, hereinafter cited as ACdeH; *La Paz* (Bogotá), February 23, 1869.

82.   *La Prensa* (Bogotá), March 5, 1869; *El Heraldo* (Medellín), March 18, 1869; another broadside strongly in favor of separation was attached to *La República* (Bogotá), March 31, 1869.

Editorial activity concerning separation peaked along with Mosquera's candidacy and dwindled as his prospects for election disappeared. But the threat of separation was never totally absent during the remainder of the federation period. Even though concrete plans for separation were never under active consideration after 1869, thoughtful Colombians periodically expressed a fear that the nation could not long remain intact under the existing constitutional framework. A year after the controversy over separation had died out, the following commentary appeared in a Conservative paper of Bogotá: "The idea of national unity has been almost totally lost. . . . Colombia is no longer a *patria común.*"[83]

Conservative and Mosquerista elements repeated the effort to end Radical hegemony in 1873. The anti-Radical candidate was Julián Trujillo, a prominent Liberal commander in the civil war of 1860–1862, former governor of Cauca, and ardent supporter of Mosquera. As Colombian diplomatic agent in Ecuador in 1870 he had commented favorably on that country's system of religiously supervised primary education. The Conservatives consequently supported Trujillo, but besides Antioquia and Tolima, only Cauca voted for him.[84]

The last major electoral struggle to dislodge the Radicals from the presidency occurred in 1875. Conservative-Mosquerista cooperation which had defined the opposition in 1869 and 1873 continued to operate, but only as a secondary, muted theme. The Radical golpes of 1867 and 1868 which had given substance to the opposition in 1869 were no longer adequate for coalition formation by 1875. Regional interest provided a more effective basis upon which to form an anti-Radical position. Opposition leaders in 1875 focused their attack on how the Radicals employed their power, *i.e.*, on their policies of regional discrimination. The candidate named in 1875 to restore regional parity by ending Radical hegemony was Rafael Núñez.

83. *El Bien Público* (Bogotá), July 29, 1870.

84. Gómez Barrientos, *25 años de Antioquia*, 183; Antonio José Rivadeneira Vargas, *Don Santiago Pérez, biografía de un carácter* (Bogotá, 1966), 59–60.

Chapter III

The Costeño Challenge To the Cachaco: The Election of 1875

Rafael Núñez belonged to that outstanding generation of Colombians who began their careers at mid-century and in a burst of reformist activity profoundly altered the course of national development. After several years of experience in local and provincial government, Núñez began a decade of impressive, often controversial, political activity at the national level in 1853. He went abroad in 1863, and a decade of traveling, writing, and intellectual activity followed. Núñez' political experience, intellectual stature, and opportune absence from Colombia destined him to lead the assault against Radical domination when he returned to his homeland in the mid-1870s. In directing this attack he became a regionalist candidate seeking to end control of the national government by the eastern mountain region. He was, it must be emphasized, the only costeño ever to overcome the disability of north coast origins and gain election to the Colombian presidency.

The election of 1875 posed the most serious challenge to the Radicals since they established their political ascendancy in 1867. As a direct result of this bitterly fought contest, the Liberals became deeply divided along regionalist lines between the Radical-dominated interior and the coastal periphery led by Núñez. Victory by the Radicals in 1875 ushered in the final, brief phase of their political hegemony. Despite Núñez' defeat, he became the central political figure of Colombia within five years.

Cachaco literally means a dandy, a term of derision used by costeños, residents of the north coast region, in referring to a person from the interior, usually a Bogotano.

Colombia's tropical north coast provided the setting for Núñez' early development, his formal education, and the inauguration of his political career. He was born to a family of moderate distinction but little means in 1825 in Cartagena, a tropical seaport surrounded by walled fortifications which symbolized both the city's important colonial past and its legendary endurance. Shortly after earning a law degree from the University of Cartagena, Núñez established ties with Panama which he maintained throughout his lifetime. Through his father's friendship with Tomás Herrera, prominent military and political figure of Panama, Núñez received an appointment as judge in David, a small town in the western part of the Isthmus. On occasional visits to Panama City he became well acquainted with Herrera and the influential Arosemena family, and during his residence in David from 1846 to late 1848 he cultivated friendly relations with José de Obaldía, one of the most prominent Panamanians of the period. Obaldía offered Núñez his friendship and introduced him to the Gallegos family, major landowners of western Panama. Núñez formalized these ties a few years later when he married a Gallegos daughter, a sister-in-law of Obaldía.[1]

A few months after Núñez returned to Cartagena in 1849, a Liberal election victory embarked Colombia on a turbulent period of reform which covered the years 1849 to 1853. This circumstance offered him opportunity to launch a political career and to attain significant stature as a political figure. In 1849 he both organized a local Democratic Society and founded a newspaper, *La Democracia*, to provide a forum for the young Cartagena Liberals, to disseminate reformist doctrine, and to generate support for President José Hilario López. As a result of Núñez' leadership of the Cartagena Liberals, he was appointed secretary in 1849 to the newly arrived provincial governor, General José María Obando, the extremely popular Liberal military figure just returned from seven years of exile. That appointment was a major step in Núñez' career, because Obando's popularity marked him for the presidential succession. From 1849 to 1852 Núñez served as secretary to four different governors of Cartagena, including Obando, Tomás Herrera, and General Juan José Nieto, Liberal boss of the province. In addi-

---

1.   Castillo, *El primer Núñez*, 40, 49, 62–66.

tion to these activities, Núñez taught at the National College of Cartagena and in 1852 was designated rector.[2]

Núñez' close relations with Obaldía, Obando, and Nieto and his reservations on the question of federalism suggest that he was a Moderate Liberal, but some of the ideas expressed in his speeches and articles identify him with the Radicals. In an early issue of *La Democracia* Núñez attacked a group of Bogotá artisans for petitioning Congress for tariff protection. The editorial displayed typical Radical condescension toward the artisans and opposed protection because of the fear that it would lead to formation of monopolies. Another Radical trait evident in *La Democracia* was an exaggerated reverence for key words such as *democracy*, *socialism*, and *republicanism*. One editorial described democracy as the "reign of reason, the doctrine which Christ preached and sealed with his blood on Calvary, and which has civilized the world to its present level." Other numbers of *La Democracia* endorsed the abolition of slavery, extinction of the tobacco monopoly, and expulsion of the Jesuits, those "bastard sectarians of Loyola." In 1851 Núñez glowingly endorsed a law recently enacted by the Radicals which, in the name of equality, suppressed the titles associated with university degrees as well as other titles of distinction.[3]

Núñez built a political career during these years on his own innate abilities and the support of influential friends. The experience of public office and acquaintance with the practical problems of operating a provincial government partially dissipated the romantic views of the young reformer and instilled a degree of pragmatism and flexibility. For example, while serving as rector of the National College of Cartagena in 1852 he reversed his earlier endorsement of the suppression of university titles.

Núñez traveled to Panama in May 1851 and in June married Dolores Gallegos.[4] This marriage strengthened his ties with Obaldía and brought immediate political benefits. The aspersion that Núñez acted out of political self-interest is hardly tenable, since that opinion would

2. *Ibid.*, 78–81, 83, 106, 117–18; Lemos Guzmán, *Obando*, 379–80.

3. *La Democracia* (Cartagena), April 20, May 1, 1849; June 6, 1850; January 2, February 20, 1851. These editorials were generally unsigned, but if Núñez did not write them he certainly endorsed them.

4. Castillo, *El primer Núñez*, 112, 107, 109.

appear to accept romance as the usual basis for marriage at a time when such a notion was uncommon.[5] Núñez brought substantial assets to the marriage in the form of a rapidly developing career and excellent prospects for a successful political future. Since 1846 he had gained social status and extended family support, and he had built a local and regional political network with contacts reaching to the national level. Through Obaldía's influence the province of Chiriquí, Panama, in 1851 elected Núñez to its assembly and to the Colombian House of Representatives. Spending 1852 in Cartagena with his bride, he postponed taking his seat in Congress. Early in 1853 he departed for Bogotá.[6]

As the Liberal party divided into Radical and Moderate factions, Núñez resisted full identification with either. His ability to maintain a measure of independence was severely tested during the 1853 session of Congress when debate on the new constitution generated enormous pressures from both extremes of the party.

From the time of Núñez' arrival in Bogotá until his departure abroad in 1863, he was centrally involved in many of the decade's pivotal events. He first attracted public attention by opposing the decentralizing provisions incorporated in the 1853 constitution, a document he helped formulate as a member of the House. During the political crisis of 1854 he fought against the Melo dictatorship and helped restore legitimate government. From 1855 to 1857 Núñez wielded a determining influence in the tariff debate because of his position as secretary of hacienda in the coalition cabinet of President Manuel Mallarino.

Núñez argued for tariff reduction from fear that public opinion would force complete elimination of customs duties, the most productive revenue source available to the national government. Hoping to destroy contraband trade and boost Colombian industry, he proposed reducing the general rate and adding items to the duty-free list.[7] In the 1857 report to Congress the secretary sought a substantial reduction of duties on rough cotton textiles, because the existing duties were "al-

5. For views favorable to Núñez see ibid., 85, 109, and Fernando de la Vega, A través de mi lupa (Bucaramanga, 1951), 151–52. Biographies critical of the marriage frequently quote Pablo Arosemena, Escritos (2 vols.; Panama, 1930), II, 122.
6. Castillo, El primer Núñez, 111, 117.
7. La Discusión (Bogotá), March 12, 19, 1853; Memoria de Hacienda, 1856, 11–12.

most exclusively paid by the people of the Atlantic coast, Chocó, and some southern regions." Núñez presented his practical arguments in favor of tariff reform within an ideological framework. He urged continued progress in the movement toward free trade, argued that increased foreign competition would help combat the "lethal influence of privilege," and concluded his 1857 report with a reasoned endorsement of classical Liberalism: "Our public finances are scarce; but when this scarcity derives from a moderation of taxation, when it does not impede the progress of an administration which is reduced to its natural limits . . . then this scarcity signifies well-being; because it clearly demonstrates that the action of industry does not have to be frequently obstructed in its operations by those artificial obstacles which tend to divert the stream of wealth from its legitimate pathway, an infallible means of destroying it."[8]

After the inauguration of President Mariano Ospina Rodríguez in 1857, Núñez returned to Panama, where he remained for nearly three years. During this relatively tranquil period he engaged in some minor business activities, held a seat in the Panama assembly, and won election as vice-governor. In early 1860 Núñez returned to Bogotá as senator from Panama.[9] His political activities from then until leaving Colombia were defined by his ambiguous relationship with General Mosquera.

Núñez assumed his post in the Senate while the storm of civil war gathered. He worked assiduously with Conservative senators to avert war by enacting a compromise election law, but because of Mosquera's obduracy the effort failed. Núñez made public his opposition to Mosquera's conduct, and he remained aloof from the war until 1861 when the tide of battle forced him to decide between the victorious Mosquera and the legitimate Conservative government. Núñez attended the Senate during its opening sessions of 1861, but the lack of a quorum prevented the Conservative majority from legally sanctioning the election of its presidential candidate. As other congressmen arrived it became evident that Núñez' presence would suffice to complete the

---

8. *Memoria de Hacienda, 1857*, 72, 13, 20.
9. Castillo, *El primer Núñez*, 215–21; Arosemena, *Escritos*, II, 123; Rafael Núñez to Manuel Ancízar, October 22, 1858, in private collection of Jorge Ancízar-Sordo, Bogotá, hereinafter cited as CdeJA.

quorum. At that point he ceased attending and sent a medical certificate stating that he "suffered certain chronic illnesses which compelled him frequently to attend the satisfaction of some natural necessities." When the Senate resolved to meet in Núñez' home, he hid himself in the home of a friend for four months until "rescued" by the arrival of Mosquera and his troops in Bogotá.[10]

Núñez had thrown in his lot with Mosquera by absenting himself from the Senate. Mosquera demonstrated his appreciation of this important if belated adherence by appointing Núñez director of national credit in July 1861 and by elevating him to the cabinet a few months later. As a cabinet member Núñez displayed compliant loyalty to the new master of Colombian destiny. While serving as secretary of treasury, Núñez gained renown by carrying out Mosquera's 1861 decree for the disentailment and disposal by public auction of church and corporate property.[11] In his "Circular Explaining What Is Disamortization," Núñez stated that the purposes of the measure were to bring inert property into circulation, to amortize the public debt, and to try to solve the problem of inequitable property distribution. He offered the following justifications for this drastic measure: "Disamortization is simply a move forward, a way station on the road we have traveled since 1810, a way station following those at which we have already witnessed other similar transformations, such as the abolition of *autos de fe* and torture, of entailed estates, of differential duties, of slavery, etc., etc., and a precursor of others which only God knows what we will see, always on the same route of progress toward liberty."[12]

Uncertainty and skepticism marked the last years of this phase of Núñez' career. In order to remain at the forefront of political developments he found it necessary to identify closely with the Mosquera regime, which came to power by means of violence. Another cause of inner conflict was the failure of his marriage by 1860 and the civil divorce which followed several years later. In the early 1860s in Bogotá he became amorously associated with a married woman whom he followed abroad in 1863. The inevitable scandal seriously tarnished his

10. Castillo, *El primer Núñez*, 256–57.
11. Núñez to Manuel Ancízar, April 2, 1862, CdeJA; Otero Muñoz, *Núñez*, 43.
12. *Registro Oficial* (Bogotá), July 18, 1862.

reputation and brought his honor into question.[13] During this period of self-doubt and inner turmoil he articulated his uncertainty in the following two stanzas of his poem "Que sais-je?", written in 1861:

Ignoro si mejor es el verano
De la existencia que el invierno cano,
Ser Titán o pigmeo, hombre o mujer;
Si es mejor ser humilde que irascible;
Si es major ser sensible que insensible,
Creer que no creer.

. . . .
No sé lo que deseo, lo que busco;
A veces con la luz misma me ofusco,
A veces en tinieblas veo mejor;
A veces el reposo me fatiga;
Cuando me muevo, a veces se mitiga
De mi sangre el hervor.[14]

As though to personify publicly this uncertainty, Núñez ended this stage of his political life with a lackluster performance as a Panamanian delegate to the 1863 Rionegro convention. The denouement came when a new regime in Panama canceled his credentials and he could not sign the new constitution. On this note of frustration Núñez returned to Bogotá and prepared for immediate departure abroad.[15]

During the 1853–1863 decade of political flux, Núñez adapted his

13. Castillo, *El primer Núñez*, 217–21, 279–80; Núñez to Manuel Ancízar, February 17, 1864, CdeJA.

14. *Poesías de Rafael Núñez* (Bogotá, 1914), 5, 8.

I do not know if the summer
Of life is better than grey winter,
To be titan or pigmy, man or woman;
If it is better to be humble than irascible;
If it is better to be sensitive than insensitive,
To believe than not to believe.

. . . .
I do not know what I desire, what I seek;
At times light itself confuses me,
At times I see better in darkness;
At times rest wearies me;
When I move, my uneasiness
At times is soothed.

15. Otero Muñoz, *Núñez*, 51; Castillo, *El primer Núñez*, 286.

policy concepts to shifting currents of opinion. After vigorously opposing the federalist views of the Radicals, and particularly those of
Florentino González, he reversed himself and from 1855 espoused federalism. He was more consistent in his adherence to laissez faire economics and again enunciated his position by attacking the views of
Manuel Murillo, the Radical leader, who advocated stripping wealthy
landowners of their unused land and giving it to the poor. Núñez
opposed such a drastic agrarian reform with the counter-argument:
"In economics, as in politics, the solution of all problems is in liberty;
and governments recognizing this have had to adopt, after a long opposition, that shining doctrine of laissez faire which has come to
redeem the people."[16] Despite this devotion to laissez faire, Núñez
exhibited enough pragmatic sense to moderate the extreme implications of this doctrine. For example, he favored free trade in principle
but advocated a revenue-generating *ad valorem* import duty of about
20 percent.

Operating from a political base in Panama and Bolívar, Núñez
weathered a decade of national political activism during which he had
cooperated closely with Conservatives as well as with both Liberal factions. He was swept into the mid-century current of reformism but resisted full identification with either Liberal faction. Although noted
for his espousal of laissez faire economics and federalism, he demonstrated a high degree of ideological flexibility and an instinct for political survival. Núñez thus remained near the center of Colombian political developments. When he departed for the United States in 1863, he
had established a reputation as a free thinker, a talented poet, a practical politician, and somewhat of a philanderer.

Upon leaving Colombia, Núñez went to New York City, where he
worked for nearly two years as a correspondent for Latin American
newspapers. From 1865 to 1874 he served as Colombian consul at Le
Havre, France, and then at Liverpool, England.[17] In 1874 he published
Ensayos de crítica social, a selection of his letters and newspaper articles written after 1864 on history, economics, and social questions of
Europe and the United States. The essays demonstrate Núñez' breadth

16.   *La Discusión* (Bogotá), April 23, 1853.
17.   Castillo, *El primer Núñez*, 279; Otero Muñoz, *Núñez*, 52–56.

of knowledge, erudition, and his spirit of free inquiry as well as the trend of his intellectual development while abroad.

During his twelve-year absence from the turbulence of Colombian political life, Núñez experienced more immediate exposure to current European thought and had opportunity to observe centralizing trends in Germany, France, and Italy. He remained faithful to the principles of federalism and free trade, but he abandoned his opposition to governmental participation in economic matters. In the preface to his essays he republished the following paragraph from an article written a year earlier:

In a confederation the economic mission of the government is so much more important and urgent, the more because it is especially needed to strengthen the national tie, so necessarily weakened in the political sense. If the confederation is composed of groups of people as scattered as ours, that importance and urgency increase in intensity. . . . It is the genuine economic constitution which can give true sanction to the political constitution. To the centrifugal force of local independence, it is necessary to place in counterbalance a powerful and very visible incentive which functions as a centripetal force.[18]

Núñez thus favored the application of laissez faire economics only to trade policy. His guiding principle in political economy during the 1850s and 1860s had been: "The economic truth is one with the political truth."[19] That truth was classical Liberalism. But by 1874 he was convinced that the political weakness of national government in a federal system must be countered by assigning a more active economic role to the federal government.

Comparison of Núñez' writings of the 1853–1863 period with his 1874 essays reveals a growing emphasis on scientific inquiry and a more critical attitude toward the church. Changes in his concept of progress reflected the increasing importance of science in his thinking. When speaking of progress in the 1850s he most frequently referred to a rather vaguely defined political or intellectual progress. In an 1871 article he urged the adoption of a new educational curriculum based on the study of science. "Science is truth, and outside of it, that which is good in its purest sense cannot be found, because where there

18. Rafael Núñez, *Ensayos de crítica social* (Rouen, France, 1874), vii.
19. Núñez, "El libre cambio en Francia," May 31, 1868, reprinted in *Ensayos*, 84.

is no truth there is error."[20] By 1874, Núñez closely linked the concept of progress with material development and scientific accomplishment. As his conception of progress crystallized, he became more critical of the church. Writing on conditions in Spain he observed: "The miracles of human effort, which are those which have established modern industry, are incompatible with those of the mystical order." In a subsequent attack on Catholicism he concluded that it was not a religion but a theocracy which had lost its reason for being. Núñez believed in a moral order, but concluded that "the moral order and the theological order are . . . diverse entities, and even on occasion opposites."[21] Despite his attacks on the church, Núñez considered progress and religious belief perfectly compatible under the right circumstances, for he had observed their compatibility while abroad.

Exposure to life and intellectual trends in the United States and Western Europe produced a discernible impact on the Colombian. Aside from the obvious broadening of his interests and knowledge, he was impressed with the achievements of industry and science. Problems created by these developments brought a perceptible retreat from Liberalism in Europe by the 1870s, and this retreat was faintly echoed in Núñez' writings during his last years in England. Classical Liberalism no longer accurately described his ideological position, because he inclined toward governmental intervention in economic affairs.

During his residence abroad Núñez effectively used his published articles and private correspondence to register his continuing interest in Colombian affairs and to demonstrate an intellectual fitness for high public office. In 1870 President Eustorgio Salgar offered him the position of secretary of war, but preferring to remain abroad he turned it down. Núñez was one of several Liberals suggested as a presidential candidate prior to the nomination of Santiago Pérez in 1873, and rumors circulated that the north coast states were voting for Pérez in return for the promise that the interior would vote for Núñez in 1875.[22]

20. Núñez, "Las ciencias aplicadas a la industria," September, 1871, reprinted in Ensayos, 335.

21. Núñez, "La revolución económica en España," January 31, 1869; "La causa de las causas," August, 1873; "Cinco años después," August 1, 1873, reprinted in Ensayos, 154, 404, 180.

22. El Republicano (Socorro), May 6, 1875; El Elector Nacional (Barranquilla),

Pérez won the 1873 election, defeating the Moderate Liberal candidate, Julián Trujillo, but the state of Bolívar assured Núñez of a public platform by electing him to the Senate. Núñez excused himself from attending the 1874 session of Congress, but in response to urgings from political supporters he expressed a desire to attend in 1875. His eagerness to return to political activity also reflected an anxiety that time was running out. In late 1873 he wrote: "I already find myself nearly in the winter of life, and I cannot play with my time."[23] While still in Europe, Núñez made the decision to return home to seek the presidency.

Núñez arrived in Colombia late in 1874 with the prestige of an Old World sophisticate. His intellectual stature had grown during his absence because of the distribution of his book and the regular appearance of his articles in Colombian newspapers. A Liberal from Cauca noted that "these collected articles powerfully contributed to increase his prestige in Colombia, especially among the young people."[24] His prolonged absence from the intense struggles within the Liberal party had enhanced his political prospects by diminishing old hatreds and avoiding new ones. Except for a private life vulnerable to attack, Núñez possessed the qualifications required for leadership in a campaign against the Radical domination of the eastern mountain region.

In Núñez' view the active support of General Tomás Cipriano de Mosquera constituted an essential ingredient in fulfilling his presidential ambitions. To obtain this support Núñez had to make another of those unpleasant reversals in his relationship with the durable old general. Shortly after Mosquera's exile in 1867, Núñez had made efforts to disassociate himself from the former president by demonstrating that, although he earlier had served in Mosquera cabinets, his political views did not always coincide with the general's. In the mid-1870s Mosquera was again a man worth cultivating because of his

---

March 15, 1875; Teodoro Valenzuela to Luis Bernal, February 20, 1872, in private collection of Horacio Rodríguez Plata, Bogotá, hereinafter cited as CdeHRP.

23. "Senado, 1874," Vol. IX, folio 17, Archivo del Congreso, Bogotá, hereinafter cited as AC; Núñez to Aquileo Parra, November 4, 1873, CdeHRP; Arosemena, *Escritos*, II, 124; Núñez to Tomás Cipriano de Mosquera, June 26, 1874, in Sala Mosquera, Archivo Central del Cauca, Popayán, hereinafter cited as ATCM.

24. Otero Muñoz, *Núñez*, 58; José María Quijano Wallis, *Memorias autobiográficas, histórico-políticas y de carácter social* (Grottaferrata, Italy, 1919), 244.

seemingly powerful influence in Cauca. He had returned to Colombia in early 1871, won election as governor of Cauca for the 1871–1873 term, and helped elect one of his most devoted followers, Julián Trujillo, as his successor. In Núñez' 1874 correspondence with Mosquera, he flattered the general and discussed topics certain to stimulate his interest and win his favor.[25]

In justifying his candidacy to Mosquera, Núñez focused on the question of discrimination against the north coast states by the Radical-controlled national government. In a letter Núñez confided: "I certainly think politics demands that the continual exclusion of costeño candidates from presidential elections cease—even for a moment. We will see what the political manipulators of Bogotá think in the next campaign." Mosquera eagerly supported any effort aimed at ending Radical hegemony, and he endorsed the regional basis of Núñez' appeal. He cited the need to elect "a citizen from the Atlantic States" as a principal reason for aiding the Cartagenero. Shortly after Núñez returned to Colombia he reaffirmed his earlier assessment of coastal feelings by noting that "sectional sentiment is somewhat wounded because of the permanent exclusion of sons of the coast from the presidency."[26] By early 1875 Núñez had established a working alliance with Mosquera, and he determined to direct his appeal to wounded regional sentiment.

Plans for launching Núñez' candidacy as president for the 1876–1878 period took shape well before he returned to Colombia, and they assumed a distinctively regional basis. In mid-1874 a group of sixteen congressmen from Bolívar, Magdalena, and Panama met in Bogotá and organized a "Society of Representatives from the Coast." The society established procedures for selecting a Liberal presidential candidate

25. Núñez proposed to his friend Manuel Ancízar, who had also served in Mosquera cabinets, that they write a pamphlet containing examples of their written policy recommendations to Mosquera that had not been accepted; see Núñez to Ancízar, November 2, 1867, CdeJA. One way Núñez sought to ingratiate himself with Mosquera was by writing of his efforts to get Mosquera's pension restored and promising to continue working for its restoration if elected president; see Núñez to Mosquera, April 17, December 1, 1874, March 10, 1875; Froilán Largacha to Mosquera, May 26, 1875, ATCM.

26. Núñez to Mosquera, April 17, 1874, ATCM; Mosquera to César Conto, December 2, 1874, January 13, 1875, MS. #113, in Biblioteca Luis-Angel Arango, Bogotá, hereinafter cited as BLAA; Núñez to Mosquera, December 1, 1874, ATCM.

who would look out for the interests of the three north coast states. Nomination of the society's candidate was to occur at a convention held in Barranquilla at the end of the year and attended by three delegates from each of the three states. The delegates were required to arrive with powers obtained from their state governments enabling them to endorse a candidate. After a delay of several days the Barranquilla convention met in early January, and the nine delegates, among whom were men of national prominence, unanimously nominated Rafael Núñez as the Liberal candidate for president. Within a few days of the nomination, mass meetings were held in Barranquilla to generate enthusiasm for the candidate and to express support for "the Núñez candidacy and the rights of the coast."[27] Initiation of the Núñez candidacy was thus strictly a costeño operation.

Nomination by means of formal convention represented an unusual practice in this period of Colombian history. Personal friends of an office seeker generally assumed the initiative for inaugurating a candidacy by publicly advocating it through public meetings, broadsides, or articles in the political press. Supporters often formed societies and established newspapers whose sole purpose was to foment the candidacy. State assemblies occasionally launched a candidacy by passing resolutions endorsing a favorite son. Neither legal procedures nor binding tradition circumscribed the flexibility of the nomination process.[28] A standard feature of a candidate's build-up was the publication in sympathetic newspapers of adherences which consisted of endorsements of a candidate followed by the names of individuals pledged to vote for him. Candidates regarded the frequent publication of adherences containing numerous names as essential to a successful campaign. Early in 1875 Núñez urged Mosquera to obtain more adherences from Cauca, noting with more hyperbole than reality that a large number of adherences early in the campaign were more important than the state's vote later in the year.[29]

27. El País (Bogotá), March 6, 1875; El Progreso (Panama), January 24, 1875; La Palestra (Mompós), January 20, 1875.
28. Use of the term nominate is misleading, because it implies a higher degree of formality than existed. The verb usually employed when discussing the nominating process was lanzar, meaning to launch.
29. For an example of a typical pro-Núñez adherence see El Escudo Nacional (Cartagena), March 9, 1875. Núñez to Mosquera, March 10, 1875, ATCM; for a more

Bitter debate between the Nuñistas and their opponents broke out after dissemination of news about the Barranquilla convention, and it focused on the regional nature of the Núñez candidacy. Besides alleging that the convention was unrepresentative and fraudulent, the anti-Núñez press accused it of threatening to dissolve the Colombian union. One Bogotá paper incorrectly reported that the convention passed a resolution to "proclaim and sustain the separation of the three states" if Núñez lost the election through fraud or intervention by the national government.[30] Such a palpable lie hardened costeño determination to place one of their native sons in the presidency.

The Nuñista press, particularly that of the north coast, responded to such attacks by asserting that a long history of discrimination against their region warranted the election of Núñez: "Until 1810 when Colombia was a colony of Spain, no Colombian merited the confidence of the crown for governing this territory. The same has occurred to the Atlantic coast since 1810. . . . The states of the coast have been looked upon with a type of disdain which, if union is desired, must no longer continue."[31] One paper which specialized in promoting economic development in the coastal region concluded that "our great men of Bogotá know as much of the topography of our coasts as of China's." Many costeños attributed the region's slight economic progress to their lack of political power in Bogotá. A Barranquilla paper declared that coastal interests "have not been well attended up to now, because a son from these shores has not been permanently seated in the presidential office." The contrast of the general neglect of the Magdalena River with the large sums spent by the government on railroads in the interior especially vexed the costeños.[32]

During the four months following the Barranquilla convention the

---

detailed discussion of adherences and the nominating process see Helen Delpar, *Red Against Blue: The Liberal Party in Colombian Politics, 1863–1899* (University, Ala., 1981), 101–104.

30. *La América* (Bogotá), January 20, 1875; *El País* (Bogotá), March 6, May 11, 1875.

31. *El Escudo Nacional* (Cartagena), February 5, 1875; for expressions of similar sentiments see *ibid.*, January 25, 1875; *La Unión Colombiana* (Bogotá), February 1, 1875; *El Promotor* (Barranquilla), February 6, 1875.

32. *El Promotor* (Barranquilla), May 8, February 20, 1875; *El Elector Nacional* (Barranquilla), March 15, 1875; *El Escudo Nacional* (Cartagena), April 25, 1875.

Núñez campaign in the three north coast states seemed formidable. Coastal newspapers published numerous adherences and endorsements from prominent figures of the region. Núñez optimistically reported to Mosquera that the convention "definitely adopted me, and this has produced a great impression." Prospects looked particularly good in Bolívar and Panama, the two states which had provided Núñez with a political base in the early years of his career. Twelve of the sixteen congressmen from those states had signed the 1874 accords preparatory to the nominating convention.[33] The governors of both states, Gregorio Miró of Panama and Eujenio Baena of Bolívar, had empowered delegations to attend the Barranquilla convention to work for Núñez' nomination, and they continued to support him throughout 1875. Continuation of their terms of office through the 1875 election dates provided an additional basis for Núñez' optimism.

Although Magdalena joined in nominating Núñez at Barranquilla, divisions and personal animosities weakened the state's Liberal party. José Ignacio Díaz Granados had been governor since 1873, and he had refused to authorize delegates to attend the convention. To assure Magdalena's representation, Joaquín Riascos, mayor of Ciénaga, hastily summoned a meeting which named three delegates, including himself, to go to Barranquilla. The convention admitted the Ciénaga delegation and excluded rival delegates elected by an anti-Núñez body in Santa Marta. After returning to Magdalena, Riascos seized a state arms shipment, to which he added weapons purportedly obtained from supplies in Barranquilla owned by the government of Bolívar. By the end of January he posed a military threat sufficient to induce Governor Díaz Granados to resign. Riascos, as first designate, assumed the governorship on February 15, thus apparently securing Magdalena in the Núñez column. His conduct, however, inflamed anti-Núñez sentiment throughout the country and evoked charges that Bolívar had intervened in the political affairs of its neighbor.[34]

Traditional economic rivalry between Bolívar and Magdalena pro-

33. Núñez to Mosquera, January 5, 1875, ATCM; El País (Bogotá), March 6, 1875.
34. El País (Bogotá), March 16, May 21, 1875; El Magdalena (Santa Marta), January 19, 1875; El Ferrocarril del Magdalena (Santa Marta), January 24, 1875; El Escudo Nacional (Cartagena), February 25, 1875; El Elector Nacional (Barranquilla), March 15, 1875; José Ignacio Díaz Granados, Rectificación histórica (Barranquilla, 1899), 5–11. The author of the latter was the son of Governor Díaz Granados.

vided an underlying cause for the difficulty in securing Magdalena's loyalty to the Núñez cause. One coastal correspondent submitted to a Santander paper the following assessment of opinion in Magdalena: "[The feeling has been growing that] the presidency of Núñez would not improve the condition of the state, and, perhaps, it would worsen it. . . . The new president will find that, due to a sense of gratitude and love of his own region, it will be necessary to promote the project which by receiving preference above all others will attract all the trade. What project could this be? The Canal del Dique, doubtless, or the railroads projected in Bolívar, and these projects will be the death of Santa Marta as the Barranquilla Railroad presently is."[35] Editorial comment from some of the press in the interior, such as the assertion that "the protectorate of Bolívar will never be accepted by Magdalena," strengthened resistance in Magdalena to the clamor for north coast unity under the Núñez banner.[36] Political conditions in the state, nevertheless, remained quiescent for several weeks.

In addition to the difficulty of maintaining political unity along the north coast when economic competition divided the region, Núñez also faced the problem of developing a strategy which could provide him with the votes of at least two of the other four Liberal states. Cauca represented an obvious target because of its anti-Radical tradition, General Mosquera's influence, and an unaccustomed sense of second-class status which had been gnawing at the state's Liberal leaders since 1867. In the Radical-governed states of Santander, Boyacá, and Cundinamarca only the latter had shown any significant degree of independence from Radical control. If the Radicals contested Núñez' bid for power and fought to retain their grip on national government, few of the Liberal states, coastal or interior, would escape an intense political struggle.

Late in January, members of the Radical "oligarchy" announced the selection of Aquileo Parra, secretary of hacienda since 1872, as their presidential candidate.[37] The "oligarchy," a term of derision em-

35. El Republicano (Socorro), March 5, 1875; see also El Ferrocarril del Magdalena (Santa Marta), February 24, 1875.
36. El País (Bogotá), April 6, 1875.
37. Diario de Cundinamarca (Bogotá), January 25, 1875.

ployed by the opposition, consisted of a coterie of the most influential men in the Radical administrations from 1867 to 1875. Its principal members included Manuel Murillo, twice president, implacable foe of Mosquera, and acknowledged ideological spokesman for the Radicals; Santiago Pérez, president and leader of the ouster of Mosquera in 1867; Felipe Pérez, his brother, former governor of Boyacá, and reputedly "minister without portfolio" in the Pérez administration; Jacobo Sánchez, secretary of interior and foreign relations; and Aquileo Parra. Parra credited Murillo with planting the first seed of his candidacy, but President Pérez served as his key backer in 1875.[38]

Parra's political background closely identified him with the Radicals, and his personal virtues made him a formidable candidate. From the beginning of his political and business careers in the 1850s he had maintained close ties with his native state of Santander, the stronghold of Radical Liberalism since mid-century. Throughout his political life as assemblyman in the 1850s, delegate to the Rionegro convention, senator in the 1860s, and minister of hacienda in the 1870s, he supported the constellation of Radical programs. In the latter position he became best known as an exponent of free trade and government support for major transportation projects designed to stimulate Colombia's import-export trade. By his own account he had risen economically through various business enterprises in Santander such as the export of cotton and quinine and the cultivation of other export commodities. Parra's character and personal life were above reproach and invited contrast with Núñez' reputation for moral laxity. One Conservative evaluated the Liberal candidates in the following terms: "Of moderate learning, much practical knowledge, irreproachable conduct, a private life without blemish—that represents Parra. Of much learning, erudite in theory, experienced in seduction, with the face of a fool behind which is hidden a slippery and ambitious soul—that is Núñez."[39]

Parra and Núñez maintained a cool and distant relationship, but no evidence of animosity exists. They first met in 1855 when Núñez

38. Parra, *Memorias*, 624; *El Sufrajio Libre* (Bogotá), June 17, 1875; Núñez to Mosquera, March 31, 1875, Manuel de J. Barrera to Mosquera, October 23, 1875, ATCM.
39. Parra, *Memorias*, 415–19, 426–27, 507, 542, 562–63, 592–95; "Diario de Quijano Otero," *Boletín de Historia y Antigüedades*, XIX (June, 1932), 399–400.

was secretary of hacienda, and, except for briefly cooperating at the 1863 Rionegro convention, they had since found no occasion to work together. In the early 1870s they exchanged a few letters in which Núñez reservedly supported Parra's favorite project, the Northern Railroad. He wrote to Parra in 1874: "My opinion is that you should make every rational sacrifice for the opening of that important route; *but nothing that is not rational.*" Because of Núñez' favorable attitude toward the railroad, Parra urged him to return to Colombia and assume his seat in the Senate.[40]

The Radical leadership perceived railroad construction and the type of progress it symbolized as a winning issue in 1875. This conviction directly led to Aquileo Parra as the logical choice for Radical standard bearer. Parra's intimate identification with the most important railroad project of the period, the Northern Railroad, made his candidacy uncontested within the ranks of the "oligarchy." Parra testified in his *Memorias* that he had accepted the position of secretary of hacienda in 1872 and retained it until early 1875 specifically to promote the railroad. In 1874 he had been elected governor of Santander for the term beginning the following year, but instead of immediately assuming office he obtained a leave of absence which enabled him to continue working on the project. When finally sworn in as governor in mid-year, he simultaneously accepted a directorship in the company chartered by the government to build the railroad.[41] The merits of the Northern Railroad thus became a principal issue of the 1875 campaign.

Plans for the Northern Railroad evolved from 1871 to 1875 under the influences of an expanding import-export trade, growing federal revenue, and a fascination for material progress of the kind represented by large-scale transportation projects. By providing direct rail linkage from Bogotá through Cundinamarca, Boyacá, and Santander to a navigable point on the Magdalena River, the Radicals hoped to increase the nation's exports, open new lands for settlement, and unite more closely the three eastern mountain states.[42] The Radicals viewed

40. Núñez to Parra, February 2, 1874, CdeHRP; see also Núñez to Parra, November 4, 1873, CdeHRP; Parra, *Memorias*, 317, 328, 684, 687.

41. Parra, *Memorias*, 595, 666; *Gaceta de Santander* (Socorro), April 1, May 20, 1875.

42. See Chapter II, 66–67.

the railroad as a redemptive work for the Colombian interior. "This railroad could be a canal, a ligament [uniting an area] formed by 1,000,000 inhabitants of the interior. . . . This railroad could transform . . . the topographical conditions of Colombia, until now the despair of all colonial and independent governments." Although the Radicals purported to see railroads in general as "the only hope for the Republic," they focused the attention and resources of the national government on the Northern Railroad. By 1875 they had authorized the construction of five different railroads but attempted to provide adequate funding only for the Northern Railroad. No railroad received more than $100,000 from the government in 1875 except the Northern Railroad, for which the government was negotiating a $15 million loan in London.[43]

By 1875 Núñez apparently decided that such lavish expenditures on one railroad were not "rational." Although he did not speak out on the issue, his partisans charged that the railroad was unconstitutional, anti-federal, and contrary to the best interests of most states. They correctly perceived the Northern Railroad as a notorious example of regional favoritism. One pro-Núñez paper charged: "It will benefit only a strip of territory and some few inhabitants of the union, placing over all the republic a crushing burden of debt."[44] The Radicals used the issue to oppose Núñez, labeling him "the candidate of the men who deny the Northern Railroad as Peter denied Jesus, . . . who nourish territorial rivalries between Bolívar and Magdalena and between all of the coast and the interior."[45] The railroad question thus became closely tied to the issue of regionalism. Nuñistas held that the Northern Railroad would benefit only the Radical core of eastern mountain states and that the other projected railroads were conceived only for vote-getting purposes. On the other hand, the Parristas justified their transportation program as necessarily piecemeal in the early stages but as ultimately national in scope and benefit.

Though the Liberal factions in several states bitterly debated the

43. *Diario de Cundinamarca* (Bogotá), July 2, September 25, January 9, May 20, 1875.
44. *La Unión Colombiana* (Bogotá), April 10, February 24, March 24, 1875; *El Escudo Nacional* (Cartagena), April 25, 1875.
45. *Diario de Cundinamarca* (Bogotá), March 18, 1875.

railroad issue, the election results hinged on the question of who held political power at election time. Campaign issues served to delineate the Liberal factions and highlight state and national problems, but control of the governorships, state assemblies, and election juries often proved decisive. Until enactment of a constitutional amendment in 1876 making the presidential election date uniform throughout the country, the dates varied from state to state, ranging from May to November. The three eastern mountain states representing Parra's core of support balloted in July and August. Santander and Boyacá followed expectations in 1875, but Cundinamarca underwent a period of turmoil directly resulting from the election. Cauca's balloting, held in October, proved highly significant. The state belonged to neither candidate's core of support, but both Parra and Núñez heavily counted on Cauca's vote. Two of the three north coast states voted early, but events later in the year upset all calculations for that region.[46]

The Nuñistas in Santander organized early, founded a newspaper, and published several adherences in support of their candidate. Early in the campaign Núñez wrote that "Santander is showing itself partially disposed in our favor." By May he gave up on Boyacá but felt it still possible to win Santander's vote. Núñez persisted in his optimism because of cooperation between his supporters and the Conservatives and some success in ascribing responsibility to the Radical state government for a trend toward centralism and away from the revered tradition of municipal autonomy.[47] In reality, Santander could hardly have been expected to vote for a costeño if a native son were available. While disparaging the north coast's desire for a costeño president, the *Diario de Cundinamarca* advised the voters of Santander of their great fortune in having as a candidate a man who is "expert in your interests and necessities, desirous of your good development, and eager for your progress."[48] In the final analysis Santander belonged to Parra, who was a native son, the governor, and chief sponsor of the vaunted Northern Railroad.

46. *La Ilustración* (Bogotá), June 22, 1875. Election dates for each state are in this issue.
47. Núñez to Mosquera, February 29, May 5, 1875, ATCM; *El Tradicionista* (Bogotá), July 16, 1875; *Diario de Cundinamarca* (Bogotá), July 14, 1875; *El Federalista* (San Gil), May 7, June 11, 25, 1875.
48. *Diario de Cundinamarca* (Bogotá), May 21, 1875.

Though Cundinamarca had favored Radical Liberalism since 1868, the Radicals there had never wielded such overwhelming control as they did in Santander. In early 1875, however, several factors suggested that Núñez could obtain the state's vote. The governor, former president Eustorgio Salgar, had been considered a possible presidential candidate, but in December 1874 he withdrew his name from contention and let it be known that he favored Núñez.[49] Three Bogotá newspapers supported Núñez, and residents of the capital were alleged to be "enthusiastically decided for Núñez." In January the Cartagenero wrote that "the vote of Cundinamarca is assured," and in the following month a Conservative paper, La América, reported that the state leaned toward Núñez.[50]

The railroad question posed one of the few substantive issues dividing the Cundinamarcan Liberals. Whereas Parra's support for the Northern Railroad served him well in Santander and Boyacá, it produced rancorous debate in Cundinamarca. The controversy focused on the question of which of two principal railroad routes to follow from Bogotá to the Magdalena River. The northern route (Northern Railroad) possessed the advantage of circumventing those portions of the middle Magdalena River considered most hazardous for navigation. Enormous cost and time requirements for construction, however, loomed as major disadvantages. The alternate western route would pass only through Cundinamarca and terminate on the river at Honda, Girardot, or Ambalema. This shorter and cheaper route would more immediately benefit Cundinamarca, but it magnified dependence on the notoriously fickle river. Favoring the western route, the Nuñistas argued that the northern route would be of "almost impossible realization, an enterprise devouring of our credit and resources, of frightful prospects which can compromise even our national unity."[51] The Diario de Cundinamarca summarized the Parrista position as follows:

49. Froilán Largacha to Mosquera, January 6, 1875, ATCM; El Escudo Nacional (Cartagena), January 25, February 5, 1875.

50. Froilán Largacha to Mosquera, February 10, 1875, ATCM. The pro-Núñez papers were El Correo de Colombia, La Unión Colombiana, and El Cronista; two Bogotá papers supported Parra, Diario de Cundinamarca and El País. Núñez to Mosquera, January 3, 1875, ATCM; La América (Bogotá), February 23, 1875.

51. La Unión Colombiana (Bogotá), April 10, 1875; see also ibid., February 24, 1875.

"What would be most suitable for Cundinamarca would be to save all its resources in order to help more rapidly in the construction of the unrivaled Northern Railroad."[52]

Despite well organized campaigns, publication of numerous adherences, and discussion of the issues, fraud and violence determined Cundinamarca's vote. The fact that Bogotá served as the seat of government for Cundinamarca and for the nation made the state government highly vulnerable to pressure from national authority. In most cases this pressure was subtle, but occasionally, as in 1868, the national government directly intervened in state political affairs. The Nuñistas held a majority of one vote on the state election jury which had the responsibility for tabulating the ballots. Shortly after the election, which was marred by violence in Bogotá, the national government arrested one of the Nuñista jury members. A political struggle then ensued between the election jury and the Radical-controlled state assembly. Under the leadership of Murillo and Felipe Pérez, the assembly usurped the election jury's function and declared Parra the winner of Cundinamarca's vote. The Nuñistas vigorously contested such proceedings, and the state finally sent two different delegations to Congress, where the final presidential voting took place.[53]

Cauca's vote was essential to Núñez, and it appeared certain he would receive it both because of Mosquera's support and a commonality of interests shared with the north coast states. The Nuñistas made a determined effort to associate Cauca more closely with the north coast by recalling shared political traditions and emphasizing the similarity of economic problems neglected by the national government. Writing from Cartagena, Núñez reported to Mosquera: "Here it is expected that the four coastal states will vote in the same way." In an article reprinted in several Nuñista papers throughout Colombia, one Cauca writer asserted: "The interests of Cauca are united with the coastal states; they are the natural allies of Cauca."[54]

52. Diario de Cundinamarca (Bogotá), September 25, January 15, 1875; El País (Bogotá), April 6, 1875.

53. Froilán Largacha to Mosquera, August 18, 1875, ATCM; Diario de Cundinamarca (Bogotá), July 14, August 2, October 6, 18, 1875; La Unión Colombiana (Bogotá), August 6, 1875; Galindo, Recuerdos, 194–96.

54. Núñez to Mosquera, December 1, 1874, ATCM; La Unión Colombiana (Bogotá), April 10, 1875; see also El Telégrafo (Palmira), May 6, 1875.

As in Cundinamarca, the Cauca Liberals divided over the railroad issue. The national government had signed a contract in 1872 with a foreign firm for the construction of a railroad linking the port of Buenaventura and the Cauca River. A new contract was negotiated in late 1874, but no significant work had been accomplished by 1875. All of Cauca's Liberals supported construction of this railroad, but the Nuñistas accused the national authorities of having signed the Cauca Railroad contracts solely to stifle opposition to the Northern Railroad. "In order to overcome opposition and assure a parliamentary majority a very simple thing was dreamed up: improvising a contract for the Cauca Railroad. [It] has been nothing other than a fiction to give a passport to the Northern Railroad." One of Mosquera's correspondents wrote from Bogotá that the government signed the new Cauca Railroad contract simply "to obtain the benevolence of Cauca in the next election."[55]

Political events of the last half of 1875 marked the end of a historic era in Cauca, the era of Mosquera's dominance. The total eclipse of the general's influence was quite unexpected. Since 1874 he had been actively engaged in guaranteeing the election of his brother-in-law, César Conto, as successor to Governor Trujillo, whose term expired in mid-1875.[56] Prior to his inauguration as governor, Conto served as a justice on the Supreme Court, and he remained highly circumspect in his opinion regarding the presidential candidates. In response to enormous pressure from Mosquera to join the Núñez camp, he replied that he had no "inclination in the candidacy question." Because of his reticence and the importance of his opinion in influencing the election, speculation ran wild as to whether he would favor Núñez or Parra. All conjecture ceased within a few days of his inauguration. Conto supported Aquileo Parra. Furthermore, Parristas controlled the state assembly, which in turn selected the election jury. An additional indication of the political trend in Cauca occurred when Eliseo Payán, who had recently switched his support from Núñez to Parra, defeated Mosquera in the contest for president of the state assembly.[57]

55. Ortega, *Ferrocarriles*, II, 456–60; *La Unión Colombiana* (Bogotá), February 20, 1875; Froilán Largacha to Mosquera, January 6, 1875, ATCM.

56. César Conto to Mosquera, January 20, 1875, ATCM; Mosquera to César Conto, May 27, October 28, December 2, 1874, MS. #113, BLAA.

57. César Conto to Mosquera, May 5, 1875, Andrés Cerón to Mosquera, April 21, 1875, Juan de Dios Restrepo to Mosquera, June 8, 1875, Gabriel Montaño to Mos-

César Conto's support for Parra dealt a fatal blow to Núñez' hopes in Cauca. The nature of the governor's political power is well illustrated in this observation from a reident of Barbacoas, which had been one of the first cities in Cauca to publish an adherence for Núñez: "Many of those who spontaneously signed that adherence, hoping to obtain some public positions from the new governor, Dr. Conto, thought of changing from night to day and offering the vote of Barbacoas to Dr. Parra as a means of being able to remain in charge of the city's public administration." Evidence suggests that Núñez obtained a substantial majority of the vote cast in Cauca, but the election jury refused to declare him the winner. On the other hand, it lacked the audacity to give the Cauca vote to Parra. After extended deliberations it declared that Cauca would not cast its ballot in the voting for president.[58]

While events in Cauca moved toward their indecisive conclusion, the national government delivered a mortal blow to Núñez' candidacy in his own region. As early as January, 1875, a newspaper in Cartagena predicted that the national government would intervene in Magdalena and Panama on behalf of the Parra faction.[59] The period from May to October witnessed the bloody fulfillment of the prophecy. The first sign of trouble occurred in February when President Pérez demanded the resignation of any army officer who refused to sign a pledge of neutrality in the presidential campaign. Several, including the commander in chief, General Solón Wilches, refused to make such a commitment. The secretary of war, General Ramón Santo Domingo Vila, objected to the president's conduct, and as a result both he and Wilches were dismissed.[60] Laudable as was this seeming attempt to neutralize an officer corps notoriously pro-Núñez in sentiment, it departed from a tradition of political activism by military officers. Indeed, Pérez had benefited from the endorsement of army officers in the 1873 campaign, as had Murillo in 1871.[61]

---

quera, July 20, 1875, ATCM; La Unión Colombiana (Bogotá), March 20, May 18, 1875; Diario de Cundinamarca (Bogotá), July 14, August 12, 1875.

58.   M. S. Barreiro to Mosquera, July 17, 1875, ATCM; Quijano Wallis, Memorias, 248; Los Principios (Cali), November 19, 1875; [Ernesto Cerruti], Aventuras de un cocinero (Ernesto Cerruti): crónicas de Cauca (Bogotá, 1898), 20.

59.   El Escudo Nacional (Cartagena), January 15, 1875.

60.   Diario Oficial (Bogotá), February 14, 1875; La Unión Colombiana (Bogotá), February 13, 20, 1875; El Escudo Nacional (Cartagena), March 9, 1875.

61.   La Unión Colombiana (Bogotá), February 13, 1875; see broadside signed by

The ouster of Wilches and Santo Domingo Vila particularly alarmed the Nuñistas, because both men had publicly endorsed the Cartagenero. Santo Domingo Vila had established his military reputation during the 1860–1862 civil war, and during the following decade he served as senator and governor of Bolívar, and he acquired a reputation as a champion of costeño interests.[62] A broadside circulating in Bogotá in February reflected the state of alarm in the Núñez camp. It charged that the "oligarchy" concocted the dismissals in preparation for "sending battalions to Panama and Magdalena. . . . The states of the coast and Cauca must arm and wait, because now there neither can nor should be further vacillation: 'be free or die.'" Núñez and five other congressmen from Bolívar openly urged the state assembly to vote swords of honor to Wilches and Santo Domingo Vila. Late in February the Nuñistas hosted a special banquet in Bogotá to honor both men, and it was attended by leading lights from the Núñez camp, including the candidate himself.[63] The tension slowly subsided in the following weeks, but events in Magdalena renewed it in May.

Fighting erupted in Magdalena when Conservatives and Radicals joined forces to overthrow Governor Riascos. To defend his government, Riascos purchased arms from the friendly government of Panama and enlisted the support of Santo Domingo Vila. In the course of the conflict Riascos violated federal laws by removing customs officials in Santa Marta and interrupting the mail service. President Pérez responded by sending federal troops from Panama to Magdalena and by replacing the Nuñista head of the Atlantic army head-quartered in Panama with a more politically reliable commander, General Sergio Camargo. When Camargo arrived in Panama City, Governor Miró placed him under arrest. Miró justified his brazen action on the grounds that he was convinced that Camargo's mission was to "provoke conflicts in the state and to make sure that the vote for president of the republic be cast in favor of Dr. Parra."[64] By the end of May the national government had

---

Wilches and Santo Domingo Vila dated February 13, 1875, in *El Escudo Nacional* (Cartagena), March 9, 1875.

62. José P. Urueta, *Cartagena y sus cercanías* (Cartagena, 1912), 432–34; Parra, *Memorias*, 606–10. Santo Domingo Vila was born in Cuba but came to Colombia in his youth.

63. *El Escudo Nacional* (Cartagena), March 9, 1875; *La Unión Colombiana* (Bogotá), March 3, 1875.

64. Gregorio Miró to Mosquera, May 28, 1875, ATCM.

ample grounds for justifying the anticipated intervention in the north coast states.

President Pérez responded to the crisis by sending two peace commissioners and federal troops to the north coast. All three states remained in turmoil until October. Peace was restored only after federal forces defeated the defiant state militias led by Santo Domingo Vila and occupied Barranquilla, Panama City, and Santa Marta. Through help received from the federal army, the rebel units in Magdalena toppled Riascos and installed a Conservative government. Later in the year Magdalena cast its vote for Parra. In October Radical insurrectionists in Panama overthrew the Nuñista governor with the tacit help of General Camargo. The state earlier had held its elections and voted for Núñez, but the new government ordered new elections and declared Parra the winner. Panama, like Cundinamarca, thus sent two different delegations to Congress. Of the three north coast states only Bolívar remained firmly in the Núñez column.[65]

Political passions in the interior became inflamed against the north coast because of rumors that the region planned to declare its independence from the rest of Colombia. Editorial comment, letters to the editor, and circulating broadsides nourished the rumors. In June the prestigious *Diario Oficial* published a statement signed by fifteen customs employees dismissed from their posts in Santa Marta by Governor Riascos. The statement concluded with the following accusation: "The disturbances of this state are not purely local; they represent the prologue of the revolution which will go under the name 'Independence of the Coast.'" *La Ilustración* of Bogotá complained that the Núñez candidacy was proclaimed "to shield the threat of separation of the coastal states, and Núñez consents with his silence." The *Diario de Cundinamarca* added to the sentiment against the coast by asserting: "The words 'separation of the coast' have not yet been written in public documents signed by Baena, Riascos, Santo Domingo,

65. For a pro-Radical account of these events see Nicolás Esguerra, *Certificación del secretario de hacienda i fomento sobre los acontecimientos de la costa* (Bogotá, 1875), 1–51; *Diario de Cundinamarca* (Bogotá), May 7, June 4, 16, 17, 30, July 6, August 31, September 23, October 12, 20, November 26, 1875. Nearly every issue of *El Escudo Nacional* (Cartagena) and *El Elector Nacional* (Barranquilla) from May to July contains useful information from the north coast view.

and Miró, but those words have been pronounced with more or less emphasis for some time now." A week later it added what could have been taken as a racial slur to political stigma by announcing that all of the loyal states "are preparing to oppose the allies of the coast who want to make of the republic a *merienda de negros*."[66]

As the electoral implications of the year's political turbulence emerged, it became evident that Núñez' only possibility for winning the presidency lay in obtaining the votes of the two Conservative states, Tolima and Antioquia. Expectation of Conservative support was not unreasonable, because both states had voted for the Moderate Liberal candidate, Julián Trujillo, in 1873. As a result of Liberal party division the Conservatives were in a position to elect either Núñez or Parra. The Conservatives, however, were as badly fragmented as their rivals and unable to formulate a position acceptable to all of the state party organizations. Local and state issues determined the party's position, so its stance varied from state to state. In Magdalena the Conservatives took the lead in the armed movement against Governor Riascos, and they supported Parra for president. In Santander they supported Núñez in an effort to break Radical control exercised by the "masonic center of Socorro."[67] Conservatives in Cundinamarca and Cauca were divided by local issues and unable to agree whether to endorse Núñez or Parra.

Since 1867 Antioquia and its "satellite" Tolima had maintained a special relationship with the Radical governments of Bogotá, and this alliance was strengthened by the support each party gave to the favorite railroad project of the other. Conservative members of Congress supported the Northern Railroad, and the national government provided an initial appropriation for the Antioquia Railroad which was expected to cost $1 million. The death of Governor Pedro Justo Berrío of Antioquia in early 1875 gave rise to hope in the Núñez camp that this Radical-Conservative accord could be broken.[68]

Despite Núñez' fear that the Radicals "had bought the vote of An-

---

66. *Diario Oficial* (Bogotá), June 19, 1875; *La Ilustración* (Bogotá), August 24, 1875; *Diario de Cundinamarca* (Bogotá), August 14, 21, 1875.

67. *El Tradicionista* (Bogotá), July 16, 1875.

68. Carlos E. Restrepo, *Orientación republicana* (Medellín, n.d.), 14–15; Parra, *Memorias*, 665.

tioquia with a million pesos," he exerted special efforts to gain Conservative support. Responding to public criticism of his well-known religious skepticism, he addressed a letter early in the year to *El Tradicionista* in which he denied being anti-Catholic. In August he directed an important letter to Carlos Martínez Silva, prominent Conservative writer, which appeared in the same newspaper. In this conciliatory letter to the "Government of Antioquia and all the members of the Conservative party" he promised that if elected he would continue the financial support for the Antioquia Railroad, divide cabinet and military posts equally between Liberals and Conservatives, keep the federal government out of religious matters, and seek constitutional reform allowing for state control of individual rights, elections, and public education.[69] Núñez' private sentiments accorded with his public stance, for in a letter to Mosquera he concluded that the only hope for success was "to cultivate the benevolence of the Conservatives." The eagerly sought benevolence was withheld. Núñez' proposals were rejected, and Antioquia and Tolima voted for a Conservative candidate, Bartolomé Calvo.[70] When Antioquia cast its ballot in November, the act symbolized both a renewed assertion of Conservative political identity and the demise of the Núñez candidacy.

Several factors account for the failure of the proposed Nuñista-Conservative alliance. Núñez appears to have given little serious thought to the cultivation of Conservative ties until driven to that consideration by the deterioration of his electoral strategy. In addition, Nuñistas in Congress and the pro-Núñez press unsuccessfully opposed federal appropriations for the Antioquia Railroad at mid-year, and Núñez' subsequent promise to aid the railroad did little to assuage Antioquia's distrust of him.[71] Fighting on the north coast and reports that the costeños were threatening regional independence also led Conservatives to reject Núñez. Ignacio Gutiérrez Vergara complained

69. Núñez to Mosquera, March 31, 1875, ATCM; *El Tradicionista* (Bogotá), February 9, 1875; Carlos Martínez Silva, *Por qué caen los partidos políticos* (Bogotá, 1934), 3–5.

70. Núñez to Mosquera, December 1, 8, 1875, ATCM; Quijano Wallis, *Memorias*, 246; Otero Muñoz, *Núñez*, 62; Manuel Briceño, *La revolución, 1876–1877: recuerdos para la historia* (Bogotá, 1947), 13.

71. Ignacio Gutiérrez Vergara to Recaredo de Villa, May 12, 1875, Recaredo de Villa to Gutiérrez Vergara, May 11, 1875, Gutiérrez Vergara collection, ACdeH.

that the Nuñistas of the north coast were attempting to take advantage of the disturbances there in order "to realize their gilded dream of making the north coast independent and taking over the customhouses as they have always wanted to do." Another Conservative asserted that the nation could never consent to the desire of the "mulattoes" for regional separation and for control of the Atlantic customshouses. There is also evidence that some Conservatives were already contemplating insurrection and that the best posture for the party in 1875 was to work for party unity by supporting a Conservative candidate rather than either Parra or Núñez.[72] Despite the pro-Núñez sentiment of some Conservative leaders such as Miguel Antonio Caro and Carlos Martínez Silva, their view was a distinctly minority view, and the party was too divided to allow the application of effective pressure on that key Conservative state, Antioquia. And Antioquia's Conservative leadership was moving toward a political assertiveness which contributed to the outbreak of civil war a few months after the election. Although Núñez' gestures toward the Conservatives were fruitless in 1875, they were highly significant as the initial step toward the Nuñista-Conservative alliance that a few years later brought him to national leadership.

Prior to enactment of the anticlimactic final scene of the electoral drama in Congress, Núñez' mood ranged from shock, to hope, to despair. In November he concluded: "What is happening is unreal, but true." By the end of the year he felt hope still remained, because neither he nor Parra had obtained the five states required for election. A month before the congressional balloting he proposed the withdrawal of himself and Parra from contention, thus leaving to Congress selection of a designate to fill the presidency. An intermediary made the proposal to Parra, but Parra rejected it.[73]

Congress convened February 1, 1876, and began a month-long process of maneuvering and bargaining which concluded with the election of Aquileo Parra. The Conservatives and Nuñistas attempted to

72. Gutiérrez Vergara to Ignacio Gutiérrez Ponce, August 13, 1875, Gutiérrez Vergara collection, ACdeH; Miguel W. Quintero to Sergio Arboleda, May 8, 1875, Fortunato Cabal to Sergio Arboleda, June 16, September 30, 1875, in Sala Arboleda, Archivo Central del Cauca, Popayán, hereinafter cited as ASA; La América (Bogotá), November 3, 1875.

73. Núñez to Mosquera, November 3, 1875, ATCM; Salvador Camacho Roldán to Parra, December 18, 1875, CdeHRP.

establish a working alliance, but the effort collapsed when the Conservatives withdrew at the last minute. Congress compromised the problem of dual delegations from Panama and Cundinamarca; it admitted the Nuñista delegation from Panama and the Parrista representation from Cundinamarca. The following results of the voting by state failed to give any candidate the required majority:

Voting for Parra . . . . Boyacá, Cundinamarca, Santander,
                                                       Magdalena
Voting for Núñez . . . . Bolívar, Panama
Voting for Calvo . . . . Antioquia, Tolima
Not voting . . . . Cauca

All members of Congress then voted individually, and the final result was forty-eight for Parra and eighteen each for Núñez and Calvo.[74]

The Nuñistas attributed their defeat to the use of fraud and violence by the Radical "oligarchy." Indeed, in the most critical states, Cundinamarca and Cauca, the Nuñistas were deprived of victory by Radicals occupying strategic positions of power who decisively employed that power. Such an analysis, however, was too self-serving, for Nuñistas had played the same game in Magdalena and lost. Núñez and his lieutenants must bear much of the blame for the year's reversals. In a campaign seeking to rectify a pattern of discrimination against the Colombian periphery, political unity of the coastal region in support of that concept was essential. Economic rivalry along the coast and the inadequacies of such regional Nuñista leaders as Miró and Riascos disrupted the region's limited political unity and provided the Radical leadership in Bogotá with the justification for intervention it sought. In addition, the theme of regional discrimination was popular in the four coastal states, but it was damaging in the remaining three Liberal states. The warranted costeño desire for just treatment became too easily twisted in the Colombian interior into a threat of national dismemberment. In Cauca miscalculation of the true dimensions of Mosquera's political influence substantially contributed to defeat. The Nuñista coalition of costeños and Mosqueristas failed, because each of its components failed in the area of its alleged strength, the costeños

74. Quijano Wallis, Memorias, 251–55; Parra, Memorias, 720; Galindo, Recuerdos, 196.

on the north coast and the Mosqueristas in Cauca. Another error
stemmed from disregard of a Conservative movement toward political
assertiveness led by Antioquia. Trujillo had won the Conservative
states in 1873, and the Nuñistas too easily assumed they would simi-
larly benefit from Conservative support.

What appears most striking about the 1875 election debates was
their lack of ideological substance. Issues that had divided the Liberal
party since mid-century were of slight consequence in 1875. Within a
few months of Parra's victory, the question of church-state relations
and attitudes toward the Conservative party became of such moment
that they directly led to civil war. But in the 1875 campaign, the
church-state issue was insignificant. Centralism versus federalism, another traditionally divisive issue, also assumed a minor role in the debates of 1875. The contenders made little mention of any need to moderate the existing federal system by means of constitutional reform.
Both Radicals and Nuñistas supported free trade and both had abandoned economic federalism in favor of an expanded economic role for
the national government. Disagreement on the railroad issue in 1875
thus centered not on the desirability of government financing, but
rather on questions of feasibility and location. These questions in turn
became involved in the argument over regional discrimination. The
deep fissures in the Liberal party revealed by the election campaign
resulted not from debate of ideological principles but instead from regional rivalries and the desire to end Radical hegemony. In making regionalism a central issue of the election, the Nuñistas simply sought
access to power for themselves and for their region. But in the process
they exposed the fragile state of national unity. From this revelation
would come a reexamination of the system of political federalism, and
it would be led by Núñez.[75]

---

75. This analysis of the 1875 election is in substantial agreement with the conclusions of Helen Delpar but for the greater emphasis here on the role of regional rivalry; see Helen Delpar, "Aspects of Liberal Factionalism in Colombia, 1875–
1885," *Hispanic American Historical Review*, LI (May, 1971), 255–64.

Chapter IV

The Conservative Party and the War of 1876–1877

Conservatives played a key role in enabling Rafael Núñez to solidify and extend the Regeneration in the mid-1880s. The history of the evolution of the Conservative party from its utter defeat in the war of 1860–1862 through its failed attempt to recapture power in the war of 1876–1877 to its victory in the war of 1884–1885 must be set forth because the principles under which the party fought in 1885 are the principles that ultimately triumphed through the leadership of Núñez. Most histories of the Colombian federation period, 1863–1885, ignore the Conservative party except for its role in the ouster of President Tomás Cipriano de Mosquera in 1867 and its actions during the months leading up to the war of 1876–1877. Historical literature also gives the impression, plausible but false, that the Conservative party of 1885 had undergone little change during the previous two decades.[1] In the 1860s and early 1870s Conservatives were divided on basic issues, uncertain about tactics, and unable to maintain a leadership structure. But when Núñez opened the door for a Conservative return to power in 1885, the party was united, well led, and prepared to exploit that rare opportunity. Once back in power the Conservatives remained in control of the national government until 1930.

Defeat in the 1860–1862 war left the Conservatives leaderless, dis-

---

1. Henao and Arrubla, *Historia de Colombia*, 707–42, 763–71; Pérez Aguirre, *25 años de historia*, 296–97, 389–97; José Ramón Vergara, *Escrutinio histórico: Rafael Núñez* (Bogotá, 1939), 275–76, 310–11; Indalecio Liévano Aguirre, *Rafael Núñez* (Lima, 1944), 240.

pirited, and divided over questions of political strategy and fundamental principles. The Conservative gains in Antioquia and Tolima in the 1860s complicated the effort to achieve party unity by allowing Antioquia to challenge Bogotá's leadership of the party. Little progress was made in resolving party difficulties until the following decade, when it came in reaction to Liberal policies of recentralization of authority and reform of public education. Recentralization of authority threatened the few gains Conservatives had made, and educational reform undermined traditional church prerogatives in education. These Liberal policies of the early 1870s became the catalyst for Conservative unification, and they propelled the party toward a more openly federalist stance and toward identification as a religious party, as a political arm of the church. The Liberal program thus provoked a collision with Conservatives determined to resist further attacks against state sovereignty and against the church. Conservatives also opted for war in 1876 because they felt the moment was opportune to exploit Liberal party divisions which the 1875 election had deepened.

The critical turning point in the evolution of the party was the war of 1876–1877. Party leaders used the opportunity provided by defeat to restructure the party and to adopt a set of principles significantly different from those that had guided Conservatives during the previous decade and a half. The war of 1876–1877 also acquires significance because it ended a decade of Radical Liberal domination, provided Núñez with access to the presidency, and revealed once again the powerful influence of exaggerated regional sentiment. Although the war lasted only nine months, it wrought considerable destruction and exacted a high death toll.[2]

Lack of effective leadership posed one of the most immediate problems facing Conservatives during the 1860s. Many of the party's most prominent figures were forced into exile following the 1860–1862 war, and others voluntarily took up residence in other countries.[3] Perhaps the most egregious loss was the wartime death of Julio Arboleda, a

2. McGreevey, *An Economic History*, 88.

3. Former president Mariano Ospina Rodríguez escaped from prison following the war and fled, along with his brother, Pastor Ospina, to Guatemala, where he remained for a decade. Bartolomé Calvo, who headed the last Conservative government during its final weeks, left for Ecuador, where he resided until his death in the 1880s. Pedro Alcántara Herrán, president in the 1840s and a Conservative com-

noted Conservative from Popayán and commander of forces from Cauca.

In addition to the loss of political and military leadership, the Conservatives suffered from their close ties with the church, because the church came under severe attack through the Liberal-sponsored anticlerical measures of the early 1860s. Conservatives helplessly witnessed the forced exile of some of their strongest political allies when the government moved against church leaders who resisted implementation of these laws. Mosquera ordered Archbishop Antonio Herrán into exile in 1861, but under the plea of illness the government relented and allowed him to remain in Bogotá. The subdued archbishop counseled his clergy to swear obedience to the offensive anticlerical laws while working to have them tempered, but the bishops of Cartagena and Medellín publicly refused to comply with the laws. Consequently, the government ordered the two bishops out of the country. José Manuel Groot, the respected Colombian historian, privately railed against the submissiveness of the archbishop who, he claimed, "is frightened to death." And when the bishop of Popayán, Pedro Antonio Torres, a Mosquera crony, signed a formal accord agreeing to comply with the religious inspection law, the Conservative press attacked him.[4]

Defense of the church and the effort to bolster resistance to the anticlerical measures thus became issues of central preoccupation to Conservatives. A typical expression of this concern is the following statement from a letter to the editor of El Conservador: "There is only one fundamental question among us—the religious question. And that question cannot have any satisfactory solution if it is not resolved in favor of Catholicism." Conservatives espoused this view because of their conviction that the goal of Liberalism was "the destruction of Catholic Christianity, and the establishment of communist theory as a social base."[5]

---

mander during the 1860–1862 war, spent most of the 1860s in Lima, New York City, and Paris. Leonardo Canal lived in Lima for four years, and Ignacio Gutiérrez Vergara lived in Madrid until 1865. See La Restauración (Medellín), August 18, 1864, and El Símbolo (Bogotá), May 31, 1865.

4. Bishop of Cartagena, Bernardino Medina y Morena, to Gregorio José Díaz, October 21, 1864, MS. #354, Bishop of Medellín, Domingo Antonio, to Archbishop Antonio Herrán, February 17, 1865, MS. #392, BLAA; José Manuel Groot to Ignacio Gutiérrez Vergara, October 13, 1864, Gutiérrez Vergara collection, ACdeH; El Conservador (Bogotá), September 26, 1863.

5. El Conservador (Bogotá), September 13, 1863, March 17, 1865.

An issue even more widely debated by Conservatives in the mid-1860s concerned the question of how to return to power. Anticipation of the election of Mosquera in 1865 for the presidential term, 1866–1868, triggered the debate which revolved around the question of following one of three courses of action: abstain from all elections, support only Conservatives, or aid the Liberal party faction led by Manuel Murillo. *El Conservador* initiated the debate early in the Murillo administration by criticizing those Conservatives who counseled cooperation with Murillo because of his conciliatory gestures toward the church and his attempts to heal the nation's wounds. Nicolás Pontón, editor of *El Conservador*, attacked the "weakness of some NOTABLES of the Conservative party" and those who "have not had the character or courage to uphold their beliefs, and who sanctioned the GOLGOTICA Constitution of 1858." In his view the fundamental error of the party had been its abandonment of principles in the 1850s, specifically the abandonment of centralism. *El Conservador* concluded that the only proper course of action was to work for unity, return to basic principles, and abstain from the elections because they were fraudulent, and the existing national and state governments were "offspring of a criminal revolution."[6] Pontón staked out an extremist position by declaring that he and his supporters reserved the right to resort to war against a government which came to power by means of violence.

Two other Conservative papers of Bogotá and one from Medellín, representing more moderate elements in the party, vigorously opposed this belligerent stance. But the principal role in promoting the moderate course was assumed by Carlos Holguín, an ambitious and practical-minded party organizer and publicist then in his early thirties. Holguín argued that a political party "has one single goal—to gain power," and it can do so either through elections or war, but because of the recent war the Conservative party had no choice but to follow the election route. Holguín's position in the months-long debate with *El Conservador* gained adherents mainly because the party was unprepared for war, but also because the fact was that some states offered reasonably free elections, and the arguments set forth in *El Conservador*

6. *Ibid.*, June 3, 1864, October 7, 1864; see also *ibid.*, November 18, 1864, August 18, 1865, March 28, 1866.

seemed intemperate and conducive to disunity. The issue was finally resolved in mid-1865 at a meeting of more than four hundred Conservative delegates in Bogotá, where a large majority voted to participate in the upcoming elections and to support Leonardo Canal for president. Within a year of this meeting the two principal papers which had sustained the debate ceased publication for the sake of party unity. Party leaders of Bogotá had met and decided to replace both papers with an official organ of the party, La Prensa. Carlos Holguín was its first editor.[7]

Several months before this debate over tactics, the violent change from Liberal to Conservative control of the government of Antioquia took place, an event which would greatly complicate the problem of party unity. President Manuel Murillo, acting against strong pressure from Congress, granted formal recognition to the new state government of Antioquia in April 1864.[8] He chose this course of action rather than war apparently because he realized that an attempted invasion of Antioquia would be a costly undertaking and because he had a genuine interest in preserving the peace. Murillo was also probably persuaded that renewed fighting would strengthen the position of the Mosqueristas within the Liberal party.

Shortly after recognizing Antioquia's Conservative government, Murillo began a long-lasting personal correspondence with Governor Pedro Justo Berrío of Antioquia, a cautious businessman who jealously protected the interests of Antioquia during his governorship, 1864 to 1873.[9] In a test of Murillo's good faith Berrío asked the president to help the government of Antioquia obtain a shipment of arms imported from abroad which had been illegally intercepted and held by the Liberal government of Magdalena. Antioquia received the arms through Murillo's assistance, and in return the president asked for Berrío's help in muting the outbursts by Conservatives and extremist

7. El Símbolo (Bogotá), October 18, 1864, June 21, 28, 1865; El Conservador (Bogotá), July 28, 1865, June 5, 1866.
8. Gómez Barrientos, 25 años de Antioquia, 4–10, 23–27; La Restauración (Medellín), August 4, 1864; El Conservador (Bogotá), January 16, April 2, 23, 1864.
9. These letters from Murillo to Berrío, which cover the period 1864–1872, were made available by Berrío's son to La República of Medellín, where they were published in 1910 and 1911.

members of the clergy who seemed eager to provoke war between Antioquia and the national government.[10]

An unexpected test of the developing understanding between Murillo and Berrío and of the latter's influence within the Conservative party occurred in the closing months of 1865 when impatient Conservatives began insurrections against the Liberal governments of Cauca, Tolima, and Cundinamarca.[11] In response to these events Murillo advised Berrío that he was raising the federal troop level and sending troops to the affected areas, and he requested the governor of Antioquia to supply a contingent of forces to act in cooperation with national units to prevent the conflict from becoming a generalized war. He astutely advised Berrío that if Conservative leaders disavowed the use of force and cooperated with the national government, there would remain little to arouse "the restless spirit of General Mosquera." Berrío declined to provide the requested troops, but he denounced the resort to force by Conservatives and proclaimed the neutrality of Antioquia.[12] Within a few weeks the insurrectionists were defeated in all three states.

The precipitate action of these eager rebels had placed the government of Antioquia in an extremely awkward position. Conservatives throughout the country looked upon Antioquia as the wellspring of their eventual salvation. A few weeks before the fighting erupted, a Conservative paper of Bogotá expressed this sentiment by noting that "it is in Antioquia where the moral force and the material force of the Conservative party are found." And in the midst of the fighting, El Conservador proclaimed it the duty of Conservatives to divert Liberal forces by rising up in arms throughout the country while Antioquia came to the aid of Conservatives in the principal areas of fighting. Shortly after the Conservative defeat, the same paper upbraided the gov-

10. El Conservador (Bogotá), August 26, 1864; Murillo to Pedro Justo Berrío, July 6, 1864, reprinted in La República (Medellín), October 29, 1910; Murillo to Berrío, August 15, 1864, reprinted in La República (Medellín), November 3, 1910.

11. Arboleda, Revoluciones, 13–18; El Conservador (Bogotá), October 13, 1865; La Restauración (Medellín), November 9, 1865.

12. Murillo to Berrío, November 17, 1865, reprinted in La República (Medellín), November 12, 1910; see also Murillo to Berrío, October 10, 1865, reprinted ibid., November 5, 1910. La Restauración (Medellín), October 29, 1865.

ernment of Antioquia for its cowardly posture: "The policy of Antioquia was reduced to writing a new protest of neutrality every day . . . a protest which brought a smile to Doctor Murillo who ordered it inserted in the *Diario Oficial*. . . . [Antioquia] could have saved the Confederation in 1860, and it did not want to; it could have saved it in 1865, and it has not wanted to." *La Restauración* of Medellín responded to this and other attacks by denying that "egoism is the motive" for Antioquia's policy.[13] The paper attributed the growth of party disunity to the federal system which it claimed was fragmenting the national parties. Most Conservative leaders accepted Antioquia's conduct as the only reasonable course to be followed given the state's lack of preparation for war. Several months after the end of the fighting when passions had moderated, a noted contributor to the Conservative press expressed a commonly held view of Antioquia's role in the Conservative party. "Unlike some of our party colleagues who believe that Antioquia is essentially egoistic and that it has broken all unity with the rest of the party, we believe, on the contrary, that Antioquia is where we must look for everything."[14]

Thus began a decade-long debate over Antioquia's role in the Conservative party. Quick failure of the 1865 insurrections demonstrated that Conservatives could accomplish little without the full support of Antioquia. But the government of Antioquia was hardly eager for wild, hopeless ventures led by extremist elements within the party. Antioquia held an effective veto over any major undertakings contemplated by the party leadership. The state's leaders and press periodically urged upon other Conservatives a policy of restraint and patience and warned against "the ultra-Conservatives," that is, those who sought an early, violent end to Liberal domination.[15] A degree of tension thus existed between the government of Antioquia and Conservative leaders in other states, particularly Conservatives in the capital who had been accustomed to setting party policy.

Antioquia demonstrated its dominance in the shaping of Conserva-

13. *El Símbolo* (Bogotá), August 30, 1865; *El Conservador* (Bogotá), November 8, 29, 1865; *La Restauración* (Medellín), November 9, 1865.

14. *El Conservador* (Bogotá), April 18, 1865; the contributor was Alberick, a pseudonym for Salomón Forero.

15. *La Restauración* (Medellín), May 10, 1866.

tive policy in the crisis of 1867, when a Radical Liberal and Conservative coalition removed Mosquera from the presidency and exiled him following his assumption of dictatorial power. Months before the crisis between president and Congress reached a climax, Governor Berrío raised the state troop level and informed Conservatives that Antioquia would resist a Mosquera dictatorship and would cooperate with Radicals in this endeavor. Berrío also opened correspondence with the Radical governor of Santander and specified which actions by Mosquera would trigger a call to arms by Antioquia. Berrío kept Murillo informed of his intentions, and Murillo encouraged him to act in conjunction with Liberal forces.[16] When the exile of Mosquera and the defeat of pro-Mosquera forces signaled the end of the crisis, Berrío advised other Conservatives "to give loyal and decided support" to the successor administration of General Santos Acosta.[17]

Antioquia's policy prevailed over conflicting advice from other Conservatives such as those who had been enticed by Mosquera's offers of friendship and support shortly before his ouster. One Conservative reported from Bogotá at the peak of the crisis that "several of our party colleagues here have concluded that it would be more useful to support Mosquera than the Gólgotas, because greater advantage can be obtained from him than from them." Another Bogotá Conservative attempted to persuade Berrío that the Radicals could never be trusted and that an alliance with them would lead to disaster. Instead, he argued, the Conservatives should act alone under Antioquia's leadership, because "Antioquia is today an immense national armory . . . a treasure; it is your duty to convert it into an active force, a fund of wealth for all of society."[18] On the other hand, prominent Conservatives such as Carlos Holguín and Leonardo Canal strongly defended Antioquia's actions. In the crises of 1865 and 1867 Antioquia had uni-

16.   Berrío to Leonardo Canal, January 11, 1867, Berrío to Domingo Paredes, January 11, 1867, Gutiérrez Vergara collection, ACdeH; Murillo to Berrío, June 23, 1867, reprinted in *La República* (Medellín), November 15, 1910; Murillo to Berrío, August 4, 1867, reprinted in *La República* (Medellín), November 17, 1910.

17.   Berrío to Sixto Hernández, n.d. but about June, 1867, Gutiérrez Vergara collection, ACdeH.

18.   *La Prensa* (Bogotá), April 30, July 5, 1867; Sixto Hernández to Nepomuceno A. Torres, April 30, 1867, Juan A. Ricaurte to Berrío, April 30, 1867, Gutiérrez Vergara collection, ACdeH.

laterally shaped Conservative policy in the face of divided party opinion, and its actions had received the endorsement of influential party figures from other parts of the country.

By August 1867 peace was restored in all states but Tolima, a Mosquera stronghold. Mosquera's removal from the national scene initiated an intense struggle for control of the state government. The picture that emerges in the press and in personal correspondence of participants in the struggle from mid-1867 until early 1868 is extraordinarily confusing, for it involved shifting alliances among two Conservative factions and two Liberal factions and intervention by Conservative forces from Cauca as well as by national forces.[19] Antioquia again came under pressure to uphold Conservative interests, but instead of following a belligerent course, Berrío arranged for a personal conference with the newly elected governor of Cauca, Julián Trujillo, a Mosquerista, so that the two states could work together to avoid a generalized conflict. Berrío also ordered the shipment of several hundred rifles to Conservative forces, and this together with the arrival of some Conservative troops recruited in Cauca was enough to bring victory. Although late in 1867 a Conservative won election as governor, not until March 1868 could he report that peace was restored, that the Conservatives were united, and that the government was well armed.[20] Tolima's Conservatives controlled the state government for the next decade but remained dependent upon Antioquia for support.

Overthrow of Mosquera also resulted in significant political change in Cundinamarca. Because of distrust between the two Liberal factions, Conservatives won a surprising, clear-cut victory in special elections in late 1867 for the assembly and governorship. Ignacio Gutiérrez Vergara, a veteran administrator, was elected governor despite problems in unifying the party behind his candidacy. One Conservative fac-

19. For background accounts of the events in Tolima see *La República* (Bogotá), September 4, 1867, January 29, 1868. The bulk of the correspondence in the Gutiérrez Vergara collection, ACdeH, for the early months of 1868 concerns Tolima—see especially the letters from Domingo Caycedo.

20. Berrío to Gutiérrez Vergara, January 28, 1868, Domingo Caycedo to Gutiérrez Vergara, January 19, March 30, 1868, Adolfo de Silvestre to Gutiérrez Vergara, December 20, 1867, Gutiérrez Vergara collection, ACdeH; *La Restauración* (Medellín), November 28, December 26, 1867.

tion in Bogotá headed by Jorge Isaacs and Luis Segundo de Silvestre, editors of *La Patria*, refused to support formation of a Conservative committee or the attempt to gain Conservative backing for a single slate of candidates.[21] Bogotá Conservatives, nevertheless, organized a three-member Directing Committee to serve as "an organ of intelligence and communication between Conservatives in the capital and those in the rest of the Republic." Its members were Gutiérrez Vergara, Carlos Holguín, and Manuel María Mallarino, the former president. In addition to opposition in Bogotá to its organizational efforts, the Directing Committee, during its year-long existence, received a less than enthusiastic response from other states to its call for the formation of state committees. Leonardo Canal informed the committee that because of the party's weakness in Santander he would instead continue to strengthen ties with one of the Liberal factions and thus strive for the creation of a truly national party of coalition. Joaquín Vélez, a leading Conservative of Cartagena, offered an impressive list of problems facing the party in Bolívar and concluded that "the Conservative party of Bolívar does not find itself suitably prepared for elections or for war."[22] The occasion of Gutiérrez Vergara's candidacy and election thus failed to spark a revitalization of the party.

Gutiérrez Vergara entered office without difficulty and enjoyed a tranquil six months until mid-1868, when new elections for state assembly were won by the Liberals. Conservative commentators agreed that they had lost because of apathy, intraparty rivalry, and a failure to agree upon a uniform slate of candidates. *La Prensa* reported that the Liberals' triumph had been "the exclusive work of the Conservative party. As long as its members believe that their *only* duty consists of religious practices, they are lost as a political party." Governor Berrío blamed the defeat on "egotistic Conservatives." Liberals in the assem-

21.   *La Prensa* (Bogotá), December 13, 1867; *La Restauración* (Medellín), November 21, 1867; *La República* (Bogotá), September 4, 1867; *La Patria* (Bogotá), September 13, 1867; Jorge Isaacs and Luis Segundo de Silvestre to Gutiérrez Vergara, October 2, 1867, Gutiérrez Vergara collection, ACdeH. For an account of the problems between the Liberal factions see *La República* (Bogotá), January 1, 1868.
22.   Lázaro María Pérez to Gutiérrez Vergara, October 21, 1867, Leonardo Canal to Sixto Hernández, December 6, 1867, Gutiérrez Vergara collection, ACdeH; Joaquín Vélez to Conservative Committee of Cundinamarca, October 14, 1868, MS. #30, BLAA.

bly used their majority to strip the governor of his power by abolishing his right to appoint mayors, limiting his police powers, and requiring the appointment of some officials from lists drawn up by the assembly. As the likelihood of armed conflict intensified, Gutiérrez Vergara requested from Berrío a shipment of arms and the use of "some Antioqueño military leaders." Berrío limited his support to the shipment of 1,000 rifles.[23] In early October Gutiérrez called up the state militia, and four days later he set aside the state constitution and announced a date for elections for a constituent assembly. The following day President Santos Gutiérrez, who had succeeded Santos Acosta, yielded to Liberal pressure and ordered the arrest of Governor Gutiérrez Vergara.[24] Cundinamarca thus returned to Liberal rule, leaving Conservatives in control of only Antioquia and Tolima.

Antioquia played a critical role in shaping the outcome of those events that determined Conservative fortunes from 1863 to 1868—establishment of Conservative regimes in Antioquia and Tolima, defeat of Conservative insurrectionists in 1865, and removal of Mosquera. Antioquia's inaction in the ouster of Governor Gutiérrez Vergara was also considered decisive by party members. A Conservative of Bolívar claimed that the state party was ready to act, but "our preparations have as an essential basis a decisive attitude by Antioquia without whose assistance we can do no more than deplore in silence the evils of the country." Consequently, the role of the government in Medellín in defining national Conservative policy became an issue of growing contention. Ensuring the survival of Conservative rule in Antioquia was Berrío's principal guide in setting policy. In practice this meant upholding the principles of federalism, maintaining correct relations with the national government, avoiding undue risks, and working for party unity. A senior official of the Berrío government privately offered a persuasive argument for Antioquia's prudent policies in a letter to a

23. *La Prensa* (Bogotá), June 9, 1868; Berrío to Gutiérrez Vergara, June 18, 1868, August 18, 1868, Gutiérrez Vergara collection, ACdeH; *El Heraldo* (Medellín), January 21, 1869.

24. For details of the events leading up to the arrest of Gutiérrez Vergara see Holguín, *Cartas políticas*, 81–102; Parra, *Memorias*, 510–41; *La Prensa* (Bogotá), July 24, August 11, 25, September 1, 29, October 13, 1868; *La República* (Bogotá), September 2, October 14, 1868.

Bogotá Conservative. He argued that if war came and Antioquia were defeated, "Antioquia will forever be trampled under foot by the reds, every hope will be ended, and the fate of Conservatives throughout the Republic will be a thousand times worse than now."[25]

Events surrounding the 1869 elections marked a low point in Conservative fortunes and cast Antioquia in a different role from what it had previously assumed. Mosquera Liberals and some key Conservatives initiated a move to elect Mosquera president for the 1870–1872 term. Preparations by his supporters were under way by early 1869 when a letter he wrote from exile in Lima appeared in a Conservative paper of Antioquia. The paper commented favorably on his proposals for a constitutional convention to revise the 1863 charter and for moving the nation's capital to Panama. A formal Pact of Union organizing a National party surfaced several months later bearing the signatures of three Liberals and three Conservatives; the latter were Recaredo de Villa of Antioquia, Leonardo Canal of Santander, and Luis Segundo de Silvestre, now editor of La República of Bogotá. The Pact of Union called for working for an end to Mosquera's exile and Gutiérrez Vergara's imprisonment, voting for Mosquera for president, granting equal representation in Congress and the state assemblies to both parties except in Cauca and Antioquia, negotiating a concordat with the Holy See to resolve religious questions, guaranteeing political rights to the clergy, and reforming the constitution through a convention in which each party would be equally represented. If either Antioquia or Tolima failed to vote for Mosquera in the upcoming election, the Pact of Union was to be annulled. In a letter to the nation published at mid-year Mosquera added to these provisions by stating that a revised constitution should retain the principles of federalism.[26]

Those Conservatives most diligent in their efforts on behalf of the National party were Leonardo Canal and Carlos Holguín. Through pressure and persuasion they elicited endorsements of Mosquera from Bogotá's two Conservative papers, La Prensa and La República. Mos-

25. Manuel C. Bello to Conservative Committee of Cundinamarca, November 28, 1868, MS. #30, BLAA; Néstor Castro to Sixto Hernández, October 10, 1867, Gutiérrez Vergara collection, ACdeH.

26. El Heraldo (Medellín), January 28, 1869; La República (Bogotá), August 25, 1869; La Prensa (Bogotá), July 2, 1869.

quera's supporters also counted on an overwhelming majority of Conservatives in Congress. In a vote to end Mosquera's exile Conservatives joined with the Mosquera Liberals to pass the measure in the House; it failed by only one vote in the Senate.[27] Pro-Mosquera Conservatives acted under the authority of a Central Election Committee formed by congressional Conservatives to promote the general's candidacy. The committee sent commissioners to all of the states to inform party members of measures taken on behalf of Mosquera and to try to enlist support for him. Holguín himself went to the north coast, and from there he planned to proceed to Lima to obtain Mosquera's personal approval for the Pact of Union.[28]

Practical politics was the strongest rationale given in the Conservative press for support for the "League of 1869," the name given to the pro-Mosquera coalition, but vengeance was the underlying motive. Carlos Holguín argued in an unsigned article that Conservative abstention from the elections offered no solution to the problems facing the party and the nation. He admitted that Mosquera might be evil but asserted that the Radical government was even worse. La República reasoned that Conservatives should support Mosquera because they were too weak to elect a president themselves; they must oppose the existing government and support for him was a logical consequence of the ouster of Gutiérrez Vergara.[29] The latter argument suggests the most credible basis for the League of 1869—vengeance against the Radicals by Mosquera Liberals for the ouster of their leader and by Conservatives for the arrest of Gutiérrez Vergara.

The only significant Conservative opposition to Mosquera's candidacy was organized by party members from Popayán, Mosquera's birthplace. Under leadership of his nephew, Sergio Arboleda, the

27. Rafael Arboleda to Sergio Arboleda, June 9, 1869, ASA; Mosquera was also supported by El Nuevo Mundo, a Bogotá paper begun by Liberals specifically to endorse him. La Prensa (Bogotá) June 11, 1869; Leonardo Canal to Tomás Cipriano de Mosquera, May 15, 1869, ATCM.

28. La Prensa (Bogotá), April 16, 1869; Leonardo Canal to Mosquera, June 3, 1869, Canal to Members of the Conservative party in Bolívar and Magdalena, June 8, 1869, ATCM.

29. La Prensa (Bogotá), June 1, 1869; for evidence that this article was by Holguín see Rafael Arboleda to Sergio Arboleda, June 9, 1869, ASA. La República (Bogotá), April 21, 1869.

Popayán Conservatives issued a manifesto which simply declared that the signers would support neither Mosquera nor Eustorgio Salgar, the Radical candidate, because neither represented Conservative principles. Other prominent Conservatives to oppose the League of 1869 included Joaquín María Córdoba, José Manuel Groot, and Pedro Alcántara Herrán. Groot privately noted, however, that Mosquera's Conservative supporters were the most ambitious and most active of the party's members.[30]

Antioquia's position on the League question was critical, for the Pact of Union would be annulled without its support for Mosquera. Early in the year it appeared likely that Antioquia would support him, because a majority of the state's congressional delegation joined the Central Election Committee and voted to lift his exile. Governor Berrío sought to maintain correct relations both with the national government and the pro-Mosquera government of Cauca, and in attempting to minimize divisive public debate on the issue he informed General Herrán that he had done what he could to hamper discussion of the League question.[31] Whatever Berrío had done to limit debate proved inadequate. Néstor Castro, his former secretary of interior and current editor of the semi-official state paper, *El Heraldo*, wrote a strong anti-Mosquera editorial and submitted it to Berrío for approval before publishing it. According to Castro, "he told me that, although he, too, believed that the League was lamentable, he did not consider it prudent that that paper, published by the government press and considered semi-official, speak out so directly." In accordance with Berrío's wishes *El Heraldo* maintained its neutral stance and Castro resigned as editor. Later in the year, however, Castro and a Conservative colleague began editing a new paper in Medellín, the *Boletín Eleccionario*. Ten issues of the paper appeared, and its sole purpose was to combat the League and expose those officials which supported it.[32]

30.   *La Prensa* (Bogotá), June 1, 1869; Rafael Arboleda to Sergio Arboleda, May 26, 1869, Manuel González to Sergio Arboleda, May 18, 1869, ASA; José Manuel Groot to José María Torres Caycedo, May 15, 1869, Gutiérrez Vergara collection, ACdeH; *La República* (Bogotá), September 22, 1869.

31.   Berrío to Pedro Alcántara Herrán, June 1, 1869, Pedro Alcántara Herrán collection, Archivo de la Academia Colombiana de Historia, Bogotá, hereinafter cited as H-ACdeH. For evidence of Berrío's caution see Berrío to Herrán, February 4, August 24, November 27, 1869, H-ACdeH.

32.   Castro to Sergio Arboleda, May 4, 1869, ASA; see weekly issues of *Boletín*

Antioquia's Conservatives departed markedly from the generality of the Conservative party in 1869. The state cast its vote for Pedro Alcántara Herrán, and it was the only state to vote for him. Antioquia voted essentially against the League rather than for Herrán, because little effort was made to generate support for him outside of the state. Furthermore, state officials had planned to vote for Gutiérrez Vergara, but when the despised opposition paper, the *Boletín Eleccionario*, endorsed him first, the government decided to endorse its own candidate. Mosquera obtained the votes of Cauca, Tolima, and Bolívar, and Salgar thus received the five votes necessary for victory. The Radical administration took no chances with the Mosquera candidacy, however, for when Carlos Holguín was in Panama, enroute to Lima for a conference with Mosquera, federal officials ordered his arrest, charged him with plotting with Mosquera to foment "a general revolution in Colombia," and imprisoned him in Bogotá.[33]

The attempt by leading Conservatives to ally their party with the Mosqueristas was an act of political desperation which mirrors the extent to which party fortunes had fallen by the end of the decade. It seemed highly unlikely that the party would ever recover if leadership remained in the hands of the faint-hearted such as Berrío or opportunists such as Holguín and Canal. Conservative support for Mosquera was born of the desire for vengeance against the Radicals, it was transparently opportunistic, and it showed the desire for office to be more compelling than adherence to principle. Seldom had the party been so deeply divided. The two Conservative-governed states, Tolima and Antioquia, voted for different candidates, and Conservatives within Antioquia were in sharp disagreement about how to respond to the Mosquera candidacy. But from the debacle of the 1869 election came the beginning of a major reevaluation of party principles and structure.

During the early 1870s, debate among Colombian Conservatives assumed a more serious tone and dealt with more fundamental issues than it had in the previous decade. Conservatives were shaken by the evidence of expediency and disarray in the party which the events of

---

Eleccionario (Medellín), October 21 to December 23, 1869. For an account of this episode see Abraham García to Sergio Arboleda, September 6, 1870, ASA.

33.   Abraham García to Gutiérrez Vergara, December 27, 1869, Gutiérrez Vergara collection, ACdeH; *La República* (Bogotá), September 1, 1869.

1869 had exposed. In addition, alarming reports of European developments confirmed their worst fears of the consequences of an unchecked Liberalism. Accounts of the seizure of Rome by Italian nationalists in 1870, the self-imposed seclusion of the pope in the Vatican, the bloodletting of the Paris Commune, and the execution by the Communards of the archbishop of Paris in 1871 were reported in detail in the Colombian press.[34] The following editorial in a Medellín paper provides a sample of the sense of alarm with which these events were treated: "Day after day we feel frightened when thinking that the excesses of those passions can reach the point of inundating us in the materialism of the period and making of this poor Colombian society a colony of the Paris Commune or of the International."[35]

Because of the frustrations felt by Colombian Conservatives and the reports of threatening European developments, a Conservative faction emerged which sought to return the party to what were regarded as basic principles. The first clear articulation of this reevaluation appeared in a broadside published in Bogotá in mid-1869 and republished in a Medellín paper late in the year. The unknown author advocated a program of total abstention from politics, formulation of a moral and political creed, and dissemination of Conservative doctrines through education and through the press. The highly respected historian and editor José María Quijano Otero also called upon Conservatives to return to basic principles. He deplored the actions of those party colleagues who, "forgetting our ancient banner," supported the League of 1869 and formed "an alliance which had no more bond of union than hatred nor object other than revenge." At the beginning of the decade a new Conservative paper, El Derecho, appeared in Bogotá, and although it lasted only six months it served as the principal organ defending "the Catholic Conservative school." Its early issues contained an important article by a member of the rising generation of Conservative leaders, Carlos Martínez Silva of Santander. Martínez Silva held that the party was worse off than a decade earlier because of the loss of party leaders and because the younger generation

---

34. La Ilustración (Bogotá), October 26, 1870; El Bien Público (Bogotá), August 18, 1871; La Unión Católica (Bogotá), September 17, 1871; La Caridad (Bogotá), October 26, 1871.
35. El Heraldo (Medellín), November 3, 1871.

was "nourished on perfidious utilitarian doctrines without religious beliefs and without moral principles." He insisted that the principal task of the party should be social rather than political—firm establishment of Catholic principles followed by the organization of genuine political parties. In conclusion Martínez Silva argued that "in order to cement a social order there is only one effective means—Catholicism; therefore our party is and must be essentially Catholic." These concepts were subsequently given strong endorsement by articles in El Heraldo, El Bien Público, and La Unión Católica; the latter was founded in 1871 to sustain the concept of a Catholic party by José María Vergara y Vergara, a man of letters and author of a major history of Colombian literature.[36]

The premier articulator of party reorganization along strictly Catholic lines was Miguel Antonio Caro, who began editing El Tradicionista in late 1871. Caro was born in Bogotá of a distinguished family, and he early acquired a sound reputation as a Latin scholar, poet, translator of Virgil, and a founder of the Colombian Academy of Language. Within days of the appearance of El Tradicionista Caro turned twenty-eight years old. In informing Sergio Arboleda of the appearance of the paper, he asserted that it was destined to serve as an "organ of the Catholic party in this capital." In one of its early issues Caro stated that the program of the Catholic party would include the propositions that the pope is infallible, Rome belongs to the pope, governments in Catholic countries should be Catholic and "the people, the clergy, and the learned classes should be represented in Congress."[37] Caro revealed another dimension of his well-ordered conceptual system in an article, "Our Error," written three years earlier. He referred to the "error" committed during the Independence period of rejecting traditions inherited from Spain such as the form of government, the religious tradition, and the literary tradition and replacing them with federalism and

36.   The broadside was published in serial form in Boletín Eleccionario (Medellín), October 21, 28, November 4, 11, 1869. José María Quijano Otero to Sergio Arboleda, November 21, 1869, ASA; El Derecho (Bogotá), March 18, 29, 1870; El Heraldo (Medellín), October 21, 1870; El Bien Público (Bogotá), July 9, 1872; La Unión Católica (Bogotá), September 24, November 19, 1871.

37.   Guillermo Torres García, Miguel Antonio Caro: su personalidad política (Madrid, 1956), 22–27; Miguel Antonio Caro to Sergio Arboleda, November 7, 1871, ASA; El Tradicionista (Bogotá), November 21, 1871.

utilitarianism. "The result has been a series of revolutions, unmistakable announcements of malaise. . . . We have arrived at the perfection of our reforms, and in the political sphere threats of dismemberment are already beginning to be noticed." Caro also expressed alarm over the potential threat to Colombia posed by what he regarded as the products of Liberalism in Europe such as the International—"a menace more imminent, a danger more real and closer than what we generally imagine."[38]

Several Conservatives challenged Caro's views, but none spoke out more vigorously or consistently in opposition than Manuel María Madiedo. A mulatto born in Cartagena during the Independence period, Madiedo received his education on the north coast, in the United States, and in Bogotá, where he obtained a law degree. He worked as a professor at several *colegios* in the capital, wrote many literary and philosophical works, and edited three Bogotá papers during the 1860s and 1870s.[39] Madiedo held views diametrically opposed to those of Caro on salient issues under debate, and he expressed those views contentiously (and with scant respect for distinguished, well-connected party leaders) in the pages of *La Ilustración*, which he founded in 1870 and continued to edit until mid-decade. Bereft of eminent lineage of his own, he ridiculed the great importance Colombian society placed on ancestry and family ties, often wrote on behalf of popular causes, and defended democracy, republicanism, and separation of politics from religion. In an article first published in 1867 to which Madiedo frequently referred he attributed the problems of the Conservative party to the presence in party ranks of an anti-republican, anti-American, *godo* (gothic) element. He contended that the party had little chance of recovery as long as it was embraced by "that pestilential cadaver of the Spanish colony which constitutes the godo element." In an early issue of *La Ilustración* Madiedo charged that the marriage between the Conservative party and the church had been harmful to both and that the clergy should be silenced in matters of politics; he derisively observed that "neither political influence nor public power will be achieved

38. *La Fe* (Bogotá), November 7, 1868; *El Tradicionista* (Bogotá), August 31, 1872.
39. Joaquín Ospina, *Diccionario biográfico y bibliográfico de Colombia* (3 vols.; Bogotá, 1927–39), II, 611–12.

praying." Three years later he was still insisting that a major goal of the party should be to rid itself of its "sacerdotal monomania." Madiedo also attacked centralism as a disastrous inheritance of the colonial past, and he criticized that "egotistic circle" of party leaders in Bogotá which had led the party to its deplorable condition.[40] Despite bitter attacks against Madiedo by Conservatives, he continued for several years to write at a prolific rate in a similar vein.

Simultaneous with these debates, leading Conservatives in Bogotá again attempted to formalize a structure of party leadership. Conservative congressmen together with other prominent Conservatives resident in the capital met in early 1870 and named a three-member Directory consisting of Gutiérrez Vergara, Manuel María Mallarino, and Ignacio Ospina. The Directory appointed agents for each state and announced a moderate program of rejecting war as a means to power, working for fair elections, and supporting the constitution despite its defects.[41]

Response to the initial circular sent out by the Directory was tentative in the key states of Antioquia and Cauca. The directors authorized Governor Berrío to name the Antioquia representative to the Directory, but he replied that he would delay making the appointment because it could cause problems. Sergio Arboleda, the agent named to represent Cauca, responded that he had to know more about the Directory's programs and methods before accepting the appointment. Several months later he indicated that some unspecified areas of disagreement yet existed between his ideas and those of the Directory. A year after organization of the Directory, its appointed agent in Bolívar, Joaquín Vélez, complained of a lack of leadership and of a sense of "abandonment in which our friends from the interior have placed us."[42]

The Conservative Directory helped unify the party's performance

40. *El Mensajero* (Bogotá), February 15, 16, 1867; *La Ilustración* (Bogotá), January 28, 1870, May 27, 1873, March 8, 1870.

41. One of the motives for forming the Directory was to undercut that faction of the party represented by *La Ilustración*; see Rafael Arboleda to Sergio Arboleda, March 30, 1870, ASA.

42. Berrío to Gutiérrez Vergara, May 10, 1870, Sergio Arboleda to Gutiérrez Vergara, May 25, October 19, 1870, Vélez to Gutiérrez Vergara, March 26, 1871, Gutiérrez Vergara collection, ACdeH.

in the presidential elections of 1871, although its action came late. When the campaign began, *El Bien Público* endorsed Sergio Arboleda, *El Heraldo* supported Manuel María Mallarino, and *La Ilustración* favored either abstention or support for an acceptable Liberal. North coast Conservatives under the leadership of Vélez supported a regional Liberal willing to grant concessions to the Conservatives, because, according to Vélez, the north coast states "have an avidity to elevate a son of the coast to the presidency." When the Directory finally announced its support for Mallarino most party members quickly fell into line. Although Manuel Murillo, the Radical candidate, easily won election as president for the 1872–1874 term, Conservatives in general and the states of Antioquia and Tolima cast their ballots for Mallarino in accord with instructions from the Directory.[43]

During the 1873 presidential election, Conservatives again avoided the extreme disunity which had characterized their performance in the previous decade. Although they issued conflicting counsel during the early stages of the election process, by mid-year the Conservative press and spokesmen agreed to work for the election of the Liberal, Julián Trujillo.[44] Because of his close ties to Mosquera, Conservative support for Trujillo evoked charges that the party sought to revive the League of 1869. Conservatives backed Trujillo primarily because he had, while in Ecuador in 1871, written praise of the religious-based system of public instruction initiated there by the Christian Brothers' Schools in the mid-1860s. Antioquia's Conservatives also supported him because they considered him an active defender of federalism in contrast to the Radical candidate, Santiago Pérez, whom they saw as an apostle of the move toward centralism which had characterized recent Radical governments. During the final months of the election all of the Conservative papers which took a position on the candidates endorsed Trujillo, a result of the efforts of Holguín, Arboleda, and Berrío. Trujillo

43. *El Bien Público* (Bogotá), January 17, 1871; *El Heraldo* (Medellín), April 21, 1871; *La Ilustración* (Bogotá), January 21, 1871; Vélez to Gutiérrez Vergara, March 27, 1871, Gutiérrez Vergara collection, ACdeH; Néstor Castor to Sergio Arboleda, May 2, 1871, ASA.

44. *La Ilustración* (Bogotá), March 15, 1873; *La Caridad* (Bogotá), September 25, 1873; *El Tradicionista* (Bogotá), January 2, 1873; *La América* (Bogotá), January 4, 1873; Bartolomé Calvo to Gutiérrez Vergara, March 6, 1873, Gutiérrez Vergara collection, ACdeH.

carried the states of Cauca, Tolima, and Antioquia, but before the final ballots were counted he shocked the Conservatives by his complaints of their "exaggerated pretensions."[45] Those Conservatives who had endorsed Trujillo and who felt they had an understanding whereby they would receive appointments and other considerations could not again be easily induced to support a Liberal candidate. The last-minute appeal by Rafael Núñez for Conservative backing in 1875 thus had little chance of acceptance.

In addition to establishing a central leadership structure, Conservatives attempted to formulate a statement of party principles under the urging of Holguín, Caro, and Arboleda.[46] During a series of discussions among Conservatives in Bogotá a tentative program was drawn up and sent to key party figures for comment. Progress in the matter required the support of Berrío, but he again displayed caution. He advised Gutiérrez Vergara that he had done nothing about the program since receiving it because he felt it contained some unacceptable points. He specifically objected to placing restrictions on a free press and to the lack of a firm commitment to federalism. More ominously, Berrío suggested that Medellín rather than Bogotá be designated headquarters of the party. To Holguín he proposed that all prominent Conservatives should have a voice, through commissioners, in formulating a program, a procedure which Holguín interpreted as "the same as resolving that we do nothing." A few months later Holguín wrote that Berrío was complaining of the "apathy" and "indifference" of Bogotá's Conservatives and that Berrío now preferred to issue a statement of general principles rather than a detailed program.[47]

Early, unauthorized publication of the program forced the abandonment of the project. Despite commitments by Conservatives not to publish the program until a final version was agreed upon, José María Quijano Otero, who began editing the Conservative paper *La América*

45. *El Tradicionista* (Bogotá), November 7, 1871; *El Heraldo* (Medellín), October 10, 1873; Carlos Holguín to Sergio Arboleda, October 1, 1873, Abraham García to Sergio Arboleda, November 17, 1873, ASA.

46. Joaquín Vélez to Sergio Arboleda, June 27, 1872, ASA; Tomás Pizarro to Gutiérrez Vergara, March 8, 1872, Gutiérrez Vergara collection, ACdeH.

47. Berrío to Gutiérrez Vergara, July 15, 1872, Gutiérrez Vergara collection, ACdeH; Berrío to Sergio Arboleda, July 17, 1872, Holguín to Sergio Arboleda, July 22, 1872, September 4, 1872, ASA.

in mid-1872, published the program and thus provoked a months-long polemic among Conservative factions. He admitted that he had attended only two of the meetings at which the program was discussed, but he found himself in total disagreement with the majority on some points. For example, unlike the majority, he favored separation of church and state, freedom of religion, and an explicit endorsement of the constitution, and he opposed reestablishment of the death penalty.[48] Quijano Otero violated a clear understanding with party colleagues apparently in an effort to prevent adoption of what he considered impolitic principles and because of his personal hatred for Caro. Gutiérrez Vergara offered a more charitable assessment of the publicly aired debate between Caro and Quijano Otero when he wrote that Quijano Otero, "although a Conservative, is not as orthodox as Caro, and the politics of accommodation does not disgust him as it does Caro."[49]

Several factors, including petty personal acrimony, aggravated party factionalism, which was but temporarily masked during the 1871 and 1873 elections. The feud between Caro and Madiedo surpassed the Caro–Quijano Otero dispute in its vitriolic quality. Both Caro and Madiedo published historical backgrounds of their feud, and Madiedo correctly claimed that Caro's father, as a young man, had been a materialist and an atheist and, further, that he, Madiedo, had converted him to Christianity. A measure of the gulf separating Madiedo from more prominent party leaders was offered by Holguín, who wrote cuttingly that Madiedo "does not conform because he is not white and rich."[50] An increase in the number of Catholic and Conservative papers published on a regular basis also contributed to party discord. La Caridad, the premier journal of that genre, counted eleven such papers in 1872. The opportunity for a full airing of conflicting views was thus extensive. Debate also intensified because by the early 1870s many Conservatives had returned from abroad, and they were eager to par-

48.   Rafael Arboleda to Sergio Arboleda, September 25, 1872, ASA; La América (Bogotá), September 4, 7, 11, 14, 1872, June 26, July 7, 10, 1873.
49.   Holguín to Sergio Arboleda, September 4, 1872, ASA; La América (Bogotá), June 18, 1873; Gutiérrez Vergara to Ignacio Gutiérrez Ponce, September 27, 1872, Gutiérrez Vergara collection, ACdeH.
50.   La Ilustración (Bogotá), December 10, 19, 1872; El Tradicionista (Bogotá), August 10, December 17, 1872; Holguín to Sergio Arboleda, September 4, 1872, ASA.

ticipate in the shaping of party policy. At the same time Conservative leadership was passing to a younger generation impatient for substantive change and a redefinition of party principles; during the first half of 1872 three leading Conservative figures died—Pedro Alcántara Herrán, José María Vergara y Vergara, and Manuel María Mallarino.[51]

Debate of three issues by Conservatives in this period helped delineate party factions. The issues were the political role of the clergy, attitudes toward the Gabriel García Moreno regime of Ecuador, and support for the Cuban struggle for independence. Debate on the first issue was sparked by the death and burial late in 1873, in a Catholic cemetery, of Ezequiel Rojas, a noted Liberal and outspoken nonbeliever. An article in El Tradicionista deplored this desecration of church land, but the archbishop's secretary asserted that according to church doctrine no desecration had occurred. Caro retorted by disputing the doctrinal question and by suggesting that church leaders should cast aside their timidity and assume more vigorous leadership of the faithful. José Manuel Groot joined the debate in defense of Caro, and several priests then charged him with attempting to disrupt the peace. In this worsening situation the archbishop summoned Caro and Groot to a meeting at his palace. It led to an immediate end to the public debate, a public apology by Caro to the archbishop, and a halt to further discussion of church dogma in the pages of El Tradicionista.[52]

The religious issue again caused problems when the ecclesiastical Provincial Council convened the following year. Three measures were voted on, and tie votes were cast in each case. The bishops of Medellín and Popayán opposed the more politically compromising archbishop and his supporters who favored endorsing the public education reform law, restricting the right of Catholic laity to write on religious matters, and limiting the right of the clergy to intervene in political matters. Shortly thereafter the archbishop issued a pastoral letter advising the clergy to stay out of purely political questions unless the interests of the church were directly involved. Caro and José Joaquín Ortiz, editor of La Caridad and long-time Catholic educator and publicist, sided

51. La Caridad (Bogotá), August 22, 1872; El Heraldo (Medellín), May 17, 1872.
52. El Tradicionista (Bogotá), September 30, October 4, 7, 14, 1873, February 10, 1874; La Sociedad (Medellín), October 25, 1873.

with the dissenting bishops and argued that the pastoral meant that the clergy must intervene in elections to prevent the election of anti-Catholic candidates. Madiedo took the opposite position and chided Ortiz: "You believe that there cannot be a Conservative party . . . if that party does not consist of bishops, canons, abbots, and abbesses."[53]

Conservatives also sharply differed in their attitudes toward the piously oppressive government of Gabriel García Moreno in Ecuador. Caro assumed the lead in marshaling support for the regime by writing laudatory editorials, reprinting favorable articles from other papers, and printing García Moreno's addresses. La Caridad labeled him "a magnificent magistrate," and Vergara y Vergara, shortly before his death, praised the Ecuadorian government for limiting the rights of non-Catholics, eliminating freedom of the press, and establishing church-state unity. He even deplored Colombia's military victories over Ecuador in the early 1860s.[54] In contrast, three other Conservative papers which commented on the government of Ecuador castigated it for its dictatorial methods, persecution of its enemies, and mistreatment of Indians and of Colombians living in Ecuador.[55]

The question of support for Cuba's fight for independence in the 1870s also provoked deep disagreement among Colombian Conservatives. Debate on the issue intensified upon the arrival in Colombia in early 1873 of General Manuel Quesada, a Cuban exile who was traveling throughout Latin America raising funds for the struggle. Most Colombians warmly received him and supported his efforts, but Arboleda and Caro regarded him as an adventurer whose presence threatened to compromise Colombian neutrality. As a result of Quesada's activities Congress enacted a law which authorized payment of $50,000 to Cubans who fled the island because of the war. Several congressmen signed a letter to President Murillo urging him to aid Cuba "clan-

53. Los Principios (Cali), April 10, 1874; El Tradicionista (Bogotá), July 21, 1874; La América (Bogotá), July 17, 1874; La Sociedad (Medellín), June 27, 1874; La Ilustración (Bogotá), June 16, 1874.

54. El Tradicionista (Bogotá), September 14, October 8, 1872, September 11, 1873, January 17, 1874; La Caridad (Bogotá), October 23, 1873; La Unión Católica (Bogotá), February 11, 18, 1872.

55. La Ilustración (Bogotá), April 17, 1873; Los Principios (Cali), August 31, 1873; La América (Bogotá), September 25, 1873.

destinely," and the government formally urged other American republics to cooperate in the effort to obtain Spanish recognition for Cuban autonomy.[56] These actions led to a public dispute between José María Quijano Otero, who ardently supported Cuban independence, and Arboleda, who opposed it. Arboleda argued that Colombia had no legal right to interfere in the matter, that Cuban independence in no way assured the well-being of the island, that Cuba might be absorbed by the United States if it gained independence, and that much of the sentiment for a free Cuba was based on a hatred for Spain. The closing commentary on the issue and, incidentally, one of the most egregious examples of scurrilous journalism was the following announcement in *El Tradicionista*: "To the Public: Is it true that General Quesada, before leaving, lost $6,000 gambling? Whoever knows, answer."[57]

By the mid-1870s four factions could be distinguished in the Conservative party. The most proclerical and doctrinaire faction was led by the editors of *El Tradicionista* and *La Caridad*, Caro and Ortiz, plus Sergio Arboleda and Carlos Martínez Silva. In their view the most critical question facing Colombia was the religious question; they sought to make the party the political arm of the church and to unify church and state. Madiedo, editor of *La Ilustración*, headed the smallest and most marginal faction of the party. An effective gadfly of the Catholic-Conservative faction, Madiedo espoused a form of Christian socialism, but he favored strict separation of politics and religion and a spirit of cooperation between Liberals and Conservatives. The party's most amorphous faction was led by political activists who strove to organize and structure the party so that it could peacefully return to power. Its major members included Quijano Otero, Manuel Briceño, Carlos Holguín, and Leonardo Canal; *La América* served as its principal organ. Some members of this faction, such as Holguín and Canal, were willing to ally with Liberals as a means to return to power, whereas Briceño argued that it was foolish to aspire to govern until the party

56. Law 27 of April 17, 1873, *Leyes de Colombia, 1863–75,* 927; *El Tradicionista* (Bogotá), February 1, April 1, 1873.

57. *El Tradicionista* (Bogotá), January 28, February 1, 1873. For arguments by Conservatives who favored Cuban independence see *El Bien Público* (Bogotá), January 30, 1872; *La América* (Bogotá), March 15, 1873; *El Heraldo* (Medellín), November 14, 1873. *El Tradicionista* (Bogotá), May 1, 1873.

had achieved unity. These three factions had as their locus of power, Bogotá; the fourth faction, headquartered in Medellín, was the Antioquia wing of the party.[58]

The Antioquia faction was distinguished from other factions by its primary loyalty to the state party rather than to the national party, its strict adherence to federalism, and its inordinate fear of the anti-Catholic thrust of Liberalism. Because Antioquia's Conservatives, unlike other state parties, had held power for over a decade, they pursued a risk-aversion policy which placed a premium on self-preservation. This largely explains the state's strong support for federalism. When Antioquia moved toward a federalist stance in the 1850s, it did so to create in Antioquia a haven safe from the "leprosy of Liberalism." Uninterrupted Liberal dominance of the national government since 1862 and the political turbulence of the period confirmed Antioqueños in their endorsement of federalism. To uphold federalism Antioquia opposed any modification of the public-order law prohibiting federal intervention in the states in case of armed conflict and challenged any threat by the national government to interfere in a state. When such threats seemed real against Tolima in 1873, Governor Berrío requested authority from the state assembly to defend Tolima's sovereignty with force.[59] Antioquia also appointed special diplomatic agents to the other states to help maintain good relations with them and to encourage them to defend the principle of state sovereignty. Non-Antioqueño Conservatives such as Caro and Carlos Martínez Silva, who preferred centralism, bowed to the logic of Antioquia's position. In his straightforward fashion Caro observed that the party could not proclaim the principle of centralism, because "Antioquia, force and nerve of the ancient Conservative party, is eminently federalist."[60]

At mid-decade Antioquia occupied an unusual position in the Colombian federation. It was a stable Conservative stronghold in a turbulent nation governed by Liberals. It enjoyed a reputation as the wealthi-

---

58. For articles which discuss divisions within the Conservative party see *Diario de Cundinamarca* (Bogotá), August 1, 8, 22, 1873; *La Caridad* (Bogotá), October 23, 1873; *La Ilustración* (Bogotá), October 28, 1873.

59. *El Tradicionista* (Bogotá), April 2, 1872, August 12, 1873; *La América* (Bogotá), August 18, 1873.

60. *La Ilustración* (Bogotá), January 4, 25, 1872; *El Tradicionista* (Bogotá), May 31, 1873.

est state in Colombia, stemming in large part from an economy based on gold mining. Close harmony prevailed be:ween Antioquia's political and religious leaders.[61]

Antioquia's exceptional situation and achievements nourished a spirit of pride which led to disdain for the rest of Colombia. This disdain was implied by the Cundinamarcan, former President Mariano Ospina Rodríguez, resident in Medellín since his return from exile in 1872, who wrote in 1875: "In Antioquia we have a government which gives guaranties, and an order of things which inspires confidence in peace; but Antioquia is a state of the Colombian Confederation." The contrast between Antioquia and the rest of Colombia was explicitly drawn in the following editorial comment by La Unión of Medellín: "One of the greatest benefits which Antioquia offers the country today is . . . that which comes from the contrast between it and the other states of the Union. Here [we have] order, stability, progress; outside of our borders a distressing outlook, a struggle between intransigent factions." Dissemination of such ideas induced significant numbers of Antioqueños to conclude that they would be better off without Colombia. To dampen such separatist sentiment, one Medellín paper admonished: "For now, for a long time, [Antioquia's] topography, rough terrain, and scarcity of inhabitants make it incapable of assuming the role of an independent nation."[62]

Such trumpeting of Antioqueño superiority generated animosity and criticism from other Colombians. A widely discussed article in a Liberal paper asserted that since 1863 Antioquia has remained "apart, isolated, segregated, dissident, creating a society distinct from society in general; a Conservative republic in the heart of a democratic republic." A Bogotá Conservative criticized the "coldness and timidity of the quasi-international relations of Antioquia with the other states and with the general government." In a private letter a Tolima Conservative complained that Antioqueños take care of themselves first but do nothing for others.[63] Antioquia's conduct during the 1875 war on the north coast earned additional enmity. During the conflict, the state

61. El Heraldo (Medellín), November 28, 1873.

62. Mariano Ospina Rodríguez, Artículos escogidos (Medellín, 1884), 140; La Unión (Medellín), April 4, 1876; El Deber (Medellín), April 20, 1876.

63. Revista de Colombia (Bogotá), December 19, 1873; La Unión (Medellín), April 24, 1876; Tomás Pizarro to Sergio Arboleda, April 25, 1873, ASA.

appointed Luis M. Restrepo peace commissioner to the national government, and Restrepo solidly placed Antioquia on the side of federal intervention. Antioquia abandoned its traditional policy of defending state sovereignty because of fear that the north coast conflict could lead to a general war and because of concern about the safe arrival of a shipment of arms ordered from abroad and scheduled to pass through customs at Sabanilla and proceed up the Magdalena River. Restrepo's public assessment of his state's contribution to peace reflected typical Antioqueño self-esteem. From his modest role in the peace settlement, a settlement brought about by force of arms, Restrepo concluded: "I sincerely believe that in the nation's present state of decomposition, Antioquia exercises a powerful influence and will be called upon, in the not too distant future, to be the safeguard of our institutions."[64]

Antioquia's posture in 1875 in favor of federal intervention and in opposition to the Núñez candidacy seriously antagonized prominent party leaders in the capital. Bogotá Conservatives had muted their centralist leanings in deference to Antioquia's adamant stance in favor of federalism, so the state's support for intervention came as a rude shock. Unswerving opposition to Núñez also thwarted the strategy of leading Conservatives such as Caro and Martínez Silva who abandoned their previous doctrinaire positions and endorsed the Cartagenero in hopes of taking advantage of the deep division in the Liberal party. In the resulting climate of growing animosity among Conservatives it seemed to Manuel Briceño that Antioquia had assumed a position of "armed neutrality contrary to the interests of the Conservative cause." To such charges, the Antioquia press retorted: "The Conservatives of Cundinamarca ought to resolve not to expect everything from Antioquia and to do something themselves for their liberty, if that is what they desire."[65]

The dialogue between Antioquia and its critics had degenerated by 1876 to an exchange of absurd racial and cultural slurs. José María Samper leveled a series of charges against Antioquia to which the state government made a formal reply. In response Samper delivered the following retort: "There being no purpose whatsoever in refuting the manifesto of the orthodox protestant Israelites of Antioquia, we will

---

64. *Diario de Cundinamarca* (Bogotá), January 24, 1876; *Boletín Oficial* (Medellín), November 22, 6, 1875.
65. Briceño, *La revolución*, 21; *La Unión* (Medellín), April 4, 1876.

only note . . . that because the fact of the infusion of Jewish blood in Antioqueño society is historical and obvious . . . we find no reason for Antioquia's governors to be irritated by the appellation 'Israelites' which we gave them." Mariano Ospina Rodríguez, like Samper, not an Antioqueño, replied in kind. He noted that though Antioqueños could not boast of Jewish origins, they should welcome the appellation; for it suggested that their antecedents, unlike those of other Colombians, were not a cause of shame. "What could be flattering or truly useful in having for a grandfather a Galician patron or a dull, miserable, and apathetic Indian, rather than a calculating and energetic Jew; or for a grandmother a wretched Negress, careless and confused, hunted like a gorilla in the Congo or Guinean forests, rather than an intelligent daughter of Sarah and Rachel?" [66]

Antioquia had become remarkably isolated by 1876. In the previous year it had needlessly antagonized the coastal states. It was ideologically at odds with the national government and the seven Liberal states. Its bishop was averse to the archbishop's policies of compromise with the Liberal government. The state's Conservatives constituted but one faction of the party, and their instincts for self-preservation made them unsuitable for national party leadership. Nor would they readily submit to direction from Bogotá. The Antioqueños, tactless in dealing with other Colombians, smug in their accomplishments, and aloof in their pride of character, aroused a dangerous antipathy in their countrymen.

Politically frustrated, Bogotá's Conservatives organized a National Conservative Committee in 1875. Its purpose was to formulate a national party policy, coordinate party activities in the nine states, and gain some political benefit from the power base and economic wealth available in Antioquia by pressuring the state to adopt a more national outlook. Late in 1875 the committee commissioned its secretary, Manuel Briceño, to travel to each state, study and report on the party's status, and help reorganize it where necessary. [67]

While Antioquia came under Conservative demand to alter its isolationist course, the long-quiescent church-state issue was revived in a way that no state could escape its consequences. In 1870 the Radicals

66. *Boletín Oficial* (Medellín), May 8, 1875; *El Ciudadano* (Medellín), June 24, 1875; *La Sociedad* (Medellín), July 3, 1875.
67. Briceño, *La revolución*, 42–43.

had launched a basic educational reform program which created a national system of compulsory public education placed under the direction of the federal government. Conservative reaction against this program became the principal lever used by Briceño to coerce Antioquia into providing vigorous national direction for the Conservative party.

Educational reform was carried out on two broad fronts—establishment of normal schools and promotion of primary education. To prepare teachers in the most modern methods of instruction, nine professors were recruited in Germany by the Colombian government to establish normal schools in each state and to operate model primary schools. The Germans arrived in 1872 and by the end of the year had opened normal schools in all nine states. Seven of the nine professors were Protestants, a disability only slightly mitigated by their pledges to avoid involvement in political and religious questions. Promotion of primary education came under the central control of the General Directorate of Public Instruction. Despite numerous obstacles, the reform program accomplished much between 1871 and 1876. Educational facilities were expanded, better trained teachers were graduated, and the number of primary schools and students increased substantially. The national government introduced modern pedagogical techniques and became firmly committed to the promotion of universal education.[68]

Because the reform program envisioned a basic revamping of Colombian education, it generated heated opposition. Critics attacked those provisions of the program which placed curriculum content under the centralized control of the national government, charging that such measures directly violated state sovereignty. Compulsory school attendance for all children between ages six and fourteen was branded excessively coercive and certain to create economic hardships for poor families. The principal opposition arose from loyalty to the deeply rooted tradition of clerical domination of education. To assure a totally secular basis for education, the reform decree prohibited the government from providing religious instruction. In an effort to minimize Catholic opposition, the reform measure permitted priests to offer religious instruction after regular school hours to children of parents requesting it.[69]

68. Loy, "Primary Education," 279, 286–88, 293–94.
69. Ibid., 280, 283.

Provisions for after-class religious instruction represented a sufficiently generous concession to Catholic sensitivities to induce important members of the church hierarchy to support full implementation of the reform program. Archbishop Vicente Arbeláez assumed leadership in the effort to reconcile Catholic opinion to educational reform. He won additional concessions from the national government through negotiations carried out in mid-1876. Under the terms of the resulting agreement, in those cases in which priests were not available to offer religious instruction, teachers were authorized to provide it using texts approved by church authorities. In a letter to the bishop of Panama, Archbishop Arbeláez urged support of public schools, because schools permitting religious instruction were not, in his opinion, lay schools in the sense intended by Pope Pius IX in his *Syllabus of Errors*. In advocating implementation of the agreement that he had negotiated with the national government, the archbishop concluded: "This procedure is the one that has been observed here in my diocese and with very good results in the parishes where the priests have taken an interest in the progress of the schools."[70]

Despite the archbishop's efforts on behalf of conciliation, many prominent Conservative spokesmen and some bishops adamantly opposed the public schools. *El Deber* of Medellín charged: "The lay schools are the virgin fields which impious liberalism has chosen for sowing sensual paganism, the bestial cult of the material." Manuel Briceño noted that although priests were allowed to teach religion in the schools, "the corrupting teacher continued infiltrating into the heart of the children the poison which would kill both their religious ideas and political traditions." Carlos Bermúdez, bishop of Popayán, obdurately labeled the public school teachers "notoriously irreligious or immoral," and asserted that the children attending those schools would become "rebellious sons, enemies of the church, a terror of society."[71]

The most vigorous opposition to the educational reform program came from Cauca, where superheated passions generated by the controversy ignited the war of 1876–1877. Cauca contained more Conser-

70. Galindo, *Recuerdos*, 199–200; Archbishop Arbeláez to Bishop José Telésforo Paúl, June 17, 1876, MS. #97, BLAA.
71. *El Deber* (Medellín), May 18, 1876; Briceño, *La revolución*, 8; Gonzalo Uribe V., *Los arzobispos y obispos colombianos desde el tiempo de la colonia hasta nuestros días* (Bogotá, 1918), 82.

vatives than any other Liberal-governed state. They predominated in the state's southern highlands and in areas north and northwest of Cali, where Antioqueño immigrants had settled during recent decades and continued to settle.[72] Popayán, the state capital, rivaled Bogotá as a traditional center of church power in Colombia; thus, a pronouncement by the bishop of Popayán commanded respectful attention. Close contact between southern Cauca and Ecuador kept the Caucanos abreast of the remarkable gains registered by the church in the neighboring country under the regime of García Moreno. These achievements inspired emulation among devout Catholics. Most important in explaining reaction to the reform program in Cauca was the active leadership against public schools provided by church leaders in Cauca and Antioquia.

Bishop Carlos Bermúdez of Popayán spearheaded the opposition to public, lay education in Cauca. The equally partisan Bishop Manuel Canuto Restrepo of Pasto and the bishop of Medellín endorsed his stance, though by openly repudiating Archbishop Arbeláez' recommendations for compromise they deeply divided the church hierarchy in Colombia. Arbeláez felt that "the bishops of Pasto and Cauca have given to the *Syllabus* an interpretation which it does not have," but he was powerless to impose his will on them. Bishop Bermúdez adamantly held that the public schools fell within the proscriptions of Pope Pius IX, and in mid-1875 he ordered parents in his diocese to withdraw their children from the schools under threat of excommunication. In refusing to yield on the school issue during discussions with state officials, Bermúdez reportedly exclaimed: "It does not matter that the country be converted into ruins and debris so long as the banner of religion may rise triumphant over it."[73]

The most effective measure employed by Bermúdez in his campaign against the public schools was the establishment of Catholic societies of laymen throughout Cauca. Under his guidance priests organized numerous locally based societies in late 1875 and early 1876, exerting considerable pressure on all Catholics to become active members. A resident of Buga reported: "Each priest in his respective parish

---

72. *La Ley* (Bogotá), April 21, 1876; Parsons, *Antioqueño Colonization*, 75–77, 83–86.

73. Arbeláez to Bishop Paúl, June 17, 1876, MS. #97, BLAA; Uribe V., *Los arzobispos*, 82–83; Quijano Wallis, *Memorias*, 221.

has organized a society in which all who wish to save themselves are inscribed!"[74] The societies propagandized against public schools as well as against the populist Democratic societies which Liberals had recently reactivated to generate support for the embattled schools. In several localities the Catholic societies opened parochial schools which competed so effectively with the public schools that the latter were forced to shut down. Dámaso Zapata, sent on a fact-finding mission to Cauca by President Aquileo Parra in mid-1876, reported that in Tuluá, where Liberals controlled the municipal government, only twelve students attended the public school, "while more than seventy children attend the horrible Catholic school."[75]

What imparted major significance to the campaign against the public schools in Cauca, besides its success, was its generalization into a fanatic Catholic crusade of ominous proportions. A friend of Mosquera wrote from Palmira, after a nine-year absence in Ecuador, "I have found Cauca highly fanaticized with some resemblance to Ecuador." Governor César Conto wrote in the same month: "The reaction of allied conservatism and ultramontanism formidably continues through these lands; they are marvelously taking advantage of this season of Lent and Holy Week which is a harvest for them."[76] At the end of one of his reports to President Parra on conditions in Cauca, Zapata despairingly exclaimed: "What savagery and superstition there are among the country folk of this Valley! I did not think that fanaticism could reach this extreme." A resident of Palmira, although writing in 1875, described an incident which characterized the atmosphere prevailing in many localities by 1876. One Sunday afternoon about four hundred people, both Conservatives and Liberals, gathered in the central plaza, but the only shouts heard from the crowd were, "'long live religion' and 'long live the priest.' Nobody dared shout a hurrah to the Liberal party," not even when a Liberal merchant offered $200 to anyone who would do so.[77]

74. *Los Principios* (Cali), January 21, 28, February 18, March 3, 1876; *La Ley* (Bogotá), June 13, 1876; *Diario de Cundinamarca* (Bogotá), February 29, 1876.

75. Dámaso Zapata to Aquileo Parra, May 10, 1876, CdeHRP.

76. Rafael González Manzano to Mosquera, April 28, 1876, ATCM; César Conto to Manuel Ancízar, April 5, 1876, CdeJA.

77. Zapata to Parra, April 29, 1876, CdeHRP; Juan E. Conde to Mosquera, April 22, 1875, ATCM.

The aspect of the Catholic crusade which most alarmed the state government was its attraction of Liberals into the Catholic societies. During the early months of 1876, Liberals from throughout Cauca documented an alarming defection from their ranks. A resident of Popayán reported in February: "The fanatic party increases greatly and we Liberals lose from day to day." In March the mayor of Palmira wrote that, although he had worked ceaselessly for Liberal party unity, "these are the most fanatic people of Cauca and the voice of the priest enormously harms us." A writer from Cartago offered the following summary of the process under way throughout the state: "The Catholic reaction advances with giant steps. Cauca is lost. The masses who constitute the majority or the force of the Liberal party are abandoning it, because the priest, through the Catholic societies and with the pretext of defending religion, today has the people at his side."[78]

Besides this general erosion of Liberal strength, a series of events had occurred in Cauca after César Conto's inauguration in August 1875 which gave his administration an increasingly beleagured outlook. The turbulence of the 1875 election had heightened political passions and deeply divided the Liberal party. Liberal factionalism had reached such an extreme that anti-Radicals plotted a coup against the Conto government in late 1875. Prominent Nuñistas of Bogotá such as José María Samper, Carlos Martín, and Alejo Morales secretly wrote to their confederates in Cali and Popayán urging them to cooperate with Conservatives in launching the coup: "We believe it of indispensable necessity for the total success of the movement, and also for justice, that the Conservatives be given all proper participation and that they receive whatever just concessions are required to obtain their cooperation."[79] The coup never materialized, but by early 1876 the Conto government had learned details of it. An outbreak of violence in the state's southern highland region in late 1875 also threatened the survival of the Conto government. That predominantly Conservative section had harbored separatist sentiments since independence, and now that the

78. José M. Iragorri to Mosquera, February 9, 1876, F. Iragorri to Mosquera, March 3, 1876, Jesús María López to Mosquera, April 5, 1876, ATCM.

79. José María Samper, Carlos Martín, and Alejo Morales to General Peregrino Santacoloma, December 10, 1875, ATCM; see also Santacoloma to Mosquera, December 11, 1875, ATCM.

Radicals governed Cauca a rupture in the state's unity became a genuine fear in Popayán. Zapata submitted the following report in May on conditions in the southern region: "Concerning the municipalities of the south, it is evident that the administrative action of the government does not reach there, and although they are not in rebellion against the authorities, they obey only Bishop Canuto and whatever the Conservatives order. Since the events of January the south has remained almost independent."[80]

Ever-escalating threats to the Cauca government in combination with Conto's anti-Catholic predispositions produced an extremist reaction matching that of the Catholic opposition. Conto intimated the type of program his administration would pursue when in May 1875 he privately asserted that Cauca's major problem was "the godo-fanatic reaction." In early 1876 Conto appointed Jorge Isaacs, author of the famed romantic novel *María*, director of public instruction in Cauca. Catholics regarded the appointment as a declaration of war because of Isaacs' recent, but well-deserved reputation as an unreasoning Radical extremist and a rabid anti-Catholic.[81] Conto further alarmed Catholics when he attempted to enforce a new state law which centralized control over the educational system depriving municipalities of any supervision over local schools. Ambiguities did not cloud his perception of the threat facing Colombia. "Either the government of the union and the states rule in the country or the Curia Romana rules." Conto reveled at the prospect of a civil war which could once and for all curb the surge of reaction. "What glory for me to be at the front of this struggle, the last that the republic will have to sustain, and to conquer or succumb with honor!"[82] By May 1876 it could hardly be asserted that the Catholics excelled Cauca's Radicals in fanaticism.

Conto's provocative attitude is explained, in part, by his conviction that President Parra would guarantee the survival of the Radical re-

---

80. *Diario de Cundinamarca* (Bogotá), April 15, 1876; Mosquera to Conto, November 30, 1875, ATCM; Zapata to Parra, May 10, 1876, CdeHRP.

81. Conto to Mosquera, May 5, 1875, ATCM. For insight into Isaacs' views see Isaacs to Parra, July 28, 1876, CdeHRP. Note that Isaacs switched loyalties from the Conservative to the Liberal party in the mid-1870s.

82. *Los Principios* (Cali), February 18, March 17, 1876; Conto to Parra, March 15, 1876, May 10, 1876, CdeHRP.

gime in Cauca. The basis of the guaranty was established when the Cauca delegation voted for Parra for president in the congressional balloting of February 1876. Although most of the Cauca congressmen favored Núñez, at the last minute they abandoned him, rejected various schemes for cooperation with the Conservatives, and voted for Parra. This switch occurred under the influence of alarming reports from Cauca of the growing Catholic threat to the Liberals. General Mosquera, senator from Cauca, assumed a major role in the reversal. Less than two months after Parra was elected he signed a law restoring to Mosquera the pension which the government had stripped from him nine years earlier. Parra also carefully considered Conto's insistent requests that the national government dispatch arms and troops to Cauca and enact a law on religious inspection. Such a law would permit the government to supervise religious activities and thus, presumably, arrest the further growth of the Catholic menace.[83]

Liberal party disunity dictated the course followed by Parra during his first months in office when some Nuñista leaders attempted to organize opposition to his administration. José María Samper sought to establish what he termed a Republican party based on an alliance of Nuñista Liberals and moderate Conservatives. Although conceding that it was too early for a true fusion, Samper reasoned that such an alliance should be effected in order to oppose the extremists in each of the two traditional parties.[84] Similar probes exploring the possibility of alliance formation were extended independently of Samper's efforts. Nicolás J. Collante and Santo Domingo Vila, Nuñista Liberals from Bolívar, made contact with Manuel Briceño and offered to confer with him about future cooperation. Briceño and Santo Domingo Vila met in March and agreed to form a committee in Bogotá composed of one Liberal and one Conservative from each state. The general purpose of the

---

83. Quijano Wallis, *Memorias*, 248; Briceño, *La revolución*, 33; Mosquera to Parra, February 19, 1876, CdeHRP; law 11 of April 5, 1876, *Leyes de los Estados Unidos de Colombia espedidas en el año de 1876* (Bogotá, 1876), 14–15; volumes in this series are hereinafter cited as *Leyes de Colombia* followed by year of publication. For examples of Conto's requests see Conto to Parra, March 15, April 5, 19, May 10, 24, 1876, CdeHRP.

84. For a statement of party principles and discussions of them see *La Ley* (Bogotá), March 28, 1876, and *El Tradicionista* (Bogotá), January 21, 1876.

proposed committee was to establish a basis for Conservative-Liberal cooperation in opposing the Parra government. Although the plan never materialized, its mere discussion suggests the seriousness of the problem faced by Parra. Until after the outbreak of war it remained uncertain whether the Nuñistas would support the Conservatives or the Parra administration. As late as June 1876 Núñez himself was undecided about which course to follow. "Should we lean toward the oligarchs from fear of the Conservatives? Should we unite, in so far as possible, with them [the Conservatives] although later being dominated by the theocratic element?"[85] Núñez' future answer to these questions gained additional significance when he was elected governor of Bolívar in mid-1876 and inaugurated on October 1.

In an effort to restore party unity Aquileo Parra made a conciliatory inaugural speech and appointed the costeño Luis Robles secretary of treasury; as secretary of interior he named Manuel Ancízar, a man highly respected by all Liberals. In his correspondence with state party leaders, Parra emphatically urged them to work to reunite Colombian Liberalism. No evidence exists that Parra directly appealed for Núñez' support, but in at least one instance Parra clearly signaled his friendly disposition toward the Cartagenero. In May Núñez wrote to his friend Manuel Ancízar asking him to use his influence to transfer Núñez' younger brother, Ricardo Núñez, from his current position as customs inspector at Sabanilla to a post in accounting. On June 21, 1876, President Parra appointed Ricardo Núñez accountant-auditor of customs at Sabanilla.[86]

Because the future conduct of the Nuñista Liberals remained so much in doubt, Parra proceeded cautiously in responding to appeals for support from Cauca. The president authorized Dámaso Zapata, the agent he had sent to Cauca in April on a fact-finding mission, to promise Conto that federal arms would be shipped on formal request. In May Parra signed into law a bill increasing the size of the standing army from 1,225 to 2,585 men, but he resisted Conto's pleas for the

85. Briceño, La revolución, 50; Núñez to Juan de Dios Restrepo, June 8, 1876, MS. #99, BLAA.
86. La Ley (Bogotá), April 4, 1876; Parra, Memorias, 727–32; Núñez to Ancízar, May 6, 1876, CdeJA; Diario Oficial (Bogotá), November 8, 1877. Accountant-auditor is translated from contador-interventor.

sending of federal troops. Several months later the president offered the following explanation for his conduct: "If the Colombian army did not go to Cauca at the time the Cauca delegation demanded that I send it, it was so as not to give the revolution a banner, and above all because that measure would have impeded the achievement of Liberal unity." Parra also declined to yield to pressure from both Conto and Mosquera to support passage of a law on religious inspection, a law which Mosquera labeled "indispensable."[87]

Resolution of the Cauca problem and avoidance of a general war hinged on the actions of Antioquia. Liberals were most alarmed at the possibility that Antioquia would intervene in Cauca under the pretext of defending the Catholics and thereby establish control over a potentially powerful region in western Colombia—the states of Antioquia, Tolima, and Cauca. In a letter to President Parra requesting federal troops, Conto exclaimed: "Think of the predicament the Liberal party of the Republic would be in with the three states of Antioquia, Cauca, and Tolima in the power of the Conservatives." In June the Democratic Society of Cali passed the following resolution: "The Democratic Society rejects with all the energy of which it is capable the type of protectorate or pupilage which the ultramontane government of Antioquia aspires to exert over a state such as that of Cauca." The usually tranquil General Trujillo also voiced the concern of Cauca Liberals toward Antioquia's ambitions. He warned that the people of Cauca "cannot accept the groundless preponderance which [Antioquia] pretends to assume over all the nation and especially over this state."[88]

As religious and political tensions intensified, Conservatives seized upon Catholic anxieties to pressure Antioquia into assuming leadership for the anticipated revolution. Manuel Briceño visited several states on behalf of the National Conservative Committee, but he focused his attention on Antioquia. During discussions he held in February with Governor Recaredo de Villa of Antioquia, a Medellín banker and businessman who had succeeded Pedro Justo Berrío to the gover-

87. Zapata to Parra, April 29, 1876, May 10, 1876, CdeHRP; *Leyes de Colombia, 1863–75*, 1151; *Leyes de Colombia, 1876*, 23; Parra to Conto, October 11, 1876, MS. #113, BLAA; Mosquera to Parra, June 5, 1876, CdeHRP.
88. Conto to Parra, April 5, 1876, CdeHRP; *La Unión* (Medellín), July 13, 1876; Julián Trujillo to Parra, June 28, 1876, CdeHRP.

norship in 1873, the governor pledged, "Antioquia would consider the following acts as a *casus belli*: armed intervention of the general government in the domestic struggles of the states, repeal of the law of public order, and passage of a law on [the inspection of cults]." Antioquia also agreed to provide necessary arms to the Conservatives and to "fix its attention" on Cauca. After studying conditions at first hand in Cauca, Briceño returned to Antioquia and informed Villa that war was inevitable and that the shipment of arms to Conservatives there should begin immediately. At the same time one of Briceño's lieutenants from Manizales in southern Antioquia advised Villa: "For us, the possession of Cauca means triumph in the Republic, for the Liberals, loss of it means defeat." To the dismay of Briceño and the Antioqueños living in the border areas near Cauca, Governor Villa announced that Antioquia would remain neutral and would not send arms to Cauca. The southern Antioqueños, however, defied his orders and did what they could to supply weapons to their confederates in Cauca.[89]

Recaredo de Villa's apparent lack of resolution stemmed from conflicting pressures exerted on the one hand by the militant Conservatives and on the other by the national government. The former were represented by Caro and Briceño and by the Conservative press outside of Antioquia such as *El Tradicionista* of Bogotá and *Los Principios* of Cali. An even more compelling factor on the Conservative side of the equation was the emergence of political opposition to Villa within Antioquia which directly complemented the efforts of the militants. Villa's leadership had been under organized attack since January 1876, when Conservative opponents in the state established their own newspaper. Through this medium they effectively threatened the Villa government by launching the gubernatorial candidacy of the popular military leader Marceliano Vélez. Such a procedure was unusual both because it bypassed the customary closed system of candidate selection and because Villa's term did not expire until late 1877. The anti-Villa Conservatives of Antioquia emphasized the divisions in the Liberal party and demanded that the state lead the way toward a nationwide Conservative regeneration by means of armed intervention in

---

89. Briceño, *La revolución*, 48–49, 57–59; *Diario de Cundinamarca* (Bogotá), June 3, 1876; Trujillo to Parra, June 30, 1876, CdeHRP.

Cauca. They issued advice to Villa which he could hardly ignore if he wished to retain party unity in Antioquia: "[Radical strategy consists of] defeating the Catholic party piecemeal in order to impede the force that would arise from the coalition of the three reunited states. We hope that the government of the state . . . will not allow itself to be deceived by the promise of the oligarchs who seek to maintain harmony with Antioquia so it will withhold the help it should offer . . . to the two neighboring states."[90]

While Villa faced mounting pressures for action from his own party and state, President Parra forced him to define more precisely Antioquia's attitude toward Cauca. In May, Parra appointed Ramón del Corral to go to Medellín to discuss the Cauca problem and to obtain Antioquia's cooperation in curbing Conservative hostility toward the public schools in Cauca. Antioquia defined its policy in a lengthy position paper presented by Luis M. Restrepo, Corral's counterpart in the discussions. Restrepo asserted that Antioquia maintained valuable interests of all kinds in Cauca and that the surge of events there could not be arrested because they reflected the operation of "moral laws." Restrepo concluded his exposition with the warning: "The neutrality which the government of Antioquia has observed and observes with strictness has as its just and natural limits the strict observance of the same neutrality by . . . the national government." To remove any ambiguities, Restrepo noted that the national government would be in violation of its neutrality if it sent arms or troops to Cauca, passed a law on religious inspection, or interfered with legitimate expressions of opinion in Cauca. Corral found it impossible to get Antioquia to moderate its stand, and the talks ended when he refused to sign the protocol summarizing their substance.[91]

Antioquia and the national government edged closer to direct conflict when in June Congress repealed the 1867 law on public order. The overturned law stated: "When any proportion whatsoever of the citizens of a state revolt for the purpose of overthrowing the existing govern-

90.   La Unión (Medellín), April 4, 1876; El Deber (Medellín), April 20, July 15, 1876.
91.   Boletín Oficial (Medellín), May 22, 1876; Recaredo de Villa to Parra, May 16, 1876, CdeHRP.

ment and organizing another, the national government must observe the strictest neutrality between the belligerents." A constitutional limitation on the use of national forces remained, but it was lightly regarded and had seldom been observed. Conservatives and Radicals interpreted the repeal of the law on public order as a step toward a war which powerful elements in both camps welcomed. The *Diario de Cundinamarca* concluded that Congress acted in order to free the national government for decisive action in the event that Antioquia carried out its ambitions against Cauca. "It is unquestionable that conflict is coming." *El Deber* of Medellín matched this militancy by publishing a letter containing the following advice: "Our country is like a tree; if the government instead of having the wisdom which nourishes, is a parasite which undermines, let us destroy it." [92]

War broke out in Cauca when Conservative forces attacked the municipal authorities of Palmira on July 11. Conto immediately placed the state on a war footing, but fighting quickly spread throughout Cauca. President Parra responded to the crisis by dispatching an army to Cauca overland by way of Tolima. Antioquia maintained an overt posture of neutrality until August 8, when Governor Villa declared Antioquia to be in a state of war. Villa justified his action by charging that "national forces were moving by way of Honda across the southern frontier for the purpose of attacking the states of Antioquia and Tolima and of intervening in the domestic struggle taking place in Cauca." Tolima followed Antioquia's lead, and on August 16 the war became general when President Parra declared the public order disturbed throughout the country. [93]

The heaviest fighting of the war of 1876–1877 occurred in Tolima, Cauca, and Antioquia, where Liberal and Conservative armies of thousands of men maneuvered against each other. The first major battle took place at Los Chancos in Cauca when in late August a Conservative force of Caucanos and Antioqueños under the command of Joaquín

92. *Boletín Oficial* (Medellín), June 7, 1876; D. Viana to Parra, June 13, 1876, CdeHRP; *Leyes de Colombia, 1863–75*, 434; Pombo and Guerra (eds.), *Constituciones*, IV, 135; *Diario de Cundinamarca* (Bogotá), June 23, 1876; *El Deber* (Medellín), July 15, 1876.

93. *Boletín Oficial* (Medellín), August 8, 1876; Briceño, *La revolución*, 156–60; *Diario Oficial* (Bogotá), July 14, 19, August 17, 1876.

María Córdoba headed south into the Cauca Valley. Liberal forces under General Julián Trujillo defeated the Conservative army but failed to deliver a decisive blow; immediately after the initial victory, Liberal troops in a festive mood scattered and returned to their homes thus depriving Trujillo of more than half of his army. Los Chancos secured Cauca for the Liberals, elevated Trujillo to the status of a national hero, and induced the Antioqueños to assume leadership in directing the war. Governor Villa appointed Marceliano Vélez Conservative commander, his second choice for the position, and Vélez operated under the orders of the governor.[94] The second major confrontation occurred at Garrapata in Tolima when Conservatives under General Vélez gathered in preparation for a breakthrough into Cundinamarca and on to Bogotá. The Liberal army defeated the Conservatives during several days of fighting in November and forced them to retreat into Antioquia. Garrapata was followed by a sixteen-day armistice and a series of fruitless negotiations aimed at ending the war. General Vélez then retired to Manizales, where the bulk of the Conservative forces were concentrated for a decisive battle in early April. General Trujillo led the Liberals in the successful siege of Manizales. Antioquia capitulated on April 5 thus bringing the war to a close.[95]

Fighting which took place in other parts of Colombia was less significant, because it was peripheral to the fate of Antioquia. Conservative guerrillas in Cundinamarca were particularly active in disrupting government communications and generally hampering Liberal prosecution of the war. After Garrapata, Conservative guerrilla units in

94.   Trujillo to Parra, October 4, 1876, CdeHRP. Recaredo de Villa stated in a letter written twenty years after the war that when the fighting began he sent a letter to Leonardo Canal asking him to take command of Antioqueño forces and that he never received a reply. He speculated that the letter was intercepted by Liberals. Vélez was thus his second choice for the command position. See Villa to Ignacio Gutiérrez Ponce, May 12, 1896, Gutiérrez Vergara collection, ACdeH.

95.   Among the many accounts of the war of 1876–1877 the following are the principal ones: Briceño, La revolución; Constancio Franco V., Apuntamientos para la historia: la guerra de 1876 i 1877 (Bogotá, 1877); José María Barona Pizarro, Bosquejo histórico de la última revolución (1876 a 1877) (Panama, 1877); Marceliano Vélez, Las memorias del señor Camilo A. Echeverri y mis actos en la revolución de 1876 (Medellín, 1878); Ricardo Ordóñez (ed.), Episodios de la campaña de occidente en 1876 tomados del 'Diario histórico' de aquel ejército abnegado i valiente (Bogotá, 1877).

the three eastern mountain states assembled in northern Santander as one army in an effort to give General Vélez time to reorganize his army by diverting federal forces from the interior. In two major battles of January and February Liberal forces under the commands of Generals Solón Wilches and Sergio Camargo defeated the Conservatives assembled in Santander.[96]

The war of 1876–1877 had its immediate origins in Cauca. Both sides to the dispute viewed the struggle as one centering on ideological issues not susceptible to compromise, and both looked upon war as the only means of resolving the issues. The fanaticism characterizing the dispute in Cauca stemmed from ideological commitments; this fanaticism was given license by tacit guaranties of support offered to the contenders by two external interested powers, Antioquia and the national government. Localized conflict quickly escalated into general war because both external guarantors saw their vital interests linked to the fate of Cauca. By intervening in Cauca the national government acted as it had in 1875 against the north coast states, but with greater justification. Antioquia, on the other hand, reversed its 1875 position of supporting federal intervention. In 1876 it regarded any form of federal aid to the government of Cauca as a violation of state sovereignty.

The weakness and disarray characteristic of the Conservative party in the 1860s had been replaced by 1876 by a high degree of unity, effective leadership, and broad agreement on general principles. Impetus for this turnaround of the early 1870s came from a reaction against the expedient support given by Conservatives to Mosquera and the League of 1869, a growing fear of the consequences to Colombian society of the sweep of Western Liberalism, and a determination to resist the Liberal program of recentralization of authority and secularization of education. A new generation of Conservative leaders including Caro, Holguín, Briceño, and Martínez Silva effectively employed these issues to revitalize the party and to link it closely to the defense of state sovereignty and of religion. The emotionalism of the secular versus reli-

---

96. Accounts of the guerrilla activities and the battles in Santander are available in: Enrique de Narváez, *Los mochuelos* (Bogotá, 1936); Solón Wilches, *Hechos de la última guerra* (Cúcuta, 1878); Alejo Morales, *Campaña del norte i batalla de la Donjuana* (Bogotá, 1877); "Diario de Quijano Otero," *Boletín de Historia y Antigüedades*, XIX (February–August, 1932), 585–98.

gious education question proved powerful enough to reduce substantially the factional boundaries within the party; that question together with the Radical Liberal threat to state sovereignty was used by party activists in Bogotá to induce Antioquia to assume the risks for leadership of the longed-for Conservative regeneration of Colombia.

Antioquia's inconsistent policy on federal intervention, its unsure leadership, and its political miscalculations caused the war in Cauca to become nationwide. The arrogance, aloofness, and tactlessness which marked Antioqueño behavior ill served the state in its reluctant quest for national leadership. Such behavior persisted during the war, as noted by Briceño, who charged that the Antioqueños "tried to make of a national cause the cause of Antioquia."[97] Recaredo de Villa neither maintained the degree of understanding with the national government which the relationship between Berrío and Murillo had allowed nor did he assume firm control over the Conservative party required by war. He was a weak leader, too pliable under the influence of militants who threatened his leadership of Antioquia. To secure his control of the state he acquiesced to their bid for national power. He yielded to the militants who saw in the religious issue a chance for Antioquia to attain its due status either as head of a powerful bloc of the three western states or as initiator of a successful national revolution.

Antioquia's major political miscalculation was in assuming that the Liberal division of 1875 would persist to the extent that the Nuñistas would either support the rebellion or remain neutral. One Conservative correctly noted, however, that by giving the war such a strongly religious character, the Conservatives made it virtually impossible for any Liberals to withhold support from the national government. Among the prominent Nuñista Liberals of 1875 only José María Samper and Camilo A. Echeverri joined the Conservative cause. When the war began, Antioquia dispatched an agent to confer with Núñez in an effort to obtain his support, but the mission proved futile. Two days after the national government declared the country in a state of war, Núñez wrote to President Parra and pledged his full support.[98]

97. Briceño, La revolución, 245. For a similar complaint by another Conservative see "Diario de Quijano Otero," 592.

98. "Diario de Quijano Otero," 587; Núñez to Parra, August 18, 1876, CdeHRP.

From the day of his inauguration as governor in October 1876 until the close of the war, Núñez demonstrated loyalty to the Liberal cause. Although not a military man by training or inclination, he displayed a sufficiently martial spirit to earn general applause for his conduct during the war. The relationship which developed between Núñez and Parra during the conflict was surprisingly friendly in view of their political rivalry. Núñez exhibited remarkable candor in his correspondence with Parra and sought to extract favors and concessions both for himself and the state of Bolívar. In one letter he advised Parra to order federal officers to stay out of the internal affairs of Bolívar, and he followed this with a broad hint that he would gladly accept an appointment as general.[99]

As an immediate result of the war the Liberals acquired a degree of political power they had not enjoyed since 1864 when Conservatives seized control of Antioquia. Following the end of hostilities the triumphant Liberals replaced the Conservative regimes of Antioquia and Tolima with military governments, enacted a law on religious inspection, and ordered the exile of the bishops of Cauca and Antioquia. The exigencies of war quelled factionalism among the Liberals, and they appeared to be on the threshold of an era of harmony until faced with the problem of choosing a successor to President Parra.

The spirit of Liberal unity generated by the war provided the Nuñistas an opportunity to bring the era of Radical hegemony to a close. After General Trujillo's victory at Los Chancos, Núñez led the way in publicly calling for the election to the presidency of this popular general who was politically identified as a Nuñista Liberal. By the early and repeated advocacy of the Trujillo candidacy during the war, Núñez placed the Radical leadership in a dilemma. To avoid the general's candidacy Manuel Murillo advised Parra to deny Trujillo the glory of receiving the final Conservative capitulation at Manizales. He warned the president that "behind Trujillo will come Núñez, and behind Núñez the Conservatives."[100] Parra demurred, fearing that by depriving Trujillo of the final victory he would revive Liberal factionalism. Radical

99. *Diario de Bolívar* (Cartagena), November 23, 1876; Núñez to Parra, November 6, 1876, CdeHRP.
100. *Diario de Bolívar* (Cartagena), November 7, 1876; Quijano Wallis, *Memorias*, 296–98.

fears that Trujillo's election would provide Núñez a passport to the presidency proved well founded.

Battlefield victory brought political defeat for the Radicals, whereas for the Conservatives their military defeat provided the impetus for successful political reorganization. Elimination of Antioquia as a Conservative power left Bogotá's Conservatives in undisputed charge of party affairs. Under their guidance in the postwar years the party's orientation became nationalist rather than regionalist, centralist rather than federalist, and secular rather than religious. The decision to mute the religious question and to use nonreligious issues to rally the party faithful removed a major obstacle to a possible future alliance with a Liberal faction.

The war of 1876–1877 fed a growing discontent with the existing form of Colombian federalism. The loose federal structure had allowed Antioqueño regionalism to flourish, and it had permitted Antioquia to carry state sovereignty to an extremity. In responding to this regionalist threat to the federal structure, the national government exercised a degree of power which the architects of the 1863 Constitution had sought to obviate. The war of 1876–1877 was but one phase in the unresolved contest between regionalism and central authority, a contest being waged because of the apparent incompatibility of regionalism and national unity.

Chapter V

Transition from Radicalism to the Regeneration, 1877–1880

Colombia underwent a remarkable transition in its political configuration from Radicalism to the Regeneration during the presidency of Julián Trujillo, 1878–1880. The Radicals had already governed the country for a decade when, in 1877, their defeat of the Conservatives on the battlefield extended their control to eight of the nine states. Bolívar, under the governorship of Rafael Núñez, remained the only state free from Radical domination. But by 1880 Radical hegemony was shattered by the political turbulence and economic dislocations which swept over Colombia in the wake of war. Under the guidance of Núñez and with the support of a revived Conservative party, the Regeneration emerged from the turmoil of the postwar years.[1]

Military challenge from the Conservatives in 1876 had induced the Radicals to share political and military power with the Nuñista Liberals—also known as Independents in this period—many of whom gained prominence in the war. The election to the presidency of Trujillo, one of the newly prominent Independents, assured that the national government would look with benevolence on Independent efforts to end Radical domination in the states. A core of Independent leaders, thrust to prominence by war, led the struggle against Radicalism at the state level, and they curried Conservative support in their

1. Historical literature generally refers to the Regeneration as the period beginning in 1885 when Núñez consolidated his power through military defeat of the Radicals. Contemporary documents, however, mark its initiation with the first Núñez administration in 1880.

efforts to gain and consolidate power. After winning control of state governments, the Independents launched spectacular projects which were promoted as panaceas for postwar economic problems.

In the interval between Trujillo's election and his April 1878 inauguration, lingering hopes for Liberal unity dissipated. Revived factionalism in several states late in 1877 alerted the Radicals to the threat posed by politically ambitious Independents.[2] Governor José del Carmen Rodríguez of Boyacá warned President Aquileo Parra: "*Draconianismo*, as you know, is coming, and it is necessary to prevent it from gaining momentum." The persistence and strength of factional loyalty became apparent in February when Congress, under Radical control, convened. A heated struggle in the House over the election of officers initiated the session on a note of confrontation which persisted until adjournment at mid-year. Factionalism prevented Congress from carrying out the normally routine function of electing a presidential designate for the year. Núñez and Parra were the candidates for the post, but neither could gain a majority and neither faction would support a compromise candidate. Congress could only agree to leave the position vacant for one year.[3]

Conflict between Radicals and Independents marked the Trujillo presidency from the day of its inauguration. The first dispute resulted from a speech Núñez, in his capacity as president of the Senate, delivered during the inaugural ceremonies. He criticized the Radicals for having misgoverned the nation so seriously that the new administration faced the choice of either "fundamental administrative regeneration or catastrophe." The Radical press strongly upbraided Núñez, and the Senate by a twelve to eight vote censured him for delivering a speech which was not "compatible with the established constitutional regime."[4] Conflict intensified between Congress and President Trujillo

2. In previous chapters the pro-Núñez faction of the Liberal party has been labeled Moderate or Nuñista. It will henceforth be labeled Independent, because during the postwar period it increasingly became referred to by that name and as a party rather than as a faction of Liberalism.

3. José del Carmen Rodríguez to Aquileo Parra, November 5, 1877, CdeHRP; Froilán Largacha to Tomás Cipriano de Mosquera, March 6, 1878, ATCM; *Diario de Cundinamarca* (Bogotá), February 20, 27, March 6, 1878; *Diario Oficial* (Bogotá), June 5, 1878.

4. *La Palestra* (Mompós), April 30, 1878; *El Promotor* (Barranquilla), April 27, 1878; *Diario de Cundinamarca* (Bogotá), April 2, 1878.

when he appointed Núñez secretary of hacienda and named three other Independents to the four-member cabinet. A majority of the Senate voted to confirm the appointees, but disturbances created by pro-Trujillo mobs occupying the galleries made the accompanying debate tumultuous.[5]

During the 1879 session of Congress, the Radicals succeeded in electing Felipe Pérez as presidential designate, and they rejected three prominent Independents appointed by Trujillo to diplomatic and administrative posts. The most spectacular of these confirmation battles occurred when the Senate refused confirmation of Núñez as Colombian minister to the United States. Shortly thereafter, Trujillo attempted to fill two cabinet vacancies with Núñez partisans, Pablo Arosemena and Luis Carlos Rico. The Senate rejected Arosemena but failed to muster a majority against Rico. The final Radical victory occurred when the Senate rejected the appointment of Narciso González Lineros as head of the Office of National Statistics because of his position as editor of the Nuñista paper La Reforma. Such tactics brought considerable discredit to the Radicals and achieved little of importance.[6]

By May 1879 Liberal factionalism in Congress produced violence. Anti-Radical mobs began filling the Plaza de Bolívar and the congressional galleries daily. On May 7 shooting erupted in the House chamber, and mob violence persisted throughout the day in Bogotá. Rock-throwing crowds pursued prominent Radicals through the streets of the capital. The military did little to restore order, and the Radicals walked out of Congress demanding as a condition of their return that the administration provide for their protection and security. Calm was gradually restored, but the Radicals could not agree on their next course of action. As a result of their group indecision, they individually filtered back to Congress thus restoring the quorum. Former Governor Rodríguez of Boyacá expressed the despair of Radical leaders at the party's inability to agree on a united course of conduct. "The behav-

5. Diario Oficial (Bogotá), April 8, 1878; Largacha to Mosquera, April 3, 1878, ATCM; José Herrera Olarte, La administración Trujillo: juicio histórico (Bogotá, 1880), 18–20.
6. El Promotor (Barranquilla), March 15, 1879; El Debate (Bogotá), March 6, 1879; Parra to Luis [Bernal], February 23, 1879, Aquileo Parra collection, Box #1, ACdeH; "Ministerio de Hacienda," Vol. 382, pp. 833–35, Archivo Nacional, Bogotá, hereinafter cited as AN; Núñez to Luis Carlos Rico, April 17, 1879, MS. #99, BLAA.

ior of a majority of the Radicals has been very egotistic in my view, and from that has come the growth of Independentism, that is, of anarchy."[7]

Evidence abounded that Radical power had seriously eroded by 1879. Manuel Murillo, the party's ideological leader, suffered from senility, and former president Parra lived in semi-retirement in Santander. Early in 1879, El Relator, one of the two most important Radical papers in Colombia, went out of business. Its editor, Felipe Pérez, bitterly complained: "The Liberals have not helped even with the payment of their subscriptions. They all want to read it free of charge; others carry their disdain for it to the point of not reading it, and others, the majority, were angered because it lacked respect for the present government." Later in the year Jorge Isaacs, the Radical partisan from Cauca, observed: "The silence of the Radical press in Bogotá is maddening."[8]

An underlying cause of this intense Liberal factionalism was the formulation by the Trujillo regime of a program which significantly differed from Radicalism. During his first month in office Trujillo sent messages to Congress indicating the areas in which he sought to depart from Radical policy. His public works program constituted one such departure. The moment for change was propitious because the overly ambitious Radical program, centering on vast interstate railroad projects conceived, promoted, and financed by the national government, had achieved few concrete results, and it seemed impossible of realization in the postwar years of financial stringency.

Epitomizing the Radical program ·was the railroad linking the Pacific port of Buenaventura with Bogotá and extending northward through the three eastern mountain states to the lower Magdalena River. Feasibility of the Bogotá-Magdalena River linkage, the so-called Northern Railroad, had been a major campaign issue between Núñez and Parra in 1875, and former president Parra remained strongly committed to the project. Preparations for construction were well advanced

7. Diario Oficial (Bogotá), May 10, 14, 1879; La Nueva Era (Medellín), May 31, 1879; Herrera Olarte, Trujillo, 77–97. A good firsthand account of the violence is Rodríguez to Parra, May 10, 1879, CdeHRP. Rodríguez to Parra, June 28, 1879, CdeHRP.

8. Felipe Pérez to Parra, February 21, 1879, Jorge Isaacs to Parra, June 18, 1879, CdeHRP.

in 1876 when war broke out, making it impossible to obtain the necessary foreign loans. Immediately after the war, Congress ordered the liquidation of the Northern Railroad Company, but it remained intact for two more years because of complicated negotiations over transfer of property to a construction company headed by the English contractor Henry Ross. Upon the conclusion of the war, the Parra government signed a contract with Ross's company to build the Central Railroad from Bogotá to the Magdalena River. The principal difference between the Central and Northern Railroads was that the former was scheduled to pass through the population centers of the three eastern mountain states rather than reach the Magdalena River by the shorter, more direct northern route.[9] In the immediate postwar period the Radicals thus continued to pursue the fantasy of "redemptive" public works projects of such vast scope as to be financially beyond the nation's reach.

President Trujillo liquidated the Northern Railroad Company as required by law and abrogated the Ross contract when the contractor found it impossible to obtain adequate financing. The Independents suffered slight criticism for abandoning these projects which had become increasingly subject to general opprobrium. In early 1879, one Conservative paper concluded that the promotion of large-scale railroad enterprises by the Radicals had resulted in "the discredit of those enterprises, the squandering of much money, the disillusionment of the credulous, and to a large extent the calamities of civil war."[10]

Political success demanded that the Independents do more than merely obstruct fulfillment of the Radical public works program. The task of formulating a new program was assumed by Trujillo's first two secretaries of hacienda, Rafael Núñez and Luis Carlos Rico, an intimate friend of Núñez. In an 1877 article, Rico outlined the public works program the Independents implemented the following year. He argued for greater local and regional initiative and asserted: "Decentralization of public works is the most fruitful part of *self government*. . . . Sectional initiative has not fully responded to the high duties which fed-

9. *Leyes de Colombia, 1877,* 35; *Diario Oficial* (Bogotá), September 20, 1879; Ortega, *Ferrocarriles,* II, 427–28, 532–33.

10. *El Deber* (Bogotá), February 7, 1879; *Diario de Cundinamarca* (Bogotá), June 28, 1878; *El Relator* (Bogotá), July 16, 1878.

eration imposes." President Trujillo presented to Congress a public works message based on the concepts of Rico and Núñez. The message, written by Núñez, advocated continuing the high level of federal expenditures on public works but placing greater emphasis than had previous administrations on the responsibility of state governments. Núñez concluded the message with the observation: "This change in the system of administering the department of public works . . . perhaps maintains more harmony than that followed up to now with the spirit, if not with the letter, of our constitution which has entrusted the most substantial portion of political power to the good sense and the interests of the nine states which form the union."[11]

Congress enacted a law on public works in 1878 which embodied the decentralized approach envisioned by Núñez and Rico. The law allocated designated sums to each state for construction projects which in most cases were specified by the law. In the likely event that the Northern and Central Railroad projects failed, the law provided funds for intrastate railroads such as those of Antioquia and Cauca. To finance these projects the national government was authorized to contract a loan of up to $2 million. Interstate railroads thus were abandoned. General applause greeted the new orientation set forth in the law, but some Radicals characterized it as marking the "abandonment of large material enterprises—works of national unity, of strength, and of probable realization—for the support of enterprises of a sectional character favored with direct aid, the results of which only God knows."[12]

The church-state issue constituted a second area in which the Trujillo administration departed from Radical policy. Congress, in 1877, had enacted three punitive laws against the church for its alleged support of the Conservatives during the 1876–1877 war. These laws established religious inspection by the government, exiled the four bishops of Cauca and Antioquia, and halted the compensatory payments made to the church for the 1861 disamortization of church property. In early 1878 the remaining Colombian bishops and the archbishop of Bogotá began lobbying Congress for repeal of these laws.[13] Radicals regarded

11. Diario de Cundinamarca (Bogotá), October 27, 1877; Diario Oficial (Bogotá), April 29, 1878.

12. Leyes de Colombia, 1878, 111–14; El Relator (Bogotá), June 14, 1878.

13. Leyes de Colombia, 1877, 8–9, 28–31; José Telésforo Paúl, Exposición que hace al congreso de los Estados Unidos de Colombia el obispo de Panamá (Bogotá,

the pressure as an insolent effort to reverse one of the positive achievements of the war. That conflict had significantly altered Radical policy, which prior to 1876 had favored religious liberty and church-state separation. During a Senate debate on the religious issue in mid-1878, Manuel Murillo summarized the postwar Radical position: "The last revolution has modified my ideas on religious liberty; I now believe that it should not be absolute, because it is a peril to the Liberal party."[14]

Trujillo sided with the church against the Radicals on the religious issue. In April, he urged Congress to repeal the three 1877 anticlerical laws. In a letter to Mosquera, Trujillo explained that his purpose was simply to bring an end to a dispute which had created so many problems for the nation. Núñez served as the administration spokesman during Senate debate on the issue. He ridiculed the attempt to cope with religious fanaticism through suppression and advocated unrestricted competition of ideas as the best antidote. The Radicals defeated the effort to repeal the three laws and passed a resolution declaring that it is "neither opportune nor proper to legislate now on religious matters."[15]

Despite the attention attracted by developments in the capital such as the struggle by the Trujillo administration to implement an Independent program, the executive-legislative conflict, and the violence and street riots, the national political trend in the postwar years was shaped by events in the states. Political and economic initiative clearly shifted from Bogotá to the states during the postwar period. Prolonged stalemate between Congress and the president politically weakened the national government. Economic disruptions caused by the war, declining exports, and the unavailability of foreign credit financially crippled the national government. The principle of state sovereignty, sanctioned by the 1863 constitution, achieved full expression during this period. Six months after Trujillo's inauguration, one paper observed: "The hope of good citizens, frustrated in large part by Congress, has already turned toward the states, looking to them for the

1878); Archbishop Vicente Arbeláez to Bishop José Telésforo Paúl, January 17, 1878, MS. #97, BLAA.

14.   La Reforma (Bogotá), June 12, 1878.

15.   Trujillo to Mosquera, May 8, 1878, ATCM; La Regeneración (Cartagena), June 26, 1878; Diario Oficial (Bogotá), May 20, 1878.

dawn or even for a glimmer of the longed for *Regeneration.*" [16] At the time of Trujillo's election the Radicals controlled the government of every state except Bolívar, where Núñez served as governor from 1876 to 1879. Through election upsets the Independents established their domination in Boyacá, Santander, and Cundinamarca. Resort to arms enabled them to seize control of Cauca, Magdalena, and Panama. By 1880 only Tolima and Antioquia remained under Radical rule. This dramatic shift from Radical to Independent control of the state governments prepared the way for the political reorientation beginning in 1880 which was called the Regeneration.

Events in Antioquia during the postwar years highlighted both the Liberal split and the decline in Radical fortunes. The Liberals acquired control of Antioquia as a result of the 1876–1877 war but found the task of governing a state with such Catholic, Conservative traditions onerous. Liberal rule also suffered from an early division into Radical and Independent factions and from a lack of personnel with government experience. The three governors from 1877 to 1880 were all generals with out-of-state origins. General Trujillo governed until the end of 1877 and was succeeded by the Independent General Daniel Aldana of Cundinamarca. Within three months Aldana stepped down, and General Tomás Rengifo assumed the office, which he held for nearly two years. Rengifo was a little-known Radical from Cali who served under Trujillo in the 1876–1877 war. Shortly before Rengifo became governor, a prominent Conservative of Medellín complained to President Parra that the elevation of another Caucano to power would revive "racial hatreds between Antioqueños and Caucanos." [17] In a gesture of frustration a small group of Conservatives began a revolt against Rengifo in January 1879, and they received some backing from Independents who wanted to restore Aldana as governor. Within a few days Rengifo defeated the main body of rebel forces. His victory propelled him to national prominence at an opportune moment, for the Radicals had reached a stalemate in their attempt to select a presidential candidate for the 1880–1882 term. [18]

16.   El Deber (Bogotá), October 11, 1878.
17.   Trujillo to Parra, May 7, September 4, 1877, CdeHRP; Abraham García to Parra, February 26, 1878, MS. #218, BLAA.
18.   Herrera Olarte, *Trujillo*, 42–54.

Since late in 1878 the Radicals had tried and failed to agree on a presidential candidate.[19] Their anxiety intensified as it became apparent that Núñez would enter the campaign with the nearly unanimous support of the Independents. Within days of the dissemination of reports that Rengifo had defeated the rebels thus preserving Antioquia for the Radicals, party leaders embraced him as candidate for president. Of Rengifo's military victory Parra wrote: "[It] can save us, because it will bring to the campaign scene a new man who can reunite the opinion of all Radicals." Rengifo's candidacy became official in March when the *Diario de Cundinamarca* endorsed him and began printing adherences.[20]

The Radicals had acted hastily. Simultaneous with the formation of a consensus among party leaders in support of Rengifo, he was conducting the final phase of military operations. The insurrectionists, after brief, scattered fighting, capitulated at Santarosa de Osos and agreed to surrender formally the following day. During the night they fled, and Rengifo avenged the deceit by ordering the immediate execution of Guillermo MacEwen, the village prefect who, having no ties with the rebels, remained behind. By the end of March a storm of protest against Rengifo appeared in all but the most partisan Radical press of Colombia. Former governor Marco Estrada of Santander notified Parra that "some Radicals are withdrawing from the Rengifo candidacy." Another party leader wrote that a committee had been formed in Bogotá "to put things in order"; it drew up a list of eight candidates, but Rengifo's name did not appear on the list.[21] Despite strong sentiment in favor of selecting another candidate, it was too late to abandon Rengifo. The Independents and Conservatives adroitly riveted public attention on the MacEwen affair for several weeks. The Independent governor of Boyacá sent a letter to the Senate urging Congress to order "the judgment and punishment of him who at Santarose de Osos has

19.   Potential candidates considered but rejected by the Radicals included Sergio Camargo, Aquileo Parra, Manuel Murillo, and Ezequiel Hurtado.

20.   Parra to Luis [Bernal], February 15, 1879, Parra collection, Box #1, ACdeH; *Diario de Cundinamarca* (Bogotá), March 14, 1879.

21.   Herrera Olarte, *Trujillo*, 56–57; D. Viana, *La muerte de MacEwen* (Medellín, 1880), 1–12; Estanislao Gómez Barrientos, *25 años a través del estado de Antioquia; segunda parte* (Medellín, 1927), 172–82; Marco Estrada to Parra, April 18, 1879, Rodríguez to Parra, April 18, 1879, CdeHRP.

attempted to make himself superior to the institutions of his nation." Nuñista members of Congress formulated motions of censure against Rengifo, trumpeted the charges throughout the land, and prolonged debate on the issue. The Radicals mustered a majority to defeat the motions, but the pro-Núñez press continued airing the controversy during the campaign.[22]

The debacle of the Rengifo candidacy was the most manifest sign of the eclipse of Radicalism, a process which unfolded at the state level during the postwar period and which was hastened by Núñez' role as an energetic and successful governor of Bolívar, 1876–1879. Núñez established a pattern of administration in Bolívar followed in one major respect by colleagues who became governors of other states during the postwar Independent surge. He directed his attention to the problems of economic recovery. Núñez energetically promoted one spectacular public works project, the reopening of the Dique Canal. In addition to stimulating economic progress, its promotion was designed to bring political dividends.

The Dique Canal, a cleared ex-channel of the Magdalena River, had been opened in the mid–seventeenth century across a one-hundred-kilometer stretch of swamps and lowlands lying between Cartagena and the Magdalena River. Neglect of the canal during the nineteenth century had made it unfit for regular navigation and had brought the eclipse of Cartagena's commercial preeminence. Santa Marta surpassed Cartagena in the early Republican period and maintained its commercial dominance until the early 1870s, when completion of the Bolívar Railroad thrust Barranquilla into the role of Colombia's major port. The rail connection between Barranquilla, the river port, and Sabanilla, the ocean port lying about twenty kilometers to the northwest, permitted circumvention of the Bocas de Ceniza, the treacherous sand bars in the mouth of the Magdalena River. Barranquilla's commercial supremacy was further enhanced in 1878 when a natural shift in the river bed deepened the channel at the Bocas de Ceniza. For the next several years ocean-going vessels could sail up the river directly to Barranquilla.[23]

---

22. "Senado 1879; Negocios Pendientes," Vol. V, pp. 38–40, AC; *La Nueva Era* (Medellín), May 3, 1879; *La Opinión* (Bogotá), November 10, 1879.

23. Mauricio N. Visbal, "Apuntes históricos sobre del Canal del Dique," *Boletín*

Reopening the Dique Canal became an enterprise upon which Núñez staked his political reputation. The last serious effort to excavate the canal prior to Núñez' governorship was undertaken by a fellow Cartagenero, Antonio del Real, in the early 1870s. Real's persistent efforts yielded a measure of success when Congress enacted a law in 1876 guaranteeing payment of $96,000 to any company which excavated the canal and made it sufficiently navigable to satisfy the government of Bolívar. Within a month of Núñez' inauguration, he signed a state law which supplemented the federal appropriation by $24,000 and outlined the contract requirements. War postponed the project, but a few weeks after the signing of peace Núñez issued an executive decree specifying that the state government rather than a private company under contract would excavate the canal.[24] Because the national law authorized funds for the project only if undertaken by a private contractor, the Núñez plan meant that Bolívar would have to bear all of the costs. Núñez' explanation to his constituents of how Bolívar, through proper management of state funds, could undertake such a large enterprise bore evidence of his self-confidence and his regional pride. He also calculated that substantial progress on the project by the state would enhance its position in future negotiations for federal aid. Núñez traveled to New York in mid-1877 to contract for the necessary personnel and equipment. In announcing his departure he wrote: "I am undertaking this trip . . . with my own personal resources and am motivated exclusively by a sense of philanthropy, because I have a deep conviction that this project is almost a question of life or death for us." During his two-month absence he gathered engineering information and made important contacts in New York but accomplished nothing conclusive. Upon returning to Cartagena he shepherded a law through the assembly that provided $100,000 for the canal and authorized the state to seek a federal grant of $96,000.[25]

Historial (Cartagena), LXXXVI (May, 1945), 1–10; Nichols, "The Rise of Barranquilla," 158–69; *El Promotor* (Barranquilla), January 19, March 2, 1878.

24. Visbal, "Canal del Dique," 12; *Leyes de Colombia, 1876*, 79–80; *Diario de Bolívar* (Cartagena), May 30, November 6, 1876, May 12, 1877. For a more detailed study of the Núñez governorship see James W. Park, "Preludio a la presidencia: Rafael Núñez, gobernador de Bolívar, 1876–1879," *Boletín de Historia y Antigüedades*, LXIII (October–December, 1976), 519–35.

25. *Diario de Bolívar* (Cartagena), May 14, July 19, August 2, 1877. While in New

Núñez displayed rare political skills in securing federal funds for the canal. He won election as senator from Bolívar in 1877, and early the following year he obtained a leave of absence from the governorship. Before departing for Bogotá he contracted in New York for the purchase of a dredge and pile driver, and for the services of a hydraulic engineer. As senator, Núñez introduced the bill providing for the payment of $96,000 to Bolívar for work on the canal, and he helped enact it into law. After serving for two months in the Senate, the newly inaugurated president, Julián Trujillo, appointed him secretary of hacienda. During his three-month stint in the cabinet, Núñez signed the executive decree ordering payment of $96,000 to Bolívar. By September the versatile Cartagenero was back in Bolívar, where he resumed his duties as governor. Núñez continued to focus his attention and the state's resources on the Dique Canal during his final year as governor. When his term expired, the dredging work was progressing satisfactorily, and his successor pledged to continue giving priority to the project.[26] The best assurance, however, that navigation would be reestablished on the canal was Núñez' election to the presidency in 1880.

In promoting the Dique Canal and the interests of Cartagena, Núñez had to move cautiously lest his political ambitions founder on the commercial rivalry between Cartagena and Barranquilla. The fading grandeur of his native city caused him genuine anguish, and he shared the typical Cartagenero's disdain for that squalid village on the banks of the Magdalena River. Although Núñez publicly portrayed the canal project as benefiting the entire state, he privately argued to the contrary. In a letter to President Parra, Núñez maintained: "The towns

---

York Núñez married Soledad Román, a Cartagenera, in a civil ceremony. Núñez' first wife, Dolores Gallego, continued living in Panama, and although she and Núñez had separated years earlier, that marriage remained valid under church law. Not until Dolores Gallego died in 1889 did Núñez and Doña Soledad marry in a religious ceremony. Serious political repercussions from Núñez' marital status first surfaced during the Senate debate in 1879 concerning his appointment as Colombian minister to the United States. The issue remained alive during the following decade. See Julio H. Palacio, "El segundo matrimonio de Núñez," Revista Colombiana, VII (November, 1936), 321–33.

26.   Diario de Bolívar (Cartagena), September 6, 1877, May 4, 31, July 12, September 7, 1878, October 13, 1879; "Senado 1878; Antecedentes de Leyes 1," Vol. I, p. 146, AC.

most directly interested in this enterprise are precisely those in which the pure Liberal element of Bolívar dominates. Barranquilla (between the two of us) is a center of all manner of Judaism." [27]

Preferential treatment for Cartagena evoked the strident voice of Barranquilla "boosterism" which could not be long ignored. Merchants and other prominent residents of the river port petitioned Congress in 1877 and 1878 for federal funds in support of a variety of municipal projects such as a normal school, charity hospital, water system, and duty-free importation of construction material for a theater.[28] One of these petitions concluded as follows: "[Barranquilla now is a] grand, rich matron, proud of her triumphs over those two maiden daughters of the Caribbean Sea—Santa Marta and Cartagena—who seem designated by the finger of God to wear the rags of misery, after having been the proud queens of the Atlantic under the domination of Spain." [29]

When navigation through the Bocas de Ceniza became possible in 1878, Barranquilla merchants organized a committee to lobby for federal aid for a scientific study of the river entrance and for major channel and dock improvements at the river port. Such pressure compelled Núñez to respond. In mid-year, while serving as secretary of hacienda, he notified Barranquilla that the new budget provided funds to hire a hydrographic engineer to study the Bocas de Ceniza. When a ship ran aground there later in the year, he visited Barranquilla and promised that money would be provided for dredging operations as soon as the engineer completed his study. Núñez further redeemed his standing in Barranquilla when he helped pass a law in 1879 which authorized the expenditure of up to $100,000 of federal funds on improved harbor and dock facilities for the city.[30]

---

27.   Núñez to Parra, March 6, 1877, CdeHRP. For an assessment by a Cartagenero of the city's decline since the 1860–62 war see Pedro Maira to Mosquera, June 15, 1877, ATCM. Núñez to Parra, December 25, 1877, CdeHRP.

28.   "Senado 1877; Antecedentes de Leyes," Vol. I, pp. 29–30; "Senado 1877; Asuntos Varios," Vol. VI, pp. 340–41; "Senado 1878; Antecedentes de Leyes," Vol. I, p. 35; "Senado 1878; Antecedentes de Leyes," Vol. II, p. 52, AC.

29.   "Senado 1877; Antecedentes de Leyes," Vol. I, pp. 29–30, AC.

30.   Diario de Bolívar (Cartagena), July 19, 1878; El Promotor (Barranquilla), December 7, 21, 1878; Leyes de Colombia, 1879, 17–18.

Núñez' term as governor greatly enhanced his reputation as a political leader. One Radical paper in the state correctly attributed his success to a public works program which served as his "battlehorse." Aside from the major navigation projects at Cartagena and Barranquilla, he promoted several less costly enterprises such as construction of a road between Sincelejo and the port of Tolú.[31] He devoted attention to the creation of a state agricultural society and provided state funds for the introduction of new tobacco strains from Cuba, the dissemination of coffee seeds, and the establishment of experimental farms. Núñez' success rested on his ability to finance these programs by raising state revenue and attracting federal funds. Budgeted income for the state government increased from $254,800 in 1875 to nearly $400,000 in 1879.[32] The bulk of the increase came from federal appropriations and a new state tax on foreign imports destined for use in Bolívar.

Núñez took full advantage of his political offices to secure positions in Bolívar for a corps of loyal followers. As noted previously, he obtained the appointment of his younger brother, Ricardo, as accountant-auditor of customs at Sabanilla. By writing directly to President Parra, Núñez procured the placement of Antonio del Real as principal administrator of the national Department of Hacienda in Cartagena. Real was an early promoter of the Dique Canal and served as state treasurer during the first months of the Núñez governorship. While Núñez served as secretary of hacienda in mid-1878, President Trujillo appointed José María Campo Serrano administrator of the Bolívar Railroad in Barranquilla, a position within the Department of Hacienda.[33] Campo Serrano was one of the three delegates from Magdalena to attend the 1875 Barranquilla convention which nominated Núñez for president. Before leaving the cabinet, Núñez added four new positions to the customs staff in Cartagena. A year later his successor and close

31. La Palestra (Mompós), September 23, 1878; Diario de Bolívar (Cartagena), January 9, 1879, October 4, 1878; El Promotor (Barranquilla), August 16, 1879.

32. Diario de Bolívar (Cartagena), January 4, 1875, January 26, February 21, December 20, 1878; El Promotor (Barranquilla), February 23, March 30, April 13, 1878.

33. See Chapter IV, 143. Núñez to Parra, January 3, 1877, CdeHRP; Diario de Bolívar (Cartagena), April 18, October 6, 1877; Diario Oficial (Bogotá), September 14, 1878.

friend Luis Carlos Rico created two more positions in Cartagena. One appointment of great benefit to Núñez, but for which he was not responsible, was the assignment of Colonel Manuel D. Montúfar to Barranquilla as chief of staff of the Third Army Division. Montúfar gratuitously avowed his political loyalty to Núñez and served as a valuable source of intelligence on events in Panama and Magdalena, where he had several political as well as military ties.[34] In addition to exerting his influence in the filling of appointive positions in Bolívar, Núñez saw to the election of well-disposed congressional delegations and selected one of his early supporters, Benjamín Noguera, to succeed him as governor.

While Núñez directed his efforts toward promoting economic development in Bolívar and creating a network of personal loyalties along the north coast, nonviolent political turnovers shifted Boyacá and Santander from Radical to Independent control.

Four months prior to Trujillo's inauguration, the long period of Radical domination of Boyacá came to an unexpected conclusion. The two-year term of Governor José del Carmen Rodríguez ended in December 1877, and the assembly elected Sergio Camargo to succeed him. Camargo instead accepted appointment by Parra as Colombian minister to England and France, and the first designate, José Eusebio Otálora, was inaugurated in his place. Otálora had identified with the Radicals from the beginning of his political career in the 1850s until the election of 1875, when he supported Núñez. During the war of 1876–1877, Otálora rose to the rank of general; his military record and the lingering wartime spirit of Liberal unity underlay his election as first designate.[35]

Otálora's immediate concern centered on political survival, particularly during the early months of his administration when the Radicals remained in control of the national government. While Radicals in Bogotá maneuvered to annul his election, he prepared forcibly to resist any such attempt. He solicited a promise of military support from

34. *Diario de Bolívar* (Cartagena), May 7, 1878, June 26, 1879; Manuel D. Montúfar to Núñez, May 18, 1878, Copiador de Cartas de Manuel D. Montúfar, ACdeH, hereinafter cited as CCM-ACdeH.

35. *El Boyacense* (Tunja), October 20, 22, November 26, December 10, 1877; Carlos A. Otálora, *Homenaje a la memoria del doctor José Eusebio Otálora en su centenario* (Tunja, 1929), 94, 136–44.

his wartime colleague General Solón Wilches of Santander, and encouraged the general to lead an anti-Radical political movement in that state. Otálora accepted support from the Conservatives beginning early in his administration. That support grew in significance during his first term and provided an important element in his successful bid for reelection in 1879.[36] Another ingredient in Otálora's political survival was his formulation of a program to cope with Boyacá's serious economic problems.

Boyacá was one of the poorest states of Colombia. It possessed no major industry, produced few exports, and was the most isolated state in the nation. Its Indian and mestizo masses subsisted on small-scale agriculture, household leather and textile production, and local commodity exchange. A common nineteenth-century Colombian saying was that "the *Boyacenses* are good only for cannon fodder," because the state served as a principal supplier of soldiers during periods of revolution and civil war. The state's economy consequently suffered from the manpower drain during the 1876–1877 war despite the absence of fighting in Boyacá. Income to the state government from the normal revenue sources declined by about two-thirds during the 1877 fiscal year.[37]

Otálora's political future largely hinged on his treatment of Boyacá's economic ills. His first priority was to increase state revenue. A month before his inauguration the assembly authorized the 1878 budget, which provided for an income of $191,937. Two years later Otálora approved a state budget which anticipated an income of $582,933. The great bulk of this increase came from funds provided by the national government. Otálora displayed persistence and ingenuity both in collecting past-due federal funds and in obtaining new federal appropriations. Throughout the first half of 1878 he concentrated on cajoling the national government into paying the money Congress had earlier au-

36.   José Eusebio Otálora to Solón Wilches, January 23, February 25, 1878, reprinted in Gustavo Otero Muñoz, *Wilches y su época* (Bucaramanga, 1936), 287–88, 291–92; Rodríguez to Parra, December 3, 1877, CdeHRP; *El Deber* (Bogotá), December 5, 1879.

37.   *El Empresario* (Tunja), January 15, 1880. This source estimated that three-fourths of the men and officers in the Colombian army were from Boyacá. *El Boyacense* (Tunja), October 6, 1877.

thorized but never appropriated. He met with total failure and was informed by the secretary of hacienda that the money simply did not exist. Otálora then advised President Trujillo that he had just dispatched his secretary general to Bogotá to collect the debt to Boyacá and had commissioned two prestigious Bogotá legal firms to discuss with the national government the terms of payment. A month later Otálora announced a partial victory to the assembly; President Trujillo had promised that half of the federal debt to Boyacá would be paid in the current fiscal year.[38] Governor Otálora also obtained the cession to Boyacá of the nationally owned emerald mines of Muzo. He then used the cession to cajole the national government to appropriate funds for a railroad project in Boyacá. In a letter to President Trujillo, Otálora explained the importance of the railroad and pointedly added that Boyacá could provide some of the necessary money "through the sale of the emerald mines in one of the European markets." Within three weeks Congress authorized a substantial grant for the railroad.[39]

Otálora unveiled a project in 1878 designed to advance his own political future and Boyacá's economic development. He proposed the establishment of a large ironworks at Samacá, a village situated a few miles southwest of Tunja near deposits of coal and iron. Since the 1850s, various entrepreneurs had struggled to establish a small ironworks there, but the ventures all failed. In 1874, Congress authorized the president to promote the construction of an ironworks at an undesignated location, but the executive failed to show any interest.[40] By the time Otálora proposed the Samacá project, Colombia's unfortunate experience with railroad construction had shaken this complacent attitude toward iron production. In mid-1878, Otálora established, by executive decree, the Samacá Ironworks Company. The state government purchased the existing property, buildings, and machinery at Samacá for the new company and provided $75,000 of the initial $200,000 in capital. To organize and operate the ironworks, Otálora recruited two experienced engineers employed by the Passaic Rolling Mill Company

38. *El Boyacense* (Tunja), December 18, 1877, December 18, 1879, August 13, 14, October 5, 1878.
39. *Ibid.*, June 23, 1879; *Leyes de Colombia*, 1879, 72–75.
40. Ospina Vásquez, *Industria y protección*, 270–71; *Leyes de Colombia*, 1863–75, 1096–97.

of Patterson, New Jersey. The engineers together with fourteen iron workers also recruited in the United States arrived in Colombia in October 1878. Early the following year Otálora urged Congress to provide funds to enable the workers' families to immigrate to Colombia, a step which he felt would assure "for an indefinite time the success of the enterprise." Congress generously appropriated $100,000 for the ironworks company and $25,000 to underwrite travel expenses for the workers' families.[41]

Despite delays in rail production, the Samacá project fulfilled part of its purpose, for Otálora won his bid for reelection, thus securing to the Independents control of Boyacá. To safeguard the state from Radical incursions across the border from Santander, Otálora encouraged his wartime colleague General Solón Wilches to assume leadership of the Independent drive for power in that state.

Wilches was the undisputed choice of Independents to topple Santander's Radical regime of two-decades' duration. In the early 1870s he had served a two-year term as governor, but in the hotly contested presidential election of 1875 he championed Núñez. As a result of his efforts in support of Núñez, President Pérez dismissed him from his position as commander in chief of the Colombian army. Wilches regained national attention during the 1876–1877 war through his service as commander of Santander's Liberal forces. He emerged from the war a genuine military hero.[42]

Prospects for Santander's Independents in the mid-1878 elections for governor and state assembly were promising, because Governor Marco Estrada's impolitic leadership of the war effort and his role in reviving the church-state issue produced widespread discontent. Santander was not a major battleground during the war, but the guerrillas and small Conservative units operating in the region proved elusive. In addition, the governor often worked at cross-purposes with his field commanders. Following the Conservative surrender at Mutiscua in February 1877, General Wilches granted amnesty to the defeated soldiers so they could return to their homes, and he issued passports for

---

41. *El Boyacense* (Tunja), June 17, 18, 22, October 3, 1878, February 3, 1879; *Leyes de Colombia*, 1879, 23–24.
42. Otero Muñoz, *Wilches*, 240–45, 279–80.

travel to Venezuela to the Conservative commanders in return for their promise to remain out of Colombia until the end of the war. Estrada countermanded this conciliatory gesture and ordered the recapture of the pardoned Conservatives. Such actions stiffened Conservative resistance and prolonged fighting in Santander three months beyond the April capitulation of Antioquia. At mid-year the acting president, Sergio Camargo, informed Parra that he had sent two peace commissioners to Santander, "where things have reached the bad situation they are in today because of the complete misgovernment or anarchy with which that state proceeds."[43] One of these peace commissioners reported that the forced loans levied by the state during the war were excessive and likely to cause political trouble in the future. Also, the church-state issue became bitterly contested when the bishop of Pamplona and several parish priests publicly labeled as unconstitutional the law on religious inspection passed by Congress during the closing weeks of the war. State authorities responded by arresting several priests and exiling the bishop. These intemperate measures provoked the clergy to close the churches throughout Santander. The state government then retaliated by enacting a law that sharply curtailed the political rights of the clergy.[44] Hatreds generated by the war thus persisted through the final months of Santander's Radical regime.

Despite Radical control of the Santander government, the Independents elected Wilches as governor and gained a majority of seats in the assembly. A decision by the Conservatives to support Wilches rather than to abstain or launch their own candidate proved significant but not decisive in the election outcome. Besides benefiting from Radical misrule and Conservative support, the Independents prepared well for the election. Shortly before the balloting, Núñez expressed his support for Wilches and asserted: "The crux of the general situation is in [Santander]." Nationally prominent Independents such as Lino Ruiz and Antonio Roldán who maintained valuable contacts in Santander,

43. Ibid., 268–69; Adolfo Harker Mutis, Mis recuerdos (Bucaramanga, 1954), 101; Sergio Camargo to Parra, June 18, 1877, CdeHRP.

44. "Ministerio de Hacienda," Vol. 393, p. 937, AN; Estrada to Parra, September 23, 1877, CdeHRP; Otero Muñoz, Wilches, 340–42; Gaceta de Santander (Socorro), October 29, 1877; José Joaquín García, Crónicas de Bucaramanga (Bogotá, 1896), 180–82.

though no longer living there, organized adherences, wrote letters in support of Wilches, and established newspapers in his behalf.[45]

In his first political act as governor, Wilches sought to curry Conservative favor by resolving the church-state dispute, which had reached a total impasse under the Radicals. He granted a general pardon to all who had taken up arms against the government, and he urged the clergy to open the churches which had been closed for nearly one year and to return to the public exercise of their functions. The assembly in 1879 repealed the 1877 law restricting the political rights of the clergy, and it urged Congress to reform the law on religious inspection. Wilches favored the return of the bishop of Pamplona, but Congress delayed lifting his exile until 1880.[46] By the end of Wilches' first term he had defused the religious question which had plagued the state since 1876.

Wilches tailored his economic program to Santander's traditional role as a producer of exports. Coffee, cacao, and tobacco represented the state's principal exports in the 1870s, but the collapse of the tobacco market at mid-decade and a period of falling coffee prices beginning in 1878 and lasting until 1885 added to the economic distress of the postwar years. In the search for a new export commodity following the end of the tobacco boom, attention centered on quinine, a product processed from cinchona bark which in Colombia was generally obtained from stands growing on vacant government lands, tierras baldías. The value of Colombian quinine exports grew substantially during the 1870s as shown in Table 5, and by 1881 it represented about one-third of the total annual value of exports. Santander provided a major portion of this increased production as a result of the discovery of new stands in the late 1870s and 1880. The good quality of the Santander product combined with high world market prices to produce a feverish boom in the Bucaramanga region by 1880.[47]

Wilches relied on the anticipated quinine bonanza to increase state revenues. To establish the quinine industry on a sound basis, the

45. El Corresponsal (Bogotá), June 27, 1878; El Deber (Bogotá), December 10, 1878; Núñez to Wilches, May 16, 1878, Lino Ruiz to Wilches, June 26, 1878, reprinted in Otero Muñoz, Wilches, 319–20, 300–306.

46. Otero Muñoz, Wilches, 337–43; García, Bucaramanga, 184.

47. Robert C. Beyer, "The Colombian Coffee Industry: Origins and Major Trends, 1740–1940" (Ph.D. dissertation, University of Minnesota, 1947), 38–41, 59; García, Bucaramanga, 204–207; Horacio Rodríguez Plata, La inmigración alemana al estado soberano de Santander en el siglo XIX (Bogotá, 1968), 16–18.

assembly in 1879 enacted a law under which the state government would begin the scientific cultivation of cinchona. In the following year the Wilches government signed with George von Lengerke, a German immigrant who headed a commercial firm in Bucaramanga, a contract for the exploitation of 12,000 hectares of the state's tierras baldías. The contract established a partnership between the state government and the Lengerke Company and provided that, in return for the exclusive right to extract quinine from government land, the company would share its profits with the state and buy shares in a state railroad project. To ensure the flow of funds into state coffers from the quinine trade the assembly levied a heavy tax on shipment of the product within the state.[48]

Having apparently overcome the revenue problem, Wilches turned his attention to a project long desired by Santandereanos, the provision of cheap, reliable transportation linking the state's population centers to external markets. The Radical administrations had also supported this goal, but they were committed to massive, interstate railroad projects funded by the national government. In the postwar months of 1877, Governor Estrada clung to the hope that the Central Railroad remained a viable project. Wilches, on the other hand, promoted two smaller railroads within the state, the Cúcuta and the Soto railroads. The Cúcuta Railroad was a short line destined to link the rich agricultural region around Cúcuta to the Zulia River, which flowed northeastward through Venezuelan territory into the Gulf of Maracaibo. An 1876 contract provided for construction of the Cúcuta Railroad, but work was delayed until 1879. Early the following year the first eleven kilometer stretch was completed and opened to service. The longer, more important Soto route extended from Bucaramanga and the quinine zone to the Magdalena River. This line would free Santander from the whims of Venezuelan customs officials and greatly facilitate the export of quinine. Work on this railroad did not begin until Wilches' second term, but by 1880 he was actively promoting it as Santander's most important public works project and as the first major result of the lucrative quinine traffic.[49]

By 1880 Wilches was in firm political control of Santander. Timely

48. *Gaceta de Santander* (Socorro), November 8, 1879, October 8, 1880, February 18, 1881; Rodríguez Plata, *La inmigración*, 123; Otero Muñoz, *Wilches*, 366–67.

49. Estrada to Parra, October 13, 1877, CdeHRP; Luis Febres Cordero, *Del antigua*

concessions to the Conservatives had won their tacit support. The beginning of the quinine boom during the last year of his first term improved the outlook of the region's economy and brought political dividends. An increase in state revenues permitted him to convert the rhetoric of redemptive railroad projects into the reality of construction. At mid-year Wilches convoked a constitutional convention which extended the governor's term from two to four years, just in time for his reelection.[50]

Independents governed Bolívar, Boyacá, and Santander and held the Colombian presidency at the close of 1878. Despite the importance of these peacefully achieved gains, they were insufficient to ensure the election of Núñez as successor to President Trujillo. To secure his election and their own politial careers, the Independents resorted to violence in 1879. Because the Radicals had already lost control where they were stronger, in Boyacá and Santander, the Independents were certain to challenge them in the coastal states where the Radicals lacked a traditional, loyal following. Among the four coastal states, the Independents of Cauca were the first to act.

The war of 1876–1877 produced a more profound impact on Cauca than on any other state. Deeply rooted hatreds—some racial—between Liberals and Conservatives led to widespread violence, confiscations, and property destruction. During the war a resident of Popayán observed that despite government decrees regulating expropriations, "the cases are legion of brutal, massive destruction of rural property, large and small."[51] An incident illustrating the degree of passion vented by the war occurred on December 24, 1876, when Liberal forces under the command of General David Peña recaptured Cali from the Conservatives who had taken it six days earlier with only a handful of men. Peña was from Cali, where he had established a Liberal following through his activities in the Democratic Society. With the approval of General Peña the Liberal troops plundered and destroyed Conservative and foreign property and killed many civilians. Several days after the tragedy, Mosquera's brother reported, perhaps with exag-

---

Cúcuta: datos y apuntamientos para su historia (Cúcuta, 1918), 495–97; *Gaceta de Santander* (Socorro), September 30, 1879, October 8, 1880.

50.   Otero Muñoz, *Wilches*, 361–62.

51.   Joaquín Mosquera to Tomás Cipriano de Mosquera, January 24, 1877, ATCM.

geration, that more than 400 bodies were recovered from the wreckage in Cali.[52]

Irresponsible conduct by both Radicals and Conservatives elevated political passions during the war and in the immediate postwar period. Governor César Conto refused to heed the advice of such party stalwarts as Mosquera and Parra to postpone the elections for governor until after the war. Instead, he manipulated the elections so that his secretary of hacienda and fellow Radical Modesto Garcés won the governorship. Mosquera subsequently noted in a letter to Parra: "I have offered my help to Garcés, whom it is necessary to support although he was declared elected in that farce of an election which was carried out so irregularly."[53] As governor, Garcés was so tactless as to appoint General Peña as mayor of Cali in mid-1877. Within a few months Garcés had to threaten him with dismissal because of his demagoguery and irresponsible conduct. Garcés further aggravated political tensions by appointing as secretary of interior the politically contentious Jorge Isaacs who wanted to continue persecuting Conservatives well after the end of the war. Conservatives in southern Cauca contributed to the problem of restoring order by refusing to lay down their arms. A month after the capitulation of Antioquia, a Conservative broadside published in Pasto issued the following call to arms: "We are in war, in harsh war against the most iniquitous enemies of God and of the people; to fear them would be weakness and to doubt our triumph is sacrilege."[54]

In a series of letters sent to President Parra, Mosquera provided perceptive commentary on postwar conditions in Cauca. Mosquera had lived in Bogotá since early 1876, and when he returned to his na-

52. Manuel María Buenaventura, "El General David Peña; reseña histórica," *Boletín Histórico del Valle (Cali)*, III (September, 1932), 103–13; Manuel Sinisterra, *El 24 de diciembre de 1876 en Cali* (Cali, 1937), 9–135; Phanor James Eder, *El fundador Santiago M. Eder* (Bogotá, 1959), 283–99; César Conto to Parra, January 5, 1877, MS. #295, BLAA; Modesto Garcés to Trujillo, December 25, 1876, Julián Trujillo collection, Vol. I, AN; Manuel María Mosquera to Tomás Cipriano de Mosquera, January 10, 1877, ATCM.

53. Parra to Mosquera, January 25, 1877, B. Reinales to Mosquera, February 28, 1877, ATCM; Parra to Trujillo, January 26, 1877, Conto to Trujillo, January 27, 1877, Trujillo collection, Vol. IX, AN; Mosquera to Parra, October 18, 1877, CdeHRP.

54. Garcés to Mosquera, November 2, 1877, ATCM; broadside, May 8, 1877, Trujillo collection, Vol. IV, AN.

tive state in September 1877 he was clearly shocked by what he observed. In addition to the economic disruptions caused by the war, Cauca suffered from drought and locust plagues in 1877 and 1878. Shortly after his arrival in Cali, Mosquera submitted the following report to Parra: "A summer of fourteen months has ruined the vegetation, livestock are dying from lack of pastures, food supplies are becoming extraordinarily scarce; laborers do not have work, and the discharged or deserting soldiers of the Cauca Army which went to Antioquia have become demoralized, and you know the excesses that they have committed from Antioquia to their homes." Early the following year General Trujillo visited Cauca after a year-long absence and confirmed the persistence of these problems.[55]

Evidence of social and political anarchy evoked greater anxiety in Mosquera and other observers than did the economic problems. The anarchy recalled the excesses of members of the Democratic societies in Cali, Popayán, and Buenaventura in the early 1850s prior to establishment of the Melo dictatorship. A disdain for governmental authority, noted by both Mosquera and Trujillo, partly stemmed from the awareness that recent elections were fraudulent. Another problem arose from the return of large numbers of soldiers who were attracted by "demagogues speaking about the division of owned lands and a thousand other communist ideas."[56] Mosquera reported from Cali that the Democratic Society had just held a tumultuous session in which the members approved "a proposition under which all the Conservatives will be notified to leave the country within eight days; [the members] then went into the streets shouting, 'down with the stiff-necked whites.'" Later in the year the general warned: "In the southern portion of the municipality of Palmira the Negroes are beginning to follow in the steps of those of Cali; and some families are starting to emigrate from the parish of Candelaria."[57]

An unsated appetite for Conservative-owned property underlay

55. *El Estandarte Liberal* (Cali), May 8, 1878; *La Reforma* (Bogotá), November 6, 1878; Mosquera to Parra, September 8, 1877, Trujillo to Parra, January 26, 1878, CdeHRP.

56. Gilmore, "Federalism in Colombia," 220–21; Mosquera to Parra, September 7, 1877, CdeHRP.

57. Mosquera to Parra, September 11, October 31, 1877, CdeHRP.

the continuing tensions in Cauca. In the first month of the war, the state government had decreed a forced loan of $310,000 to be levied against "the rebels or those opposed to the government." During the postwar period the Garcés regime continued its program of confiscation and sale through auction of property owned by Conservatives who could not meet the "loans." When the national government ordered Cauca to cease its illegal policy of property confiscation, Secretary of Interior Isaacs replied that the program was necessary, legal, and would continue.[58] Governor Garcés candidly expressed his dilemma as follows in a letter to President Parra: "I can assure you that if, obeying the orders which the national government sent us, we had suspended the collection of loans assigned to Sergio Arboleda, the Pombos, Arroyo, Caicedo, etc., the people would have flogged us. The tendency in this state is to impoverish the Conservatives. In the question of auctioning the property confiscated by the government, Liberals of the greatest influence are involved. It would be extremely dangerous to the tranquillity of this state to try to snatch away from the Liberals the properties that have been auctioned." Mosquera reported that in the state's three southern municipalities, Conservative property was confiscated even if the owner offered to pay the loan levied against him. "This has become a confiscation of valuable Conservative property, and a large number of the [Conservatives] have emigrated to Ecuador."[59] The flight of Conservative families from Cauca reached alarming proportions. In November Governor Garcés estimated that about 1,000 Caucanos had emigrated to Ecuador, many of them responding to encouragement from the exiled bishop of Pasto who resided there. One historical study of Popayán concluded that this departure of prominent families "initiated an era of social and economic decadence for Popayán which was of deplorable consequences."[60]

Transfer of property from Conservative to Liberal hands was a process which proved nearly impossible to bring under control in the an-

---

58. *Registro Oficial* (Popayán), September 7, 1877.

59. Garcés to Parra, September 19, 1877, Mosquera to Parra, October 10, 1877, CdeHRP; see also Mosquera to Parra, September 7, 1877, January 23, 1878, CdeHRP.

60. Garcés to Parra, November 7, 1877, CdeHRP; Arcesio Aragón, *Fastos payaneses* (2 vols.; Bogotá, 1939), I, 282; see also "Senado 1878; Negocios Pendientes," Vol. V, pp. 67–75, 78–79, AC.

archic conditions of postwar Cauca. In mid-1878 Garcés unsuccessfully attempted to annul the auction of rural property around Pasto.
One of Mosquera's correspondents warned: "Because of the nullity of
property sales, the malcontents of Pasto will give a revolutionary cry
for the creation of a tenth state." In December the governor aimed for a
more modest goal. He decreed that property taken over by the state in
lieu of payment of forced loans was to be returned to the original owners if the state had not sold it to a third party.[61] The amount of property
not yet transferred from government control to private Liberal hands
presumably was minuscule.

Resolution of Cauca's postwar problems proved beyond the capa-
bilities of the Radicals. To restore order they called for stationing additional federal forces in the state. To halt the Conservative exodus they
placed checkpoints manned by soldiers along the routes to Ecuador.[62]
To stimulate economic recovery they revived the centuries-old dream
of providing a good transportation route between Cali and Buenaventura. Garcés, Parra, and Trujillo cooperated closely in an effort to get
the national government to underwrite the construction of a railroad
linking the two cities. In the closing weeks of the Parra administration,
the national government signed a contract with the Cuban-born engineer Francisco Javier Cisneros for construction of the Cauca Railroad.
The contract estimated the total cost at $6 million and authorized pay-
ment by the national government of $3 million. In view of the Colom-
bian experience with costly railroad projects and the Cauca experience with the rugged Buenaventura-Cali route, the promoters were
hardly realistic in regarding the project as "the key to salvation for the
Caucanos—a key sent by Providence."[63]

No substantive issues separated Radicals and Independents during

61.   Largacha to Mosquera, May 29, 1878, ATCM; see also Largacha to Mosquera,
August 21, 1878, ATCM. *Registro Oficial* (Popayán), January 1, 1879.

62.   Parra to Mosquera, November 7, 14, 1877, ATCM; Garcés to Parra, September
11, 1877, Mosquera to Parra, January 9, 1878, CdeHRP.

63.   Trujillo to Parra, September 11, 1877, Mosquera to Parra, January 9, 1878,
CdeHRP; Parra to Mosquera, November 7, 1877, ATCM; *Registro Oficial* (Popayán),
March 16, 1878; *El Progreso* (Bogotá), April 16, 1878. This contract eventually led
to success. Francisco Javier Cisneros completed the first segment of the railroad in
1882, but completion of the rail link between Cali and Buenaventura was delayed
until 1914. See Neal, "The Pacific Age," 231, 240.

the campaign to elect a successor to Governor Garcés for the 1879–1881 period. All political factions in the state favored construction of the Cauca Railroad. Radicals accused Independents of allying with the Conservatives, but the Independents simply denied the existence of any special understanding with them. Manuel Sarria, secretary of interior in the Conto administration from 1875 to 1877, was the Radical candidate for governor. The Independents nominated General Ezequiel Hurtado, who had earned high military honors under General Mosquera in the 1860–1862 civil war. Hurtado was chief of staff of the Cauca forces in 1876, and he served with Trujillo at Los Chancos and Manizales. Following the war he went to Bogotá as a senator from Cauca and was named secretary of war by President Trujillo.[64]

The election was interrupted shortly before the votes were tabulated when, in early April, General Eliseo Payán led a revolt against the Radical government. Payán's military career paralleled that of Hurtado, to whom he was related, but at the close of the 1876–1877 war he retired to the family estate near Buga in the northern end of the Cauca Valley. Hurtado, while serving as secretary of war, dispatched a battalion of national troops to Cauca, ostensibly to guard the frontier with Ecuador, but they encamped near Buga. Municipal authorities in scattered localities initiated the insurrection, but within a few days General Payán took charge of the movement. Using Cauca volunteers together with national forces, he overthrew Garcés after a month of fighting and assumed control of the state government.[65]

A month after seizing power, Payán issued a decree declaring that all property that had been expropriated as a result of the 1876–1877 war would be "unconditionally returned to its original and legitimate owners." Indemnity to the purchasers of the auctioned property was to be provided by the state government. Municipal authorities complied

64. *La Voz del Pueblo* (Cali), December 5, 19, 1878; *El Estandarte Liberal* (Cali), September 5, 1878; Gustavo Arboleda, *Diccionario biográfico y genealógico del antiguo departamento del Cauca* (Bogotá, 1962), 212, 421–23; *Diario Oficial* (Bogotá), April 3, 1878.

65. For accounts of the revolution see *Diario de Cundinamarca* (Bogotá), June 14, 1879; *El Correo de la Costa* (Buenaventura), June 1, 1879; Eder, *El fundador*, 301–303; Aureliano González Toledo, *El general Eliseo Payán, vicepresidente de la república* (Bogotá, 1887), 89–100; Modesto Garcés, *Manifiesto del presidente del estado soberano del Cauca a la nación* (Bogotá, 1879), 1–16.

with the decree. In Pasto, where much property had changed hands, the mayor reported in early 1880: "Very little property in this municipality remains in the hands of those who purchased it through auction."[66] During Payán's brief rule he also lifted the exile of the bishops and priests who had been expelled during the war. Because of these measures Payán's biographer correctly labeled him "the visible nucleus in Cauca of the union of Independents and Conservatives." The state assembly met in July, legitimized Payán's actions, and elected Hurtado governor for the period beginning August 1, 1879.[67] Cauca was thus prepared to cast its vote in September for the Independent candidate for president, Rafael Núñez.

The Independents faced fewer obstacles to power on the north coast than in any other region. Bitter party divisions of the sort which plagued Cauca's politics were alien to the north coast political scene. The region also lacked the Radical tradition of Santander or the Conservative loyalty of Antioquia. Personal ties rather than party affiliation dominated politics in Magdalena and Panama. In addition, the Independents enjoyed a base of operations in Bolívar where Núñez governed. By 1879, when Núñez was widely proclaimed a candidate for president, he had formed a network of personal political alliances extending to Magdalena and Panama. He no doubt vividly recalled his defeat of 1875 when the Radicals, through their control of the national government, brazenly employed that advantage to topple the governments of those two states. Since that contest the Radicals had dominated Magdalena, and in 1879 Luis Robles was the governor. Now it was Núñez' turn to even the score.

Preparations for a coup against Governor Robles began in early 1879. Although political reality demanded of Núñez an appearance of noninvolvement, he was the moving spirit behind the operation. In a letter written to his friend Luis Carlos Rico a few weeks before the revolt began, Núñez confided: "The need for a new regime [in Magdalena] is felt even by the rocks." In early May, Colonel Montúfar reported that Núñez was ready to station an additional battalion in Barranquilla, and that "in Magdalena things are proceeding toward a

66. *Registro Oficial* (Popayán), June 5, 1879, April 24, 1880.
67. González Toledo, *Payán*, 151; *Registro Oficial* (Popayán), July 7, August 2, 1879.

definite solution; its government will not long delay in extinguishing its fading light."[68] Montúfar and Campo Serrano, administrator of the Bolívar Railroad, operating from their official positions in Barranquilla, organized the revolt against Robles. Campo Serrano led a group of national forces from Barranquilla to Ciénaga in neighboring Magdalena at the end of May. After a month of fighting they had confined Robles and his small army to Santa Marta, where the defenders waged a stubborn resistance. Montúfar then sailed from Barranquilla to Santa Marta with additional federal forces to assist Campo Serrano. Within two days of Montúfar's arrival Robles surrendered, and Campo Serrano consolidated his political control over Magdalena by assuming the governorship and generously rewarding his accomplices.[69]

The Radical press raised a storm of protest against Núñez. He denied involvement but was quick to justify the dispatch of troops to Santa Marta on grounds that the Radicals of Antioquia, Cauca, and Magdalena had attempted to form an alliance against Bolívar. In a typically cryptic letter to Rico he came closer to admitting a role in the affair. "The truth is that I did no more than avoid being selfish toward those who, *on their own initiative*, launched the revolution of Magdalena. Parties compromise their members, who must then accept the sacrifice."[70]

In Panama the Nuñistas less directly influenced political events. The Arosemena family and Colombian army officers stationed in the state served as the principal agents advancing Núñez' cause. Personal ties rather than party loyalties shaped Panamanian politics, which were volatile and ill-defined. Writing from Panama, Montúfar well ex-

68. Montúfar to Colonel Rafael Carvajal, January 3, 1879, CCM-ACdeH; Núñez to Rico, April 17, 1879, MS. #99, BLAA; Montúfar to General Gregorio Vergara, May 8, 1879, CCM-ACdeH.

69. Montúfar to General Comandante de la División, June 25, 1879, CCM-ACdeH. The state assembly elevated Colonels Montúfar and Cecilio Rodríguez, Montúfar's principal assistant, to the rank of generals of militia. Montúfar was also elected alternate senator for Magdalena, and Ricardo Núñez was elected representative. Governor Rafael Núñez also rewarded Montúfar by appointing him general of the militia of Bolívar. See Montúfar to Juan Campo Serrano, December 16, 1879, CCM-ACdeH, and *Registro de Magdalena* (Santa Marta), September 30, 1879.

70. *La Palestra* (Mompós), June 7, July 7, 23, 1879; *Diario de Cundinamarca* (Bogotá), June 14, 1879; Núñez, *La Reforma*, II, 107; Núñez to Rico, July 7, 1879, MS. #99, BLAA.

pressed the perplexity of many observers who tried to fathom the state's political convolutions. "In this country one always senses anxiety; when it is not one thing it is another, revolutions or fiestas and vice versa. . . . Politics, above all, is a terrible thing in this country, in that everyone defends his own interests, and in that it is very difficult to achieve a consensus." Between December 1878 and June 1879 Panama experienced three revolts, but they had little relation to national political trends. It remained unclear until several weeks after the June uprising that the Nuñistas controlled the new state government.[71]

Establishment of Independent hegemony in the north coast region guaranteed Núñez' victory in the presidential elections of September 1879. His supporters, nevertheless, sought to extend their influence by gaining control of Tolima and Cundinamarca. The Independents lost the September elections for governor of Tolima, but a month later their candidate led an armed expedition from Cundinamarca against Tolima's Radical government. The effort failed when the national government, responding to urgent pleas from the Radicals for support, intervened and supervised negotiations between the rivals. At year's end the Radical candidate was inaugurated governor. In Cundinamarca the Independents peacefully ended nearly a decade of Radical domination. With Conservative backing they gained control of the state assembly, which declared the Independent candidate, Wenceslao Ibáñez, winner in the race for governor.[72] By 1880 the Independents thus governed every state except Tolima and Antioquia.

The Independent party had rapidly emerged in the postwar years, and by 1880 it was the major political force in Colombia. Its success stemmed from the bitter rivalry of the 1875 election and the opportunity made available when the Radicals were compelled by the crisis of war to share power with the Independents. Following that conflict, a core of Independent leaders, tested by war, mounted effective challenges to Radical leadership in most of the states. Radical domination, weakened by the apparent failure of its program, grave postwar eco-

71. Montúfar to Juan Campo Serrano, December 16, 1879, Montúfar to Gregorio Vergara, April 8, July 19, 1879, Montúfar to Núñez, July 27, 1879, CCM-ACdeH.
72. *Diario Oficial* (Bogotá), November 13, 14, 1879; *Gaceta del Tolima* (Neiva), January 6, 1880; *Rejistro del Estado* (Bogotá), October 16, December 1, 1879, January 6, 1880; Herrera Olarte, *Trujillo*, 113–14.

nomic problems, and enervating conflict with the church, collapsed. The Independent leaders were products of state politics, and they responded to state needs. In attacking their states' economic woes, they assumed the initiative by offering solutions which were of state rather than national origin and by launching their programs with state funds. Only after the Independent governors had established priorities and had achieved some progress toward their goals did they look to the national treasury for support.

Conservatives played a key role in the dramatic success of the Independents and the election of Núñez. Beginning in 1878, Núñez openly encouraged the revival of the Conservative party. Early in the year he publicly asserted that the nation needed a "militant Conservative party" as well as a Conservative government in Antioquia to serve as a "counterweight" to the Liberal dominance of Colombia. "I do not expect a solid moral reorganization in our party while the Conservative party is reduced to impotence," he observed. Liberals and Conservatives attached considerable importance to Núñez' attitude because of the near certainty that he would succeed Trujillo. During the remainder of the year, Núñez continued to encourage the Conservatives. Besides leading the drive for repeal of the anticlerical laws, he began corresponding with the Conservative leader Carlos Holguín. By the end of the year, Núñez confided to friends that in his bid for the presidency he anticipated receiving Conservative support in Bolívar and that he needed it in Cundinamarca.[73]

In response to this encouragement Carlos Holguín and Antonio B. Cuervo began the task of reviving and reorganizing the Conservative party. Until the election of a directorate in 1879, Holguín and Cuervo assumed the responsibility for reshaping party policy. In several respects it differed from the party's prewar orientation. Antioquia had exercised the predominant influence in party leadership prior to the war and had committed the party to support federalism and uphold the rights of the church. But beginning in 1878 party leadership became national rather than Antioqueño, favored a "centralization of public order," expressed concern "that national unity be saved," and

73. *El Relator* (Bogotá), March 5, 1878; Núñez to Rico, December 27, 1878, MS. #99, BLAA. One other Liberal of stature, Sergio Camargo, encouraged Conservative activism; see *Diario de Cundinamarca* (Bogotá), December 7, 1878.

sought to secularize the party by suppressing defense of religion as a political banner.[74] Early in the reorganization process Holguín and Cuervo initiated steps toward allying the party with the Independents. In September the two Conservative leaders sent Alejandro Posada to the north coast on a mission to persuade colleagues in that region to support such an alliance. Working through Conservative friends of Núñez, Posada informed party members in Bolívar that "the Conservative party was resolved to support Núñez, while demanding no more of him than loyalty to the institutions when he is president."[75]

Resistance within party ranks to the trend toward alliance with the Independents developed quickly. In addition to a general reluctance to aid candidates with Liberal backgrounds, many Conservatives were particularly wary about Núñez because of his alleged betrayal of the Conservative insurrection in 1876. Some party leaders countered the trend toward Núñez by advocating other Independents as presidential candidates. Carlos Martínez Silva favored Salvador Camacho Roldán, while Manuel Briceño and José María Quijano Otero suggested Sergio Camargo.[76]

The principal leaders in the struggle to unite the Conservative party behind Núñez were Holguín, Cuervo, Alejandro Posada, and José María Samper. To achieve this goal Holguín and Cuervo summoned a national party convention to Bogotá for April 1879. In a joint message to the convention they argued eloquently on behalf of an understanding with the Independents, citing the favorable treatment the party had received from Governors Núñez, Wilches, and Otálora: "In our present situation, without any friendly government, without our own resources, without any base of operations, without guaranties or political rights, in a struggle with enemies who have no moral or legal restraint, we do not see how we can escape from such a sad condition except in the shadow of our own enemies. Call it what you will, whether in peace or in war, whether it be today or tomorrow, we must arrive at an understanding with one of the Liberal factions; there is no

74. *El Deber* (Bogotá), October 15, December 24, 1878; see also *La Rejeneración* (Cartagena), November 26, 1878, and *El Guardian* (Medellín), November 2, 1878.

75. Alejandro Posada to Holguín and Cuervo, September 28, 1878, MS. #30, BLAA.

76. *El Deber* (Bogotá), September 16, 19, December 9, 1879.

other way out."[77] After heated debate the convention resolved that the party should abstain from the 1879 elections, but it conferred broad powers on the party directors to alter course as the campaign progressed. Within a few weeks the directors exercised their option by endorsing Núñez and urging Conservatives to support Independents in states where abstention would likely result in Radical victory.[78] The only major dissent from this decision came from Manuel Briceño, party director in Cundinamarca and editor of the party organ in that state, El Bien Social. The national leadership moved swiftly to isolate Briceño by prohibiting Conservatives from subscribing to El Bien Social, serving as its agents, or entering into dialogues with it. Briceño shortly thereafter resigned from his position. The Conservatives had thus finally achieved unity during peacetime. Even their most doctrinaire spokesman, Miguel Antonio Caro, endorsed the party's pragmatic approach to the elections. In the September voting Conservatives supported Núñez in seven states and abstained only in Tolima and Antioquia.[79]

Núñez handily won election as president. His victory stemmed in part from the decision of Conservatives to aid the Independents, a decision based on political expediency rather than doctrinal affinity. The Conservatives were attracted by the Independent governors' record of benevolent treatment of the vanquished in the postwar period. Public commitment by the Independents finally to resolve the church-state problem also offered a compelling argument for Conservative backing in the elections. Public acknowledgment by Núñez that Antioquia justly aspired to preserve its regional identity through Conservative rule nourished the hope that the despised Radical regime would be replaced if Núñez became president.

The visible distintegration of Radicalism in the postwar period also contributed to Independent victory. Operating from a political

77. Holguín and Cuervo to Conservative convention, April 15, 1879, MS. #30, BLAA.

78. El Deber (Bogotá), May 2, September 5, 1879; La Nueva Era (Medellín), June 28, 1879; Carlos Martínez Silva, Revistas políticas publicadas en 'El Repertorio Colombiano' (2 vols.; Bogotá, 1934), I (June 30, 1879), 118.

79. El Deber (Bogotá), September 9, October 7, December 9, 1879; La Opinión (Bogotá), September 27, 1879; La Caridad (Bogotá), September 12, 1879; La Justicia (Bogotá), November 13, 1879.

base in the eastern mountain region, the Radicals during the 1867–
1877 period extended their control to most of the country and strengthened their grip on the national government. They greatly increased the
political and economic power of the national government and tended
to rule for the benefit of their own region. As the primary architects of
the educational reform program of 1870–1876, the Radicals promoted
a system of public, secular education which centralized control in
Bogotá for policy formation and execution. Though well received in
the eastern mountain region, the reform program was odious to the
Conservatives of Antioquia and Tolima. The Radical public works program also focused power in Bogotá and worked for the principal benefit of the eastern mountain region. In essence it consisted of promoting
costly interstate railroad construction in order to facilitate the export
trade. The north coast states felt particularly slighted in the distribution of public works funds, and their political leaders accused the
Radicals of deliberate regional discrimination. Flagrant armed inter-
ventions by the national government in the north coast states in 1875
and in Cauca in 1876 further advanced the centralization of political
power and heightened grievances against Radical rule. Elimination of
the Conservative political base in Antioquia and Tolima and the installation of Radical regimes there following the 1876–1877 war climaxed this centralizing trend. From this military victory by the Radicals came their political collapse. The strong Conservative challenge of
1876 forced them to open the ranks of power to the Independents,
who, after the war, employed their newly acquired prestige for political gain. War and the economic problems of the postwar years halted
progress on the costly public works program upon which the Radicals
had mortgaged their political future.

By 1880 the transfer of power from Radicals to Independents was
accomplished. It had begun with the election of Trujillo to the presidency, but it was carried forward at the state level while Radicals and
Independents jockeyed for minor political advantage in Bogotá. The
easy victory of Núñez in his 1879 contest with Rengifo was an anti-
climax, a nearly certain consequence of trends set in motion by war
and its conclusion in 1877. Núñez would enter office with the support
of a corps of loyal colleagues who had followed his lead in establishing
a solid political base in the states. The future course of the Independent

party, however, remained unclear. It was uncertain whether Núñez would extend the experiment with state sovereignty or resume the trend toward centralism, whether he would govern in favor of the north coast region or strengthen the forces of nationalism, whether he would work to reunite Liberalism or move the Independents toward a closer alliance with the Conservatives.

Chapter VI

Nationalism and the First Núñez Administration, 1880–1882

Rafael Núñez wrought a profound change in Colombian history after his election as president for the two-year term beginning in 1880. More than any other nineteenth-century Colombian, he transformed Colombia from a loosely bound association of regions into a nation-state. Yet he exhibited neither a charismatic presence nor oratorical skills. He was a man of simple tastes displaying an unseemly casualness in his dress and appearance. Núñez possessed no substantial wealth, ill-health often plagued him, and he was further disadvantaged by his regional origins. He overcame his liabilities through well-developed political skills and an acute sense of timing to become the only costeño ever elected to the Colombian presidency. His early reputation as a noteworthy poet, his travels and residence in the United States and Europe, and his prolific writings on a variety of topics established Núñez as a man of knowledge and intellect. An analytical mind and a broad vision elevated him above his contemporaries—after the death of Manuel Murillo in 1880, no Colombian political figure matched Núñez in his ability to attract followers—and enabled him to formulate a coherent program directed toward resolving his nation's grave political and economic problems.

During his first administration, 1880–1882, Núñez established the outlines of the Regeneration. This movement, in essence, employed a variety of devices to strengthen the power of the national government. A tendency toward enhanced national authority had slowly gathered support and momentum during the decade of Radical rule, 1868–1878, but suffered an apparent check immediately following the 1876–1877 war, when political initiative shifted to the states. During the post-war years a number of talented governors, identified with the new Independent party and closely associated with Núñez, gained control of the state governments. By 1880 they were in firm political control of Colombia.

The Independent governors sponsored ambitious programs aimed at meeting the serious economic problems of the period. State resources, however, proved inadequate to carry out these programs. The growing demand for federal subsidies together with an abnormally high incidence of political violence in 1879 caused the Independent governors to look to Bogotá for economic relief and political support. As president, Núñez took advantage of this need for federal sustenance to resume at quickened pace the march toward centralized government. One of the most serious challenges to this centralizing trend came from Solón Wilches, Independent governor of Santander.

Núñez inherited a deepening economic crisis. Complaints about Colombia's economic condition had been chronic since independence, but by 1880 a new sense of urgency, of desperation, appeared in the traditional prognostications of impending collapse. An 1879 report to the Senate signed by three members of the Public Works Committee contained the following observations: "It is certain that the country is going through an afflictive economic situation; money is scarce because of the lack of exports with which to pay for our imports; transactions and enterprises are being damaged from paralysis, and, in conclusion, the national treasury and those of the states are seriously threatened by deficits." Early the following year Carlos Martínez Silva, the Conservative publicist, felt compelled to comment: "The peace that the republic currently enjoys is not nor can it be of major benefit, because it is not the result of health but rather of prostration and of annihilation. Nobody feels calm and secure; business is paralyzed; capital is hidden due to fear; there exists a general malaise." One of Colombia's most competent economic observers, Salvador Camacho Roldán, reported in 1881: "Correspondence from all parts of the republic and from abroad reports one of the most afflictive situations concerning economic activity that has been seen in this country during the last forty years."[1] Most observers of the Colombian economy

1. "Senado 1879; Antecedentes de Leyes," Vol. II, pp. 184–90, AC; Martínez

focused their attention on three specific problems: growing budget deficits, an imbalance in foreign trade, and the flight of gold from the country.

Alarming deficits in the federal budget provided the most conspicuous evidence of a troubled economy. Between 1875 and 1880 federal income increased only about 23 percent, whereas expenditures increased 89 percent.[2] Aside from the war-related expenses of 1876 and 1877, the principal cause of the rapid growth in expenditures was the appropriation of federal funds for public works construction in the states. These subsidies accounted for 34 percent of the authorized federal expenditures in 1880 as opposed to 24 percent five years earlier.[3] Because increased public works subsidies were a major cause of the deficits, reduction of the subsidies seemed the most logical method for restoring a balanced budget. Such a solution appeared politically impossible in 1880 in view of the decision by Independents in 1879 to allocate one-third of the federal budget to public works projects. Núñez thus faced a situation in which his party's dominant position in the states would be jeopardized if he attacked the deficit problem by cutting into public works appropriations. Major increases in federal revenue offered an alternate solution, but prospects for this remedy were equally discouraging. Between the mid-1860s and 1880 the per capita tax cost of federal and state government had risen sharply. The population increased by no more than 20 or 25 percent during this period, whereas total federal and state revenue rose about 130 percent.[4] Secretary of Hacienda Luis Carlos Rico reported in 1879: "In the crisis which oppresses the commerce and industry of the country it would be reckless to think of new large taxes in order to balance the budget;

Silva, *Revistas políticas*, I (February 12, 1880), 155; *La Unión* (Bogotá), September 6, 1881, reprinted in Salvador Camacho Roldán, *Escritos varios* (3 vols.; Bogotá, 1892–95), I, 665.

2. Calculated from Table 7.

3. See Table 8.

4. The last census in the nineteenth century was taken in 1870, and between 1851 and 1870 the population increased 31 percent. See Gómez, "Los censos en Colombia," in Urrutia and Arrubla (eds.), *Compendio de estadísticas*, Table 13, p. 30. Federal and state incomes for 1865/66 were obtained from Table 6; for 1880, federal income was obtained from Table 9, and state income, which totaled $3,274,000, was computed from the budgets published in the official newspapers of the states.

Table 7

Federal Income and Expenditures by Fiscal Year, 1875–1885, Based on Annual Budgets

Fiscal Year	Income	Expenditures	Deficits
1875	$4,003,728	$4,576,102	$ 572,374
1876	4,241,000	5,306,530	1,065,530
1877	4,337,800	6,643,327	2,305,527
1878	4,328,800	6,812,788	2,483,988
1879	4,938,800	5,574,583	635,783
1880	4,910,000	8,634,571	3,724,571
1881	4,787,000	10,328,638	5,541,638
1882	5,313,000	8,548,105	3,235,105
1883	5,917,000	11,352,618	5,435,618
1884	6,244,000	6,744,000	500,000
1885	6,182,921	6,344,398	161,477

SOURCES: Leyes de Colombia, 1863–75, 1102–1103, 1198. Budget figures for the 1877/ 85 period were obtained from the annual publication Leyes de Colombia, on the indicated pages of each year's volume: 1876, 112–113; 1877, 73–74; 1878, 115; 1879, 87; 1880, 221–22; 1881, 162–63; 1882, 165–66; 1883, 78–79; 1884, 121–22.

you cannot take blood from an emaciated body except at the risk of killing it."[5]

A growing imbalance in the nation's foreign trade caused more concern among informed Colombians than did budgetary deficits. Although official trade statistics showed a favorable balance of trade for every year during the 1875–1885 decade, knowledgeable Colombians knew that the value of imports was greatly understated in relation to exports.[6] Federal income heavily depended on import duties, which provided nearly two-thirds of total revenue collected during the 1870s. In 1874–1875 the high import level of the previous decade shifted downward by nearly half and remained at a low level for the next several decades.[7] Despite the import decline, customs revenue was main-

5. Memoria de Hacienda, 1879, 4.

6. McGreevey, An Economic History, 115–16; Miguel Samper, "La protección," Escritos político-económicos (4 vols.; Bogotá, 1925–27), I, 212.

7. See Table 9. McGreevey, An Economic History, 99, 114–15. There appears to

Table 8

Proportion of Federal Expenditures Authorized for Public Works by Fiscal Year, 1875–1885

Fiscal Year	(A) Total Expenditures	(B) Authorized Expenditures for Public Works	(B) as a Percentage of (A)
1875	$4,576,102	$1,018,253	24%
1876	5,306,530	1,645,500	31%
1877	6,643,327	2,135,900	32%
1878	6,812,788	1,675,200	25%
1879	5,574,583	1,014,600	18%
1880	8,634,571	2,958,200	34%
1881	10,328,638	4,170,200	40%
1882	8,548,105	1,357,120	16%
1883	11,352,618	2,525,334	22%
1884	6,744,000	875,000	13%
1885	6,344,398	1,295,976	20%

SOURCES: Federal expenditures and authorized appropriations for public works were obtained from the annual budgets. The figures for public works represent appropriations for *fomento* and *obras públicas*. See sources for Table 7.

tained at a fairly stable level from 1876 to 1884 by means of upward tariff revision in 1873, a 25 percent surcharge in 1874, and a moderate move toward protection in 1880. The trade imbalance of 1863–1874 persisted even after the sharp import decline, but in the following decade it resulted from a declining export level. By 1884 Colombian exports were at their lowest level of the previous two decades.[8] Indeed, Colombia's export problem continued until the closing years of the century when coffee began to dominate the export sector.

---

be no clear reason for this rapid downward shift, but McGreevey suggests that credit restrictions on Colombian merchants were a principal cause.

8. McGreevey, *An Economic History*, 99. A possible exception was 1867, when commodity exports, *i.e.*, not counting gold, exceeded those of 1884; but total exports were less than for 1884.

Table 9

Proportion of Federal Income Provided by Customs Revenue for Fiscal Years 1875–1885

Fiscal Year	Total Income	Customs Revenue	% of Total Income Provided by Customs
1875	$4,003,728	$2,800,000	70%
1876	4,241,000	3,000,000	71%
1877	4,337,800	3,000,000	69%
1878	4,328,800	3,000,000	69%
1879	4,938,800	3,000,000	61%
1880	4,910,000	3,000,000	61%
1881	4,787,000	3,000,000	63%
1882	5,313,000	3,500,000	66%
1883	5,917,000	4,000,000	68%
1884	6,244,000	3,800,000	61%
1885	6,182,921	4,000,000	65%

SOURCES: Federal income and customs revenue figures were obtained from the annual budgets. See sources for Table 7.

A major symptom of the export crisis was the apparent drain of gold from the country. The proportion of total export value represented by coined and uncoined gold tended to increase as the more traditional export commodities became less able to meet the cost of imports. Although the percentage of gold in the total export figure fluctuated considerably from year to year, an upward trend prevailed during the decade beginning in 1875. Gold represented about 10 percent of total exports in 1875 and 21 percent in 1884. The trend caused alarm even though it resulted primarily from a decline in total export value while the value of gold exports changed but slightly. The alarm seems even less well founded in view of the upward trend in annual gold production from the early 1860s to 1885. Because of frequent complaints of the lack of specie, it appears likely that less bullion was being coined or that a growing proportion of gold exports consisted of coinage. In the Hacienda report of 1879 Luis Carlos Rico concluded:

FIGURE 1

GOLD EXPORTS AS A PERCENTAGE OF TOTAL EXPORTS, 1872–1885

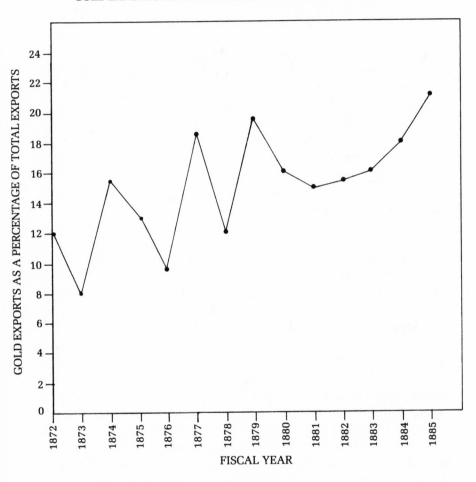

SOURCE: McGreevey, *An Economic History*; calculated from Table 12, p. 99.

"The export of gold and silver is alarming and if it continues in the same proportion as in the last fiscal period . . . it will cause grave difficulties for industry, commerce, and government."[9]

On the eve of Núñez' inauguration there was abundant cause for grave concern over Colombia's economic future. An increasing flow of federal funds to the states was seriously adding to the deficit problem. The import level, though low in relation to the level of the early 1870s, remained too high to be long sustained by commodity exports. Lack of reliable export items, a serious trade imbalance, an apparent gold drain, and imperative commitments to the states posed major economic problems whose solution signaled the end of the Liberal free trade era. Responsibility for formulating a new economic program rested with Núñez.

Núñez' reticence on the specifics of his economic program during the months preceding his April inauguration aroused considerable interest in his inaugural address. Interest was also heightened by his assurance that the speech would contain the essence of his program. In addition, it seemed likely that Núñez would depart from existing free-trade economic policies because of his known conviction that those policies were leading to disaster. In February he urged former president Aquileo Parra to cooperate with his administration, because "the country is sick, and a weak policy would just about prostrate it."[10]

In his inaugural speech Núñez presented the following somber picture of the Colombian economy: "Our agriculture is barely in its infancy. Our crafts remain stationary. Our vast territorial expanse counts only a few kilometers of railroads. Statistical tables reveal the disheartening fact that for several years we have not exported enough to pay for what we import. This economic imbalance, if it continues, will even give rise to the alarming conjecture that the Colombian people consume more than they produce. And in any case it is evident that the labor of the nation is in decay. The formidable calamity of public poverty is thus approaching our threshold." Núñez then proceeded to out-

---

9.   See Figure 1; Restrepo, *Estudio sobre minas*, 199; *Memoria de Hacienda, 1880*, 57; *Memoria de Hacienda, 1879*, 112.

10.   Núñez to Parra, March 30, 1880, CdeHRP; Núñez to Parra, February 6, 1880, as quoted in Parra to Fortunato Bernal, José M. Villamizar G., and Daniel Hernández, March 10, 1880, CdeHRP.

line the basic elements of his economic program. To promote national industry he proposed a system of protective tariffs. He announced plans to seek a foreign loan for use in establishing a national bank, which was expected to expand credit facilities and thereby stimulate economic activity. Public works projects deemed of primary importance by Núñez were the improvement of transportation between the interior and the north coast, continuation of work on current railroad projects, and improvement of Atlantic coast port facilities.[11]

Núñez' proposal for a shift to protectionism stemmed from his conviction that free trade had not only failed to benefit the export sector of the economy but that it had significantly delayed the process of national development. In his view Colombia had become impoverished because of submission to the forces of international trade. Colombia had too willingly accepted the natural-role thesis for participation in the international market. He sought to regain a measure of control over the nation's economic development by loosening the ties binding the country to external economic forces. In a series of articles written subsequent to the tariff debate, Núñez attributed the nation's economic plight to "excessive reliance on the action and foresight of commercial interests." In an article of early 1882 he observed: "It is evident that our population has grown more than our wealth, and this is proven by the fact of the incessant scarcity of all articles of subsistence. . . . What new industry has been created in the last twenty years? Indigo was a great failure. The exploitation of quinine forests is in alarming decay."[12] Núñez thus recognized the need to abandon Colombia's traditional economic role of concentrating on nontechnical, labor-intensive lines of production. He called for a program of import substitution, arguing that adherence to a free-trade program had led to dependence on foreign sources for the most simple commodities. "We do not have a paper factory; we do not have sawmills except for a few very small ones. We must thus import everything: bottles, cardboard and wooden boxes, nails, boards, etc., and even many foods of prime necessity." An additional argument in favor of protection was offered

11. *La Luz* (Bogotá), May 17, 1881, reprinted in Núñez, *La reforma*, Vol. I, Pt. 1, pp. 20–21.
12. *El Porvenir* (Cartagena), December 31, 1882, *La Luz* (Bogotá), January 10, 1882, reprinted in Núñez, *La reforma*, Vol. I, Pt. 1, pp. 306, 101.

in a report to the House of Representatives by Ricardo Núñez, the president's brother and co-author of the 1880 tariff law. He noted that a curb on imports could reduce the troublesome outflow of gold.[13] Through a policy of protectionism President Núñez thus sought to reduce dependence on foreign commodities, encourage native industry, and lay the basis for a modernization program.

A highly controversial argument offered by Núñez in support of protectionism was his assertion that it would promote social stability by strengthening the middle-level artisan groups. "Is it suitable or not that a union of artisans exists to serve as a mediating force between the social element which directs and governs and the illiterate mass which forms the base of the pyramid? This is the question in one of its principal aspects."[14] Núñez thus allied himself with the Bogotá artisans who had so ominously flexed their political muscle against the Radical-dominated Congress in mid-1879. Opponents of protection quickly drew the parallel between Núñez and the dictator General José María Melo, who seized power in 1854 in the aftermath of a series of artisan-led disorders in Bogotá.

Because the Independents held an overwhelming majority of seats in the 1880 Congress, Núñez had little difficulty in obtaining passage of the protective tariff measure. The major provision of the new law granted the president power to raise duties in the highest tariff category by 25 percent. Such an increase was mandatory for clothing, footwear, saddlery, and wooden furniture. The law also lowered the duty on some raw materials and increased it on other goods for revenue rather than protective purposes. The 1880 tariff was thus only moderately and selectively protective and was designed to encourage artisan crafts. A more sweeping reform would have worsened the always troublesome contraband problem and seriously reduced customs revenue. Because of the government's fiscal dependence on import duties, the 1880 tariff law sought to restore balance between imports and exports rather than to move away from foreign trade.[15]

13. El Porvenir (Cartagena), December 31, 1882, reprinted in Núñez, La reforma, Vol. I, Pt. 1, p. 304; El Promotor (Barranquilla), May 15, 1880.

14. El Porvenir (Cartagena), April 1, 1883, reprinted in Núñez, La reforma, Vol. I, Pt. 1, p. 390; see also El Promotor (Barranquilla), August 12, 1882.

15. Leyes de Colombia, 1880, 51–56; Bushnell, "Two Stages in Colombian Tariff Policy," 15–16; Ospina Vásquez, Industria y protección, 292.

Political opposition to the protective tariff gave the measure more significance than did its immediate economic results, which were slight. Most Conservative spokesmen criticized the tariff while the Radicals bitterly opposed it. José María Samper, former Liberal firebrand but now a Conservative leader eager to align his party with the Independents, supported the tariff; but Carlos Martínez Silva, more accurately reflecting mainstream Conservative sentiment, asserted that the tariff imposed an onerous tax on consumers and revived "the social question, full of threats and dangers of all kinds. . . . Why would one wish to return to the scenes of 1853, by now completely forgotten?" The free-trade stance in the early 1880s of Conservative leaders of the stature of Martínez Silva and Carlos Holguín and of major Conservative organs such as *El Deber* and *El Conservador* forcefully remind one that support for free trade from mid-century onward had been essentially bipartisan.[16]

Radical opposition stemmed largely from the conviction that Núñez had committed an act of political betrayal, that he had betrayed Colombian Liberalism on a matter of doctrine. After all, Núñez had been co-author of the 1861 free-trade law. Miguel Samper, who shared authorship of that landmark law with Núñez, remained loyal to laissez faire economics, and he led the attack against protectionism. He agreed with Núñez that the country "does not produce as much as it consumes," but he offered a moral rather than an economic solution: "Reestablishing the equilibrium between appetites and the means for satisfying them is, in all likelihood, a more urgent matter than reestablishing it between what we buy and what we sell abroad." The Radicals were even more alarmed than the Conservatives about the implications of Núñez' overtures to the unruly Bogotá artisans, recalling, no doubt, the artisans' role in provoking the fatal split in the Liberal party in the early 1850s.[17]

A nationalistic spirit underlay Núñez' program of protectionism.

16. Martínez Silva, *Revistas políticas*, I (April 30, 1880), 187–88; for Samper's position see *El Deber* (Bogotá), May 4, 1880. For Holguín's views see *El Deber* (Bogotá), May 11, 1980. See also *El Conservador* (Bogotá), September 5, 1882, and Ospina Vásquez, *Industria y protección*, 293.

17. Samper, "La protección," *Escritos*, I, 212–13; Helen Delpar, "The Liberal Party of Colombia, 1863–1903 (Ph.D. dissertation, Columbia University, 1967), 264; *Diario de Cundinamarca* (Bogotá), May 12, 1880; *El Promotor* (Barranquilla), May 29, 1880.

He endeavored to assert a degree of control over the nation's economic development rather than continue to allow haphazard international economic forces to shape Colombia's future. Furthermore, emphasis on free trade had weakened national unity and magnified regionalist sentiment, a linkage which is obvious today but which Núñez appears to have but dimly perceived. He did note, however, that preferential treatment of foreign trade and neglect of internal trade had produced a "permanent and universal anemia" and that internal railroad construction offered the only means of overcoming a "harsh topography which divides and confines us to small population clusters." [18] The decision to orient the nation's transportation system to the exterior had derived from dedication to export production as well as from the greater feasibility of an externally directed system as compared with an internal network. Interstate economic ties were thus sacrificed to the improvement of trade routes linking each state to its external market. Development of native industry and emphasis on production for the domestic market offered the possibility of reducing this external orientation and strengthening the economic bonds of national unity. Radicals from the interior, nevertheless, attacked the tariff law as a regionalist measure designed to promote the economic interests of the north coast. Observed the *Diario de Cundinamarca:* "Three-fourths of the import tax weighs on the states of the interior, [which are] equal to the coastal states in political rights but incredibly unequal in obligations and burdens of all kinds." Regional discrimination became a recurring theme in the Radical attacks against Núñez throughout his first administration. At one point he sharply complained: "There is not an appointment, there is not an election which falls on citizens of the coast which does not give rise to bitter criticism from those apostles of national schism." [19]

The second major element of Núñez' economic program consisted of establishing a national bank with money obtained from a large foreign loan. Operating as an agent of government, the bank could provide

18. *El Porvenir* (Cartagena), December 31, 1882, reprinted in Núñez, *La reforma,* Vol. I, Pt. 1, pp. 305–306.

19. *Diario de Cundinamarca* (Bogotá), June 29, 1880; see also *La Defensa* (Bogotá), November 18, 1880. *La Luz* (Bogotá), November 15, 1881, reprinted in Núñez, *La reforma,* Vol. I, Pt. 1, p. 82.

the credit so desperately needed by a deficit-ridden national treasury. In an article written in 1882, Núñez characterized the problem faced by his administration as follows: "The dilemma, thus, was this: exploiting *the recourse to credit or retiring the national administration.*"[20] Núñez also intended to use the national bank to establish a measure of control over interest rates, credit, and the issuance of bank notes. Colombia's experience with banks had been limited to private institutions, the first of which appeared on the national scene in 1871. By 1881 forty-two private banks existed in the country. In accord with the principles of laissez faire economics, little regulation was imposed on the banks' note-issuing privileges, and note issuance became increasingly important in the late 1870s because of the scarcity of specie. There was general dissatisfaction, however, with the services provided by the private banks, which in many cases were family businesses devoted to financing real estate transactions, import purchases, and merchant inventories.[21]

Obtaining a foreign loan was the most difficult aspect of the problem facing Núñez in his effort to establish a national bank. Congress in 1879 had granted authority to contract a $3 million loan, and Núñez received authorization from the 1880 Congress to use up to $2 million of that money to organize the bank.[22] Since the mid-1870s, Colombian governments with similar loan contracting authority had tried and failed to obtain large foreign loans for public works programs. Their failure resulted from a growing European preference for investment in Asia and Africa and from Colombia's poor credit standing in foreign money markets which stemmed from irregular servicing of the existing foreign debt.

The outcome of the loan negotiations which were conducted during the last months of 1880 had major political as well as economic consequences. One supporter of Núñez noted in a letter to General

20. *La Luz* (Bogotá), May 12, 1882, reprinted in Núñez, *La reforma*, Vol. I, Pt. 1, p. 164.
21. Camacho Roldán, *Escritos varios*, II, 338–39n; Guillermo Torres García, *Historia de la moneda en Colombia* (Bogotá, 1945), 112–13; McGreevey, *An Economic History*, 163; *Diario de Cundinamarca* (Bogotá), February 20, 1878; Robert Triffin, *Money and Banking in Colombia* (Washington, D.C., 1944), 7.
22. *Leyes de Colombia, 1879*, 72–75; *Leyes de Colombia, 1880*, 46–51.

Julián Trujillo: "If Doctor Núñez does not obtain the loan, the Independent party is going to dissolve, sad as it is to say, or at least many will switch over to Radicalism." The Radicals were keenly aware of the political import of the loan, and according to Núñez some of them made a futile attempt to sabotage the negotiations. In December 1880, the Núñez government obtained a $3 million loan in New York through an arrangement whereby the bulk of the annual lease income from the Panama Railroad Company would be assigned to the creditors until the year 1908. Upon receiving early word that the negotiations had succeeded, Aquileo Parra wrote: "If Núñez has obtained the loan [he will be an] energetic and intransigent regenerator."[23]

The National Bank opened for business in January 1881. Public subscription of shares was authorized by the 1880 bank law, but none were sold because of a boycott by holders of private bank stock. The National Bank therefore had a strictly governmental character, and the president appointed its board of governors, making it an agent of the executive branch of government. Private banking interests felt most threatened by the National Bank's authority to issue notes for circulation. The 1880 bank law stated: "The emission of notes payable to the bearer is an exclusive right of the National Bank." But private banks could continue to issue notes, provided they accepted National Bank notes as currency. The National Bank issued notes in limited quantities, and they remained convertible at par until 1885, when the war of 1884–1885 forced the government to resort to large-scale emissions.[24] Another provision of the bank law which aimed at easing the specie shortage was the authorization to mint small-denomination nickel coins. About this provision Núñez wrote: "If that money had not appeared, it would be totally impossible to meet the many expenses demanded by the economic situation of the country, the penury of the regions, and the many calamities which jointly afflict us."[25]

23. Julio Estevez B. to Trujillo, October 26, 1880, Trujillo collection, Vol. X, AN; La Luz (Bogotá), May 12, 1882, reprinted in Núñez, La reforma, Vol. I, Pt. 1, pp. 164–65; Parra to Luis [Bernal], December 5, 1880, Parra collection, Box #1, ACdeH.

24. Leyes de Colombia, 1880, 48; Triffin, Money and Banking, 3; for a discussion of the bank and its functions see Torres García, Historia de la moneda, 113–16.

25. La Luz (Bogotá), September 20, 1881, reprinted in Núñez, La reforma, Vol. I, Pt. 1, p. 67; for a Radical view see Camacho Roldán, Escritos varios, III, 734–38.

As in the case of protectionism, Radical opposition to the National Bank focused on the issue of economic doctrine. The principal spokesmen for the Radicals were Miguel Samper and Salvador Camacho Roldán. Both men were, within the Colombian context, eminent economic thinkers and articulate defenders of laissez faire economics, and their private economic interests were tied to the import-export trade and to private banking circles in Bogotá. Both men had supported Núñez since 1875, and both abandoned him when he abandoned laissez faire economics.[26] In a series of articles appearing in the Bogotá press in mid-1880, Samper asserted that the private banks satisfied the country's credit needs, that an official government bank would lead to monopoly control over credit, and that the authority to issue official bank notes would eventually lead to a flood of worthless paper currency.[27] Samper exalted the spirit of private initiative and argued: "The industrial genius of the Colombian . . . waits only for the politicians to leave him a free field to transform, in a few years, a ruined Colombia into a powerful and rich republic."[28]

Radicals correctly saw the creation of the National Bank as a giant step away from laissez faire economics. The principal thrust of the 1880 bank law was to increase the ability of government to direct the economic life of Colombia. In addition to issuing bank notes and regulating interest rates, the National Bank served as the fiscal agent and bank of deposit for the government. Operating under the authority of the bank law, Núñez hoped to employ the enhanced power of government to stimulate economic activity by making more credit available to the private sector and by lessening the specie shortage. He also looked to the bank to ease the operations of government through the provision of readily available credit.

Enactment of a seriously unbalanced federal budget in 1880 became, for Núñez, another means for enlarging the economic power of national government. The budget for fiscal year 1880/1881 authorized expenditures that were more than twice as high as anticipated income.

26. Samper, "Banco nacional," *Escritos*, III, 24–25; Liévano Aguirre, *Rafael Núñez*, 175–76.

27. Samper, "Banco nacional," *Escritos*, III, 11–96.

28. *Ibid.*, 28; for Camacho Roldán's position see Liévano Aguirre, *Rafael Núñez*, 175–76.

In absolute terms the deficit had never been larger. Instead of following the tradition of speaking reverently of the sound economic principle of the balanced budget while proceeding to unbalance it, Núñez endorsed deficit spending as an unavoidable necessity: "In order to make that [desperate fiscal] situation bearable, empiricism would have advised two known means: reduction of expenses, increase in taxes. The government did precisely the contrary; it increased expenses and reduced taxes."[29]

Aside from the obvious political importance of maintaining a steady flow of federal funds to the states, Núñez saw the deficit as a device for cultivating support for strong, stable government. The 1880 deficit required heavy internal as well as external borrowing; by regular, prompt servicing of the internal debt, political support from appreciative bondholders could, in all probability, be secured. In an article written in mid-1882 in opposition to proposed tax increases, Núñez wrote: "The internal debt . . . cultivated with care and serviced with regularity, is one of the great means for giving stability to governments—by virtue of the bond, established for the conservation of peace, between the public entity and the interests tied to its tranquil and normal existence."[30]

Appropriation of vast sums for public works projects in the states was a primary cause of the 1880 deficit. Congress designated an incredibly large proportion of the budget, about 40 percent, for public works.[31] The decision to stress public works in the 1880 budget represented a continuation of the previous year's policy whereby the Independents allocated sums to favored state projects for the purpose of securing political control over the states. Most of the outlay for public works in 1880 went to projects that had been initiated during the postwar period, such as the Samacá ironworks, Dique Canal, and Cauca Railroad. The only major new project authorized in 1880 was the Western Railroad, a route destined to link Bogotá with Girardot, a port on the upper Magdalena River. This railroad had been under discussion for years as an alternative to the interstate Northern Railroad, but Con-

29. For deficits in the 1875–1885 period see Table 7. *La Luz* (Bogotá), August 19, 1881, reprinted in Núñez, *La reforma*, Vol. I, Pt. 1, p. 50.
30. *La Luz* (Bogotá), July 21, 1882.
31. See Table 8.

gress did not provide funds for the Western Railroad, a purely Cundi-namarcan route, until mid- 1880, a few months after the Independents gained control of the Cundinamarcan government.[32]

Núñez implemented an additional measure signaling his unortho-dox economic views when, by executive decree, he substantially low-ered the price of salt produced in the government-owned salt works. Income to the government from the salt monopoly ranked second only to that from import duties. Salt prices usually fluctuated widely, be-cause the government relied on the monopoly as a source of revenue for emergency purposes during periods of war or financial crisis. At such times the official price of salt reached exorbitant levels.[33] The price re-duction on salt, an article of prime necessity, enabled Núñez to take credit for easing the tax burden on the average Colombian consumer.

With such measures as the salt price reduction in mind, Núñez of-fered the following justification for his fiscal program in an article written in 1881: "The fiscal policy of the present administration has been based, then, in substance on practices of the civilized world. It has sought resolutely to escape the vicious circle of tax increases, which temporarily alleviate the anguish, to make it much more grave a little later; there has been no slow-down toward the goal of promoting the development of communication routes, notwithstanding the afflic-tions of the national treasury, because it is very well understood that on that development depends the solid and increasing prosperity of the republic."[34]

Núñez' economic program was bold, innovative, and imbued with a spirit of nationalism. His decision to combine defined evils into a coordinated program for good was dictated, in part, by a basic desire to survive politically during a period of economic distress. With little forewarning he directly attacked the well-entrenched principles of laissez faire economics. He sought to end Colombia's economic crisis through governmental action. To overcome economic stagnation Núñez directed the power of government toward a policy of inflation.[35] The

32. *Leyes de Colombia, 1880,* 119–20; *El Deber* (Bogotá), July 8, 1881.

33. *Diario Oficial* (Bogotá), April 15, 1880; *Memoria de Hacienda, 1910,* 36–37.

34. *La Luz* (Bogotá), August 19, 1881, reprinted in Núñez, *La reforma,* Vol. I, Pt. 1, p. 53.

35. Monetary inflation was adopted by Núñez essentially in response to fiscal ne-

specific measures designed to bring this about included deficit spending, an increase in bank note emissions, and nickel coinage. By lowering the salt price he eased the financial burden on consumers, and through protectionism he hoped to slow the gold drain. His policy of moderate protectionism was designed to stimulate national industry through import substitution and thus to achieve a degree of national self-sufficiency. Núñez expressed his goal as follows: "As we achieved political independence, we have to achieve economic independence."[36]

Núñez not only increased control of the economy through credit and currency mechanisms, but he also bolstered the administrative and political powers of the national government. Implementation in April 1880 of a new law which enlarged the cabinet from four to seven members, thus increasing the function and reach of government through greater specification and larger staffing, symbolized the shift toward a strengthened federal power. Núñez had personally advocated this measure since the convening of Congress in February, and the Independent majority dutifully responded to his wishes. The new president named one Conservative, Gregorio Obregón, and six Independents to the cabinet. The latter included such successful state leaders as José Eusebio Otálora from Boyacá and Eliseo Payán of Cauca as well as trusted colleagues such as Luis Carlos Rico and Justo Arosemena.[37]

Appointment of Arosemena as secretary of foreign affairs unexpectedly raised the question of constitutional reform. At the time of his appointment, Arosemena was serving as Colombian minister to the United States. In a rather amazing letter to Núñez, widely published in the Colombian press, Arosemena emphatically declined the cabinet appointment. He refused to participate at such a high level in any government operating under the burden of the 1863 constitution. In his attack on the constitution he charged that the institutions created by it "foment disturbances" and "demoralize, impoverish, and discredit

---

cessity, and although it may have been a major stimulus to the coffee industry, that was not its purpose. See Miguel Urrutia M., "El sector externo y la distribución de ingresos en Colombia en el siglo XIX," *Revista del Banco de la República*, No. 541 (November, 1972), 1983.

36. *La Luz* (Bogotá), October 18, 1881, reprinted in Núñez, *La reforma*, Vol. I, Pt. 1, p. 80.

37. *Diario Oficial* (Bogotá), April 13, 1880; *Leyes de Colombia, 1880*, 11–12; *Diario de Cundinamarca* (Bogotá), February 17, 1880.

our country, as its history of the last twenty years shows." Arosemena favored the strengthening of central government by amending the constitution, a method of reform made nearly impossible by the requirement that the states unanimously ratify proposed amendments. Despite several attempts to reform the constitution between 1863 and 1880, the only amendment adopted was that of 1876, which made the presidential election date uniform in all states.[38] Arosemena's criticisms of the constitution were particularly noteworthy, because he had assumed a major role in formulating that document during the Rionegro convention in 1863.

Arosemena's letter voiced at a high political level at a significant moment a desire for reform aimed at tipping the balance of power away from the sovereign states and toward the national government. "Organized anarchy" became a favorite phrase used by many commentators to emphasize the absurd extreme to which the doctrine of federalism had been carried since 1863. Most observers of the Colombian scene— Liberals, Conservatives, and foreign visitors—concurred with the judgment of *El Deber* that under the Constitution of 1863 "national unity does not exist in Colombia, except in name." The Argentine minister to Colombia concluded that the doctrine of state sovereignty was a basic error in Colombia's system of political organization, and that "Colombians must be persuaded of the necessity of giving strength and cohesion to national sentiment, of converting that sort of league, which one gust of wind can topple, into a compact human group with an ideal, with a concept identical to patriotism." Núñez, too, favored basic reform, but he was highly cognizant of the obstacles posed by the amending procedure. "A constitution which does not assure peace does not satisfy the most important of its natural purposes; and here we have an argument which has been made in requesting the reform of said code," observed Núñez.[39] But instead of futilely struggling for constitutional reform, Núñez opted for the established Radical practice of reinterpretation of key articles of the constitution by legislation.

38. *La Palestra* (Mompós), August 24, 1880; Pombo and Guerra (eds.), *Constituciones*, IV, 176–77.

39. *El Deber* (Bogotá), January 9, 1880; see also *Diario de Cundinamarca* (Bogotá), March 1, 1881. Miguel Cané, *Notas de viaje sobre Venezuela y Colombia* (Bogotá, 1907), 120; *La Luz* (Bogotá), August 2, 1881, reprinted in Núñez, *La reforma*, Vol. I, Pt. 1, p. 31.

Núñez achieved de facto constitutional reform through enactment of a law on public order. In 1867 Congress had passed a law on public order which required the national government to maintain absolute neutrality in the event of rebellion within a state. Shortly before the outbreak of civil war in 1876, Congress repealed the law in order to free the federal authorities from any legal restraints against military intervention in Cauca and Antioquia. The 1880 law on public order, passed by Congress at Núñez' request, declared that the national government "will prevent every attempt at invasion against any of [the states] as well as all internal violence against the government of any state, provided that in the latter case the intervention of the national government is requested by the state assembly, or, if it is in recess, by the executive power." Debate on the bill was heated, and opposition came principally from the Radicals, who regarded Núñez' interpretation of the public order authority in the constitution as a clear indication of his commitment to centralism. Now that they were out of power, the Radicals became more ardent in their defense of political and economic federalism. Felipe Pérez' paper, El Relator, quoted with mordant satisfaction from a Conservative paper of Antioquia which characterized the law as "a brusque attack on the autonomy of the states."[40] Except for the strongly federalist Antioqueño wing of the Conservative party, most Conservatives supported the law. Carlos Martínez Silva endorsed it by noting that "even though the national constitution does not permit the intervention of the general government in the internal struggles of the states, this precept of our absurd political organization has in fact now been reformed."[41]

The worst fears of the Radicals were realized within a few months of passage of the law on public order. In two specific instances Núñez used the law as the basis for an attempt at undermining state power and increasing federal power. He tried first to abolish the traditional rights of the states to import arms and munitions, and secondly he greatly increased the size of the national army.

40. Leyes de Colombia, 1880, 21; Senado de Plenipotenciarios de los Estados Unidos de Colombia, Debates del proyecto de lei sobre orden público (Bogotá, 1880), 1–252; El Relator (Bogotá), September 26, 1881. For another expression of Radical opposition see Diario de Cundinamarca (Bogotá), August 27, 1880.

41. Martínez Silva, Revistas políticas, I (April 30, 1880), 188. For another Conservative view see El Deber (Bogotá), April 30, 1880.

In August 1880 Antioquia gave formal notice to the national government that a shipment of 1,000 rifles purchased in the United States was expected at Barranquilla. The 1880 tariff law, which permitted the duty-free importation of arms and munitions, required that notification of such imports be given to the national government. To the amazement of Antioqueño authorities, Secretary of Hacienda Antonio Roldán replied: "During the operation of law 19 of 1880 on public order, the state governments of the union cannot import arms and munitions of war without permission from the federal executive power." Never before under the 1863 constitution had federal authorities attempted to deprive all the states of a right explicitly guaranteed even to individuals. In justification of this broad interpretation of the public order law, Roldán asserted that "the impotence of the states" impelled the federal power to assume responsibility for preserving the "legal regime."[42]

Opposition to this limitation on state authority was widespread, organized, and successful. Salvador Camacho Roldán privately expressed the widely held view that the secretary of hacienda's resolution "demonstrates the intention of destroying the federal system and returning to centralism." The governments of Antioquia, Santander, and Cundinamarca formally protested that the resolution was a gross infringement on state sovereignty.[43] Faced with mounting opposition, Núñez retreated. In February 1881 he revoked the resolution, noting that the law on public order "cannot in practice have the full extension which the executive power sought to give it in the resolution of the secretary of hacienda." A month later Núñez signed a new law which stated: "The government of the union recognizes that under the federal constitution the states have the right to buy, import, and possess arms and war materials."[44]

While yielding on the issue of state arms purchases, Núñez urged Congress to enable the government to fulfill its obligations under the public order law by authorizing a high troop level for the national

42. *Memoria de Hacienda, 1881*, document #LXXXVI, 122–24.
43. Camacho Roldán to Trujillo, October 13, 1880, Trujillo collection, Vol. X, AN; "Senado 1881; Antecedentes de Leyes," Vol. I, pp. 79–80, 94–97, AC; "Correspondencia de Antioquia y Cundinamarca," Vol. I, pp. 796–804, AN; *La Palestra* (Mompós), February 10, 1881; *La Bandera Federal* (Socorro), April 12, 1881.
44. *Memoria de Hacienda, 1882*, document #XII, 48–49; *Leyes de Colombia, 1881*, 18–19.

army and by increasing military appropriations. In arguing on behalf of a strengthened military force, he mentioned the problems of unsatisfactory relations with neighboring countries and Colombia's poor system of communications, but the focus of his attention was directed to the problem of guaranteeing political stability. Núñez had obtained a troop level authorization of 5,000 in 1880, but despite his request that the same level be maintained in 1881, Congress reduced it to 4,000.[45] This level, nevertheless, was remarkably high during peacetime when compared with the levels of the 1870s. Prior to the 1876–1877 war, the troop level authorization averaged 1,200 men and never exceeded 1,500; following the war it was set at 3,000. Congress responded more generously to Núñez' request for larger military appropriations in 1881. The following table shows the military's share of the annual budgets in the fiscal years 1880 to 1882:[46]

Year	(A) Total Budget	(B) Military's Share of the Budget	(B) as a Percentage of (A)
1880	$ 8,634,571	$ 982,432	11.4
1881	10,328,638	935,737	8.0
1882	8,548,105	2,087,403	24.4

Shortly after enactment of the troop level and military appropriations measures, Núñez offered the following rationale for a strengthened military force: "The increase of the army was a collateral measure of the law which placed the preservation of public order in all the national territory under the guaranty of the general government. If peace has been maintained everywhere, which is evident, the increased expenditure made on the army represents the best of possible savings for a country traditionally tormented by the calamity of civil war."[47]

Núñez' administration secured the most peaceful two-year period Colombia had experienced since promulgation of the 1863 Constitu-

45. Diario de Cundinamarca (Bogotá), February 16, 1881; Leyes de Colombia, 1880, 45–46; Leyes de Colombia, 1881, 96–97.

46. Leyes de Colombia, 1863–75, 1283; Leyes de Colombia, 1878, 42; Leyes de Colombia, 1879, 87; Leyes de Colombia, 1880, 222; Leyes de Colombia, 1881, 163.

47. La Luz (Bogotá), August 19, 1881, reprinted in Núñez, La reforma, Vol. I, Pt. 1, p. 51.

tion. The period witnessed neither general civil conflict nor minor state-based insurrections. The most obvious reason for such abnormal tranquillity was that the Independents controlled every state government except that of Tolima when Núñez was inaugurated.[48] To ensure continued Independent domination of the states, Núñez dispensed large sums for state public works projects during the first year in office. In the second year of his term he shifted funds to the military, which he regarded as a principal "element of order." By thus bolstering the political influence and power of national government, Núñez achieved the most important goal which he had set for his administration in his inaugural address, "preventing the subversion of order."[49]

Núñez' personal style as president also played a role in the movement toward a strengthened national government. As though to display his tireless activity on behalf of national interests, in September 1880 Núñez traveled to Panama to conduct negotiations with Costa Rican officials to resolve a boundary dispute. He did not return to Bogotá until December, and during his prolonged absence he made several political stops along his travel route. A year later he journeyed to Girardot to inspect construction work on the Western Railroad. Núñez also effectively used the press to focus attention on himself and the accomplishments of his government. In addition to enjoying the support of many Independent newspapers which flourished during his first term and which frequently published his articles, messages, and letters, he founded La Luz in 1881 to serve as a semiofficial advocate for his policies.[50]

Núñez made liberal use of his powers to provide positions for his political allies and to secure the loyalties of an army of bureaucrats. The opposition press repeatedly castigated him for excessively cater-

---

48. La Luz (Bogotá), January 3, 1882, reprinted in Núñez, La reforma, Vol. I, Pt. 1, p. 93. See Arboleda, Revoluciones, 1–60, and Jorge Isaacs, La revolución radical en Antioquia (Bogotá, 1880). The Radicals regained control of Antioquia in 1881 and held control until 1885.

49. La Luz (Bogotá), August 19, May 17, 1881, reprinted in Núñez, La reforma, Vol. I, Pt. 1, pp. 51, 21.

50. El Promotor (Barranquilla), September 18, November 6, December 4, 1880, October 8, 1881; Diario de Cundinamarca (Bogotá), September 14, 1880. Other pro-Núñez papers of 1880–1881 included La Reforma (Bogotá), El Magdalena (Bogotá), El Porvenir (Cartagena), and La Balanza (Medellín).

ing to *empleomanía*.[51] Radicals and residents of the interior seemed particularly incensed by the influx of costeños into the governmental bureaucracy. One of General Trujillo's correspondents quoted a Boyacense who warned: "You have to go to Bogotá with a mosquito net because of the many costeños there." Election to the Cundinamarcan assembly of a number of well-connected Cartageneros, including Núñez' brother, nephew, and the son of his secretary of interior, reflected a diligent fulfillment of family and political obligations, but it provoked animosity.[52]

It should be noted that this extensive use of patronage by Núñez in no way violated nineteenth-century political norms in Colombia. Most political leaders of the period were charged by the opposition with nepotism and a ready response to *empleomanía*, and the charges were substantially correct. Elective office was looked upon by many as offering one of the few opportunities available for economic advancement. Consequently, political loyalties were shaped, in part, by the likelihood that an aspiring politician could offer jobs, contracts, and other favors upon his election. One interesting piece of evidence of nepotism at the state level in the 1870s is a handwritten document listing a number of government employees in Bolívar, their positions, salaries, and family ties. This curious document shows that during the governorship of Eugenio Baena in the mid-1870s twenty-two people related to Baena held official positions in the state, and like positions were occupied by seven relatives of Miguel de la Espriella, Baena's secretary general.[53] In evaluating the reasons for party identity in Colombia, one must be cognizant of the power of patronage, for it had an impact on a portion of the electorate. For example, the clear perception in 1878–1879 that Núñez would be the next Colombian president in itself attracted support to him and made his candidacy formidable. To the complexity of factors explaining the success of Núñez must be

51. *Diario de Cundinamarca* (Bogotá), July 17, 1880; *La Palestra* (Mompós), September 24, 1880; Martínez Silva, *Revistas políticas*, I (March 31, 1880), 180.

52. Manuel José Moreno to Trujillo, October 6, 1880, Trujillo collection, Vol. X, AN; *La Palestra* (Mompós), August 24, September 24, 1880.

53. This six-page unsigned, undated document is #62 in MS. folder #1, BLAA. Much of the data concerning positions and salaries was verified in issues of the *Diario de Bolívar* (Cartagena), but only a few of the kinship ties stated in the document could be substantiated.

added control of patronage by the Independents and their willingness to employ it to its fullest extent.[54]

President Núñez effectively used the tools of office to increase his political influence and to gain support for his program, the Regeneration. He not only had the will and talent to embark on an innovative program, but he also faced a worsening economy which presented him with an opportunity for change. The Regeneration was made possible by conditions of economic crisis, Independent control of Congress and the state governments, tacit Conservative support for elements of the program, and effective leadership. The economic, administrative, and political components of Núñez' program fell into a coherent pattern aimed at strengthening national government through increase and greater range of its functions. In the fullest sense the Regeneration was nationalist. Within the severe limitations of the 1863 constitution, it sought to initiate the integration of a dangerously fragmented nation.

The nationalist character of his regime and the centralizing thrust of the policies initiated by Rafael Núñez during his first year as president surprised his supporters and opponents alike. During his first bid for the presidency in 1875 Núñez ran as a regional candidate dedicated to revitalizing the federal system by obtaining for the coastal periphery a more equitable share of political power and of federal funds. When elected president in 1880, however, Núñez sought to strengthen national ties rather than govern on behalf of any particular region. During his first year in office he demonstrated a fundamental opposition to the constraints on national government imposed by the extremely federalist 1863 constitution. By 1881 President Núñez had made considerable progress toward centralization in Bogotá of administrative, political, and economic power. His program included protectionism,

---

54. This is not to accept the thesis of some writers, such as Fernando Guillén Martínez, who argues that there were no ideological differences between Liberals and Conservatives from the mid-nineteenth century onward and that the parties employed ideological pretexts simply to gain control of government funds. See *Raíz y futuro de la revolución* (Bogotá, 1963), 134, 141–43. The Colombian novelist Eduardo Caballero Calderón makes a similar argument in his historical essay *Historia privada de los colombianos* (Bogotá, 1960), 110. In his book *Patterns of Conflict in Colombia* (New Haven, 1968), 70, 295–98, James L. Payne concludes that selfishness is the driving force of Colombian politics and that political conflict stems from the quest for office rather than from ideological or socioeconomic differences.

creation of the National Bank, increased deficit spending, strengthening of the standing army, and enactment of the law on public order.

Núñez' sharp departure in 1880 from his stance of five years earlier raises the question of motivation, a question made even more compelling by the unanticipated nature of the shift. It has been argued that the Regeneration represented the implementation of a Positivist philosophy which Núñez embraced while in Europe.[55] An examination of a collection of his essays written while abroad and published in 1874 indeed reveals a perceptible change in his thinking during the previous decade and a familiarity with Positivist tenets. By 1874 he closely linked the concept of progress to material achievement, scientific education, and evolutionary development. But at the same time he remained true to the principles of federalism and free trade, and he had come to favor governmental participation in economic matters, other than trade, as a means of countering the disintegrating tendencies of federalism. It is too simplistic to label an eclectic thinker such as Núñez a Spencerian Positivist. As a perceptive observer of contemporary affairs he was keenly aware of the centralizing tendencies shaping Western Europe as well as Latin America. Even Colombia's Radicals had participated in this trend during their decade in power.

Another factor offered in explanation of Núñez' conduct was his marriage in 1877 to Doña Soledad Román, a member of a Conservative Cartagena family. The marriage brought him into closer contact with local Conservatives and helped him reestablish ties made when he openly bid for Conservative support in his 1875 run for the presidency. Though retaining his identity as a Liberal in 1880, Núñez sought to restore the Conservative party to a place of legitimacy in national politics by naming Conservatives to high government positions, by repealing anticlerical measures, and by speaking out in favor of reconciliation.[56] In view of Núñez' independence of mind and Doña Soledad's

55.   The strongest statement of this argument is Javier Ocampo López' "El positivismo y el movimiento de 'La Regeneración' en Colombia," *Latinoamérica: Anuario de Estudios Latinoamericanos*, I (1968), 81–109. Ocampo López concludes that Spencerian Positivism provided the ideological basis for the first Núñez government in 1880. On the other hand, Jaime Jaramillo Uribe argues in *El pensamiento colombiano en el siglo XIX*, 302–307, that Núñez was influenced by several nineteenth-century currents of thought including Positivism and the anti-Positivist reaction.

56.   For details of Núñez' marriage to Soledad Román see Palacio, "El segundo

denial in later life of any political influence on her husband, it is not likely that the marriage had the overwhelming influence attributed to it.[57]

In evaluating Núñez' motivation it is well to recall that when he went abroad in 1863 Colombia had just emerged from one of its major civil wars, and within months of his return armed violence defeated his presidential bid. A year later another war between Liberals and Conservatives erupted. In Núñez' view, reconciliation between Liberals and Conservatives and a reconstitution of authority were essential. In summary, Núñez' clear awareness of contemporary currents of thought and centralizing political trends together with his determination to restore national authority and a degree of interparty comity impelled him to seize the opportunity provided by the preeminent power of the Independents and the economic plight of the nation in order to implement the Regeneration.

The unheralded shifts in Núñez' posture from a regionalist to a nationalist stance and from federalism to centralism provided a major ingredient in the nation's political debate during the next several years, and the first serious challenge to his program came from a member of his own party, Governor Solón Wilches of Santander. It was entirely fitting that Santander, stronghold of Colombian Radicalism, should carry the banner of state sovereignty, even if it did so under the leadership of an Independent governor. Santandereanos gloried in their long tradition of opposition to central authority. This tradition extended from their struggle for municipal autonomy during the Comunero Rebellion of 1781 to their leadership in the drive to incorporate the principle of state sovereignty into the 1863 constitution. The centralizing tendencies of the Núñez administration aroused fears in Santander that the president intended to undermine the federal system. Governor Wilches assumed the role of defender of federalism in the renewed struggle with central power shortly after he consolidated his political

---

matrimonio," 321–33. *Diario Oficial* (Bogotá), April 13, 1880; *El Conservador* (Bogotá), October 20, 1881, January 20, 1882.

57. For the view that the marriage had a marked influence on Núñez' political thinking see Tomás Rueda Vargas, *Escritos* (3 vols.; Bogotá, 1963), I, 262. Denial by Doña Soledad of any political influence on Núñez is found in the following biography which was based on conversations with her: Daniel Lemaitre, *Soledad Román de Núñez: Recuerdos* (Cartagena, 1927), 17.

domination of Santander. He had compiled a successful record as governor during his first term, and to ensure continued control he summoned a convention for mid-1880 which promulgated a new state constitution. Among the major constitutional changes adopted were the extension of the governor's term from two to four years and the provision for his election by the assembly rather than by direct vote. In a final endorsement of Wilches, the constituent assembly reelected him governor for the term ending in October, 1884.[58] Both Núñez and Wilches enjoyed solid political support in 1880–1881, when they became locked in a rivalry which severely strained the unity of the fledgling Independent party and which symbolized the contest between central authority and state sovereignty.

Decisions by national Secretary of Hacienda Antonio Roldán precipitated the crisis with Santander and induced Wilches to convoke the state assembly into extraordinary session in November 1880. Roldán's resolution of September forbidding the states to import arms, although directed at Antioquia, elicited a more immediate and vigorous challenge from Santander than from any other state. Wilches urged the assembly to nullify the resolution which he characterized as either an utter absurdity in a federal system or an attempt to "return to centralism." The assembly complied with Wilches' request and on its own initiative provided authorization and funds for dispatching agents to the other states to induce them to follow Santander's lead. In justification of its vote of nullification the assembly declared: "With resolutions such as that of the secretary of hacienda the federation could become the most irritating sarcasm, because the *sovereign* states . . . would be converted into fiefs of the national executive power." Shortly thereafter, the assembly authorized Wilches to increase the size of the state militia to 5,000 troops and to purchase 5,000 rifles plus artillery and ammunition.[59]

A more serious conflict between the national government and Santander centered on the extraction of quinine from vacant government lands, *tierras baldías*, located in Santander. The discovery in 1879–

58.   *Gaceta de Santander* (Socorro), July 16, 1880; Otero Muñoz, *Wilches*, 361; Mantilla, *Geografía de Santander*, 37.

59.   *Gaceta de Santander* (Socorro), November 25, 26, December 29, 1880; Martínez Silva, *Revistas políticas*, I (December 31, 1880), 237.

1880 of abundant cinchona stands yielding high quality quinine produced an economic boom in central and western Santander. To prevent speculative excesses, impose a measure of control over quinine extraction, and guarantee a direct state share of anticipated profits, Governor Wilches brought the government into a commercial partnership with George von Lengerke, a German citizen of long-standing residence and a leading quinine exporter of the region. A contract of September 1880 between the Lengerke Company and the state government granted the company exclusive rights to extract quinine from 12,000 hectares of tierras baldías. In return, the company agreed to share its profits with the state and to buy shares in the Soto Railroad, a project actively promoted by Wilches and destined to link Bucaramanga with the lower Magdalena River.[60]

The Santander-Lengerke contract directly challenged the validity of a national Department of Hacienda decision favorable to a competitor of Lengerke. In August, Secretary Roldán had granted an exclusive privilege to an export company headed by a Venezuelan, Manuel Cortissoz, to extract quinine from a 20,000 hectare plot of tierras baldías in Santander. The land involved in the national and state concessions overlapped, and a protracted dispute between the two governments focused on the question of which one held legal title to the tierras baldías. As the deadlock continued, violence erupted between employees of the two companies.[61]

From the extraordinary session of the state assembly summoned in November Wilches obtained a vote of nullification against Roldán's quinine concession and passage of a law which imposed a heavy road tax on the shipment of quinine within state borders. The assembly amended the law a few days later to allow the governor to exempt from the quinine tax those "individuals or companies which extract [quinine] in partnership with the state government."[62] By means of

60.   Rodríguez Plata, La inmigración, 98–105, 128–31; Gaceta de Santander (Socorro), September 3, 1880.

61.   Memoria de Hacienda, 1881, 94–102, and document #VI, 260–77; Gaceta de Santander (Socorro), October 26, 29, 1880; Martínez Silva, Revistas políticas, I (October 31, 1880), 230; García, Bucaramanga, 204–206; Alfred Hettner, La cordillera de Bogotá; resultados de viajes y estudios, trans. Ernesto Guhl (Bogotá, 1966), 290–91.

62.   Gaceta de Santander (Socorro), November 25, December 31, 1880; García, Bucaramanga, 206; Leyes de Colombia, 1881, 317.

discriminatory tax legislation Wilches sought to secure for the Lengerke Company a monopoly over quinine extraction in Santander. Instead of openly accepting this challenge, Núñez made a public display of friendship for Wilches and sent a special commissioner to Santander for discussions which ultimately proved fruitless.[63] Núñez could well afford to appear conciliatory, for the legal aspects of the conflict were soon settled through the normal judicial process over which he exerted telling influence.

Cortissoz quickly challenged the constitutionality of the Santander quinine tax in a suit filed before the Supreme Court. It upheld the laws, but under the constitution, the Court's opinion was only advisory. The Senate made the final decision. In March and April the Senate nullified both the original and the amending laws and ordered Santander to halt collection of the tax. The laws were declared illegal because they violated the constitutional prohibition against taxing products destined for export and because they contravened the equal rights article of the constitution. The decisions were particularly frustrating for Santander because the Senate had previously upheld laws of Tolima, Cundinamarca, and Bolívar which resembled the Santander law but which imposed a much smaller tax. With ill-concealed rage Wilches ordered compliance.[64]

Núñez assumed a major role in the dispute between Santander and the national government despite his public posture of conciliation and his apparent willingness to allow the matter to be resolved by judicial process. At no time did he intend to yield to Wilches. In a letter of early 1881 to a close friend in Medellín, General Juan Nepomuceno González, Núñez wrote: "At the moment Wilches seems crazier than ever, and so that he understands that I take the matter seriously, I just replaced General Delgado with General Severo Olarte." The reference to a shift in the military command in Santander illustrates Núñez' often-used tactic of assigning the most politically trusted officers to trouble spots. His friendship with González was significant because González served as one of the two Colombian representatives of the

63. *Gaceta de Santander* (Socorro), December 31, 1880; Martínez Silva, *Revistas políticas*, I (December 31, 1880), 237.
64. *Leyes de Colombia, 1881*, 314–26; *La Bandera Federal* (Socorro), May 18, 1881; *Gaceta de Santander* (Socorro), May 4, 1881.

Cortissoz Company during its negotiations with the national government.[65] In addition to his distrust of Wilches' political pretensions, Núñez also exerted his influence on behalf of the Venezuelan-owned Cortissoz Company because Santander's discrimination against it had led the government of Venezuela to make official inquiries about the Santander tax. Venezuela feared that Santander would tax quinine shipped by Venezuelans through Cúcuta to the Gulf of Maracaibo.[66] The factors driving Núñez and Wilches into political confrontation were thus substantive. They involved international relations, fundamental questions of the powers of the national government, and ultimate control of the Independent party.

Existence in Santander of a disorganized but potentially powerful Radical opposition to Wilches gave Núñez considerable leverage in his contest with Wilches. In his *Memorias*, Aquileo Parra recalled an incident which illustrated the extreme difficulty inherent in Wilches' political position. The Radicals of Santander attempted to take advantage of the struggle between Núñez and Wilches by negotiating an agreement with Núñez whereby he would remain neutral in the event of a Radical-led revolt against Wilches. Núñez and a representative of the Santander Radicals met in early 1881. According to Parra, "Núñez agreed not only to observe the requested neutrality, but he offered to help the Radicals with a battalion of the Colombian army on condition that General Juan Nepomuceno González be Wilches' successor as governor of Santander." The Radicals saw little merit in exchanging one Independent governor for another or in risking the possibility that Núñez was maneuvering them into armed action in order later to join Wilches in crushing them. The talks thus came to naught.[67]

By mid-1881 the governor of Santander had suffered serious setbacks. Despite his best efforts to turn the quinine boom into an eco-

65. Núñez to Juan Nepomuceno González, February 5, 1881, in "Cartas del Doctor Núñez," *Boletín de Historia y Antigüedades*, XXXIV (January–March, 1947), 21; *Memoria de Hacienda, 1881*, document #VI, 260–68.

66. Núñez to Nepomuceno González, March 28, 1881, "Cartas del Doctor Núñez," 25; Venezuelan minister of hacienda to customs administrator at Táchira, January 17, 1881, in "Ministerio de Hacienda," Vol. CCCXCV, AN.

67. Parra, *Memorias*, 516n. See Núñez to Nepomuceno González, April 27, 1881, "Cartas del Doctor Núñez," 27–28, for a cryptic reference to these discussions with Domnino Castro.

nomic windfall for the state, he had failed. Within a few weeks of nullification of the quinine tax laws, the boom ended due to a rapid drop in world prices stemming from increased Asian production. The end of quinine exportation together with the continuing decline in the price of coffee, a product grown principally in Santander in this period, dealt a severe economic blow to the state.[68] Wilches had raised expectations too high in promising that quinine revenue would bring peace, prosperity, and major railroad construction. The past year, instead, had witnessed a fruitless struggle with the national government, violence in the countryside, and bitter discouragement about the economic future. Wilches' identification with the Independent party therefore became a serious political liability to the Independents.

In April 1881 Wilches launched his presidential candidacy. His principal opponent was Francisco Javier Zaldúa, a candidate selected and promoted by Núñez. Wilches' platform consisted of an endorsement of Liberal party unity, federalism, and state sovereignty.[69] The Wilches candidacy, in addition to being an escalation in the developing rivalry with Núñez and a factional struggle within the Independent party, represented a conflict between centralism and federalism.

The movement toward centralism which Núñez directed during his first term as president encountered weak and unorganized resistance. This resistance was adequate, nevertheless, when combined with the constitutionally sanctioned doctrine of state sovereignty, to prevent abandonment of federalism. Additional significant moves toward centralism would require overcoming the obstacle posed by the 1863 constitution. Whether the centralizing trend would continue depended on Núñez, who remained a key political figure in the period which followed the end of his first presidential term. The question of Núñez' ultimate intentions and of his loyalty to the constitution underlay much of the intricate political maneuvering by Independents, Radicals, and Conservatives during the 1882–1884 period.

68. La Unión (Bogotá), September 6, 1881, reprinted in Camacho Roldán, Escritos varios, I, 667.

69. La Bandera Federal (Socorro), April 6, 1881; Diario de Cundinamarca (Bogotá), April 30, June 15, 1881.

Chapter VII

A Hiatus in Leadership: Rafael Núñez in Absentia, 1882–1884

Colombia's political scene between the first and second Núñez administrations, 1882–1884, was marked by a struggle among Independents, Radicals, and Conservatives focusing on the question of whether to advance or reverse the policies initiated by Núñez in 1880. The Independents were willing to continue on the road to centralism, and they looked more and more to constitutional reform as the best vehicle for such change. But their political strength suffered erosion during the Núñez interregnum. The Radicals remained uncompromising in their opposition to Núñez, the move toward centralism, and any modification of the 1863 constitution, but they competed with the Conservatives for alliance with and eventual control over the Independents. Until early 1884 the Conservatives succeeded in maintaining a high degree of party unity in support of Núñez. The major result of the intricate competition for political advantage in these years was a stalemate, thus further spotlighting the pivotal role of Núñez.

Few fundamental issues separated the Independents and Radicals between the time of the Liberal party split in 1875 and implementation of Núñez' program five years later. They were differentiated primarily on the basis of regional origins, personal loyalties, and attitudes toward Conservatives. Independents derived mainly from Bogotá and the four coastal states; they depended on Núñez for leadership; and they favored restoration of full political rights to the Conservatives. Radical strength was centered in the three eastern mountain states; party members looked to the so-called Radical oligarchy for leadership; and the party regarded Conservative political assertiveness as subversive of the constitutional order. The Núñez program of 1880, which the Radicals unsuccessfully resisted, substantially widened the gap between the two Liberal parties.

Besides further dividing the Radicals and Independents, Núñez' program also weakened his own party. Although a majority of Independents supported his program, the abrupt departure from traditional Liberal positions signaled by the Regeneration caused the defection of several prominent Independents such as Salvador Camacho Roldán and Julián Trujillo. Rivalries among the many Independent governors for national office and for Núñez' favor disrupted party harmony and led to additional desertions. Primary reliance upon Núñez for leadership enhanced unity on policy and programs, but it constituted the party's most conspicuous weakness during his semiretirement in Cartagena between his first and second administrations. Belated organization of a party directorate by congressional leaders in early 1884 failed to fill the void in leadership caused by his absence from Bogotá.[1] Another underlying cause of Independent discord was the party's nebulous relationship with the Conservatives. Many Independents feared that Núñez intended to form a permanent alliance with the Conservatives rather than work for the restoration of Liberal party unity.

From the time Conservative leaders established a National Party Directorate in 1879 until 1884, the vast majority of Conservatives remained unwavering in their support for Núñez. José María Samper and Carlos Holguín continued to raise the most ardently pro-Núñez voices in party deliberations.[2] Other nationally known Conservatives such as Antonio B. Cuervo, Alejandro Posada, and Carlos Martínez Silva, though less enthusiastically pro-Núñez, nevertheless endorsed the decision to support him and the Independents.

In the early 1880s the Conservative party sought to end federalism, restore budgetary balance by means of reducing expenditures, and al-

1. El Conservador (Bogotá), May 20, 1884; La Epoca (Bogotá), April 29, 1884; Francisco de P. Matéus, La administración del señor Otálora (Paris, 1884), 36.

2. El Deber (Bogotá), September 28, 1880, February 1, 1881. Samper's paper, El Deber, served as official party organ from 1879 until 1881, when it was replaced by El Conservador edited by Sergio Arboleda.

ter church-state relations by obtaining governmental protection for the church. During Núñez' first administration the Conservatives objected to many of his economic policies such as protectionism, deficit spending, and large expenditures for public works, but they applauded his efforts to strengthen national authority and his conciliatory gestures toward the church. Under Núñez' prodding, Congress in 1880 abolished some of the anticlerical measures enacted during the 1876–1877 war, such as exiling several of Colombia's bishops, but Congress refused to repeal the law on religious inspection. Conservatives seemed most pleased with Núñez' respectful attitude toward the church. In early 1882 El Conservador asserted; "During the administration of Señor Núñez the cross is again honored on the pinnacle of the Capitol, and Christianity . . . again receives some homage from those who hold power in their hands."[3]

The Conservatives achieved a remarkable degree of unity from 1879 to early 1884. Such a development was surprising because the party included many talented, forceful figures who might easily come into conflict as they had in the past, and because the internal factions were doctrinally based. One such faction, centered in Medellín, tended to be regionalist rather than nationalist, federalist rather than centralist, and it wanted protection of the Catholic faith as the party's principal banner. But Antioquia's Conservatives had few adherents outside of the state, because they were held responsible for the war of 1876–1877 and its disastrous consequences. Antioqueños further discredited themselves during the postwar years by the bitter debate they conducted with Conservatives in Bogotá concerning the causes and conduct of the war. The powerful proclerical, doctrinaire faction of prewar days had become by the early 1880s a much diminished group led by José Joaquín Ortiz, editor of the religious and literary periodical La Caridad. Ortiz maintained close ties with the church hierarchy, espoused the view that the party should be the secular arm of the church, and opposed cooperation with the Núñez regime or with any Liberal government operating under the 1863 constitution.[4] Other former lead-

---

3. El Conservador (Bogotá), October 20, 1881, January 20, 1882.

4. La Tribuna (Medellín), November 6, 1880; El Relator (Bogotá), September 26, October 4, 1881; La Defensa (Bogotá), August 5, September 16, 1880; bishop of

ers of that faction had become silent following the war or prudently supported the pragmatic leadership of Holguín.

Conservative success in establishing and maintaining a high degree of party unity, despite the survival of these factions, largely derived from the authoritative leadership provided by the party Directorate. This organ consisted of three members who were elected by a body of party delegates representing each of the nine states. The delegates were chosen by indirect election in each state and assembled as a party convention in Bogotá at periodic intervals. The greater Conservative tendency to obey authority and the absence of conflicting sources of authority, such as state governments under Conservative control, greatly facilitated the Directorate's task. Although a diversity of opinion existed within the Directorate and personal conflicts occasionally broke into the open, by and large party unity was upheld.[5]

Unlike the Conservatives, the Radicals were unwilling to bide their time patiently while awaiting the right moment for a return to power. The end of Radical domination was yet recent, and the party had not suffered the humiliation of military defeat as had the Conservatives. Between 1881 and 1884 the Radicals attempted to reabsorb the Independents by touting Liberal union. They made effective use of Núñez' cooperation with the "common enemy," i.e., the Conservatives, in their attempts to persuade and coerce Independents to return to the ranks of traditional Liberalism, which the Radicals claimed to represent.

Despite a plethora of talented and politically experienced figures in the ranks of Radicalism, including former presidents, governors, and cabinet members, the party suffered from lack of leadership. Manuel Murillo, the acknowledged party head for more than two decades, died in late 1880, and former presidents Santiago Pérez and Aquileo Parra, who governed during the last four years of Radical hegemony,

---

Santa Marta to José Joaquín Ortiz, April 7, 1881, in José Joaquín Ortíz collection, Box #3, ACdeH.

5.   For an expression of the Conservative attitude toward authority see an editorial from the Conservative paper *La Verdad* quoted in *Diario de Cundinamarca* (Bogotá), March 21, 1883. For an example of a major conflict between party stalwarts José María Samper and Manuel Briceño, see the following: *El Deber* (Bogotá), February 1, 1881; *El Conservador* (Bogotá), October 20, 1881; Samper to Antonio B. Cuervo, January 11, 1881, MS. #30, BLAA.

lacked the requisite qualities for leadership. A sympathetic biographer of Pérez, who by profession was an educator, noted that Pérez "preferred his professorship and his books to men." Parra was the logical successor to Murillo as party leader, but he lacked the prestige and the inclination to command. At the end of his presidency in 1878 he had returned to Santander and dedicated himself to various family export enterprises. He maintained an active political correspondence from Santander, but even when elected senator from Tolima he remained but briefly in Bogotá. Party colleagues often implored him to return to the capital on matters of political urgency, and they sometimes complained that he shirked his party responsibility "since he went in search of quinine."[6] Felipe Pérez, brother of former president Santiago Pérez, possessed widely recognized intellectual talent, and he aspired to assume the mantle of leadership left vacant by Murillo's death. But his blatant ambition and unrestrained ego frequently placed him at odds with his brother and other major party figures.[7]

To provide the Radicals with leadership, unity, and direction during the first Núñez presidency, four former Radical presidents—Santos Acosta, Eustorgio Salgar, Santiago Pérez, and Aquileo Parra—organized the Liberal Central Committee in mid-1880. Both Acosta and Salgar had supported Núñez for president in 1875, as had several other prominent Radicals, but they returned to the Radical camp in 1880 as Núñez widened the gap between the two Liberal parties. The Central Committee provided symbolic rather than effective leadership, for it remained inactive after its formation. In early 1881 one Radical from Bogotá privately complained: "Señor Parra seems to have forgotten the responsibility he assumed in organizing the committee." Shortly thereafter a north coast Radical prodded Parra about the need for "the Central Committee to show signs of life."[8] Political action was unavoidable

6. Guillermo Camacho Carrizosa, *Santiago Pérez y otros estudios* (Bogotá, 1934), 19; Teodoro Valenzuela to Luis Bernal, March 5, 1881, Parra collection, Box #1, ACdeH. See also Luis Robles to Parra, April 26, 1881, and Ramón Perea to Parra, April 27, 1882, CdeHRP.

7. Parra to Luis [Bernal], August 8, 1881, Parra collection, Box #1, ACdeH; *El Promotor* (Barranquilla), December 17, 1881.

8. *La Defensa* (Bogotá), July 29, 1880; Teodoro Valenzuela to Luis Bernal, March 5, 1881, Parra collection, Box #1, ACdeH; Luis Robles to Parra, April 26, 1881, CdeHRP.

in early 1881 when preparations began for candidate selection for the 1882–1884 presidential period.

When Congress convened in February 1881, Núñez faced the problem of choosing a successor who possessed stature, prestige, and dedication to uphold the gains achieved thus far. On their own initiative the Independents in Congress attempted to agree upon a candidate, but none of the contenders, Solón Wilches, Pablo Arosemena, Eliseo Payán, or José Eusebio Otálora, could attract majority backing. Since late 1880, Núñez had favored Francisco Javier Zaldúa as his successor but had been unable to get Zaldúa to accept the candidacy.[9] Zaldúa, a distinguished jurist of Bogotá, had been intimately associated with Colombian Liberalism from mid-century as an assemblyman, congressman, and first president of the 1863 Rionegro convention. He was one of the leading figures in the Núñez camp when the Liberals divided in 1875. Subsequently, he served in the Trujillo cabinet, and in 1879 he won election as senator from Cundinamarca. In a warm personal letter Núñez congratulated Zaldúa on his election to the Senate, and during Núñez' first year as president he solicited Zaldúa's active support in some close Senate votes.[10] The precarious state of Zaldúa's health and the fact that he was seventy years old posed major disadvantages in electing him president.

Zaldúa forcefully declined the proffered nomination, citing the bad state of his health and noting that knowledge of his infirmity would improperly focus attention on the election of designates.[11] By late February a majority of Congress was urging Zaldúa to accept the nomination. Núñez then appealed to his sense of patriotic duty in persuasive terms: "In the name of our common fatherland permit me to inform you that if you do not accept the candidacy which has again been offered by many distinguished people, you will incur a grave his-

9. La Palestra (Mompós), February 10, 1881; El Promotor (Barranquilla), April 23, 1881; Martínez Silva, Revistas políticas, I (January 31, February 28, 1881), 251, 260–61; La Luz (Bogotá), June 9, 1882, reprinted in Núñez, La reforma, Vol. I, Pt. 1, p. 197.

10. Núñez to Zaldúa, November 10, 1879, July 24, 1880, in Francisco Javier Zaldúa collection, Vol. V, Biblioteca del Seminario Mayor, La Arquidiócesis de Bogotá, Bogotá, hereinafter cited as BSM.

11. Zaldúa to Simón de Herrera, February 12, 1881, Zaldúa to Felipe Angulo, February 24, 1881, Zaldúa collection, Vol. V, BSM.

toric responsibility, because only your name represents harmony and peace." Two days later Núñez again implored him to yield to the will of the nation. Zaldúa thereupon agreed.[12]

In Núñez' view, Zaldúa possessed many advantages not offered by other potential candidates. Zaldúa had not served as a governor since the 1840s and thus was not exclusively identified with a single region. He held the respect of all educated Colombians for his learning, his legal scholarship, and his unimpeachable character. Zaldúa's purely civilian background was a major asset in a party whose outstanding figures, aside from Núñez, had achieved status through military leadership. Perhaps the most compelling factor leading Núñez to insist on Zaldúa's candidacy was his conviction that Zaldúa would serve as a faithful, obedient lieutenant. Núñez did not want a bold, energetic innovator to succeed him. He sought instead a compliant disciple who would consolidate the Núñez program and maintain the status quo until 1884 when Núñez himself could regain the presidency. On the eve of Zaldúa's acceptance of the nomination, Núñez confided to a friend: "[Zaldúa] is the man called upon to continue the work undertaken by the present administration."[13]

Promotion of Zaldúa's candidacy by the incumbent administration was tantamount to electing him. All other Independent contenders dropped out of the race with the exception of Wilches, whose feud with Núñez led him to challenge Zaldúa. The nomination of Zaldúa placed the Radicals in a dilemma. They had no chance of electing their own candidate, and Zaldúa's election seemed to promise a continuation of the Núñez program for at least another two years. While the Radical leaders attempted to devise a suitable strategy, they openly expressed their dislike of Zaldúa because of his apparent acquiescence to Núñez' plans.[14]

In April the Radicals decided upon their course of action. It con-

12. Núñez to Zaldúa, February 28, March 2, 1881, Zaldúa to Senators Antonio González Carazo and Manuel M. Castro, March 2, 1881, Zaldúa collection, Vol. V, BSM.

13. Núñez to Nepomuceno González, February 28, 1881, "Cartas del Doctor Núñez," 24.

14. *Diario de Cundinamarca* (Bogotá), March 19, August 16, 1881; *El Magdalena* (Bogotá), August 26, 1881.

sisted of a so-called evolution, an all-out effort to entice Zaldúa away from the Independent party by offering him the nomination in the name of the united Liberal party. To convey the impression of Liberal unity, the four members of the Radical Liberal Central Committee obtained the support of four prominent Independents in issuing a manifesto calling for Liberal union. The four Independents who joined in this anti-Núñez effort, all major figures who had supported Núñez in 1880, were Julián Trujillo, Pablo Arosemena, Salvador Camacho Roldán, and Hermógenes Wilson. The maneuver was well executed at a public rally in Bogotá's Plaza de Bolívar in late April by Parra and other Liberal luminaries who spoke fervently of the need to reunite the party in the face of a revitalized "common enemy." In a speech to the crowd, Zaldúa graciously accepted the presidential nomination of the Liberal union.[15]

The principal Radical goal in launching the evolution was to gain power by absorbing the Independents, thus beating the Conservatives at their own game. Parra, who claimed major credit as architect of the plan, also used it as an argument for convincing his restless colleagues in Santander to postpone their plans for an armed revolt and give the evolution a chance to succeed. Despite the obvious advantages of the Radical strategy, not all party members supported it. Felipe Pérez opposed Zaldúa's candidacy because he felt that the Radicals should nominate someone totally dedicated to Radical principles such as himself.[16] Most Radicals, however, followed Parra's lead and supported Zaldúa.

The Liberal union gambit somewhat disconcerted the Conservatives. They blamed the Radicals for it and labeled the notion of a unity of principles between Radicals and Independents "ridiculous and disgraceful." Rather than yield to the Radical attempt to separate them from their Independent allies, the Conservatives announced that they would refrain from launching their own candidate and instead would support Zaldúa because of his honor and integrity.[17] Conser-

15.   *Diario de Cundinamarca* (Bogotá), May 3, 1881; *El Deber* (Bogotá), May 17, 1881; *La Palestra* (Mompós), May 14, 1881.

16.   Parra to Luis Bernal, August 8, 1881, Parra collection, Box #1, ACdeH; Parra to Fortunato Bernal, October 23, 1881, CdeHRP; *La Bandera Federal* (Socorro), July 8, 1881; [Agustín Camargo (?)], *Felipe Pérez* (Bogotá, 1883), 22.

17.   Martínez Silva, *Revistas políticas*, I (April 30, 1881), 287; *El Deber* (Bogotá), May 13, 1881.

vatives as well as Independents looked upon the Zaldúa presidency as a "transitory thing." One Conservative endorsement of Zaldúa noted that his election would give the Independents two badly needed years to work on party organization. To keep Zaldúa on the right track a north coast Conservative suggested that the best course available to his party colleagues was "to consolidate the prestige of Núñez."[18]

Zaldúa handily won the presidential election in September, receiving the votes of eight of the nine states. Santander alone voted for Wilches. The same election produced a large Independent majority in Congress. As Núñez' term expired, he won and accepted election by Congress to the post of first designate for the first year of Zaldúa's presidency. In addition he was elected governor of Panama and first designate in both Bolívar and Magdalena, positions he declined to occupy.[19] No matter what policies Zaldúa might pursue, the Independents held a strong political position.

Between Zaldúa's election and his April 1882 inauguration, political activity centered on the effort by Radicals and Independents to "capture" Zaldúa. The Radicals appealed to his sense of loyalty to Colombian Liberalism and emphasized the importance of Liberal unity against an assertive Conservative party seeking to perpetuate Liberal divisions. The appeal was well conceived. In a letter to Felipe Pérez written on election eve Zaldúa pledged: "I will regard every effort as truly patriotic which is directed at consolidating the unity proclaimed on April 24 and at erasing, even from memory, the names designating the factions into which the great Liberal party has unfortunately been divided." Another argument often repeated in the Radical press maintained that Núñez had selected Zaldúa only because of his conviction that Zaldúa could be easily manipulated. An editorial in the *Diario de Cundinamarca* expressed this theme as follows: "Señor Núñez believed that the age and infirmities of Señor Zaldúa made him a likely prey, and from that time forward he devoted himself to work for this candidacy which he believed the most favorable to his treacherous plans."[20]

18.   Martínez Silva, *Revistas políticas*, I (March 31, 1881), 275; *El Deber* (Bogotá), March 4, 1881; Joaquín F. Vélez to Sergio Arboleda, August 17, 1881, ASA.

19.   *El Conservador* (Bogotá), October 3, 1881; *El Relator* (Bogotá), October 27, 1881; *La Palestra* (Mompós), June 26, 1882.

20.   Zaldúa to Felipe Pérez, August 31, 1881, MS. #425, BLAA; *El Relator* (Bo-

Núñez had worked energetically to get Zaldúa to accept the nomination, and he found it necessary to intensify his efforts to retain Zaldúa's loyalty. In the months prior to Zaldúa's inauguration, Núñez attempted to strengthen the Independent claim on Zaldúa by lavishly praising him as "the most respectable member of the Independent party." Núñez correctly observed that the Independents were the real winners of the 1881 congressional and gubernatorial elections and that Zaldúa's victory was but a part of that sweep. At the same time Núñez launched an attack against the Liberal union, calling it a "wretched intrigue."[21]

Núñez' attack against the Liberal union proved to be a major miscalculation, for Zaldúa had totally embraced the concept. Furthermore, Zaldúa developed a strong personal dislike of Núñez, who never seemed fully to grasp this or to realize how strongly Zaldúa objected to his program. Shortly after his inauguration Zaldúa recorded the following observations about the Núñez presidency: "Not content with having left the public treasury ruined, with having sterilely consumed more than twenty million pesos, with having adopted corruption as a policy and means of influence, with having eliminated two important incomes, that from the salt works and that from the Panama Railroad, with having compromised customs revenue almost in its entirety, not content with all this and much more, now he is attempting to bring anarchy to the country, subvert the constitutional order, and place the high national powers in collision and conflict."[22] Zaldúa's reference to conflict between high national powers concerned the developing struggle between the Zaldúa administration and the Independent majority in Congress. The latter insisted on electing Núñez as first designate, and in view of the precarious state of Zaldúa's health this aroused grave suspicions about Núñez' intentions. In addition, Núñez remained

---

gotá), January 12, 1882; *Diario de Cundinamarca* (Bogotá), January 14, February 4, 1882.

21. *La Luz* (Bogotá), January 27, February 14, 1882, reprinted in Núñez, *La reforma*, Vol. I, Pt. 1, pp. 111, 121.

22. Undated memo entitled "Apuntes" in Zaldúa collection, ACdeH. The content of this unsigned memo shows that it was intended for the governor or other high state official of Cauca. The memo is written in the same hand as other letters in the Zaldúa collection, and it consists of twelve points which were probably to be incorporated into a formal letter.

in Bogotá for several months following the end of his term despite his well-known dislike of the Bogotá climate and the extended separation from his wife, who had remained on the north coast throughout his presidency. Early in his administration Zaldúa ominously observed: "Núñez remains secluded in his house without daring even to look out of the window, but conspiring."[23]

The 1882 session of Congress was remarkably unproductive because of the protracted dispute with Zaldúa. Congress enacted only two significant laws: repeal of the 1877 religious inspection law and an act providing for the return of property confiscated during the 1876–1877 war. The legislative-executive struggle centered on the refusal of the Senate to approve Zaldúa's appointment of Radicals to the cabinet. He initially named a cabinet of four Radicals and three Independents, giving the key posts of War and Hacienda to the Radicals. Only one Radical appointee, Miguel Samper, received early Senate confirmation. Zaldúa tried to circumvent the Senate by allowing lesser officials not in need of Senate confirmation to run the headless departments, but Congress passed a law requiring Senate approval for the appointment of a wide-ranging list of such officials.[24] Zaldúa remained without a fully constituted cabinet until early September, when the Senate approved his last appointment after a series of behind-the-scenes discussions. Within a month of installation of the full cabinet, its most prestigious member, Secretary of Hacienda Samper, resigned citing his inability to implement an economic program because of the conflict between the executive and legislative branches. The Senate also rejected several military and diplomatic appointments. In August, it disapproved the nomination of General Santos Acosta as inspector general of the army, and a month later it voted against Pablo Arosemena as minister to Venezuela.[25]

23. *El Promotor* (Barranquilla), March 4, 1882; *El Relator* (Bogotá), February 18, 1882; "Apuntes," Zaldúa collection, ACdeH.

24. *Leyes de Colombia, 1882*, 131–32, 250–51, 52; *La Palestra* (Mompós), May 12, 1882; *Diario Oficial* (Bogotá), April 4, May 27, July 24, 1882; Liévano Aguirre, *Rafael Núñez*, 208–12.

25. *Diario Oficial* (Bogotá), September 13, 1882; Martínez Silva, *Revistas políticas*, I (August 5, 1882), 361–62; *La Luz* (Bogotá), October 20, 1882; President of Senate to Zaldúa, September 11, 1882, Zaldúa collection, ACdeH; *Diario de Cundinamarca* (Bogotá), August 18, 1882.

The activities of Public Safety, a Radical organization formed in late 1881, greatly intensified political tensions in the capital. Through frequent political rallies, dissemination of inflammatory broadsides, and disruptive occupation of congressional galleries, Public Safety sought to widen the gap between Núñez and Zaldúa. Its activities also contributed to the eruption of violence. In April, armed conflict broke out at Zipaquirá, a few miles north of Bogotá, between members of Public Safety, who were attempting to seize a state arms depot, and a detachment of the Colombian army. The army unit quickly restored order, but its commander, General Alejo Morales, was killed in an exchange of fire. In August, an unsuccessful attempt was made on the life of Ricardo Becerra, leader of the Senate Independents. Another assassination attempt occurred the following month against Daniel Aldana, Independent governor of Cundinamarca. The assassin only slightly wounded Aldana but killed his companion.[26]

Conflict between Radicals and Independents in 1882 stemmed from fundamental differences between the two parties. The principal legacy of the Núñez presidency was a national government with greatly enhanced political and economic powers. Núñez had strengthened federal power by means of legislative action, executive decree, and a broad interpretation of the constitution. Throughout 1882, Zaldúa and the Radicals sought to undo this legacy. The law on public order, passed in 1880 at Núñez' behest, epitomized the struggle between Independents and Radicals. This law permitted the national government to intervene in the states, at the request of the governor or legislature, to assist in maintaining order. Of Núñez' many accomplishments as president, he took the greatest pride in the nearly unprecedented tranquillity which prevailed during his two-year term. He attributed this period of calm to the law on public order. Late in 1882 Núñez' paper, *La Luz*, made the following broad assertion about that law: "Since 1863 there has been no legislative act more beneficial or of greater importance. . . . The solidarity of public order is today the strongest tie of national unity." Radicals maintained that the public order law "leads

26. *Diario de Cundinamarca* (Bogotá), January 14, March 24, 1882; *El Promotor* (Barranquilla), April 29, 1882; Martínez Silva, *Revistas políticas*, I (April 12, September 30, 1882), 341, 379; *La Luz* (Bogotá), August 8, 1882; *El Conservador* (Bogotá), August 3, 1882.

to centralism, destroys rotation in office, and is a sarcasm flung in the face of the federation."[27] The transitory nature of this Núñez reform became apparent in late 1882 when the Independent governor of Cauca requested Zaldúa to dispatch federal forces to his state to thwart an insurrection threatened by Radicals. Zaldúa delayed, asked for more information, and finally sent a military detachment under the command of the pro-Radical general, Sergio Camargo.[28]

As a result of such undermining of the Núñez program, the Independents and their Conservative allies began to look upon constitutional reform as the only way to bring about lasting change. Specifics were often omitted in discussions of constitutional reform, but the general aim was to reduce state sovereignty and increase federal power. The Conservatives spoke out forthrightly on the issue. Their official organ asserted in early 1882: "Patriotism demands that the first political necessity in benefit of peace is reform of the constitution." Specifically the Conservatives called for guaranteed tolerance toward the Catholic Church and the elimination of state sovereignty. Independents focused on the need to extend the presidential term to at least four years. Núñez praised the six-year term of Argentina's president and the actions of Cundinamarca and Santander in extending the governor's term from two to four years.[29] Another specific reform advocated by the Independents was a constitutional change allowing the national government to aid all types of state public works projects, not merely interoceanic routes as authorized in the 1863 charter. At the close of the 1882 congressional session, La Luz complained that the Independents had nominated and elected Zaldúa so that he could continue the work of Núñez, preside over peaceful elections in 1883, and "lead the nation in the peaceful and wise reform of the constitution."[30]

Zaldúa and the Radicals absolutely rejected the idea of consti-

27. La Luz (Bogotá), November 7, 1882; La Concordia (Barranquilla), July 8, 1882.
28. La Luz (Bogotá), November 24, 1882; La Prensa Libre (Barranquilla), November 29, December 16, 1882; La Reforma (Bogotá), December 16, 1882; [Cerruti], Aventuras de un cocinero, 26–27.
29. El Conservador (Bogotá), March 16, 1882; El Porvenir (Cartagena), December 10, 17, 1882, reprinted in Núñez, La reforma, Vol. I, Pt. 1, pp. 279, 284; El Relator (Bogotá), February 3, 1882; La Concordia (Barranquilla), May 8, 1882.
30. La Verdad (Bogotá), March 17, 1883; La Luz (Bogotá), October 3, 1882.

tutional reform, for they regarded the 1863 constitution as a holy ark containing sacred Liberal doctrine. They argued that the current economic and political difficulties facing Colombia stemmed from violations of the constitution by the Independents. As strict constructionists, Zaldúa and Secretary of Hacienda Samper attacked Núñez' economic program as an extralegal attempt to undermine federalism. By reversing the economic policies of Núñez and thereby reducing the economic power of the national government, they sought to preserve the federal system sanctioned by the constitution. In a message to Congress in April, the president criticized the practice of appropriating federal funds to state public works projects: "In my concept every time that an expense has been voted which no part of the constitution demands [the government] has been outside of the constitutional order." Zaldúa proposed a drastic reduction in allocations to the states and introduction of a system whereby each state would receive a fixed percentage of the customs revenue. State fiscal responsibility and sovereignty would thus be enhanced, and Congress would be relieved of the annual task of examining a long list of public works projects requested by the states. Despite the vigorous assault mounted against the Núñez economic program by Zaldúa and the Radicals in 1882, they failed to undo any significant portion of it.[31]

Zaldúa's health became a major factor in the political struggles of 1882. In June he suffered a recurrence of an old respiratory problem, but within a few days he recovered. Shortly thereafter Congress repealed an 1880 law which had been enacted to allow the president to retain office even while away from Bogotá. Congress had passed the 1880 law to enable Núñez to travel to Panama as president during the final weeks of 1880. In July 1882 it replaced the 1880 law with one declaring that whenever the president left Bogotá, even for reasons of health, the designate would assume the presidency.[32] The first designate in 1882 was Núñez. Political pettiness, which underlay enactment of this law, prevented Zaldúa as president from traveling to lower

31. *Diario Oficial* (Bogotá), April 21, 1882; *La Luz* (Bogotá), July 21, November 3, 1882; *El Conservador* (Bogotá), August 5, September 5, 1882; *La Concordia* (Barranquilla), July 18, 1882.

32. *Diario de Cundinamarca* (Bogotá), June 17, 1882; *Leyes de Colombia, 1880*, 41; *Leyes de Colombia, 1882*, 67–68.

altitudes to recover his health. In December he died, succumbing to another respiratory infection. Because Núñez was in Cartagena, Second Designate José Eusebio Otálora, who resided in Bogotá, assumed the presidency. Núñez remained on the coast during the remaining months of Zaldúa's term thus permitting Otálora to serve as president. In this manner, Núñez retained his eligibility for reelection as president for the 1884–1886 term.[33]

The sudden death of Zaldúa appeared to relegate the Radicals to political oblivion and assure continued Independent control of the national government. Although Otálora had established his own political reputation as the first Independent governor of Boyacá, he served as a close collaborator of Núñez in the cabinet in 1880 and then in the Senate. Núñez strongly endorsed Otálora as president, supported his election as first designate for the April 1883 to April 1884 period, and publicly approved his cabinet appointments which consisted of four Independents, two Radicals, and one Conservative. Because a loyal Independent again occupied the presidency, the election of Núñez for the 1884–1886 presidential term seemed a certainty. Shortly after Congress convened in February, a majority of its members endorsed Núñez for a second term as president. Núñez' own paper, La Luz, and the pro-Otálora organ, El Estandarte, endorsed the nomination. Within a month the Conservative National Directorate issued a manifesto placing the party solidly behind the Núñez candidacy.[34]

Despite the apparent inevitability of Núñez' election, his candidacy met opposition. Governor Wilches of Santander again challenged Núñez. Wilches' candidacy had been launched several weeks before that of Núñez and received the support of two prominent Independent publicists, Lino Ruiz, editor of El Imparcial, and Narciso González Lineros, editor of La Reforma. Some Radical newspapers of the north coast also supported Wilches. At the end of March, Radicals from the three north coast states held a convention at Barranquilla and endorsed Wilches for the presidency. The convention, claiming to rep-

33. Martínez Silva, Revistas políticas, I (July 15, 1882), 358; La Luz (Bogotá), December 20, 1882, January 17, 1883; El Promotor (Barranquilla), January 13, 1883.
34. La Luz (Bogotá), January 3, 17, 1883; La Integridad (Socorro), February 9, March 30, 1883; El Conservador (Bogotá), March 10, 1883; La Verdad (Bogotá), March 17, 1883.

resent the Liberal union, based its opposition to Núñez on the fact that he was too ardently supported by the Conservatives.[35] Wilches thus had the support of north coast Radicals and a handful of anti-Núñez Independents from the interior. During the initial phase of the campaign most of the Radical press in the interior remained silent on the candidacy question.

By early April the Radical leaders decided upon a strategy of evolution, that is, an attempt to induce Otálora to accept nomination from the Liberal union. The Radicals faced several problems in implementing their strategy. Foremost of these was article 75 of the constitution, which declared: "The person who has exercised the presidency will not be able to be reelected for the next period."[36] Another problem was the lack of unity among the Radicals, some of whom were already committed to Wilches. The question of how to induce Otálora to oppose his benefactor, Núñez, posed another obstacle.

Despite these problems, the campaign to launch the Otálora candidacy began in the Radical press in early April. Radicals denied the applicability of article 75 to a first designate serving as president and maintained that only Otálora could unite the Liberals and thus prevent the Conservatives from gaining power. Shortly thereafter, Otálora, in a formal statement, equivocally declined to accept the nomination. The statement quickly became an issue between the Radicals, who claimed to see in it an inclination to accept the nomination, and the Nuñistas, who accepted it at face value and applauded Otálora for his judgment and respect for the constitution.[37] A few days later Otálora presided over a meeting at the presidential palace summoned to discuss the candidacy question. Four cabinet members, including the Conservative Alejandro Posada, spokesmen for the Radicals, and both pro- and anti-Núñez Independents attended the meeting. All participants agreed that Wilches did not have a chance to win the election and that Núñez' election was inevitable unless Otálora became an active candidate.

35.   La Palestra (Mompós), March 17, April 14, 1883; La Reforma (Bogotá), January 10, April 27, 1883; La Integridad (Socorro), January 26, 1883; La Costa Atlántica (Barranquilla), January 26, April 13, 1883.

36.   Pombo and Guerra (eds), Constituciones, IV, 154.

37.   Diario de Cundinamarca (Bogotá), April 10, 13, 17, 1883; El Conservador (Bogotá), April 10, 21, 1883; El Promotor (Barranquilla), April 28, 1883.

Only Manuel Plata Azuero, representing the Liberal Central Committee (Radical), defended the constitutionality of Otálora's reelection and urged him to become a candidate. At the end of the discussion Otálora announced that he definitely would not be a candidate, giving as a principal reason the unconstitutionality of his reelection.[38]

During the next several weeks the Radical leaders played a waiting game which in effect aborted the Wilches candidacy. Instead of adopting the logical course of action and joining the north coast Radicals in support of Wilches, they nourished the hope that Otálora's candidacy could yet be sparked. Unable to attract additional support, Wilches shortly had to give up hopes for election. Two Bogotá papers founded for the purpose of supporting him suspended operations in May. Several of his most prominent supporters, including Lino Ruiz, published an appeal to Wilches urging him to withdraw in order to unite the Independents behind Núñez. In early July, Wilches issued a manifesto requesting his friends to switch their support to Núñez.[39]

Following Wilches' withdrawal, the Radicals intensified their pressure on Otálora to accept the nomination. Late in July Felipe Zapata addressed an open letter to Otálora in the name of the Liberal Central Committee forcefully arguing the Liberal need for Otálora's reelection. On July 28, Otálora's ambition overcame his good sense. He announced his candidacy for president.[40] It was, however, one of the shortest campaigns in Colombian history. Seven days later he again changed his mind and withdrew from the contest.

Otálora's decision to accept the nomination provoked a flurry of political activity which lasted until he reversed his position. On the day of his initial announcement, a pro-Otálora majority in the House forced its adjournment, leading in turn to the adjournment of the pro-Núñez Senate, which had just begun a formal inquiry into charges that President Otálora was guilty of financial wrongdoing. Two days later

38. *El Conservador* (Bogotá), May 1, 3, 1883; *El Cauca* (Popayán), June 9, 1883; Matéus, *La administración Otálora*, 14–16.

39. *La Luz* (Bogotá), May 23, 1883; *La Reforma* (Bogotá), June 2, July 31, 1883; *La Prensa Libre* (Barranquilla), June 23, 1883.

40. *Diario de Cundinamarca* (Bogotá), July 10, August 3, 1883; *La Nueva Era* (Bogotá), June 28, July 4, 1883; *La Escuela Liberal* (Bogotá), July 31, 1883; *El Conservador* (Bogotá), August 2, 1883.

the cabinet resigned in protest against Otálora's candidacy. He then conducted a series of meetings with leading members of all political factions, seeking their advice on what course to follow. The Conservatives and Independents asked Otálora to withdraw, and a majority of the Radicals urged him to press on with his candidacy. During one of these sessions the Radicals presented Otálora with numerous hastily gathered adherences; Aquileo Parra's name appeared at the top of a list of about 1,000 signatures. Otálora agreed to step aside if Núñez did likewise, but the Nuñistas refused. Finally on August 4, Otálora announced his withdrawal from contention.[41] In return for withdrawing, the Independents agreed to endorse him as candidate for governor of Boyacá. But before accepting the offer, Otálora insisted that the Conservative National Directorate also endorse him. Under pressure from the Independents, the Conservatives agreed to do so even though both parties had already endorsed General Pedro Sarmiento, a client of the Calderón family which at the time controlled Boyacá. Some Conservative papers adamantly refused to abandon Sarmiento, but Otálora nevertheless was led to believe that the formal endorsement of both parties guaranteed his election. When the votes for governor of Boyacá were tabulated later in the year, Sarmiento emerged the winner, thus revealing to Otálora the cost of his contemplated betrayal.[42]

A month before the presidential election, the Radicals were still without a candidate. In the circumstances they had little choice but to follow the lead signaled months earlier by their colleagues from the north coast. They endorsed the defunct candidacy of Wilches, a hopeless solution. Many Radicals, therefore, simply sat out the election. Aquileo Parra well expressed the feeling of resignation felt by his colleagues in the weeks prior to election: "The calamity which we have

41. *Diario de Cundinamarca* (Bogotá), August 3, 1883; *El Conservador* (Bogotá), August 3, 1883; *El Cauca* (Popayán), August 25, 1883; *La Prensa Libre* (Barranquilla), September 6, 1883; Galindo, *Recuerdos*, 234–35; Julio H. Palacio, "La evolución Otálora," *Revista Colombiana*, VIII (May, 1937), 215–19.

42. *La Escuela Liberal* (Bogotá), October 25, 1883; *La Epoca* (Bogotá), February 26, 1884; *El Promotor* (Barranquilla), August 25, 1883; *El Cronista* (Panama), December 8, 1883; *El Conservador* (Bogotá), August 21, November 10, 15, 1883; Martínez Silva, *Revistas políticas*, I (September 30, 1883), 400–401. Conservative papers refusing to endorse Otálora included *La Ilustración* (Bogotá) and *El Repertorio Colombiano* (Bogotá).

suffered with the candidacy of Otálora has placed us at the edge of an abyss. If Wilches were a docile man and accessible to the dictates of patriotism, we would be able to do something with his help; but he is, on the contrary, a stubborn and conceited man who, like Trujillo, pays attention only to those who flatter him." Parra, nevertheless, endorsed Wilches out of fear that by playing the role of dissident he would never be able to lead the party out of what he called its "trance."[43]

In the September election Núñez obtained the votes of six states, and Wilches, despite his withdrawal from the race, received the votes of his native Santander plus those of Tolima and Antioquia. Fears of civil war were rampant during the next two months. The principal Radical newspapers provocatively asserted that Wilches won the election and that he had been cheated out of victory by fraudulent elections in Boyacá and Panama. The state of alarm gradually subsided as a result of judicious troop movements ordered by a chastened President Otálora and the strengthening of state militias by Independent governors in Cundinamarca and Boyacá.[44]

The increasingly desperate political position of the Radicals stirred many of them to regard armed action as the only available path to power. Prominent party members such as Felipe Zapata and General Gabriel Vargas Santos joined groups of the ever-restive Santander Radicals in advocating recourse to arms. A party member from Bogotá advised Parra that the choice facing the Radicals was "Núñez or war, both things criminal, but the latter less than the former, because with Núñez we will not save ourselves from the consequences of war."[45] Parra himself felt that war offered the ultimate solution but that for the moment too many obstacles faced the Radicals. In a letter to Luis Bernal he concluded: "War is, without doubt, the only remedy against the leprosy of Nuñismo, but as of now there is not a leader in sight to di-

---

43. *Diario de Cundinamarca* (Bogotá), August 8, 1883; *La Estrella del Tolima* (Neiva), August 19, 1883; Parra to Luis [Bernal], August 19, 1883, Parra collection, Box #1, ACdeH.

44. *La Reforma* (Bogotá), September 19, 1883; *Diario de Cundinamarca* (Bogotá), October 17, 1883; *La Nueva Era* (Bogotá), October 25, 1883; *El Cauca* (Popayán), October 20, 27, 1883; *El Cronista* (Panama), October 13, 1883.

45. Gabriel Vargas Santos to Parra, November 11, 1883, Temístocles Paredes to Parra, November 18, 1883, CdeHRP.

rect it." Bernal summarized the Radical position in late 1883 as follows: "A leader is needed, and there is none; arms are needed, and there are none because Wilches is not going to place those he has in Radical hands; money is needed and there is none." [46] By the end of the year the Radicals' disunity and their lack of a recognized leader and a strong base of operations led them to accept a wait and see posture.

A principal factor causing the Radicals such distress was the continuing agitation by Núñez and his followers for constitutional reform. Throughout 1882 Núñez had advocated such specific reforms as extending the presidential term and allowing the national government to aid all types of state public works projects. But early the following year he called for replacement of the 1863 constitution: "The times in which we now find ourselves require a definite program, because it is a question not simply of preserving peace at any price, and of secondary measures, but of replacing the dead Constitution of 1863 with a new one in harmony with felt needs." [47] Furthermore, Núñez assigned to the Independent party the historic mission of revamping Colombia's constitutional framework. The specific changes recommended by Núñez all tended to weaken the federal system and to bolster the powers of the national government. He recommended that responsibility for the maintenance of order throughout the country be assigned to the national government and that the states delegate to Congress their right to legislate on all matters concerning national elections. Núñez also advocated standardizing penal legislation among all the states, strengthening the guaranties for religious freedom, and broadening the Supreme Court's power. In several newspaper articles written during 1883, Núñez stressed the theme that the 1863 constitution was an underlying cause of the nation's political problems. To Núñez' supporters and opponents alike, his reelection thus became linked to constitutional reform. One Independent paper avowed in late 1883: "The effort of the Independent party . . . is the quest of a single goal: to place itself in a position resolutely to undertake reform of the constitution." [48]

46. Parra to Luis Bernal, November 13, 1883, Parra collection, Box #1, ACdeH; Bernal to Parra, November 18, 1883, CdeHRP.

47. El Porvenir (Cartagena), February 25, 1883, reprinted in Núñez, La reforma, Vol. I, Pt. 1, p. 346.

48. Ibid., 345–48; El Porvenir (Cartagena), May 6, July 8, October 14, 1883, re-

The gap between the two Liberal parties which the first Núñez administration had so considerably widened grew even broader during the following two years. Debate on the fundamental issue of constitutional reform offered compelling evidence of the increasing doctrinal difference between the two parties. Despite the repeated call by Radicals for Liberal unity, their hallowed respect for the 1863 constitution meant no compromise on the issue uppermost in importance to the Independents. The Radical attitude toward the constitution was best expressed by the *Diario de Cundinamarca*, which asserted: "The constitution is a sacred thing; it is the tabernacle of the Liberal alliance."[49]

In the period between the first and second Núñez administrations, the national government labored under a condition of stalemate which was most acute in the final six months of the Otálora administration. Otálora's political career at the national level as well as in Boyacá came to an end. His indecisiveness and blatant opportunism had alienated Independents, Conservatives, and Radicals. The press ridiculed him without mercy and Congress humiliated him at every opportunity. The Independent majority in the newly elected House chose a long-standing personal enemy of Otálora as its presiding officer. Congress denied Otálora's request for permission to travel to Girardot to inaugurate a completed portion of the new railroad linking that city with Tocaima. Shortly thereafter, the House resolved that the diplomatic credentials of the Colombian minister to France, a close personal friend of Otálora, should be withdrawn because "he does not have the confidence of the Colombian people."[50] Congress' most drastic action against the president was the initiation of impeachment proceedings. A movement to investigate Otálora's conduct began in mid-1883 as part of the tangled political maneuvers designed to force him out of the presidential race. Within a few days of the convening of the 1884 congress, a motion to proceed with the investigation passed in the House by a vote

---

printed in Núñez, *La reforma*, Vol. I, Pt. 2, pp. 23–28, 79, 125; *El Cauca* (Popayán), October 15, 1883.

49. *Diario de Cundinamarca* (Bogotá), February 9, 1883.

50. Parra to Luis Bernal, February 12, 1884, Parra collection, Box #1, ACdeH; *La Epoca* (Bogotá), February 19, 1884; *El Cauca* (Popayán), January 12, 1884; *La Escuela Liberal* (Bogotá), September 15, 1883, March 21, 1884; *El Conservador* (Bogotá), February 19, 22, 1884.

of forty-three to four. A potpourri of charges was drawn up that included ten allegations of misconduct such as signing unauthorized contracts and making illegal appointments. Debate in the House on the charges began in March and continued until the sudden death of Otálora in May.[51]

Otálora's death did not end the paralysis of the national government. On inauguration day, April 1, 1884, President-elect Núñez had not yet arrived in the capital, so in his absence First Designate Ezequiel Hurtado, former governor of Cauca, took the presidential oath. Hurtado had emerged the winner over Governor Daniel Aldana of Cundinamarca in a bitter election in Congress for the position of first designate. Congress usually cast its annual vote for first designate in early February, but in 1884 the Independent majority postponed the vote for a month, hoping that Núñez would soon arrive from Cartagena and help avoid a divisive fight. He remained aloof from the contest, however, desiring not to alienate either of the two Independent candidates. Because of the split in Independent ranks, the Radicals determined the final outcome of the vote. They disliked both candidates, but Aldana's open hostility toward them and his close cooperation with the Conservatives induced the Radicals to unite behind Hurtado.[52]

Núñez' delay was expected to last only a few days, but in early May the nation learned to its surprise that he had just departed for Curacao for treatment of an unspecified illness. The president-elect did not return to Colombia until the end of June, and further delays postponed his arrival in Bogotá an additional month. To the immense relief of his supporters he finally assumed the presidency on August 11.[53] His absence generated considerable mystery and widespread specula-

51.   La Escuela Liberal (Bogotá), August 22, 1883; La Prensa Libre (Barranquilla), September 6, 1883; El Conservador (Bogotá), November 13, 1883, February 22, March 17, 1884; Diario de Cundinamarca (Bogotá), June 4, 1884; La Epoca (Bogotá), April 23, 1884. For information on Otálora's feelings during this period see Matéus, La administración Otálora, 25–26.

52.   Diario de Cundinamarca (Bogotá), April 22, 1884; Martínez Silva, Revistas políticas, I (February 29, 1884), 425; La Epoca (Bogotá), March 18, 1884; La Escuela Liberal (Bogotá), March 21, 1884; Parra to Luis Bernal, March 3, 1884, Parra collection, Box #1, ACdeH.

53.   La Prensa Libre (Barranquilla), April 5, May 3, 1884; La Luz (Bogotá), July 30, 1884; La Palestra (Mompós), June 30, July 18, September 12, 1884.

tion as to its true cause. At mid-year Carlos Martínez Silva expressed the nation's impatience and exasperation as follows: "The only thing certain about Señor Núñez is that nothing is known of him, that he writes to no one anything that is clear or that can be shown, that he does not explain his delay or fix a time for his arrival. What mystery is there in all this? How can he thus leave the nation delivered to the torments of uncertainty? How can he abandon his party to dissolution, to confusion, and to ruin?"[54]

Hurtado presided over the third caretaker government between the first and second Núñez administrations. It was the most provisional of the three, because its duration was indeterminate and totally dependent upon the will of Núñez. Hurtado set the tone of his administration by promising to undertake no political initiatives during Núñez' absence.[55]

The intrigues and political maneuvers among Independents, Radicals, and Conservatives which had so crippled the Zaldúa and Otálora regimes continued under Hurtado. A difference, however, was that the Conservatives were more restive and created more difficulties than the Radicals. The Radicals, claiming to foresee a developing rupture between Núñez and the Conservatives, nursed the hope that he would work for Liberal unity. A north coast Radical reported to Parra that Núñez, in talks with local Radicals, seemed inclined toward an understanding with them. An Antioqueño Radical urged his colleagues to support Núñez in order to secure him in the Liberal camp, while a party member from Cali agreed with Parra's advice to promote the Liberal union and withhold criticism of Hurtado.[56]

In sharp contrast to the conciliatory attitude of the Radicals, the Conservatives expressed serious misgivings about Hurtado. Their discontent focused on the composition of Hurtado's cabinet, to which he had appointed four Independents, two Radicals, and one Conservative. Conservatives felt cheated despite the gratuitous assertion in El Con-

---

54. Martínez Silva, *Revistas políticas*, I (May 31, 1884), 434; see also *Diario de Cundinamarca* (Bogotá), May 30, 1884.

55. Martínez Silva, *Revistas políticas*, I (April 30, 1884), 427.

56. Pablo Arosemena to Parra, April 15, 1884, CdeHRP; Parra to Luis [Bernal], February 14, 1884, Parra collection, Box #1, ACdeH; Pedro Restrepo Uribe to Parra, May 1, 1884, Belisario Zamorano to Parra, June 20, 1884, CdeHRP.

servador, a day before the appointments were announced, that the Conservative party demanded nothing more from the Independents than "the faithful fulfillment of their program."[57] The lone Conservative cabinet appointee, Mariano Tanco, was a septuagenarian, inactive in party affairs. He declined the appointment on the advice of the Conservative National Directorate, which felt that the cabinet should be either entirely Independent or else should contain an equal Conservative and Radical representation. Hurtado named another Conservative to the vacant post, but he too declined the office. Despite Conservative protestations of continued confidence in Hurtado and the Independents, the general tenor of commentary in the Conservative press reflected an ill-concealed sense of betrayal. A north coast Conservative paper edited by Leonardo Canal exclaimed: "Never has perfidy been better rewarded or loyalty more punished than in the present case."[58] The only recourse available to the Conservatives, however, was to await patiently the return of Núñez and to resist Radical efforts to separate them from the Independents.

By mid-1884 the program of the first Núñez administration was yet basically intact. The struggle by Radicals to reverse it and Nuñistas to consolidate it had produced stalemate. The conflict, which caused erosion of Independent strength, highlighted the doctrinal differences between the two Liberal parties, and it sparked debate on constitutional reform, an issue not readily susceptible to compromise. Political debate in this period also emphasized the continuing pivotal role of Núñez.

President Núñez occupied a strong bargaining position at the beginning of his second administration. Both the Radicals and the Conservatives were eager for a lasting alliance with the Independents. Even though this eagerness largely stemmed from each party's conviction that it could swallow the Independents, the very fact that each wanted the opportunity to try presented Núñez with clear-cut options. Pure opportunism dictated alliance with the Radicals, reunification of the Liberal party, and the likely continuation of Liberal rule.

---

57. *Diario Oficial* (Bogotá), April 2, 1884; *El Liberal* (Bogotá), May 6, 1884; *El Conservador* (Bogotá), April 2, 1884.

58. *Diario Oficial* (Bogotá), April 26, 1884; *El Conservador* (Bogotá), April 4, 5, 14, 1884; *El Liberal* (Bogotá), April 22, May 6, 1884; *El Heraldo* (Cartagena) quoted in *El Liberal* (Bogotá), May 6, 1884.

The desire for fundamental change, a shift from federalism to centralism, and strengthened national unity dictated alliance with the Conservatives. The second choice, however, invited civil war because of the known propensity to armed action among some Radicals and the lack of effective control over the party by its weakened leadership. By August 1884 both Radicals and Conservatives were impatient for a clear signal from Núñez as to the course he would follow.

Chapter VIII

The Second Núñez Administration: Crisis, Civil War, and Reform 1884-1886

Colombians identified Rafael Núñez with a clear set of goals at the time of his second inauguration in August 1884. He sought to move the nation toward a more self-sufficient economic system by shifting from a labor-intensive, extractive economy to a capital-intensive, technologically based economy. Through such measures as inflation and such policies as protectionism and import substitution Núñez had initiated this transformation during his first administration. In addition to favoring a more active economic role for government, he wanted to strengthen federal political and administrative power in order to secure internal peace. As a thoroughgoing nationalist, Núñez strove to transform Colombia from an association of regional communities into a national republic. The Núñez program, the Regeneration, was a program of modernizing nationalism.

Opposition from the Radicals to every major element of the program had effectively stalemated it for the past two years. By late 1884 this opposition took the extreme form of an armed revolt. Núñez could overcome his opponents only by committing the Independent party to an alliance with the Conservatives. He consolidated the Regeneration only after confirming his right to govern the nation by leading his administration to military victory over the Radicals in the civil war of 1884-1885.

Núñez arrived in the capital at the end of July 1884. His forced residence in Bogotá burdened him with the vexing social problem of his marital status. Núñez' civil marriage to Doña Soledad Román in

1877 not only violated basic church law but also offended many Colombians because his first wife, whom he had married ecclesiastically,
was still alive in Panama.[1] Bogotanos viewed Núñez' second marriage
as a manfestation of the moral laxity long associated with costeño social behavior.

Bogotá society evidenced particular curiosity over whether Doña
Soledad would accompany Núñez to the capital or would remain in
Cartagena as she had done during his first administration. The Conservative press discreetly made little comment about his marital status,
but the Radicals took great delight in riveting public attention on it.
When Aquileo Parra learned that the president-elect planned to bring
his wife with him to Bogotá, he observed to a friend: "We will see what
results from this challenge to the cream of Bogotá society." A late 1883
issue of the Diario de Cundinamarca responded to an attack by Conservatives on the moral character of José María Rojas Garrido, a recently deceased Radical luminary, by posing the following series of
questions about Núñez:

Does this man attend mass? No!
Does he fast on holy days? No!
Does he confess? No!
Does he take communion? No!
. . . .
Was Rojas Garrido a bigamist? No!
Is Núñez one? Yes![2]

Bogotanos delighted in composing epigrams about Núñez and Doña
Soledad, and some of these verses enlivened political discussions
when published as broadsides surreptitiously posted throughout the
city. When Núñez and Doña Soledad reached Bogotá in July, prominent Conservatives accompanied by their wives cordially greeted the
pair. In contrast, Radicals arrived at the welcoming ceremonies unac-
companied by their spouses.[3] Such incidents may have had little po-

1. See note 25, Chapter V.
2. Aquileo Parra to Luis Bernal, February 12, 1884, Parra collection, Box #1,
ACdeH; Diario de Cundinamarca (Bogotá), November 10, 1883.
3. Diario de Cundinamarca (Bogotá), October 17, 1884; Liévano Aguirre, Rafael
Núñez, 222–23. One epigram which circulated in Bogotá after Núñez and Doña
Soledad were married in the church in 1889 was the following, found in a footnote

litical significance, but a sensitive man such as Núñez could hardly fail to take note.

As president, Núñez faced a rapidly mounting political crisis and a series of economic problems which had become acute during the governmental stalemate of the past two years. As a consequence, he came under intensified pressure from both Radicals and Conservatives during this period to abandon his equivocal stance and to commit himself and the Independents to a solid alliance with one or the other of the two contending parties.

One of the most striking features of the Colombian political scene in August 1884 was its tendency toward anarchy. The problem of unfocused national party leadership had plagued the Radicals for several years, though it had been somewhat ameliorated during the benign presidency of Ezequiel Hurtado. Radicals received some assurances from Hurtado as well as from people in contact with Núñez that the president-elect would follow a policy of unifying the Liberal party. Although the Radicals lacked a leader and a directing committee in mid-1884, a general consensus existed among prominent party figures that Núñez should be given a chance to unite the Liberal party. Despite this policy decision, the conspicuous social snub of Núñez and Doña Soledad by Bogotá's Radicals indicated that the party lacked the discipline necessary to take even the most elementary step toward reconciliation with Núñez. In addition, the Radical party in each of the nine states operated nearly autonomously from national direction. After 1878 when the Radicals lost control of the national government, the party leadership held few sanctions it could apply to state party figures to induce compliance with national policy. Santander's Radicals refrained from revolting against Governor Solón Wilches only because prominent party figures such as Santiago Pérez and Aquileo Parra got them to postpone their revolution through persuasion.

By mid-1884 the Conservatives were experiencing similar, though

---

on typed copy of letter from Parra to Luis Bernal, April 1, 1880, Parra collection, Box #1, ACdeH:

Explíquenos lo que pasa
Los Hermanos de Loyola:
Si Núñez hasta hoy se casa
Que era de antes Doña Sola?

less severe, organizational difficulties. The willingness of the party faithful to follow the Conservative National Directorate's policy of support for Núñez and the Independents was more severely strained during the Hurtado presidency than at any time since the establishment of the Directorate in 1879. After that date the party press had grown rapidly in both prestige and number of publications. This growth gave expression within the party to diverse views which were often shaped by regional events. In responding to pressure for a more relaxed control over party policy, the Directorate resolved in mid-1884 that henceforth no single paper would serve as the official party organ.[4]

Degree of compliance to Conservative national party policy varied significantly from state to state in 1884. Conservatives and Independents cooperated closely in Cauca and Cundinamarca. Independents governed both states and offered a conspicuous role to Conservatives in the state administrations. Intense Radical opposition to Governors Eliseo Payán of Cauca and Daniel Aldana of Cundinamarca greatly strengthened the Conservative-Independent alliance in their states.[5] In Santander many Conservatives openly opposed the National Directorate's policy which called for abstention in the gubernatorial election of mid-1884 to choose a successor to Wilches. The regional Conservative paper, La Voz de Ocaña, declared that to avoid a Radical victory the Conservatives would have to participate in the election. The most flagrant violation of national party policy occurred in Panama, where party labels had little significance. The Conservatives disliked the Independent governor, and when he attempted to handpick a successor in the 1884 elections, they allied with the Radicals in nominating Justo Arosemena for the governorship.[6]

4. El Conservador (Bogotá), July 19, 1884. Some of the principal Conservative organs in 1884, together with their editors, were the following: El Conservador (Bogotá), Manuel Briceño; La Voz Nacional (Bogotá), Sergio Arboleda; El Comercio (Bogotá), Rufino Gutiérrez; La Verdad (Bogotá), José María Quijano Otero; El Repertorio Colombiano (Bogotá), Carlos Martínez Silva; El Heraldo (Cartagena), Leonardo Canal; La Voz de Ocaña (Ocaña), Félix A. Merlano.

5. El Conservador (Bogotá), May 7, 1884; Diario de Cundinamarca (Bogotá), June 6, 1884; La Epoca (Bogotá), June 11, 1884; Martínez Silva, Revistas políticas, I (November 30, 1883, February 29, April 30, 1884), 415, 424–25, 432–33.

6. La Voz de Ocaña (Ocaña), July 15, August 30, 1884; El Conservador (Bogotá), January 26, June 17, July 14, August 20, 23, 1884; La Prensa Libre (Barranquilla), May 24, 1884; Martínez Silva, Revistas políticas, I (June 30, 1884), 441.

Núñez thus faced a highly fluid political situation which left him with considerable maneuverability. The national leaderships of both the Radical and Conservative parties competed with each other for an alliance with Núñez. But his postponement of a choice posed serious problems for each party. Regionally based political interest groups in each party were defying national party policy and undermining the bargaining position of party leaders in Bogotá. Núñez' delay in allying with either party magnified the danger of insurrection by Radicals in Santander, Cundinamarca, and Cauca, and to Conservatives it posed the threat of party fragmentation. Conservative-Radical competition in late 1884 intensified the struggle of each to maintain party authority while waiting for Núñez to announce a decision favoring one party or the other.

Colombia's economic problems contributed to the growing political anxieties in the months prior to Núñez' inauguration. The problems remained essentially the same as they had been at the opening of his first administration in 1880: an imbalance in foreign trade resulting from a lack of exports, an alarming gold drain, and the necessity of making a choice between balanced budgets or major federal financial support for state public works projects. After 1880, Colombian foreign trade continued to deteriorate; the quinine boom collapsed, world coffee prices declined, and gold exports assumed an ever larger proportion of total export value. Beginning in 1883, Congress made a vigorous effort to bring the budget deficit under control. The growth in customs receipts over the past decade, a result of increased import duties, eased the task. But the only feasible way to eliminate the deficit was to cut expenditures drastically. Congress approved a budget for fiscal year 1883–1884 which anticipated the smallest deficit in a decade. The budget called for major cuts in appropriations for the two categories consuming the most revenue, service on the national debt and public works projects. The 1884–1885 budget further reduced total expenditures and nearly eliminated the deficit.[7] As a result of stringencies produced by these cuts, complaints began appearing in the press that the government lagged months behind in meeting its payroll and other administrative expenses. Secretary of Hacienda Aníbal Galindo

7. Beyer, "The Colombian Coffee Industry," 368–71; El Promotor (Barranquilla), January 12, 1884; Leyes de Colombia, 1882, 166; Leyes de Colombia, 1883, 79. See Figure 1, Table 9, and Table 7.

reported to Congress in early 1884 that "the bad fiscal situation . . . is reaching extremes almost incompatible with the existence of the government."[8]

The decision to reduce federal support for public works projects reflected both a growing disenchantment with such programs and a desire to cut deficits. Despite the expenditure over the last decade of millions of pesos on public works, none of the principal projects was nearing completion. The major contractor of the period was a Cuban-born, naturalized United States citizen, Francisco Javier Cisneros, who won the contract to build the Antioquia Railroad in the 1870s. Because of his engineering competence, organizational skills, and political sensitivity, he obtained a variety of construction contracts during the following years. Cisneros merited and received considerable respect for his accomplishments, but by 1883/1884 he had become the object of serious criticism. Labor problems, shortages of material, and lack of funds caused seemingly endless delays, postponements, and contract renegotiations. If the highly qualified Cisneros could not fulfill his contracts, there seemed little hope that Colombia could achieve the economic breakthrough promised by the so-called redemptive public works projects.[9]

Colombia's experience with another enterprise, the ironworks of Samacá, contributed to the decision to curtail federal aid to state projects. Governor José Eusebio Otálora of Boyacá had actively promoted the ironworks in the late 1870s, and he reaped major political advantage from the expectation that the ironworks would spark an economic renaissance. By 1883 the continuation of federal subsidies for the project became a heated political issue, and the debate led to the formation of several commissions charged with studying the project's feasibility. The most authoritative of the studies, one authorized by Congress and conducted by the Antioqueño engineer Vicente Restrepo, concluded that the area around Samacá did not contain

8. Martínez Silva, *Revistas políticas*, I (September 30, 1883), 399; *Diario de Cundinamarca* (Bogotá), August 18, 1883; *El Conservador* (Bogotá), April 8, 1884; *Memoria de Hacienda, 1884*, 144–45.

9. Martínez Silva, *Revistas políticas*, I (October 31, 1883), 407–408; *El Comercio* (Bogotá), January 23, June 23, 1884; Hernán Horna, "Francisco Javier Cisneros: A Pioneer in Transportation and Economic Development in Latin America, 1857–1898," *The Americas*, XXX (July, 1973), 54–82.

enough high-grade iron ore to supply the ironworks for more than six months. After spending more than $500,000 on the ironworks, the government discovered its embarrassing oversight, lack of high-grade ore! The congressional committee responsible for reviewing Restrepo's findings concluded: "The Samacá ironworks is an absolutely hopeless enterprise, and after enormous expenditures the only thing that has been achieved as a final result is an irremediable disaster."[10]

As a consequence of the decision to sacrifice state public works programs for a balanced federal budget, state governments came under increasing pressure to fund the more deserving of these projects. From 1880 to 1884 total federal expenditures dropped nearly 22 percent, whereas state expenditures increased about 25 percent.[11] To obtain more funds the state governments resorted to tax increases and imposition of new taxes. Miguel Samper, a leading Liberal economic thinker of the period, wrote in 1884 a widely read pamphlet on the consequences of what he labeled the "fiscal voraciousness" of state governments. He directed his criticism to the growing tendency of states to levy road taxes on foreign goods in transit through a state, a tax explicitly forbidden by the constitution. Cundinamarca violated this provision most flagrantly, but Samper noted that Santander, Tolima, and other states were following Cundinamarca's example. "The evil of voraciousness has become contagious, as a result of which we are entering into full tariff warfare which will bring feudalism in commerce, discouraging the movement of goods and dividing the republic into small Chinas with their surrounding walls of tax collectors and guards."[12]

Evidence of this tendency toward economic fragmentation appeared in an article by Marceliano Vélez, a prominent Conservative of Antioquia. Vélez examined the problems of a growing imbalance in Antioquia's trade and the inability of its gold exports to pay for

10. Emiliano Restrepo E. et al., Ferrería de Samacá: informe de una comisión (Bogotá, 1884), 3–4.
11. See Table 7. Budgeted expenditures for the nine states totaled about $3,823,000 in 1880 and $4,775,000 in 1884. These figures were compiled from the budgets published in the official newspapers of the states. In those cases in which the fiscal period consisted of two calendar years the figures for expenditures were divided by two.
12. Miguel Samper, Nuestras enfermedades políticas (Bogotá, 1884), 8.

goods imported from abroad and from neighboring states, and he concluded: "In order to meet the cost of our imports and to overcome the monetary crisis, it is necessary for governments and businessmen to promote industries producing goods which we unnecessarily bring from other states."[13]

In the years between the first and second Núñez administrations, political and economic power tended to flow from Bogotá to the states. Conservative party leadership became less effectively centralized, and Radical leaders fruitlessly continued their efforts to impose a modicum of discipline on the state parties. Although major elements of Núñez' 1880–1881 economic program, such as protectionism and the establishment of the National Bank, remained intact, Congress reversed his policy of incurring huge deficits to finance a growing federal bureaucracy, a large standing army, and subsidies to state public works projects. The period of governmental fiscal retrenchment which followed the first Núñez administration gave license to Colombia's federalist tendencies. By mid-1884 the states were becoming more self-assertive, and national unity was again threatened.

Santander's economy by 1884 had sustained more setbacks than that of any other state. Since at least the mid-1870s the once well-to-do artisan and textile industries of Santander and Boyacá had been in a state of decay because of competition from cheaper foreign imports. The collapse of the quinine market in 1881 and the fall in coffee prices until 1885 had their greatest impact in Santander, where these two commodities represented the state's principal exports. A sharp drop in the price of wheat in 1884–1885 brought economic hardship to Boyacá, and this, in turn, reduced the volume of Santander's trade with its southern neighbor in such traditional articles of exchange as sugar and beef. Income to the Santander government, nevertheless, continued to grow because of an increasing tax burden which was approaching its political limits. Late in 1883 the state assembly authorized Governor Wilches to levy new taxes and increase existing ones. Wilches immediately imposed a slaughter tax of $5 per head on beef, a sizable tax considering that cattle had a market value of only about $25 per head.[14]

13.   El Trabajo (Medellín), June 4, 1884.
14.   McGreevey, An Economic History, 105–106; Diario de Cundinamarca (Bogotá), October 8, 1884.

The governor also levied a $10 tax on each *carga*—a muleload weighing about 125 kilograms—of imported flour, a carga being worth about $12. Other foreign imports were charged $6 a carga, a $4-per-carga tax was imposed on goods imported from neighboring states, and taxes were raised on liquor, tobacco, and stamps. The Liberal and Conservative press during the next several months contained numerous complaints about the excessive tax burden in Santander, the lack of progress on the Soto Railroad projected to link Bucaramanga with the Magdalena River, and the general misuse of tax revenue. In August 1884 a paper in northern Santander described economic conditions of that region as follows: "Industry is totally annihilated, business [is] in complete paralysis, there is no work, and poverty is felt and known."[15]

As a result of these economic problems and the approaching end of the Wilches regime, Santander's political stability became a matter of serious concern in mid-1884. Wilches chose as his successor Francisco Ordóñez, a business associate, promoter of the Soto Railroad, and political colleague. Conservatives and some Independents opposed the choice, and they attempted to pressure Wilches to adopt a candidate whom both parties could support. Each party separately sent delegations to confer with Wilches proposing alternate candidates, but he refused to abandon Ordóñez.[16]

The Radicals, despite their support for Wilches as presidential candidate in 1883, opposed his choice for governor. They nominated the prestigious Eustorgio Salgar, who at the time was serving in the Hurtado cabinet and in the past had been governor of Santander and president of Colombia. Party leaders made a serious attempt to unite their colleagues behind Salgar, but the effort to defeat Ordóñez at the polls was quite hopeless because of Wilches' control of the election machinery. A Radical from Socorro reported to Aquileo Parra that he could not even get party members to sign adherences in support of Salgar; in response to such organizational efforts they retorted: "We are not going to expose our signatures to more ridicule; give us a rifle, and

15. *El Conservador* (Bogotá), October 4, November 29, December 22, 1883; Martínez Silva, *Revistas políticas*, I (November 30, 1883), 412–13; *El Debate* (Bogotá), September 4, 1884; *La Voz de Ocaña* (Ocaña), August 30, 1884.

16. Foción Soto, *Memorias sobre el movimiento de resistencia a la dictadura de Rafael Núñez, 1884–1885* (2 vols.; Bogotá, 1913), I, 10–13; García, *Bucaramanga*, 217–18; Francisco Santos to Daniel Hernández, May 2, 1884, CdeHRP.

in that way we will help." The correspondent added: "This is the thinking of everyone, and it is necessary to take advantage of this last plan." Another Radical informed Parra that the party's prospects were hopeless because of Wilches' control of the election machinery, his intimidation of Radicals, and defections from Radical ranks. On election eve a Radical from Socorro concluded: "Nothing else remains for us except to give evidence of our virility, even going to extreme measures, in order to regain our lost renown." [17] During the weeks prior to the late July elections, Santander's Radicals arrived at a general consensus agreeing to launch a revolt if Wilches resorted to violence or the obvious use of electoral fraud to assure the election of Ordóñez.

As anticipated by the Radicals, overt acts of fraud and violence characterized the election. In the days immediately following it, they prepared to launch their long-postponed insurrection. Radicals from throughout the state advised party leaders in Bogotá of their preparations, warning that war was inevitable unless the national government acted to annul the election results.[18] Conditions in Santander thus reached a critical point in which peace could be preserved only through federal intervention. Before the newly inaugurated Núñez administration had an opportunity to act, fighting erupted in Santander.

Cabinet appointments and the inaugural speech traditionally served as indicators of the political course to be followed by a new president. In the case of the second Núñez administration, these indicators signaled conflicting courses of action. In his inaugural address Núñez declared himself "an irrevocable member of Colombian Liberalism," but he increased Conservative membership in the cabinet from one to two positions. Of the remaining five positions, two went to the Radicals and three to the Independents. All three parties seemed satisfied with the president's initial moves, or at least they withheld critical comment.[19] Núñez had, in effect, postponed a final decision on

17. I. Noriega to Parra, June 27, 1884, Ramón Angarita to Parra, June 28, 1884, Triano Albornóz to Parra, July 24, 1884, CdeHRP.

18. Soto, *Memorias sobre la dictadura*, I, 17–27; García, *Bucaramanga*, 218–19; Martínez Silva, *Revistas políticas*, I (August 31, 1884), 448–49; five residents of La Concepción to Felipe Zapata, Januario Salgar, and Temístocles Paredes, August 2, 1884, seven residents of Pamplona to Felipe Zapata, Januario Salgar, Fortunato Bernal, Nepomuceno Alvarez, Temístocles Paredes, Gabriel Vargas Santos, M. Plata Azuero, and Dámaso Zapata, August 5, 1884, CdeHRP.

19. *La Prensa Libre* (Barranquilla), August 27, 1884; *El Promotor* (Barranquilla),

whether he would ally with the Radicals or with the Conservatives. Events in Santander, however, would force his hand by the end of the year.

In responding to the Santander crisis, Núñez chose not to invoke the 1880 law on public order which would have required overt backing for the highly unpopular Wilches regime. Núñez instead sent two senators as mediators, one a leading Radical, Felipe Zapata, and the other an Independent editor, Narciso González Lineros. Federal troops under the command of Núñez' trusted friend General Juan Nepomuceno González followed the commissioners to Santander. All factions in the state were amenable to mediation, and the brief conflict ended in early September when the peace commissioners announced a formal settlement. The peace terms called for the resignation of Wilches, the temporary succession of González Lineros to the governorship, and the holding of a special election to choose delegates to a convention which would decide all questions arising from the contested election of July.[20]

In the special election the Radicals won a majority of the convention seats. When the delegates convened in November the Radicals attempted to broaden the powers of the convention and to use it to gain control of the state government. The minority coalition of Conservatives and Independents responded by walking out of the convention, thus depriving it of a quorum. Although Governor González Lineros thereupon dissolved the convention, the Radicals met privately and elected General Sergio Camargo governor of Santander and Fortunato Bernal and Daniel Hernández first and second designates. A few days later Daniel Hernández, acting on his own initiative, took up arms at Pamplona against the government of Santander. After uniting with forces under General Foción Soto of Cúcuta, Hernández and his rebel units generalized the war by crossing the border into Boyacá.[21]

August 30, 1884; *La Palestra* (Mompós), September 12, 1884; *Diario de Cundinamarca* (Bogotá) August 15, 1884.

20. *La Luz* (Bogotá), September 24, 1884; *El Conservador* (Bogotá), August 22, 1884; *La Palestra* (Mompós), September 12, 1884; Martínez Silva, *Revistas políticas*, I (September 15, 1884), 453–54.

21. *El Conservador* (Bogotá), November 12, December 19, 23, 1884; *Diario de Cundinamarca* (Bogotá), November 21, 1884; *La Voz de Ocaña* (Ocaña), December 16, 1884; *La Luz* (Bogotá), November 22, December 10, 1884, reprinted in Núñez, *La reforma*, Vol. I, Pt. 2, pp. 297–310.

Despite the frequent threats of revolution uttered by Santander's Radicals, Hernández' action found Colombia's Radical party still disorganized, unprepared, and virtually leaderless.[22] In an effort to provide the party with a prestigious leader capable of uniting all of its elements in this moment of crisis, a committee of five Radical members of Congress chose General Sergio Camargo as party leader. Camargo, recently returned to Colombia from Quito where he had served as Colombian minister, declined both the national party leadership and the governorship of Santander. He advised the committee to try to arrive at a negotiated settlement with Núñez and to obtain firm commitments of support from the Radical governments of Tolima and Antioquia, which alone could provide the necessary arms for a major revolutionary effort. Camargo then retired to his hacienda in Boyacá.[23]

The attitudes of the governments of Antioquia and Tolima were critical to party prospects, and neither government favored resort to arms. Late in December, Governor Luciano Restrepo of Antioquia offered Parra this assessment of the rebellion in Santander: "I think that, except for a providential circumstance, the patriots of that state will be sacrificed because it is not possible for them to resist all the national forces that have been sent against them."[24] The lack of revolutionary zeal in Tolima was even more striking. Governor Gabriel González evaluated events in Santander as follows: "The lack of good judgment with which our friends in Santander proceeded is to be lamented. . . . I understand perfectly that this has not been the result of a *meditated* act, deliberately and spontaneously matured in the Liberal party, but of a rash haste, inexcusable in men of judgment who ought to know that the cause which they were going to express or expound was not individual but the great cause of the Liberal party of the republic."[25]

22. For a good analysis of Radical disunity in the months prior to the war see Delpar, "The Liberal Party of Colombia," 286–88.

23. B. Herrera to Parra, October 1, 1884, Sergio Camargo to Parra, T. Paredes, J. Salgar, F. Zapata, and Luis Robles, November 28, 1884, CdeHRP; Gabriel Camargo Pérez, Sergio Camargo, el bayardo colombiano (Bogotá, 1972), 287–94.

24. Luciano Restrepo to Parra, December 24, 1884, CdeHRP; see also Restrepo to Parra, September 11, 1884, and Joaquín E. Montoya to Parra, October 30, 1884, CdeHRP.

25. Gabriel González to Parra, December 24, 1884, CdeHRP. For more on the negative attitudes of Restrepo and González toward the revolution see Soto, Memorias sobre la dictadura, I, 204.

Radicals in states under Independent rule also exhibited a lack of resolution. In Cauca the activities of Ezequiel Hurtado proved particularly disconcerting. Hurtado had returned to the state after transferring the presidency to Núñez, and he attempted to assume leadership over a united Liberal party in Cauca. His efforts were challenged by Governor Payán and by the Radicals, who could not decide whether he was a Payanista, Nuñista, or convert to Radicalism. A resident of Cali well expressed Radical perplexity at Hurtado's action in forming a Liberal Directory in Popayán. "General Hurtado, as the sphinx in the fable, continues proposing enigmas to his astonished party colleagues. Now he seems a friend of Liberal union, now a decided Payanista."[26] The irresolution of the Radicals of Cundinamarca resulted from the chastening experience of having been recently defeated in an armed struggle. In late September, a force of about 1,000 Radicals under Generals Ricardo Gaitán Obeso and Manuel Navarrete revolted against Governor Daniel Aldana. They operated in the western portion of the state for only about two weeks when national troops, immediately dispatched by Núñez, forced the Radicals to capitulate. In Boyacá the Santandereanos who entered the state under Hernández and Soto gained few adherents as they made their way toward Tunja, where they hoped to capture a major federal arms depot. Governor Pedro Sarmiento neither aided nor resisted the Radical advance, but he helped national forces transfer the arms and munitions to Bogotá just before the arrival of the invading army. Sarmiento, like Camargo, opposed the war and urged negotiations with Núñez.[27]

In Bogotá the Radical leadership could not decide what course to follow. Key figures such as Santiago and Felipe Pérez, Felipe Zapata, José María Quijano Wallis, and Aquileo Parra opposed the rebellion, but a majority of their less prominent colleagues favored support for Hernández. Late in December, Foción Soto accepted Sarmiento's advice and traveled to Bogotá to hold discussions with Núñez. The talks proved fruitless, but while in the capital Soto attempted to stimulate

26. Rafael Toro to Parra, November 14, 1884, CdeHRP. For other expressions of Radical confusion and organizational problems in Cauca see Alejandro Matión to Parra, December 1, 1884, J. Núñez to Parra, December 5, 1884, and Ezequiel Hurtado to Enrique Posada, November 17, 1884, CdeHRP.

27. *El Conservador* (Bogotá), September 27, October 4, 21, 1884; *El Liberal* (Bogotá), September 25, October 16, 1884; Camargo Pérez, *Sergio Camargo*, 298–302.

support for the rebellion among the Radical leaders. In meetings with Parra, Januario Salgar, and Francisco E. Alvarez, Soto discovered that they regarded a resort to arms precipitate and premature. Soto also attempted to obtain funds for the revolt from party members, but when he left Bogotá in early January he had collected less than $1,400. Such niggardliness led him to exclaim: "To such a level, hardly above zero, has the fervor, enthusiasm, and determination of our partisans in the capital risen!"[28]

A main obstacle to Radical unification was the desire by many party members to respond to Núñez' call for cooperation in reforming the constitution. The reform issue became increasingly important in late 1884 because it directly bore on Núñez' decision on whether to ally with Radicals or Conservatives. In several articles published in the closing months of 1884, the president stressed the reform theme, making it clear that achievement of Liberal unity depended on Radical support for substantive constitutional reform. Shortly after Núñez' arrival in Bogotá, Carlos Martínez Silva observed: "He speaks only of the necessity of reforming the constitution, although it is not known what he considers the easiest and quickest route in arriving at this result."[29] At mid-year some Radical senators joined the Independent majority in asking the state assemblies to request constitutional reform. Shortly thereafter, Bolívar's assembly complied with the Senate request and was soon joined by the Radical-dominated assembly of Tolima. Radicals in Tolima expressed a cooperative attitude toward Núñez and favored constitutional reform as a means of reuniting the Liberal party. Governor Luciano Restrepo of Antioquia also concluded that "we should not close the door to reform of the constitution." Núñez further encouraged Radical interest in reform by pledging in November that if the constitution were reformed and the presidential term extended he would not accept reelection under the new charter.[30]

28.   Parra, Memorias, 515n; Quijano Wallis, Memorias, 465–66; Soto, Memorias sobre la dictadura, I, 203, 213–14.

29.   La Luz (Bogotá), September 24, October 8, 22, November 8, 1884, reprinted in Núñez, La reforma, Vol. I, Pt. 2, pp. 249–56, 263–68, 281–87; Martínez Silva, Revistas políticas I (July 31, 1884), 447.

30.   El Conservador (Bogotá), October 18, 1884; Martínez Silva, Revistas políticas, I (August 31, 1884), 451; La Estrella del Tolima (Neiva), August 26, September 1, 1884; Luciano Restrepo to Parra, September 5, 1884, CdeHRP; La Luz (Bogotá), November 8, 1884, reprinted in Núñez, La reforma, Vol. I, Pt. 2, p. 287.

Despite the growing willingness of Radicals to consider constitutional reform, fundamental problems remained. The Conservatives and Independents wanted to abandon federalism and return to the centralist principles of the 1843 constitution, but the Radicals favored only minor reform such as strengthening the free election guaranties. In addition, the Radicals would consider reform only if carried out by Congress. The Conservatives, who were grossly underrepresented in Congress by any equitable standard, demanded that reform be accomplished by means of a constitutional convention.[31]

Discussion of constitutional reform in the critical months of late 1884 foreshadowed the course Núñez would follow. The debate highlighted the fundamental differences between Núñez and the Radicals, and at the same time it demonstrated a growing proximity between Conservative views and those of the president. In a period of increasing political and economic fragmentation, Núñez became more firmly committed to the principle of strengthened institutional authority. In an editorial of October 1884 Núñez wrote: "The principle of authority has been, among us, the target of a persistent work of demolition for a third of a century. That principle of authority is a multiple entity, because it embraces not only its most visible representation, which is political or governmental power, but also the judicial system, the educational system, social customs, and religious beliefs, which exercise such a preponderant influence. The principle of authority is the main instrument employed in the long and complicated task of civilizing the human species."[32]

As a result of the invasion of Boyacá, Radical pronouncements on the north coast, and a new call to arms in Cundinamarca by General Gaitán Obeso, Núñez made the fateful decision of inviting the Conservatives to provide military support for his regime. The Conservatives eagerly responded to the summons for which they had patiently awaited for several years. Núñez placed General Leonardo Canal in charge of the Reserve army which consisted of Conservative volunteers and which counted among its officers such experienced generals as Manuel Briceño, Antonio B. Cuervo, and Guillermo Quintero Cal-

31. *El Liberal* (Bogotá), May 6, 1884; *Diario de Cundinamarca* (Bogotá), July 30, October 21, November 12, 1884; *El Conservador* (Bogotá), October 28, 31, 1884.

32. *La Luz* (Bogotá), October 8, 1884, reprinted in Núñez, *La reforma*, Vol. I, Pt. 2, p. 252.

derón. The Conservatives had endeavored to cultivate warm relations with Núñez, and they succeeded because of their tact and their scrupulous avoidance of conflict with the Independents. General Canal, in a letter to Antonio B. Cuervo, provided the following analysis of the Conservative relationship with Núñez: "You must keep in mind that Núñez had led us to understand many times during moments of relaxation that he has given us everything that he could, and that, if we are not a bunch of fools, we ourselves must take the rest. . . . [Núñez is playing] the role of a girl in love, but shy, who does not dare to take certain liberties with her lover, but who is highly displeased if he does not take every liberty with her."[33]

Núñez' summons to the Conservatives ended the vacillation of key Radicals such as Sergio Camargo and the governors of Tolima and Antioquia, all of whom joined the rebellion in early 1885. Independent defections to Radical ranks included the governor of Bolívar, Governor Sarmiento of Boyacá, and Ezequiel Hurtado of Cauca. In the face of these defections to a united Radical party the government's prospects for survival would have been minimal without the loyalty of such Independents as Governor Aldana of Cundinamarca, Governor Payán of Cauca, Santo Domingo Vila, Antonio Roldán, José María Campo Serrano, and Solón Wilches.

In January 1885 the war spread to every state in the union, but the most decisive battles occurred in the Magdalena River valley and on the north coast where the Liberal insurgents gained a quick, early dominance. General Gaitán Obeso captured Honda early in the month and sailed down the Magdalena River to join rebel units along the north coast. Operating from a base at Barranquilla, the Liberals soon reduced the loyalists to the fortress of Cartagena. General Gaitán Obeso's forces together with other units from the interior commanded by Generals Vargas Santos and Daniel Hernández began a siege of Cartagena in March which proved unsuccessful and which they finally lifted in mid-May. A few days later Cartagena's defenders, led by Gen-

33. Canal to Cuervo, May 12, 1885, MS. #29, BLAA. For other examples of Conservative feeling toward Núñez and the Independents see the following letters in "Correspondencia privada de Leonardo Canal, 1885," ACdeH: to Marceliano Vélez, May 19, to Ismael Bernal, May 25, to Antonio B. Cuervo, May 25, to Aristides García Herreras, June 18, to Rafael Núñez, June 22, 1885.

eral Santo Domingo Vila, received reinforcements from Rafael Reyes and a body of Cauca troops who arrived by sea from Panama, which they had pacified in April and May.

General Sergio Camargo then assumed overall command of insurgent forces on the north coast. He directed his troops inland, moving up the Magdalena River, and at La Humareda they met government forces commanded by General Quintero Calderón. A bloody battle took place on June 17 resulting in victory for the Liberals, but during the night a ship carrying the bulk of their munitions and supplies accidentally caught fire and sank. This critical loss of provisions, in effect, ended the war, although the last remnants of the rebel army, a force of about 1,100 men under General Foción Soto, did not surrender until late August. To a jubilant crowd which gathered in front of the presidential palace upon learning of the disaster suffered by the insurgents at La Humareda, Núñez succinctly intoned the significance of the war of 1884–1885: "The Constitution of Rionegro has ceased to exist!"[34]

Within a few days of the restoration of peace, Núñez decreed that a council of delegates would convene later in the year to formulate the bases for a new constitutional framework. The eighteen-member council, half Conservative and half Independent, consisted of two appointed delegates from each state. In his address at the council's opening session in November, Núñez charged the delegates with the general task of formulating a constitution which would "replace anarchy with order." Núñez offered the following guideline in justifying his call for an end to federalism: "Enervating particularism should be replaced by

34.   Liévano Aguirre, *Rafael Núñez*, 262. The following are the principal accounts of the war of 1884–1885 not previously cited: Guillermo E. Martín, *Campaña del ejército del norte en 1885* (Bogotá, 1887); [Rafael Núñez], *La rebelión: noticias de la guerra* (Bogotá, 1885); Rudecindo L. Cáceres, *Un soldado de la república en la costa atlántica* (Bogotá, 1888); Martín Restrepo Mejía, *Recuerdos de 1885* (Bogotá, 1919); José María Samper, *El sitio de Cartagena de 1885: narraciones históricas y descriptivas en prosa y en verso* (Bogotá, 1885); José María Vargas Vila, *Pinceladas sobre la última revolución de Colombia y siluetas políticas* (Maracaibo, 1887); Jacobo Henríquez H., *Rectificaciones a las pinceladas sobre la última revolución de Colombia del señor J. M. Vargas Vila* (Ocaña, 1888); Luis Eduardo Villegas, *Detracción del general Foción Soto y defensa de Luis Eduardo Villegas* (Bogotá, 1913); Pedro Sicard Briceño, *Páginas para la historia militar de Colombia: guerra civil de 1885* (Bogotá, 1925); Julio H. Palacio, *La guerra del 85* (Bogotá, 1936); Aurelio Acosta, *Memorias: un sobreviviente del glorioso liberalismo colombiano* (Bogotá, 1940).

vigorous generality. The law codes which establish and define laws should be national; and the same for the public administration charged with making them effective." [35] Núñez urged the council to require that the educational system be based on Christian teachings, and he advocated restrictions on freedom of the press and on the rights of individuals to purchase arms. The constitution which emerged from the deliberations of the Council of Delegates was based on the principles enunciated by Núñez, although its principal author was the doctrinaire Conservative Miguel Antonio Caro. Authorship by Caro rather than an Independent was a fitting symbol of the fundamental change in fortunes which Colombia's two traditional parties experienced during the initial brief span of Núñez' second administration.

35. *Diario Oficial* (Bogotá), November 12, 1885.

Chapter IX

Conclusions

Promulgation of the Constitution of 1886 marked the end of a quarter century of Liberal party leadership and opened the era of the nation-state whose shaping would be primarily the work of the Conservative party until 1930. The new constitution created a highly centralized government in which sovereignty resided in the nation; the sovereign states were replaced by departments headed by presidentially appointed governors and elected legislative assemblies. In addition, the acts of *alcaldes* and municipal councils became subject to review by governors, thus bringing centralization of authority to the level of local government. Under the new charter, the president and senators were elected indirectly for six-year terms, and representatives held four-year terms. Congress met every two years. Civil rights, which had been amply enumerated in largely absolute terms but poorly observed in practice under the Rionegro charter, were subject to restriction in the new constitution. Government alone had the right to import, manufacture, and possess arms and munitions of war. The death penalty was restored for serious crimes, and although the press was declared free in time of peace it was held responsible for injury to personal honor and attacks on public peace. In discarding the federalist Constitution of 1863 Núñez replaced it with a new charter in the spirit of that of 1832.

The 1886 constitution also initiated cordial relations between church and government by declaring Roman Catholicism to be the religion of Colombia and by empowering civil authorities to enforce respect for the church. The constitution further declared that public education was to be conducted in accord with Catholic teachings, that the church could conduct its affairs without governmental inspection, and that the church was considered a juridical person in civil matters. Constitutional authorization to negotiate a concordat with the Holy See was carried out by Núñez and a formal agreement signed in 1887. It provided compensation to the church for losses suffered from the 1861 disamortization decree, a decree authored by Núñez in his youthful zeal for Liberal reform along anticlerical lines. The agreement also provided an annual subsidy to the church, affirmed the church's juridical personality and its independence from civil authority, and granted it substantial influence over education. A year before the signing of the concordat the Jesuits had returned to Colombia, and the influence of religious communities on education continued to grow and receive government support under the benevolent encouragement of Regeneration governments.[1]

The remarkable turnover from Radicalism to the Regeneration in the post-1875 decade was the result of many factors including a worsening economy, the disintegration of Radicalism, solid support of Núñez by a strong, unified Conservative party, and effective leadership by Núñez. The sharp decline in Colombian exports beginning in 1876 marked the free-trade program a failure, and the development of serious economic difficulties by the early 1880s tended to discredit the Radicals who had claimed major responsibility for that program despite the largely bipartisan support behind it. Initiation by the Radicals of a policy of providing large federal subsidies to public works projects of the states directly violated the constitution and contradicted the party's reverent attitude of ideological fundamentalism toward the principles embodied in the 1863 charter. The subsidy policy was an unacknowledged affirmation that the Radicals had proceeded too far along the way of decentralization.

The ideological and political decline of Colombian Radicalism, a process which had been under way since the election of 1875, was completed by the party's military defeat in 1885. When Manuel Murillo died in 1880, Radicalism lost its premier ideological spokesman, its

1. Liévano Aguirre, Rafael Núñez, 322–36.

cohesive factor, and its most effective political strategist. Losing the guidance which he had provided, the Radicals of national stature became opportunistic and irresolute individuals. The party's erratic behavior in the election campaign of 1883 presaged its indecisive conduct during the months prior to the outbreak of war in 1884. Without Murillo to set the ideological frontiers and to provide the coherence which held party leadership to an effective consensus, the anarchic effects inherent in absolute liberties gained the upper hand. Want of ideological order weakened commitment among Radicals, broke down party unity, and contributed to the decided lack of enthusiasm for the revolution. Defense of the 1863 constitution represented the Radicals' most uncompromising stand in the early 1880s, and yet Núñez induced them to contemplate constitutional reform. The extremist tendencies of Colombian federalism further complicated the task of unifying and leading the party. Without the patronage and funds of the national government, Radical leaders had neither the means nor the leverage to maintain coordinate national leadership over a party whose members espoused the principles of individual and state sovereignty.[2]

Vigorous Conservative support for Núñez contributed mightily to the success of the Regeneration. That support was born of the perception that the Conservative military defeat of 1877 blocked access to power unless it should come through alliance with the Independents. The party's more pragmatic leaders took advantage of the debacle of the 1876–1877 war to recast the party program, unify the leadership structure, and provide Conservatives with a realistic mission. The spectacle of Conservative discipline and strength in the mid-1880s in contrast to the moribund condition of the Independents and the disintegration of the Radicals was not lost on Núñez. This fact of Conservative strength and unity in the early and mid-1880s has eluded some historians, but as J. León Helguera has correctly noted, the Conservatives "by 1885 had built a remarkably efficient political and military organization."[3]

2. For an excellent historiographical article examining varied assessments of Colombian Liberalism from 1849 to 1885 see Helen Delpar, "The Liberal Record and Colombian Historiography: An Indictment in Need of Revision," *Revista Interamericana de Bibliografía*, XXXI (1981), 524–37.

3. J. León Helguera, "The Problem of Liberalism Versus Conservatism in Colom-

Most certainly the single most important event in the shift from Radicalism to the Regeneration was the war of 1876–1877. That conflict climaxed the centralizing trend under Radicalism and thereby glaringly exposed the inconsistency between Radical doctrine and practice, it worsened the economic plight of the nation, it sparked Conservative revitalization, and it provided the entrée to power for the Independents. Trujillo's election of 1878, a direct consequence of the war, was truly a watershed in Colombian history. Independents took full advantage of his friendly administration to displace the Radicals in control of the sovereign states. Núñez' victory in 1880 merely confirmed that sweep.

These conclusions contrast with those of Charles Bergquist, who argues in his book *Coffee and Conflict in Colombia, 1886–1910* that political developments during the last half of the nineteenth century can best be explained by economic forces. He concludes that "the success of export agriculture led to the rise and dominance of the Liberal party in Colombia after 1850" and that the decline of export agriculture paralleled the decline of the Liberal party after 1880. The heart of Bergquist's study covers 1886 to 1910, but he generalizes his thesis to the pre-1886 period. Although he acknowledges the operation of factors such as personal rivalry among Liberal leaders and deep differences between Conservatives and Liberals over noneconomic issues such as church-state relations, he argues that the ability of Liberalism to uphold its dominance was fundamentally undermined by the post-1875 crisis in exports. He concludes that "the hegemony of the Liberals' philosophy and their control of government were not challenged until the last half of the 1870s, when their ideas and policies were subjected to telling criticism and their control of politics confronted serious and ultimately successful challenge." But before the Liberals were overcome by that challenge they faced a vigorous Conservative challenge in the war of 1876–1877. That war had virtually nothing to

---

bia: 1849–85," in Frederick B. Pike (ed.), *Latin American History. Select Problems: Identity, Integration, and Nationhood* (New York, 1969), 231. Liévano Aguirre fails to discuss the causes and some important consequences of the 1876–1877 war, and this contributes to his mistaken conclusion that both parties lacked cohesion, programs, and organization in the mid-1880s. See Líevano Aguirre, *Rafael Núñez,* 240.

do with economic factors, and its outcome had a significant bearing on the subsequent failure of Liberalism.[4]

Persuasive evidence of Bergquist's thesis for the early Regeneration period would be the demonstration that the economic interests of the Liberals were closely identified with export agriculture and the importation of foreign goods and that Conservative interests were not so identified. But the evidence is weak. As Jorge Orlando Melo notes in an essay concerning the period around 1880, "the widely held idea that merchants were usually Liberals and landowners Conservatives does not have much basis, at least for this period."[5]

The victory of Rafael Núñez, the Independents, and their Conservative allies in 1886 represented the triumph of a clear set of principles. Centralism, strengthened institutional authority, and close church-state cooperation composed the doctrinal core of the Regeneration. It was in its way a return to the past, to the halcyon days of 1831–1832 when the Liberals, not yet divided into those two elements later known as Conservatives and Liberals, had provided the country with a political structure in reasonable concordance with its society, only to destroy it out of ideological passion and personal rancors. Núñez would have preferred to reorganize the country through a unified Liberal party rather than in alliance with the Conservatives. But the Radicals were in a process of disintegration, and in any case they wholly opposed the kind of changes Núñez had in mind. If Núñez was to succeed in carrying out the Regeneration, which was in accord with the current modernizing nationalism in Europe, he could do so only with the full support of the Conservative party. The Radicals' desperate resort to civil war to maintain the status quo quickly forced Núñez into an overt political and military alliance with the Conservatives, with whom he had been establishing a rapport on the form and policies of government.

One of the principal goals sought by Núñez from 1880 onward was the strengthening of national unity. He had been influenced toward this goal by events he had witnessed in Europe and by the spectacle in

4. Charles Bergquist, *Coffee and Conflict in Colombia, 1886–1910* (Durham, 1978), 7–9, 14–15.

5. Jorge Orlando Melo, "La república conservadora (1880–1930)," in Mario Arrubla (ed.), *Colombia, hoy* (Bogotá, 1978), 57.

his native land of political violence, insurrection, and civil war which at times threatened national dismemberment. Necessarily, he began his quest for the presidency as a regionalist candidate, only to reveal to his astonished fellow citizens the depth and range of his nationalism in his first administration. In his effort to prevent the national fragmentation which seemed to impend largely because of the decreasing coherence of Radicalism, he bolstered the power of the federal government to the extent possible within the limitations of the 1863 constitution. Following his return to power in 1884 he took advantage of the opportunity offered by an unsuccessful rebellion to redesign his country's institutions. Núñez thus brought to a close Colombia's existence as a disintegrating association of regional communities, and he established solid bases for Colombian nationhood.

A major consequence of the Regeneration was to shift power from the eastern mountain region to the periphery. Trujillo's election in 1878, two years before inauguration of the Regeneration, marked the turning point in this power shift to the littoral. In the two decades following 1878, six of the nine men who occupied the presidential office were from the coastal states, and they held the office for more than twelve of the twenty years in the period.[6] It is not unlikely that Núñez viewed the transfer of political power to the coastal periphery as a means of strengthening national ties where they were most fragile, in regions remote from the capital and with relatively easy access abroad.

The Regeneration encountered no effective challenge to its domination for more than a decade following adoption of the 1886 constitution. Its firm control was maintained by the unswerving willingness of Núñez and his followers to utilize the greatly enhanced power of government to thwart opposition, by a marked recovery of the economy caused by rapid growth of the coffee export sector, and by the weak, disorganized state of the opposition Liberal party. When an effective challenge to the Regeneration did materialize, as it did in 1899 through

6. The men who held the executive office as president, vice-president, or presidential designate in this period, listed in the order in which they held the office, were: Julián Trujillo (Cauca), Núñez (Bolívar), Francisco Javier Zaldúa (Cundinamarca), José Eusebio Otálora (Boyacá), Ezequiel Hurtado (Cauca), Núñez, José María Campo Serrano (Magdalena), Eliseo Payán (Cauca), Núñez, Carlos Holguín (Cauca), and Miguel Antonio Caro (Cundinamarca). For the same conclusion see Delpar, "The Liberal Party of Colombia," 291.

the outbreak of the War of the Thousand Days, it came in the wake of divisions in the ranks of the governing party, a deterioration of the coffee economy, and reinvigoration of the Liberal party. The death of Núñez in 1894 also played a part in the advent of this turn-of-the-century crisis.

Although Núñez but briefly occupied the office of president after 1886, in his actions, writings, and support for the acting presidents he displayed a determination to create a strong executive and to use all available power to maintain peace and stability. The Council of Delegates elected him to the six-year term of president, 1886 to 1892, but in that term he initially held the office only from mid-1887 until December, when he retired to Cartagena leaving Vice-President Eliseo Payán in charge of the government. Shortly after assuming power, Payán, an Independent from Cauca, demonstrated conciliatory inclinations toward the Liberals by removing press restrictions not in the constitution and by granting amnesty to all political exiles. At the behest of his alarmed Conservative colleagues, Núñez hastened back to the capital, and upon entering Cundinamarcan territory in early February he sent a tersely worded telegram to Payán informing him that he was reassuming the presidency. Three months later the vice presidency was declared vacant by the National Legislative Council.[7] One consequence of this action was to alienate the few Independents who yet remained in the National party, the name given to the governing coalition of Independents and Conservatives following the war of 1884–1885. Before Núñez' death, the National party, political arm of the Regeneration, thus became thoroughly dominated by Conservatives.

During his last months as president, February to August, 1888, Núñez saw to the enactment of measures which greatly restricted the political opposition. He issued an executive decree in February which afforded to the government the greatest power to restrict the press in time of peace that Colombia had experienced for decades. It provided that crimes against society would come under the jurisdiction of the executive, and it defined those crimes as the publication of material that attacked the church, offended the dignity of civil and ecclesiastical authorities, encouraged disobedience of the law, generated class

7. Vergara, *Escrutinio histórico*, 353–64.

hatreds, or attacked the monetary system. Penalties under this decree ranged up to permanent suspension of the offending publication, and during its lifetime, until 1896, several newspapers were suspended and their editors exiled. Another repressive measure sanctioned by Núñez, and even more odious to the opposition, was a law of May 1888, the so-called "law of the horses." This law, in force until 1898, empowered the president to prevent or repress offenses against public order and property, to inspect scientific and educational institutions, to close such institutions if they were sources of subversive propaganda, and to impose penalties ranging in severity up to imprisonment and exile.[8] Sure domination by the Regeneration in this period thus stemmed partly from the availability of the means for political repression.

Regeneration fiscal policies, though subject to damaging criticism from the opposition, provided an additional source of power for the regime. During the war emergency of 1885 the government, when confronted with a run on the National Bank, ordered a suspension of specie payments, and following the war the government decreed that National Bank bills would no longer be convertible and would henceforth constitute the only legal payment permitted in contracts. Private banks were ordered to call in their own bills. Issuance of National Bank bills was limited to $12 million by law, but by 1892 more than $21 million in such bills had been issued. These "clandestine emissions" became a subject of heated political debate, and the government was forced to open an investigation into the matter. In spite of strong opposition to emission of paper currency, these emissions by the National Bank provided a significant supplement to governmental power. By inflating the currency the government in effect imposed a forced loan on the population, protected domestic industry by making imported goods more costly, and reduced dependence on customs revenues and loans. Strong endorsement by Núñez of the National Bank and paper money emission constituted a recurring theme in his newspaper articles and private correspondence during the last years of his life.[9]

8. Delpar, Red Against Blue, 143–44.
9. Torres García, Historia de la moneda, 214–62; Núñez, La reforma, V, 55–62, 73–79, 87–96, VI, 195–201, VII, 94–103; Núñez to Miguel Antonio Caro, August 30, 1889, August 23, 1894, in Eduardo Lemaitre (ed.), Epistolario de Rafael Núñez con Miguel Antonio Caro (Bogotá, 1977), 42–43, 159.

Despite Núñez' preference for retirement in Cartagena after 1888, he remained informed and actively involved in the affairs of government until his death. A Conservative friend of long-standing, Carlos Holguín, held the presidency as presidential designate from 1888 to 1892, and Núñez ensured the election of Miguel Antonio Caro as his vice-president in 1892. Caro thus governed Colombia as vice-president from 1892 to 1898. Evidence suggests that Núñez exerted a telling influence on the shaping and execution of policy, and he directed that influence toward the enhancement of governmental authority. In a letter to Caro, Núñez confided that he had long been convinced that "political difficulties cannot be resolved but with heroic firmness." And months after leaving office for the last time, Núñez privately wrote from Cartagena: "In this Department there will be absolute decisiveness in terms of stability, in everything—which is what the constitution demands and should demand after a half century of instability." [10] Núñez freely lent his prestige to bolster his successors' power, and he employed the force of his reasoning to uphold Regeneration policies in numerous newspaper articles. Through his public and private actions Núñez thus showed a determination to keep his program on track.

Rapid expansion of the coffee economy also strengthened the Regeneration in the decade after 1885. Colombian coffee rose in value from an average price in 1887 of 10.6 cents a pound on the New York market to a peak of 18.8 cents in 1893, and in the same period coffee exports tripled. In the mid-1890s coffee represented about 70 percent of the total value of Colombian exports. Until the sharp downturn in coffee prices of the last three years of the century, the coffee boom strengthened the Regeneration by providing increased customs revenue which allowed the government to meet its obligations, maintain a large standing army, and claim credit for the economic revival. The downturn in prices likewise weakened the Regeneration and emboldened its opponents to challenge its continued hegemony. [11]

During the decade following the Liberal defeat of 1885, the Liberal party suffered from weakness and disorganization which also aided

10. Núñez to Caro, June 29, 1890, May 20, 1889, in Lemaitre (ed.), Epistolario, 48, 38.
11. Bergquist, Coffee and Conflict, 21, 23, 50.

the Regeneration in maintaining its domination. Deaths and exile debilitated party leadership, the Liberals lacked a true national organization, and a scarcity of funds made it extremely difficult to sustain a vigorous opposition press. By and large Liberal leadership until the end of the century remained in the flaccid hands of older members, men such as Santiago Pérez and Aquileo Parra, who had dominated Radicalism during its heyday in the late 1860s and the 1870s.

A question facing both Liberals and Conservatives when out of power during the second half of the nineteenth century, and one which sharply divided party members, was whether to abstain from elections, seek an alliance with dissident elements of the ruling party, or prepare for revolution. The plight of the Liberals after 1885, however, was much worse than that which earlier had faced the Conservatives— the power and willingness of the central government to restrict and suppress opposition activities were much greater under the Regeneration than in the years after 1863. In 1887 when a few Liberal leaders gathered to plan party reorganization, the government exiled several of them. Consequently, until 1891 Liberals made little effort to participate in elections, and party organization did not exist. In that year they prepared for national elections by forming a Liberal Center and attempting, without success, to cooperate with dissident Conservatives to form an anti-Regeneration coalition. Liberal abstentions were high and by 1892 the party had elected only one man to Congress. Some party members then made plans for revolution, but the government uncovered the plot and moved quickly, confiscating party funds, closing down the official party organ, and exiling Santiago Pérez, who despite his position as party leader was innocent of involvement in the plot. Despite these setbacks some Liberals launched a revolution in 1895, but it was limited in scope and the government easily crushed it in three months.[12] Colombian Liberalism, nevertheless, achieved a high degree of reintegration by the late 1890s by attracting the Liberal followers of Núñez, most of whom had abandoned him by the time of his death. Ironically, the division which developed in the National party and which ultimately threatened the demise of the Regeneration was a division between Conservatives.

12.   Julio H. Palacio, *Historia de mi vida* (Bogotá, 1942), 214–24; Helen Delpar, "Road to Revolution: The Liberal Party of Colombia, 1886–1899," *The Americas*, XXXII (January, 1976), 352–55.

This Conservative split first became evident when Antioqueño Conservatives unsuccessfully opposed the reelection of Carlos Holguín for an additional two-year term as presidential designate in 1890. It deepened the following year during the preliminary skirmishing of the presidential election. Núñez, the unchallenged candidate for reelection, planned to remain in retirement in Cartagena, so the real contest was for the vice-presidency. He early announced his neutrality in that race, but shortly thereafter the candidacy of Marceliano Vélez was announced. Vélez, an Antioqueño Conservative and commander of Conservative forces in the war of 1876–1877, was supported principally by Conservatives of Antioquia. In a letter to Núñez, Vélez audaciously and strongly criticized the Regeneration for its political repression, its practices of political fraud, its fiscal policies, and its attempt to divide several departments. Núñez subsequently abandoned his neutrality and came out in support of Miguel Antonio Caro for vice president. Vélez later gained the presidential nomination of the dissident Historical Conservatives, but the Núñez-Caro ticket easily won the contest and Caro governed until 1898. Consequently, as the Liberal party moved toward reintegration, the Conservative division between Historicals and incumbent Nationalists widened.[13]

An examination of the causes of political disagreement between Historicals and Nationalists is beyond the scope of this study, but the problems were related to the regionalist basis of Historical strength, the unbending character of Caro, and opposition to the Nationalist programs of paper money emissions and fiscal monopolies, especially the government tobacco monopoly which Caro had reestablished in 1893.

Antioquia was the heart of Historical Conservative strength, although after the mid-1890s the Historicals attracted support from other departments. The first item in Vélez' list of grievances against the Regeneration in 1891 was his complaint against a government proposal to divide some of the departments into smaller units, a proposal put forth by Holguín in 1888. This proposed constitutional change represented a special threat to the territorial integrity of large departments such as Antioquia and Cauca, where opposition to further moves against regional unity was most vigorous. One Medellín paper adopted

---

13. Vergara, *Escrutinio histórico*, 385–401; Liévano Aguirre, *Rafael Núñez*, 402–18.

the extreme position of threatening the secession of Antioquia and Cauca if the proposal became enacted. Under public and private pressure from Núñez, who regarded the proposal as grossly impolitic, Holguín withdrew it, but that did not head off the developing split in the National party.[14]

Caro's doctrinaire approach to politics also contributed to party division. The differences in style and character between Caro and Núñez were profound. Whereas Núñez was worldly, flexible, possessed of a wide-ranging intellect, and capable of arousing a loyal following through the force of his personality, Caro was insular, doctrinaire, limited in vision, devout, and scholarly. He would compromise only under extreme pressure by which point the political benefits of compromise were largely mitigated. Both men were ideologically committed to centralism, but Núñez' centralism was tempered by a greater sensitivity to the bitterness of the centralist-federalist conflict in Colombian history and by dislike for Bogotá. In a letter to Caro, the Bogotano, Núñez, the Cartagenero, wrote: "Centralization—which is not popular in itself except in Bogotá—becomes discredited and impossible if the government does not paternally attend to sectional interests." Despite considerable differences between these two men, the only evident area of policy disagreement concerned implementation of the government tobacco monopoly, which Núñez felt should be delayed until greater public support for it could be mustered. In general, Caro was a loyal disciple of Núñez, and Núñez did his utmost to ensure Caro's success. During a period of crisis within the National party and shortly before Núñez' death he wrote to Caro: "The country can soon become lost if you do not save it. Believe that your authority is *omnipotent*. . . . Today nobody counterbalances you, for I am with you *until death*, and I perceive no other hope than you."[15]

This unqualified endorsement of Caro came at a time of stiffening

14.   *La Tarde* (Medellín), July 5, 1889. The secession threat seems not to have been repeated in *La Tarde* or echoed in other newspapers. For Núñez' position see Núñez to Caro, April 22, 1889, in Lemaitre (ed.), *Epistolario*, 34–36. Discussion of the issue can be found in *La Tarde* (Medellín), March 14, 21, 28, April 11, July 28, August 29, 1889, *La Nación* (Bogotá), November 16, 1888, and *El Telegrama* (Bogotá), November 6, 8, 9, 12, 1888, November 6, December 13, 1889.

15.   Núñez to Caro, January 16, 1889, August 23, 1894, in Lemaitre (ed.), *Epistolario*, 25, 159.

opposition to Regeneration policies and rancorous debate in Congress over government fiscal policies. From mid-1894 until Núñez' death in September following a stroke, colleagues, congressmen, and ultimately Vice-President Caro himself beseeched Núñez to return to Bogotá and assume the presidency. He had resisted, pleading ill health, until shortly before the end. His decision to return to Bogotá has raised many questions concerning his attitude toward Caro and his ultimate plans, but of greater importance, it gives the lie to the assertion that Núñez had come to the conclusion that the Regeneration had failed. Núñez did know the melancholy of old age and he did on occasion yield to pessimism and despair—note for example his Bolivarian observation that it was his intimate conviction that he had "plowed the sea."[16] But his willingness to undertake the arduous journey to Bogotá and assume active leadership of country and party reflected courage, determination, and hope, and it was an acknowledgment of the trust his countrymen placed in him.

Núñez' death did not mark the end of an era, for his legacy long survived him. Conservatives continued to govern well into the twentieth century, government remained organized along centralist lines, and close church-state cooperation became an accepted feature of Colombian life. Despite the strengthening of national authority under the Regeneration, Núñez' successors failed to avert the outbreak of civil war at the close of the century, and they failed to preserve national unity when Panama separated in 1903. These twin national disasters did confirm Núñez' perception of the dangers facing Colombia in the last quarter of the nineteenth century—the repeated eruptions of internal violence and the threat of national fragmentation. But the well-conceived policies of the Regeneration were in themselves insufficient to overcome these dangers without the sure guidance required to modify and execute those policies. At that leadership task Núñez had few, if any, peers.

16. Núñez to Caro, July 16, 1890, *ibid.*, 50.

Bibliography

I. Primary Sources

A. Private Manuscripts

Archivo de la Academia Colombiana de Historia, Bogotá

Calderón, Carlos. One box of letters dated 1886 to 1890s.

Canal, Leonardo. "Correspondencia privada, 1885." A copybook of letters written by Canal in 1885.

Cisneros, Francisco Javier. Two boxes of letters dated 1880s and 1890s.

Gutiérrez Vergara, Ignacio. Several boxes of letters dealing with political and family matters from mid–nineteenth century to 1870s; includes five bound volumes of letters, 1871–76, to his son, Ignacio Gutiérrez Ponce, while the latter was in New York, London, and Paris.

Herrán, Pedro Alcántara. A large collection covering mid–nineteenth-century Colombia to the 1870s and including a few letters from Rafael Núñez.

Manrique, Juan E. A two-box collection of Manrique correspondence from 1890 to 1914; contains some misplaced letters from Rafael Núñez dated 1879–80.

Montúfar, Manuel. Contains about twenty letters dated 1878–80 including some letters to and from Rafael Núñez.

Ortiz, José Joaquín. A four-box collection covering mid–nineteenth century to early twentieth century; mostly religious matters.

Parra, Aquileo. Three boxes of letters covering 1874 to early 1880s and late nineteenth century.

Samper, José María. One volume of published documents and letters, 1850s to 1880s.

Uribe Uribe, Rafael. Thirty-one boxes of letters covering the 1880s to second decade of twentieth century.

Zaldúa, Francisco Javier. Two volumes of documents and letters, most of which are from mid–nineteenth century; contains a few letters dated early 1880s.

Archivo Central del Cauca, Popayán

Arboleda, Sergio. A large but poorly organized collection covering Conservative politics and family matters from mid–nineteenth century to 1880s.

Mosquera, Tomás Cipriano de. Well-organized collection covering from independence to 1878; an excellent source for Colombian political history.

Archivo Nacional de Colombia, Bogotá

Trujillo, Julián. "El archivo del General en Jefe del Ejército del Sur." Ten volumes of letters and telegrams dated 1876–81.

Biblioteca Luis-Angel Arango, Bogotá

A well-indexed manuscript collection is maintained; letters dated in the 1860s, 1870s, and 1880s from the following correspondents were examined:

Antonio, Domingo, Bishop of Medellín
Arbeláez, Vicente, Archbishop
Bello, Manuel C.
Conto, César
Cuervo, Antonio B.
García, Abraham
Holguín, Carlos
Medina y Morena, Bernardino, Bishop of Cartagena
Mosquera, Tomás Cipriano de
Núñez, Rafael
Pérez, Santiago
Posada, Alejandro
Rico, Luis Carlos
Salgar, Eustorgio
Samper, José María
Vélez, Joaquín
Zaldúa, Francisco Javier
Zapata, Felipe

Biblioteca del Seminario Mayor, La Arquidiócesis de Bogotá

Zaldúa, Francisco Javier. Two volumes of adherences and private and official correspondence of 1860s and 1879–82.

Private Collection of Jorge Ancízar-Sordo, Bogotá

Ancízar, Manuel. Personal correspondence from 1850s to 1880s.

Private Collection of Horacio Rodríguez Plata, Bogotá

Parra, Aquileo. Three volumes of letters written to Parra from early 1870s to mid-1880s.

B. Unpublished Government Documents

Archivo del Congreso, Bogotá

Senado. Volumes with the following titles were examined for each year from 1875 to 1884:
"Antecedentes de Leyes"
"Asuntos sin Resolver"
"Comisiones Despachadas"
"Comisiones sin Despachar"
"Expedientes de Leyes"
"Informes de Comisiones"
"Negocios Negados"
"Negocios Resueltos y Pendientes"
"Proyectos Negados"
"Proyectos Pendientes"
"Solicitudes y Asuntos Varios"
"Solicitudes Resueltas"

Archivo Nacional de Colombia, Bogotá

Volumes with the following titles were examined for the years 1875–85:
"Correspondencia de Antioquia"
"Correspondencia de Antioquia y Cundinamarca"
"Correspondencia de Bolívar"
"Correspondencia de Boyacá"
"Correspondencia de Cauca"
"Correspondencia de Magdalena"
"Correspondencia de Santander"
"Correspondencia de Tolima"
"Gobernaciones Varias"
"Ministerio de Hacienda"

C. Official Publications

Official Newspapers—National

Diario Oficial (Bogotá), 1875–86
Gaceta Oficial (Bogotá), 1856

Registro Oficial (Bogotá), 1862

Official Newspapers—State

Antioquia:
Boletín Oficial (Medellín), 1875–76, 1885
Rejistro Oficial (Medellín), 1877–84
Bolívar:
Diario de Bolívar (Cartagena), 1875–84
Registro de Bolívar (Cartagena), 1885
Boyacá:
Boletín Oficial (Tunja), 1885
El Boyacense (Tunja), 1875–84
Cauca:
Rejistro Oficial (Popayán), 1875–85
Cundinamarca:
Rejistro del Estado (Bogotá), 1875–85
Magdalena:
Gaceta de Magdalena (Santa Marta), 1875–79
Registro de Magdalena (Santa Marta), 1879–85
Panama:
Gaceta de Panama (Panama), 1875–85
Santander:
Gaceta de Santander (Socorro), 1875–83
Tolima:
Gaceta del Tolima (Neiva), 1880–84

Other Official Publications

Anales de la Convención. Rionegro, Antioquia, February 12, 1863, to June 5, 1863.

Banco de la República. Informe anual del gerente, 1 julio 1960–31 diciembre 1962. Bogotá, n.d.

Constitución y leyes de los Estados Unidos de Colombia espedidas en los años de 1863 a 1875. Bogotá, 1875.

Esguerra, Nicolás. Certificación del secretario de hacienda i fomento sobre los acontecimientos de la costa. Bogotá, 1875.

Galindo, Aníbal, ed. Anuario estadístico de Colombia, 1875. Bogotá, 1875.

Leyes i decretos espedidos por la lejislatura del estado soberano de Antioquia en sus sesiones de 1865. Medellín, 1865.

Leyes i decretos de Bolívar . . . 1865. Cartagena, 1866.

Leyes i decretos de Boyacá . . . 1865 a 1867. Tunja, 1868.

Leyes i decretos de Cauca . . . 1863 i 1865. Bogotá, 1866.

Leyes i decretos de Panama . . . 1865. Panama, 1867.

Leyes i decretos de Santander . . . 1864. Pamplona, 1865.

Leyes de los Estados Unidos de Colombia, 1876–1884. 9 vols. Bogotá, 1876–84.

Memoria de Hacienda. Bogotá, 1856–57, 1866–84, 1910. Annual reports from the minister of hacienda with varying titles, e.g., *Memoria que el secretario de hacienda i fomento presenta al presidente de la república.*

Memoria del secretario del tesoro i crédito nacional al congreso de 1873. Bogotá, 1873.

[Núñez, Rafael]. *La rebelión: noticias de la guerra.* Bogotá, 1885.

Recopilación de actos lejislativos del estado soberano del Tolima espedidos desde el año de 1862 hasta el de 1877. Bogotá, 1879.

Recopilación de leyes y decretos del estado soberano de Cundinamarca espedidos desde su creación en 1857 hasta 1868. Bogotá, 1868.

Restrepo, E., Emiliano, *et al. Ferrería de Samacá: informe de una comisión.* Bogotá, 1884.

Senado de plenipotenciarios de los Estados Unidos de Colombia. *Debates del proyecto de lei sobre orden público.* Bogotá, 1880.

D. Newspapers

The dates following the place of publication indicate the years for which issues were consulted. The most complete newspaper collection is in the Biblioteca Nacional, Bogotá, but it lacks many issues.

La América (Bogotá). 1872–75. Conservative; edited by José María Quijano Otero, Manuel Briceño, and Manuel María Paz.

La Balanza (Medellín). 1880. Pro-Núñez; edited by Camilo A. Echeverri.

La Bandera Federal (Socorro). 1881. Supported presidential candidacy of Solón Wilches.

El Bien Público (Bogotá). 1870–72. Political but largely nonpartisan; edited by José María Quijano Otero.

Boletín Eleccionario (Medellín). 1869. Sole purpose was to combat the pro-Mosquera League of 1869; edited by Ricardo Villa and Néstor Castro.

La Caridad (Bogotá). 1864–76, 1878–79. Conservative and Catholic.

El Cauca (Popayán). 1883–84. Independent Liberal; pro-Núñez.

El Ciudadano (Medellín). 1875. Independent Liberal; edited by Manuel A. Hernández and Constantino Martínez.

El Comercio (Bogotá). 1883–85. Reported business and economic news; edited by Marco A. Pizano.

La Concordia (Barranquilla). 1881–82. Radical; edited by Pedro Blanco García.

El Conservador (Bogotá). 1863–66, 1881–84. The paper of the 1860s claimed to be the organ of the Conservative party and was edited by Nicolás Pontón; the paper of the 1880s was the official organ of the Conservative National Directorate and was edited by Sergio Arboleda and Rufino Gutiérrez.

El Constitucional (Tunja). 1883. Independent Liberal; supported Calderón regime in Boyacá and edited by Pablo E. Lozano.

El Correo (Santa Marta). 1878. Supported Radical regime of Luis Robles in Magdalena.

El Correo de Santander (Socorro). 1882. Independent Liberal; supported Núñez and Governor Solón Wilches.

El Corresponsal (Bogotá). 1878. Radical.

La Costa Atlántica (Barranquilla). 1883. Edited by an anti-Núñez Independent, Bolívar J. Franco; supported presidential candidacy of Wilches.

El Cronista (Panama). 1882–84. Independent Liberal and pro-Núñez.

El Debate (Bogotá). 1878–79, 1884. Polemically anti-Radical; edited by Independent Liberal, Leonídas Flórez.

El Deber (Bogotá). 1878–81. Conservative; edited by José María Samper until February 1879 and then by Carlos Holguín; served as official Conservative organ beginning May 1879.

El Deber (Medellín). 1876. Conservative; edited by Aquilino Alvarez.

La Defensa (Bogotá). 1880. Radical; edited by Santiago Pérez.

La Democracia (Cartagena). 1849–51. Founded by Núñez; contains some of his earliest writings.

El Demócrata (Medellín). 1878. Radical; edited by Venancio A. Calle.

Diario de Cundinamarca (Bogotá). 1873–84. Most authoritative organ of Radicals; edited by Florentino Vezga.

La Discusión (Bogotá). 1853. Contains early articles by Núñez.

El Elector Nacional (Barranquilla). 1875. Pro-Núñez.

El Empresario (Tunja). 1879–80. Commercial and economic news.

La Epoca (Bogotá). 1884. Independent Liberal; opposed to President José E. Otálora.

El Escudo Nacional (Cartagena). 1875. Pro-Núñez.

La Escuela Liberal (Bogotá). 1883–84. Radical; editors included Adolfo Cuellar, Jesús Rozo Ospina, and Tomás Rodríguez Pérez.

El Estandarte Liberal (Cali). 1878. Supported Ezequiel Hurtado for governor of Cauca; edited by Benjamín Núñez.

La Estrella del Tolima (Neiva). 1882–84. Radical; supported Liberal Union.

La Fe (Bogotá). 1868. Religious and literary; edited by José María Vergara y Vergara and Miguel Antonio Caro.

El Federalista (San Jil). 1875. Pro-Núñez; edited by José María Baraya.

El Ferrocarril del Magdalena (Santa Marta). 1875. Good on relations between Magdalena and Bolívar.

La Gaceta Mercantil (Barranquilla). 1881–82. Reported commercial news.

El Guardián (Medellín). 1878. Supported Liberal government of Antioquia.

El Heraldo (Medellín). 1868–74. Conservative; editors included Néstor Castro, Ernesto M. Sicard, Juan C. Aguilar, and Demetrio Viana.

La Ilustración (Bogotá). 1870–75, 1878. Conservative; editors included Carlos Holguín, Ezequiel Canal, Nicolás Pontón, Manuel María Madiedo, and Emilio M. Escobar.

El Independiente (Bogotá). 1878. Independent Liberal; edited by Manuel Herrera.

La Integridad (Socorro). 1883. Supported presidential candidacy of Wilches.

La Ley (Bogotá). 1876. Edited by José María Samper.

El Liberal (Bogotá). 1884. Pro-Núñez; edited by Alirio Díaz Guerra.

La Libertad (Medellín). 1877–78. Supported presidential candidacy of Julián Trujillo; edited by Manuel de J. Barrera.

La Luz (Bogotá). 1882–84. Founded by Núñez; contains many of his most important articles.

El Magdalena (Bogotá). 1881. Pro-Núñez; edited by Manuel Abello Vergara.

El Mensajero (Bogotá). 1867. Contains early articles by Manuel María Madiedo.

La Nación (Bogotá). 1888. Pro-Regeneration.

El Neo-Granadino (Bogotá). 1853. Edited by Manuel Murillo and briefly by Núñez.

La Nueva Era (Bogotá). 1883. Pro-Núñez.

La Nueva Era (Medellín). 1879. Radical; supported presidential candidacy of Tomás Rengifo.

El Nuevo Mundo (Bogotá). 1869. Founded by Liberals to support the presidential candidacy of Tomás Cipriano de Mosquera.

La Opinión (Bogotá). 1879. Independent Liberal; edited by Benjamín J. Martínez and Isidoro Laverde Amaya.

La Opinión Liberal (Bogotá). 1876. Edited by Diójenes A. Arrieta.

El País (Bogotá). 1875. Radical.

La Palestra (Mompós). 1874–75, 1878–85. Good source for north coast Liberalism.

El Parlamentario (Bogotá). 1879. Radical.

La Patria (Bogotá). 1867. Conservative; edited by Luis Segundo de Silvestre.

La Paz (Bogotá). 1869. Contains articles on possibility of secession.

El Precursor (Panama). 1878–79. Radical until November 1878, when taken over by the Conservative Tomás Casís.

La Prensa (Bogotá). 1866–69. Conservative paper of high quality; edited by Carlos Holguín, Nicolás Pontón, and Salomón Forero.

La Prensa Libre (Barranquilla). 1881–84. Pro-Núñez; contains good economic information.

Los Principios (Cali). 1873–76. Supported concept of Conservative Catholic party; edited by Jaime Hurtado.

El Progreso (Bogotá). 1878. Independent Liberal; edited by Agustín Núñez.

El Progreso (Medellín). 1884. Pro-Núñez; edited by Vicente Villegas.

El Progreso (Panama). 1875. Pro-Núñez.

El Promotor (Barranquilla). 1874–85. Good for economic and commercial information; edited by Ricardo Becerra.

La Propaganda (Ocaña). 1884. Supported Francisco Ordóñez for governor.

La Reforma (Bogotá). 1878–80, 1882–84. Independent Liberal; edited by Narciso González Lineros.

La Rejeneración (Cartagena). 1878. Pro-Núñez; edited by Antonio P. del Real.

El Relator (Bogotá). 1877–78, 1881–82. Radical; edited by Felipe Pérez.

El Repertorio Colombiano (Bogotá). 1878–84. Conservative; edited by Carlos Martínez Silva.

La República (Bogotá). 1867–69. Conservative but supported Mosquera candidacy in 1869; edited by Jorge Isaacs and Luis Segundo de Silvestre.

La República (Medellín). 1910–11. Contains the Murillo-Berrío correspondence of the 1860s.

El Republicano (Socorro). 1875. Supported presidential candidacy of Aquileo Parra.

La Restauración (Medellín). 1864–68. Antioqueño Conservative party organ; edited by Isidoro Isaza.

Revista de Colombia (Bogotá). 1869. Contains articles on secessionist threat by some states.

El Semanario Comercial (Barranquilla). 1880–82. Economic and commercial news of north coast; edited by Pedro Celestino Angulo.

El Símbolo (Bogotá). 1864–66. Conservative; edited by Juan S. de Narváez.

La Sociedad (Medellín). 1873–76. Religious; edited by Néstor Castro and Alejandro Botero.

La Tarde (Medellín). 1889. Advocate of Antioqueño and Historical Conservative interests.

El Telégrafo (Palmira). 1875. Pro-Núñez.

El Telegrama (Bogotá). 1888–89. Prestigious daily with good international news.

El Tiempo (Bogotá). 1860. Radical; contains articles and letters of Núñez.

El Trabajo (Medellín). 1884. Economic news; edited by Rafael Uribe Uribe.

El Tradicionista (Bogotá). 1871–76. Conservative; edited by Miguel Antonio Caro and Carlos Martínez Silva.

La Tribuna (Medellín). 1880–81. Liberal; edited by Venancio A. Calle.

La Unión (Medellín). 1876. Represented views of Conservative government of Antioquia.

La Unión Católica (Bogotá). 1871–72. Founded to defend the church and support the concept of a Catholic party; edited by José María Vergara y Vergara.

La Unión Colombiana (Bogotá). 1875. Pro-Núñez; edited by José María Samper.

La Unión Liberal (Bogotá). 1877. Liberal; edited by Francisco de P. Matéus.

La Verdad (Bogotá). 1883. Conservative; edited by José María Quijano Otero and José M. Mallarino.

La Voz de Ocaña (Ocaña). 1884. Conservative; edited by Felix A. Merlano.

La Voz del Pueblo (Cali). 1878–79. Radical organ of Democratic Society of Cali; edited by José M. Barona Pizarro.

E. Other Primary Sources

Acosta, Aurelio. *Memorias: un sobreviviente del glorioso liberalismo colombiano.* Bogotá, 1940.

Arias Robledo, Eduardo, and Joaquín Piñeros Corpas, eds. *Acuarelas de Mark, un testimonio pictórico de la Nueva Granada.* Bogotá, 1963.

Arosemena, Pablo. *Escritos.* 2 vols. Panama, 1930.

Barona Pizarro, José María. *Bosquejo histórico de la última revolución (1876 a 1877).* Panama, 1877.

Briceño, Manuel. *La revolución, 1876–1877: recuerdos para la historia.* Bogotá, 1947.

Cáceres, Rudecindo L. *Un soldado de la república en la costa atlántica.* Bogotá, 1888.

Camacho Roldán, Salvador. *Escritos varios.* 3 vols. Bogotá, 1892–95.

———. *Mis memorias.* 2 vols. Bogotá, 1946.

[Camargo, Agustín (?)]. *Felipe Pérez.* Bogotá, 1883.

Cané, Miguel. *Notas de viaje sobre Venezuela y Colombia.* Bogotá, 1907.

Carrasquilla, Francisco de P. *Tipos de Bogotá.* Bogotá, 1886.

"Cartas del doctor Núñez." *Boletín de Historia y Antigüedades,* XXXIV (January–March, 1947), 19–33.

Cordovez Moure, José María. *Reminiscencias: Santa Fe y Bogotá.* 10 vols. 6th ed. Bogotá, 1942–46.

"Correspondencia del doctor Manuel Murillo Toro." *Revista del Archivo Nacional,* IV (January–February, 1942), 73–94.

Delgado, Evaristo. *Memoria sobre el cultivo del café en el municipio de Popayán.* Popayán, 1867.

"Diario de Quijano Otero." *Boletín de Historia y Antigüedades,* XIX (February–August, 1932), 69–80, 131–59, 215–40, 293–320, 365–400, 585–98.

Franco V., Constancio. *Apuntamientos para la historia: la guerra de 1876 i 1877.* Bogotá, 1877.

Galindo, Aníbal. *Recuerdos históricos, 1840 a 1895.* Bogotá, 1900.

Garcés, Modesto. *Manifiesto del presidente del estado soberano del Cauca a la nación.* Bogotá, 1879.

Harker Mutis, Adolfo. *Mis recuerdos.* Bucaramanga, 1954.

Helguera, J. León, and Robert H. Davis, eds. *Archivo epistolar del General Mosquera: correspondencia con el General Ramón Espina, 1835–1866.* Bogotá, 1966.

Henríquez H., Jacobo. *Rectificaciones a las pinceladas sobre la última revolución de Colombia del señor J. M. Vargas Vila.* Ocaña, 1888.

Herrera Olarte, José. *La administración Trujillo: juicio histórico.* Bogotá, 1880.

Hettner, Alfred. *La cordillera de Bogotá: resultados de viajes y estudios.* Translated by Ernesto Guhl. Bogotá, 1966.

Holguín, Carlos. *Cartas políticas publicadas en "El Correo Nacional."* Bogotá, 1951.

Isaacs, Jorge. *La revolución radical en Antioquia.* Bogotá, 1880.

Lemaitre, Daniel. *Soledad Román de Núñez: recuerdos.* Cartagena, 1927.

Lemaitre, Eduardo, ed. *Epistolario de Rafael Núñez con Miguel Antonio Caro.* Bogotá, 1977.

Madriz, F. J. *Cultivo del café o sea manual teórico y práctico sobre el beneficio de este fruto.* . . . Le Havre, 1871.

Martín, Guillermo E. *Campaña del ejército del norte en 1885.* Bogotá, 1887.

Martínez Ribón, C. *Nuevo método para el cultivo de cacao.* . . . Bogotá, 1879.

Martínez Silva, Carlos. *Revistas políticas publicadas en 'El Repertorio Colombiano.'* 2 vols. Bogotá, 1934.

Matéus, Francisco de P. *La administración del señor Otálora.* Paris, 1884.

"Memoria testamental de don José de Obaldía, Vicepresidente de la Nueva Granada." *Boletín de Historia y Antigüedades,* XXXI (March–April, 1944), 274–304.

Morales, Alejo. *Campaña del norte i batalla de la Donjuana.* Bogotá, 1877.

Narváez, Enrique de. *Los mochuelos.* Bogotá, 1936.

Núñez, Rafael. *Ensayos de crítica social.* Rouen, France, 1874.

———. *La federación.* Bogotá, 1855.

———. *La reforma política en Colombia.* 8 vols. Bogotá, 1945–50.

Ordóñez, Ricardo, ed. *Episodios de la campaña de occidente en 1876 tomados del 'Diario Histórico' de aquel ejército abnegado i valiente.* Bogotá, 1877.

Osorio, Nicolás. *Estudio sobre las quinas de los Estados Unidos de Colombia.* 2nd ed. Bogotá, 1874.

Ospina Rodríguez, Mariano. *Artículos escogidos.* Medellín, 1884.

Palacio, Julio H. *Historia de mi vida.* Bogotá, 1942.

Parra, Aquileo. *Memorias de Aquileo Parra.* Bogotá, 1912.

Paúl, José Telésforo. *Exposición que hace al congreso de los Estados Unidos de Colombia el obispo de Panamá.* Bogotá, 1878.

Poesías de Rafael Núñez. Bogotá, 1914.

Pombo, Manuel Antonio, and José Joaquín Guerra, eds. *Constituciones de Colombia.* 4 vols. Bogotá, 1951.

Quijano Wallis, José María. *Memorias autobiográficas, histórico-políticas y de carácter social.* Grottaferrata, Italy, 1919.

Restrepo Mejía, Martín. *Recuerdos de 1885.* Bogotá, 1919.

Samper, José María. *Historia de un alma.* Medellín, 1971.

———. *El sitio de Cartagena de 1885: narraciones históricas y descriptivas en prosa y en verso.* Bogotá, 1885.

Samper, Miguel. *Escritos político-económicos.* 4 vols. Bogotá, 1925–27.

———. *Nuestras enfermedades políticas.* Bogotá, 1884.

Sicard Briceño, Pedro. *Páginas para la historia militar de Colombia: guerra civil de 1885.* Bogotá, 1925.

Soto, Foción. *Memorias sobre el movimiento de resistencia a la dictadura de Rafael Núñez, 1884–1885.* 2 vols. Bogotá, 1913.

Vargas Vila, José María. *Pinceladas sobre la última revolución de Colombia y siluetas políticas.* Maracaibo, 1887.

Vélez, Marceliano. *Las memorias del señor Camilo A. Echeverri y mis actos en la revolución de 1876.* Medellín, 1878.

Viana, D. *La muerte de MacEwen.* Medellín, 1880.

Villegas, Luis Eduardo. *Detracción del general Foción Soto y defensa de Luis Eduardo Villegas.* Bogotá, 1913.

Wilches, Solón. *Hechos de la última guerra.* Cúcuta, 1878.

II. Secondary Sources

A. Books and Pamphlets

Alarcón, José C. *Compendio de historia del departamento del Magdalena de 1525 hasta 1895.* Santa Marta, 1898.

Aragón, Arcesio. *Fastos payaneses.* 2 vols. Bogotá, 1939.

Arboleda, Gustavo. *Diccionario biográfico y genealógico del antiguo departamento del Cauca.* Bogotá, 1962.

———. *Historia de Cali.* 2 vols. Cali, 1956.

———. *Historia contemporánea de Colombia.* 6 vols. Cali, Bogotá, and Popayán, 1919–35.

———. *Revoluciones locales de Colombia.* Popayán, 1907.

Arosemena, Justo. *Constitución de los Estados Unidos de Colombia con antecedentes históricos i comentarios.* Le Havre, 1870.

Bergquist, Charles W. *Coffee and Conflict in Colombia, 1886–1910.* Durham, 1978.

Caballero Calderón, Eduardo. *Historia privada de los colombianos.* Bogotá, 1960.

Camacho Carrizosa, Guillermo. *Santiago Pérez y otros estudios.* Bogotá, 1934.

Camargo Pérez, Gabriel. *Sergio Camargo, el bayardo colombiano.* Bogotá, 1972.

Cárdenas Acosta, Pablo E. *La restauración constitucional de 1867.* Tunja, 1966.

Castillo, Nicolás del. *El primer Núñez*. Bogotá, 1971.

[Cerruti, Ernesto]. *Aventuras de un cocinero (Ernesto Cerruti): crónicas del Cauca*. Bogotá, 1898.

Cordero, Luis Febres. *Del antigua Cúcuta: datos y apuntamientos para su historia*. Cúcuta, 1918.

Correa, Ramón. *La convención de Rionegro: páginas históricas de Colombia*. Bogotá, 1937.

Delpar, Helen. *Red Against Blue: The Liberal Party in Colombian Politics, 1863–1899*. University, Ala., 1981.

Díaz Granados, José Ignacio. *Rectificación histórica*. Barranquilla, 1899.

Eder, Phanor James. *El fundador Santiago M. Eder*. Bogotá, 1959.

Fajardo, Luis H. *The Protestant Ethic of the Antioqueños: Social Structure and Personality*. Cali, n.d.

García, José Joaquín. *Crónicas de Bucaramanga*. Bogotá, 1896.

Gómez Barrientos, Estanislao. *25 años a través del estado de Antioquia*. 2 vols. Medellín, 1918, 1927.

Gómez Picón, Alirio. *El golpe militar del 17 de abril de 1854*. Bogotá, 1972.

González Toledo, Aureliano. *El general Eliseo Payán, vicepresidente de la república*. Bogotá, 1887.

Guillén Martínez, Fernando. *Raíz y futuro de la revolución*. Bogotá, 1963.

Hagen, Everett E. *On the Theory of Social Change: How Economic Growth Begins*. Homewood, Ill., 1962.

Henao, Jesús María, and Gerardo Arrubla. *Historia de Colombia*. 8th ed. Bogotá, 1967.

Jaramillo Uribe, Jaime. *El pensamiento colombiano en el siglo XIX*. Bogotá, 1964.

Lemos Guzmán, A. J. *Obando, de Cruzverde a Cruzverde*. Popayán, 1959.

Liévano Aguirre, Indalecio. *Rafael Núñez*. Lima, 1944.

Mantilla, Eladio. *Geografía especial del estado de Santander*. Socorro, 1880.

Martínez Silva, Carlos. *Por qué caen los partidos políticos*. Bogotá, 1934.

McGreevey, William P. *An Economic History of Colombia, 1845–1930*. Cambridge, 1971.

Molina, Gerardo. *Las ideas liberales en Colombia, 1849–1914*. Bogotá, 1971.

Monsalve, Diego. *Colombia cafetera*. Barcelona, 1927.

Nieto Arteta, Luis Eduardo. *Economía y cultura en la historia de Colombia*. Bogotá, 1942.

Nieto Caballero, Luis E. *Murillo, escritor*. Bogotá, 1916.

Ortega, Alfredo. *Ferrocarriles colombianos*. 2 vols. Bogotá, 1920–23.

Ospina, Joaquín. *Diccionario biográfico y bibliográfico de Colombia*. 3 vols. Bogotá, 1927–39.

Ospina Vásquez, Luis. *Industria y protección en Colombia, 1810–1930*. Medellín, 1955.

Otálora, Carlos A. *Homenaje a la memoria del doctor José Eusebio Otálora en su centenario*. Tunja, 1929.

Otero Muñoz, Gustavo. *Un hombre y una época: la vida azarosa de Rafael Núñez*. Bogotá, 1951.

————. *Wilches y su época*. Bucaramanga, 1936.

Palacio, Julio H. *La guerra del 85*. Bogotá, 1936.

Parsons, James J. *Antioqueño Colonization in Western Colombia*. Berkeley, 1949.

Payne, James L. *Patterns of Conflict in Colombia*. New Haven, 1968.

Pérez, Felipe. *Geografía general, física y política de los Estados Unidos de Colombia y geografía particular de la ciudad de Bogotá*. Bogotá, 1883.

————. *Jeografía física i política de los Estados Unidos de Colombia*. 2 vols. Bogotá, 1862–63.

Pérez Aguirre, Antonio. *25 años de historia colombiana, 1853 a 1878: del centralismo a la federación*. Bogotá, 1959.

Pérez Ayala, José Manuel. *Antonio Caballero y Góngora, virrey y arzobispo de Santa Fe, 1723–1796*. Bogotá, 1951.

Restrepo, Carlos E. *Orientación republicana*. Medellín, n.d.

Restrepo, Vicente. *Estudio sobre las minas de oro y plata de Colombia*. Bogotá, 1952.

Restrepo Euse, Alvaro. *Historia de Antioquia desde la conquista hasta el año 1900*. Medellín, 1903.

Rivadeneira Vargas, Antonio José. *Don Santiago Pérez, biografía de un carácter*. Bogotá, 1966.

Rivas Groot, José María. *Asuntos constitucionales, económicos y fiscales*. Bogotá, 1909.

Rodríguez, Gustavo Humberto. *Santos Acosta, caudillo del radicalismo.* Bogotá, 1972.

Rodríguez Piñeres, Eduardo. *El olimpo radical: ensayos conocidos e inéditos sobre su época, 1864–1884.* Bogotá, 1950.

Rodríguez Plata, Horacio. *La inmigración alemana al estado soberano de Santander en el siglo XIX.* Bogotá, 1968.

Rueda Vargas, Tomás. *Escritos.* 3 vols. Bogotá, 1963.

Safford, Frank. *Aspectos del siglo XIX en Colombia.* Medellín, 1977.

———. *The Ideal of the Practical: Colombia's Struggle to Form a Technical Elite.* Austin, 1976.

Samper, José María. *Derecho público interno de Colombia.* 2 vols. Bogotá, 1951.

Sierra, Luis F. *El tabaco en la economía colombiana del siglo XIX.* Bogotá, 1971.

Sinisterra, Manuel. *El 24 de diciembre de 1876 en Cali.* Cali, 1936.

Torres García, Guillermo. *Historia de la moneda en Colombia.* Bogotá, 1945.

———. *Miguel Antonio Caro: su personalidad política.* Madrid, 1956.

Triffin, Robert. *Money and Banking in Colombia.* Washington, D.C., 1944.

Uribe V., Gonzalo. *Los arzobispos y obispos colombianos desde el tiempo de la colonia hasta nuestros días.* Bogotá, 1918.

Urrutia M., Miguel, and Mario Arrubla, eds. *Compendio de estadísticas históricas de Colombia.* Bogotá, 1970.

Urueta, José P. *Cartagena y sus cercanías.* Cartagena, 1912.

Vega, Fernando de la. *A través de mi lupa.* Bucaramanga, 1951.

Vega, José de la. *La federación en Colombia, 1810–1912.* Bogotá, 1952.

Vergara, José Ramón. *Escrutinio histórico: Rafael Núñez.* Bogotá, 1939.

B. Dissertations

Beyer, Robert C. "The Colombian Coffee Industry: Origins and Major Trends, 1740–1940." Ph.D. dissertation, University of Minnesota, 1947.

Davidson, Russ Tobias. "The Patronato in Colombia, 1800–1853: Reform and Anti-Reform in the Archdiocese of Santa Fe de Bogotá." Ph.D. dissertation, Vanderbilt University, 1978.

Delpar, Helen V. "The Liberal Party of Colombia, 1863–1903." Ph.D. dissertation, Columbia University, 1967.

Gilmore, Robert L. "Federalism in Colombia, 1810–1858." Ph.D. dissertation, University of California, Berkeley, 1949.

Helguera, J. León. "The First Mosquera Administration in New Granada, 1845–1849." Ph.D. dissertation, University of North Carolina, 1958.

Johnson, David C. "Economic and Social Change in Nineteenth Century Colombia: Santander, 1850–1885." Ph.D. dissertation, University of California, Berkeley, 1975.

Neal, James H. "The Pacific Age Come to Colombia: The Construction of the Cali–Buenaventura Route, 1854–1882." Ph.D. dissertation, Vanderbilt University, 1971.

C. Articles

Buenaventura, Manuel María. "El General David Peña; reseña histórica." *Boletín Histórico del Valle (Cali)*, III (September, 1932), 103–13.

Bushnell, David. "Two Stages in Colombian Tariff Policy: The Radical Era and the Return to Protection (1861–1885)." *Inter-American Economic Affairs*, IX (Spring, 1956), 3–23.

Delpar, Helen. "Aspects of Liberal Factionalism in Colombia, 1875–1885." *Hispanic American Historical Review*, LI (May, 1971), 250–74.

———. "The Liberal Record and Colombian Historiography: An Indictment in Need of Revision." *Revista Interamericana de Bibliografia*, XXXI (1981), 524–37.

———. "Road to Revolution: The Liberal Party of Colombia, 1886–1899." *The Americas*, XXXII (January, 1976), 348–71.

Gilmore, Robert L. "Nueva Granada's Socialist Mirage." *Hispanic American Historical Review*, XXXVI (May, 1956), 190–210.

Harrison, John P. "The Evolution of the Colombian Tobacco Trade, to 1875." *Hispanic American Historical Review*, XXXII (May, 1952), 164–74.

Helguera, J. León. "The Problem of Liberalism Versus Conservatism in Colombia: 1849–85." In *Latin American History. Select Problems: Identity, Integration, and Nationhood*, edited by Frederick B. Pike. New York, 1969.

Horna, Hernán. "Francisco Javier Cisneros: A Pioneer in Transportation and Economic Development in Latin America, 1857–1898." *The Americas*, XXX (July, 1973), 54–82.

Loy, Jane Meyer. "Primary Education during the Colombian Federation: The School Reform of 1870." *Hispanic American Historical Review*, LI (May, 1971), 275–94.

Nichols, Theodore E. "The Rise of Barranquilla." *Hispanic American Historical Review*, XXXIV (May, 1954), 158–74.

Ocampo López, Javier. "El positivismo y el movimiento de 'La Regeneración' en Colombia." *Latinoamérica; Anuario de Estudios Latinoamericanos*, I (1968), 81–109.

Orlando Melo, Jorge. "La república conservadora (1880–1930)." In *Colombia, hoy*, edited by Mario Arrubla. Bogotá, 1978.

Palacio, Julio H. "La evolución Otálora." *Revista Colombiana*, VIII (May, 1937), 215–19.

―――. "El segundo matrimonio de Núñez." *Revista Colombiana*, VII (November, 1936), 321–33.

Park, James W. "Preludio a la presidencia: Rafael Núñez, gobernador de Bolívar, 1876–1879." *Boletín de Historia y Antigüedades*, LXIII (October–December, 1976), 519–35.

Rodríguez Piñeres, Eduardo. "Páginas olvidadas en 'El olimpo radical': la liga de 1869." *Boletín de Historia y Antigüedades*, XXXVIII (April–June, 1951), 252–73.

Safford, Frank. "Significación de los antioqueños en el desarrollo económico colombiano: un examen crítico de la tesis de Everett Hagen." *Anuario Colombiano de Historia Social y de la Cultura*, II (1965), 18–27.

Twinam, Ann. "Enterprise and Elites in Eighteenth-Century Medellín." *Hispanic American Historical Review*, LIX (August, 1979), 444–75.

Uribe Uribe, Rafael. "La necesidad de los grandes partidos nacionales." *Revista Argentina de Ciencias Políticas (Buenos Aires)*, IV (1912), 54–61.

Urrutia Montoya, Miguel. "El sector externo y la distribución de ingresos en Colombia en el siglo XIX." *Revista del Banco de la República*, No. 541 (November, 1972), 1974–87.

Visbal, Mauricio N. "Apuntes históricos sobre del Canal del Dique." *Boletín Historial (Cartagena)*, LXXXVI (May, 1945), 1–10.

Index
